AF539282

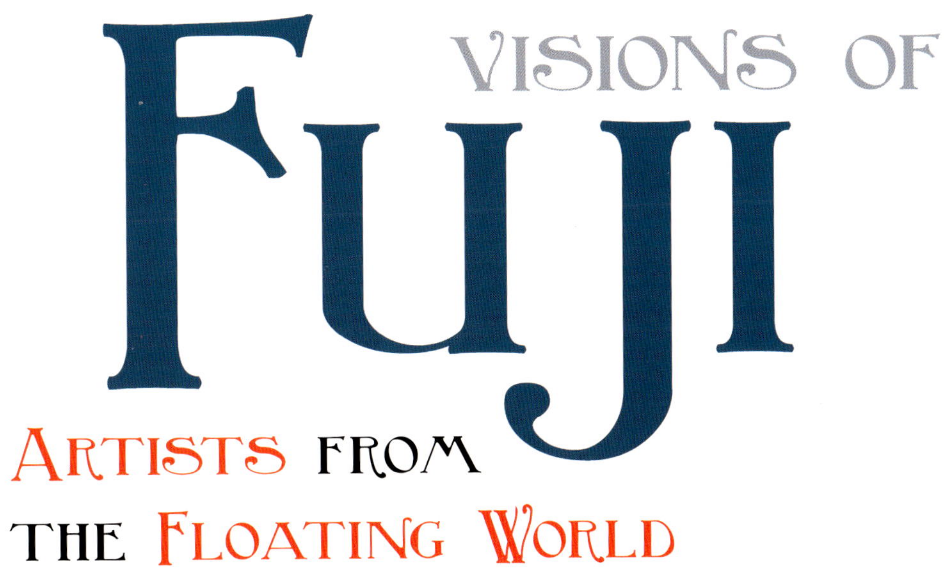

Visions of Fuji

Artists from the Floating World

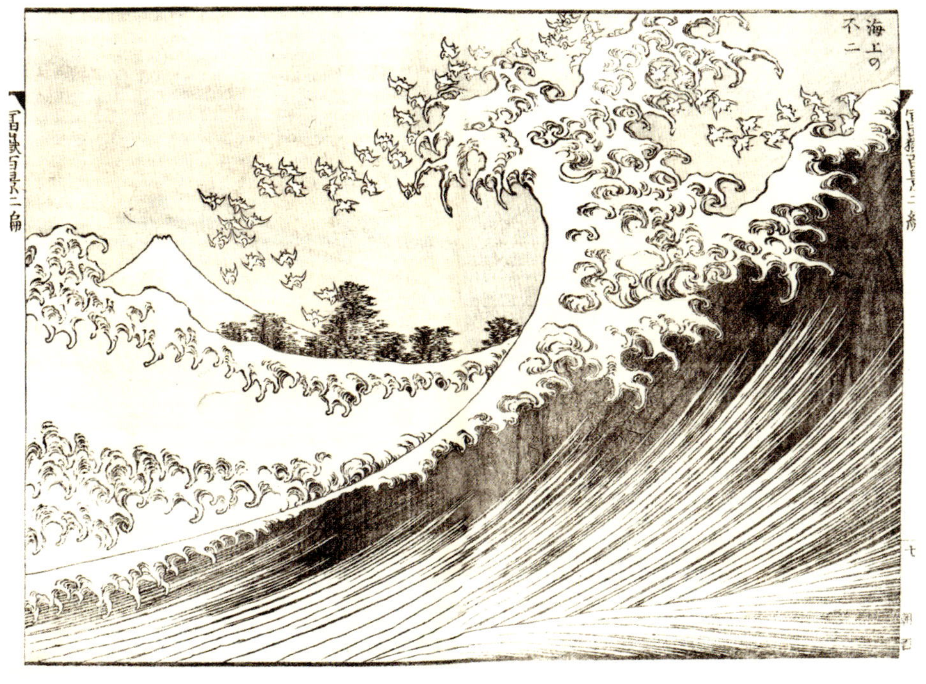

Note to the reader on names and spellings

Japanese words given in the book tend to use the most common romanized spellings (without accents), which, it should be remembered, are necessarily approximate, being based on a transliteration of an entirely different script. Artists' names are given with the family name first, in the Japanese style.

Notes to the reader on images

Works shown are in the woodblock print medium unless otherwise stated.
Unitalicized titles are contemporary descriptions rather than the artist's own/historically accepted.
Illustrations in the book may reproduce impressions from the first print run of a series, or may be later prints – such as reprints by Takamizawa (1890–1940) or by Adachi from the Showa period (1926–1989). The age/edition of a particular print is not always known, so any dates given in captions are the dates of original creation/publication unless otherwise noted (with 'printed later' for instance).

Publisher and Creative Director: Nick Wells
Commissioning Editor: Polly Prior
Senior Project Editor and Picture Research: Catherine Taylor
Art Director: Mike Spender
Copy Editor: Ramona Lamport
Proofreader: Dawn Laker

FLAME TREE PUBLISHING
6 Melbray Mews
Fulham, London SW6 3NS
United Kingdom

www.flametreepublishing.com

First published 2016

16 18 20 19 17
1 3 5 7 9 10 8 6 4 2

ISBN 978-1-78361-989-4

A CIP record for this book is available from the British Library upon request.

Printed in China

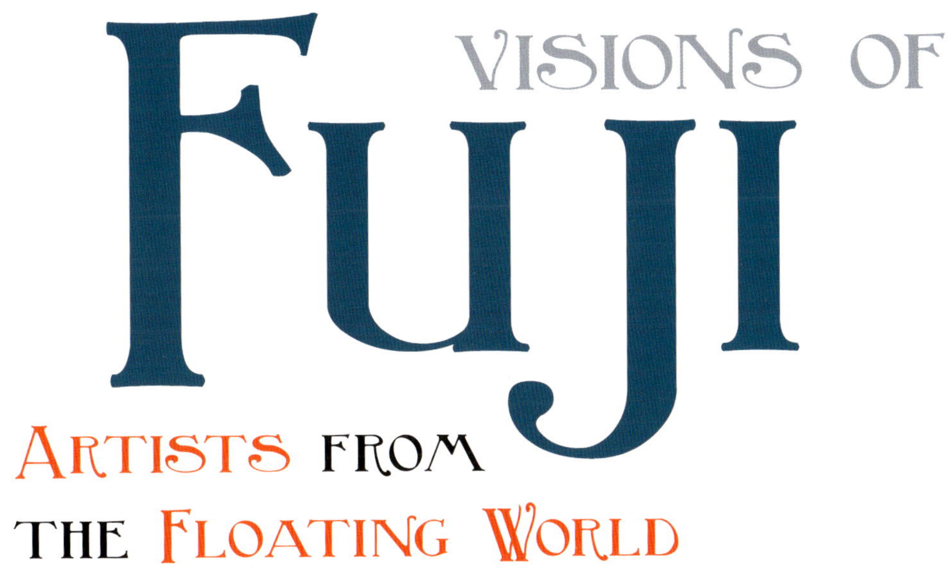

Visions of Fuji

Artists from the Floating World

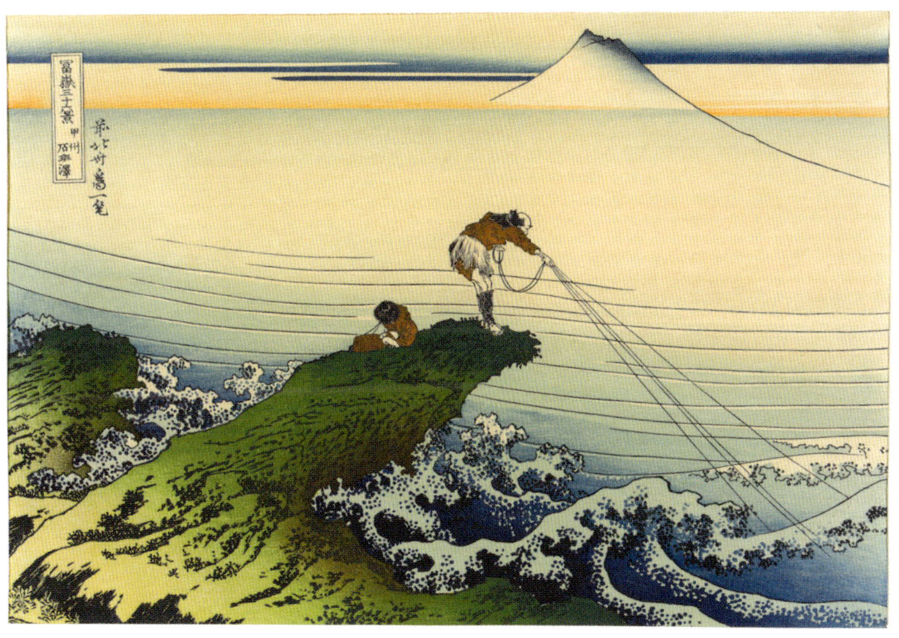

Michael Kerrigan

FLAME TREE
PUBLISHING

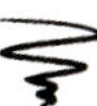

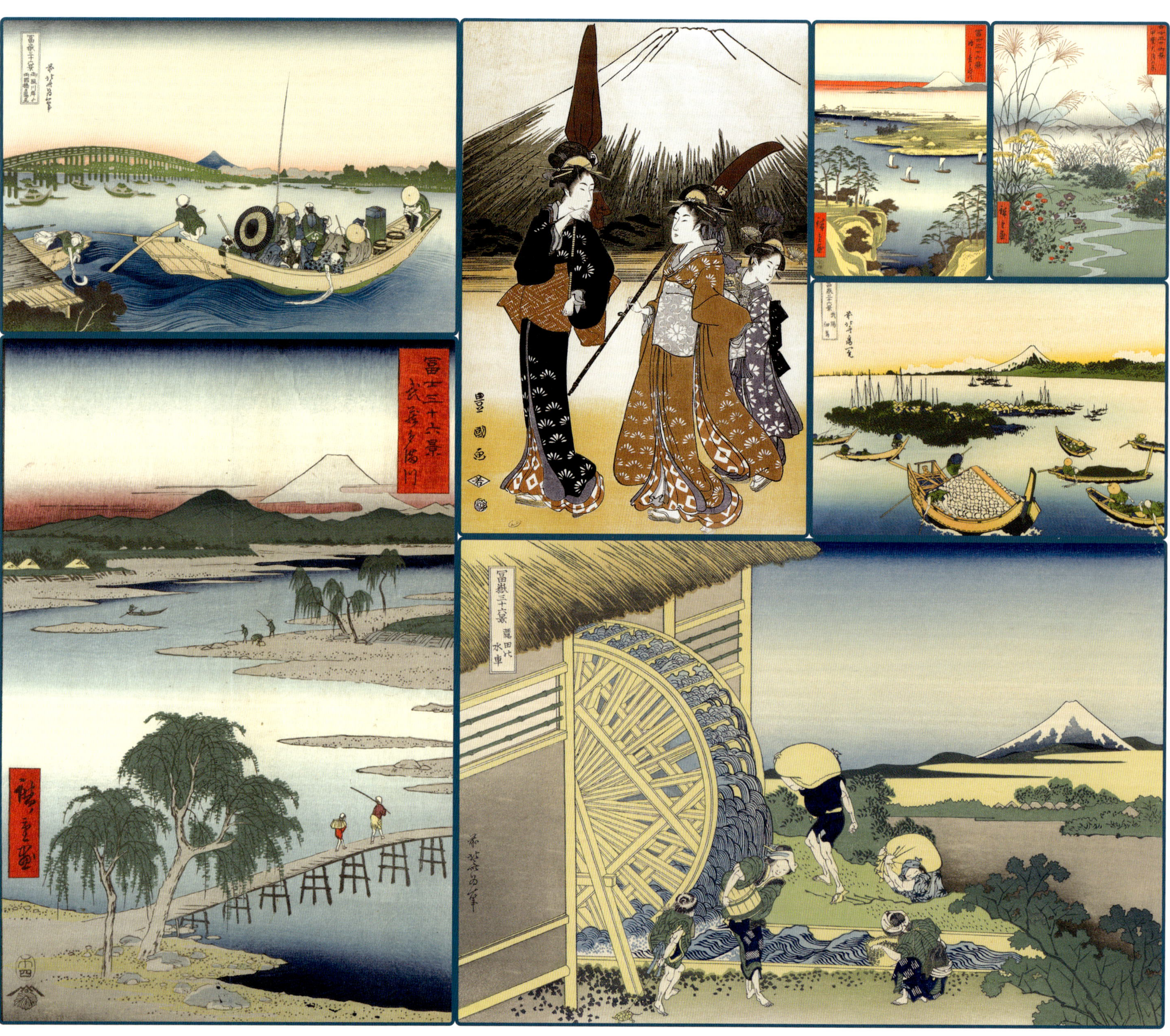

ABOVE **Katsushika Hokusai (1760–1849) and Utagawa Hiroshige (1797–1858)** Various prints from each artist's 'Thirty-six Views of Mount Fuji' (1826–33 and 1858 respectively), plus **Suzuki Harunobu (1725–70)** *Walk Towards Mount Fuji* (1765)

Contents

Introduction

'Setting out along Tagonoura Beach,
I look across to see the snow still falling steadily
on the slopes of Fuji, white as washi.'

Yamabe no Akahito (*fl.* 724–36) composed this little poem around the middle of the eighth century – the earliest known written reference to Japan's most famous mountain. Tagonoura Beach, which runs across the northern edge of Honshu Island's Suruga Bay, is celebrated for its beauty – and its views of Fuji – to this day. The white-fibred *washi*, with which the poet compared Fuji's snowy slopes, is also still familiar; made from the bark of the 'paper mulberry' tree, it is used (as its English name suggests) for making a fine paper or coarse cloth.

It goes without saying that the mountain known to the Japanese as Fujisan is solid and permanent; some 3,776 m (12,389 ft) high and 50 km (31 mi) across at its base, this near-perfect cone of accumulated lava would take some shifting. But it has lasted less literally too, enduring in the Japanese imagination as an emblem of beauty and perfection, of symmetry and spiritual balance; of soaring aspiration and grounded stability. Above all, perhaps, it has been an emblem of endurance itself. Days, years, centuries may pass – but Fujisan remains the same.

Eternal Youth

Fuji's very name proclaims this immortality: its etymological origins may be obscure, but it sounds exactly like another ancient phrase, fu-shi, which means 'never dying'. No more than a linguistic coincidence, this is nevertheless a linguistic coincidence of the kind that has always fascinated the Japanese (as it has the Chinese and other Far Eastern cultures).

Fuji has been there, says Akahito in another poem, 'since the sky was separated from the earth' – but it is actually extremely young as mountains go. Although apparently ever-present, it erupted out of otherwise almost level land some 100,000 years ago. If that makes it about as old as humankind, it is the blink of an eye in the geological scheme. In any case, that was a former Fuji – thought to have been not much more than half the present mountain's mass. The cone we see today was formed by a fresh eruption only 10,000 years ago.

The violence of its creation of course contributed to its later air of serenity; its abruptness shaped the seeming 'perfection' of its form. Fujisan stands in solitary splendour, its tapering outline elegantly framed by its surrounding land- and seascape, its contours comparatively unaffected by erosion.

Still pristine, then; inspirationally so. For as long as chroniclers have made observations, the volcano – its vents, its cratered summit and a number of

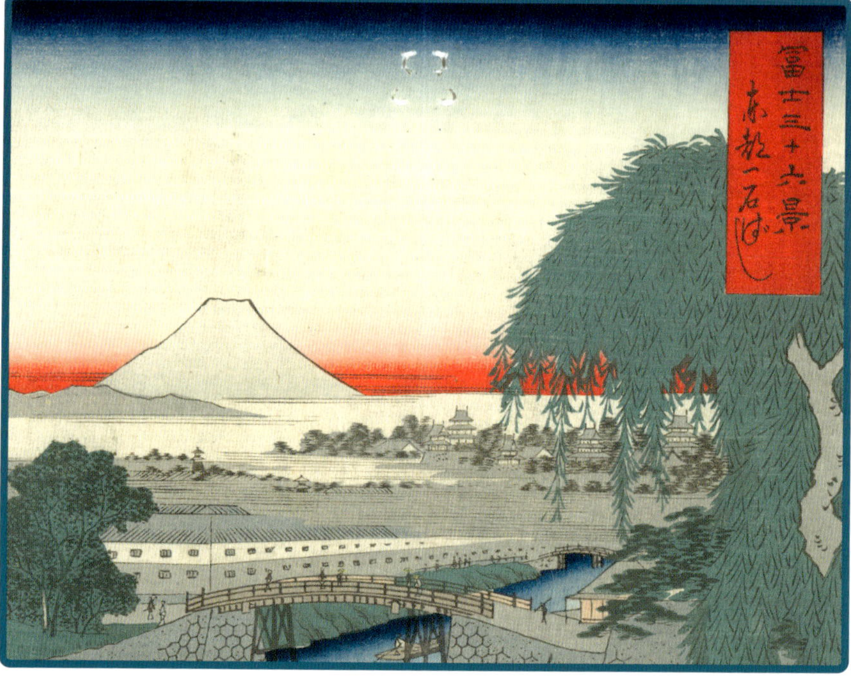

Above Utagawa Hiroshige (1797–1858) *Ichikoku Bridge in the Eastern Capital* (detail), from 'Thirty-six Views of Mount Fuji' (1858)

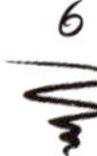

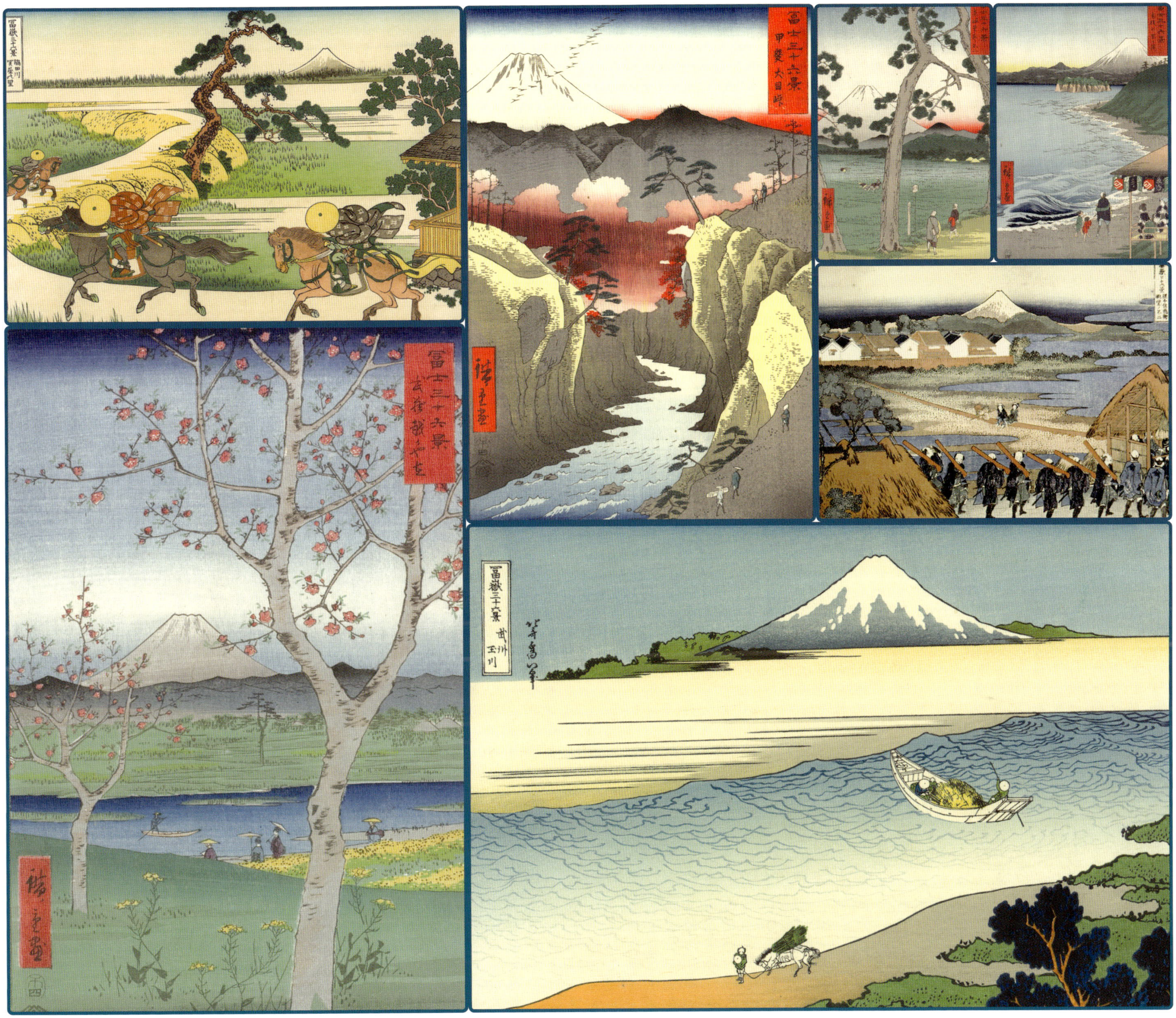

ABOVE **Katsushika Hokusai (1760–1849) and Utagawa Hiroshige (1797–1858)** Various prints from each artist's 'Thirty-six Views of Mount Fuji' (1826–33 and 1858 respectively)

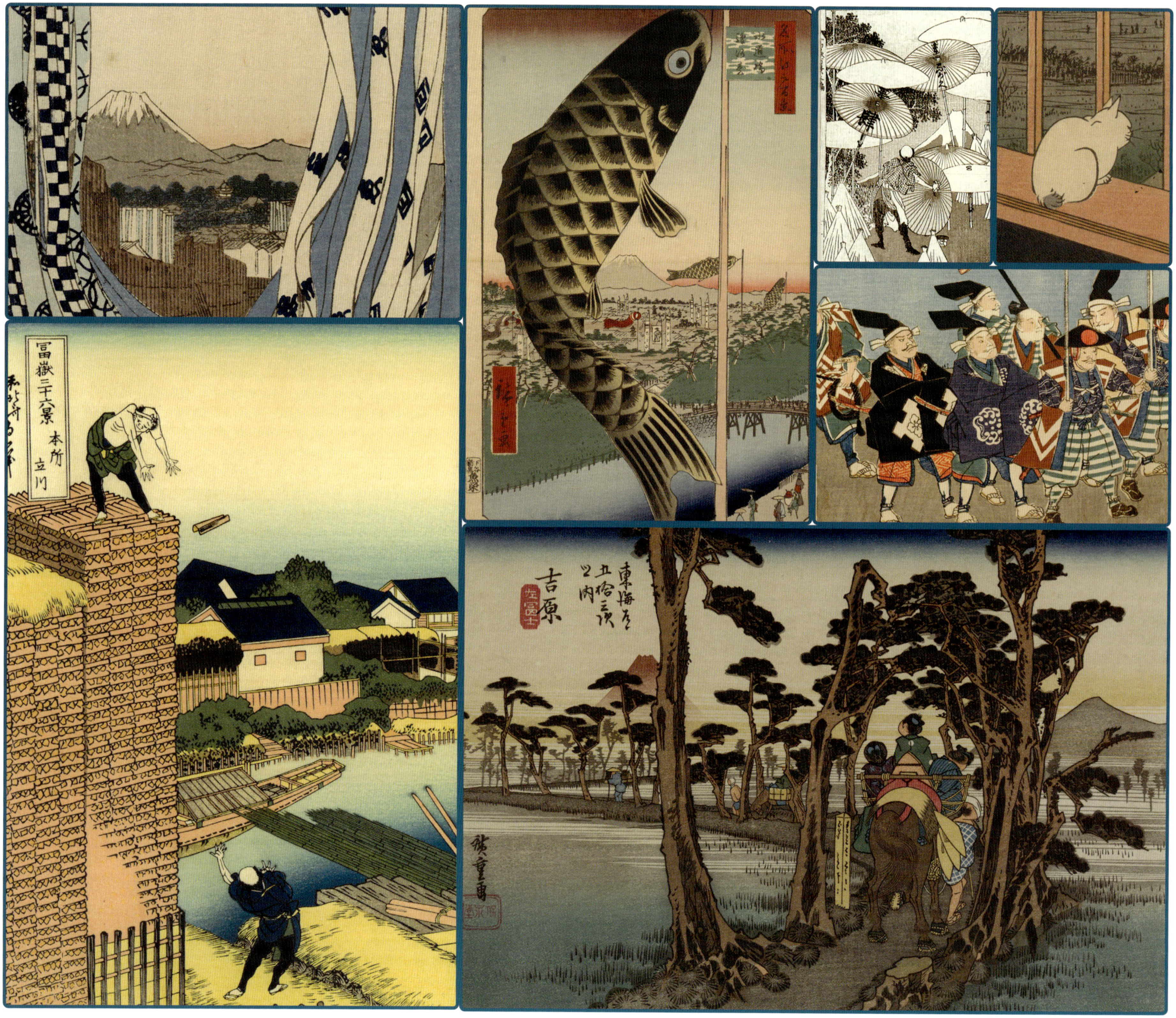

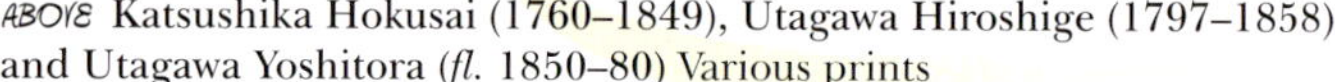

Above Katsushika Hokusai (1760–1849), Utagawa Hiroshige (1797–1858) and Utagawa Yoshitora (*fl.* 1850–80) Various prints

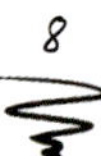

shrines in the vicinity of its base – has been an important place of pilgrimage for the Japanese. Pious visitors have flocked here for centuries, making their way up these smooth, steep slopes to Fuji's dizzying summit in the hope that some of its immortality will rub off on them. They still keep coming in their tens of thousands – no fewer than 320,000 in 2012 alone (ironically, 25 of those seekers after eternal life were killed during their climb; a mountain of this size is not to be trifled with).

Always the Background?

But if the slopes themselves are bustling, that is not how Mount Fuji is stereotypically seen. Much more often it has been there as a distant prospect. Visible from Tokyo, its cloud-swathed summit and snow-clad slopes have stood as a symbolic protective presence, serene and still, counterbalancing the business of the worldly, the everyday. In art, the mountain's mystic form has become the quintessential background to a foreground of vivid, vibrant, present life.

Here it is Akahito, setting out along the Suruga sands, but in poems and paintings ever since it has been there on the horizon, the quiet custodian to a thousand lively scenes. A traveller stops to rest his packhorse on the shores of a lonely lake; a fishing boat plies the waters of an empty bay; a ferryboat filled with laughing, chatting passengers sets out across a strait of water; a fine lady promenades with her retinue; peasants work in rice paddies; merchants make their way to market; young beauties board a boat to take a pleasure cruise….

A Blank Sheet

It is appropriate that Akahito should have seen white *washi* in Fuji's snow-cloaked slopes, for this cloth-like paper was important as a support for works of art. What canvas would be for Western painters, *washi* was to Japanese artists – the blank base on which they would capture the most extravagantly colourful flights of their creative minds.

In its more oblique, more subtle and symbolic way, the form of Fuji was to do this as well. Its unchanging stillness seems somehow to anchor the wilder effusions of Japanese art. It recurs in painting after painting – especially in the landscape art of the Edo Period (1603–1867), in which it is practically a fixture – in which it seems to 'fix' the fluid dynamism of a thousand scenes. So insistently, so obsessively even, is it recreated that it passes right through the realm of cliché and out the other side – no more hackneyed than a classic trope or standard pose in Western art.

There it is, a companionable, a talismanic, even perhaps an admonitory presence in painting after painting, print after print, by some of the greatest masters of Japanese art. Katsushika Hokusai (1760–1849) and Utagawa Hiroshige (1797–1858) made the mountain the subject of some of their most important and ambitious works. And, as the wonders of oriental art filtered through to the West in modern times, it also became a feature of the European artistic scene.

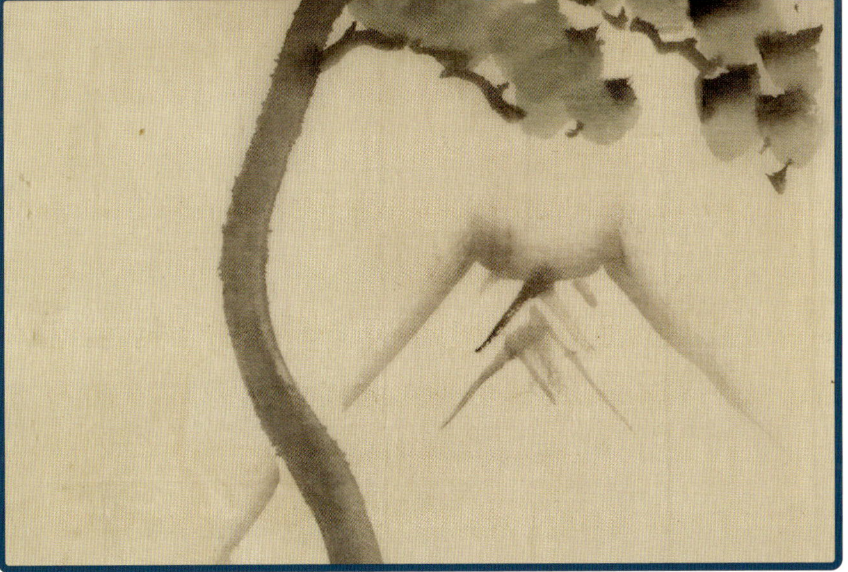

ABOVE Hokusai School (mid-19th C) *Untitled* (detail) (1830–50), ink wash and colour on paper

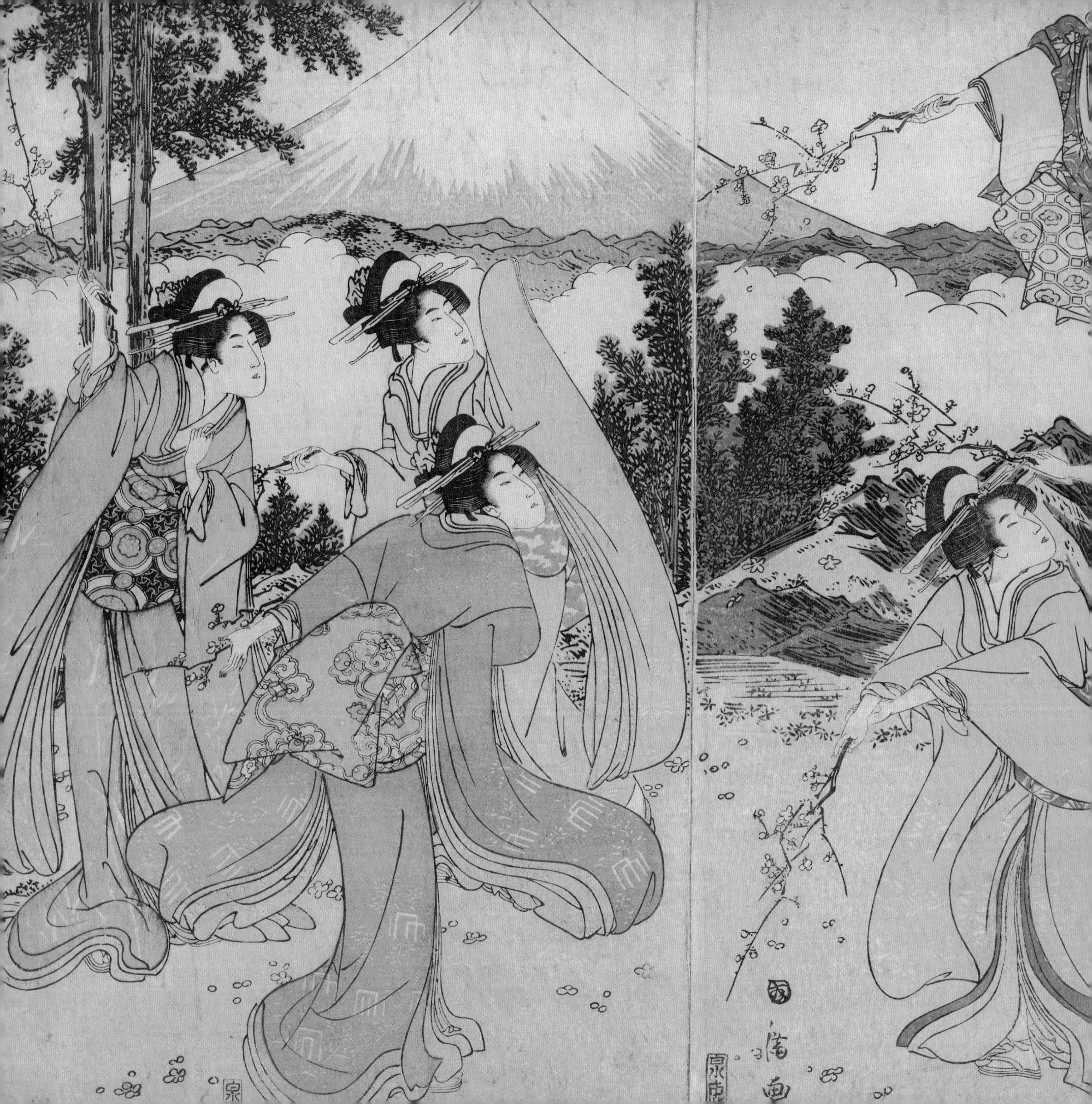

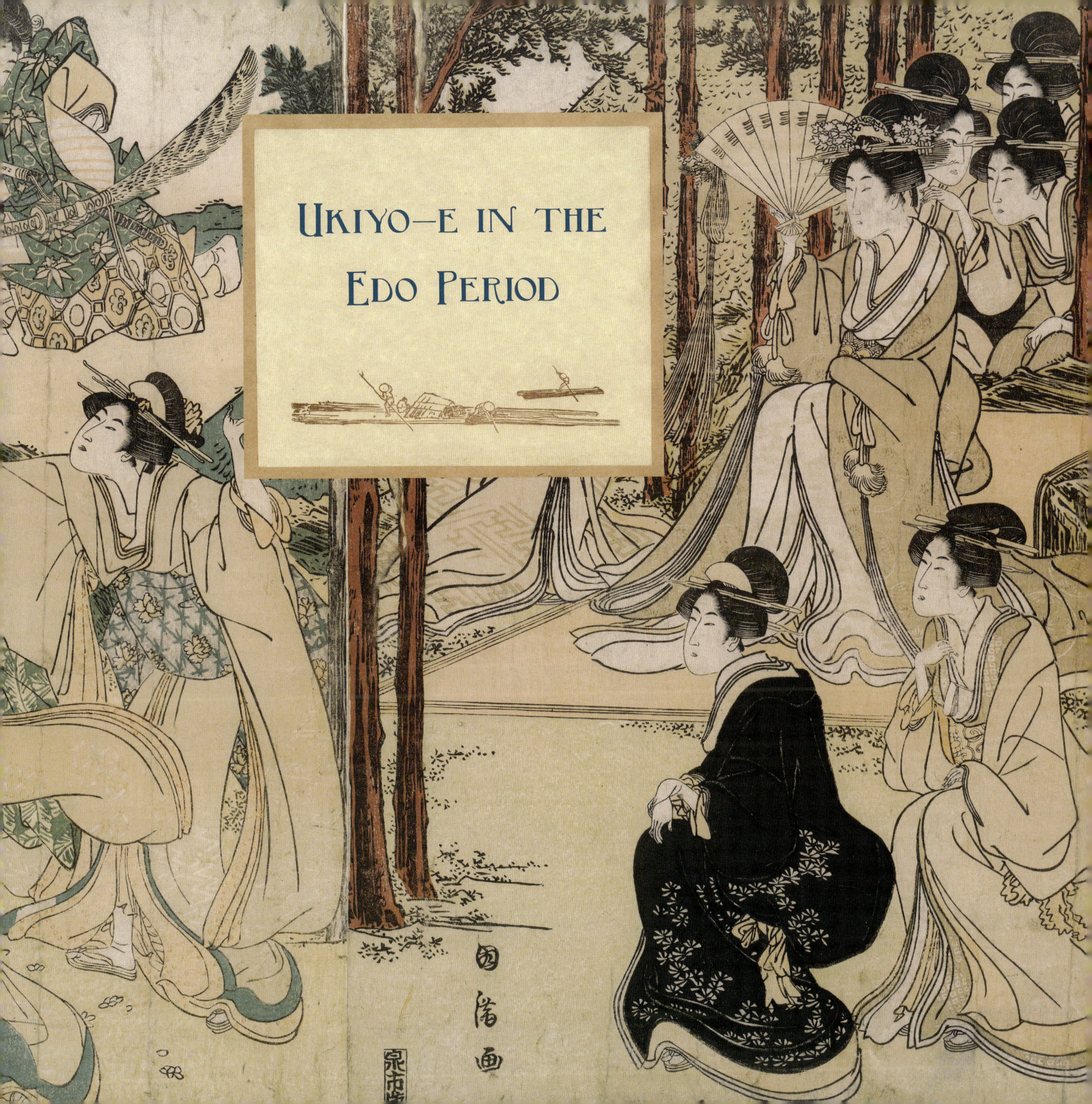
Ukiyo-e in the
Edo Period

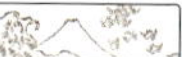

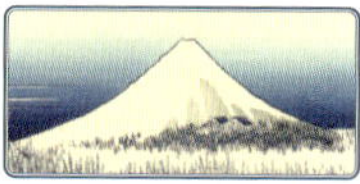

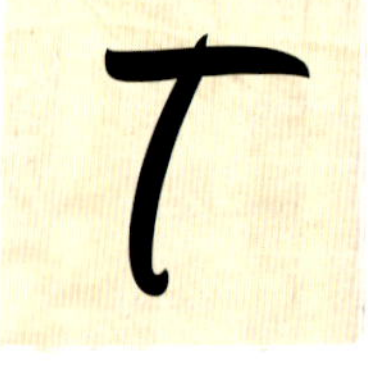

TOKYO TODAY is not so much a city as the urban principle in apotheosis, the ultimate metropolis, awe-inspiring in its size. It is immense by just about any imaginable measure, whether population (pushing 14 million); urban area (2 million square kilometres/772,204 square miles); political importance, financial significance or cultural wealth; as well as in traffic congestion, air pollution and its disorientating newness. Wartime firestorms only finished the job that centuries of earthquakes had set in motion, leaving Tokyo a tabula rasa without any historic monuments or special places of memory or mystique – no chronological dimension at all, indeed. Just new-build glass-and-concrete and neon lighting at every turn.

A Civilization at Sea

The result was as alienating as it was thrilling. Nearly half a century ago, in 1967, Abe Kobo's novel, *The Ruined Map*, was sketching out a cityscape in whose teeming vastness and complexity it was becoming barely possible to find one's way. An experienced detective, Kobo's protagonist (who, fittingly, is not named himself) is set to search for a missing man. As he combs the streets of the city, however, he slowly but surely comes to realize that he is the one who is lost – and not just geographically, but emotionally, existentially, adrift on that disorientating sea of normlessness which seems to have been characteristic of urban life in the modern era and which the French sociologist Emile Durkheim (1858–1917) called 'anomie'.

A later French thinker, Roland Barthes (1915–80), was to find himself adrift in the Japanese capital himself – just a year before Kobo's novel was published. Barthes, by contrast, found the sense of self-dissolution he experienced in Tokyo liberating, which he described in his own book,

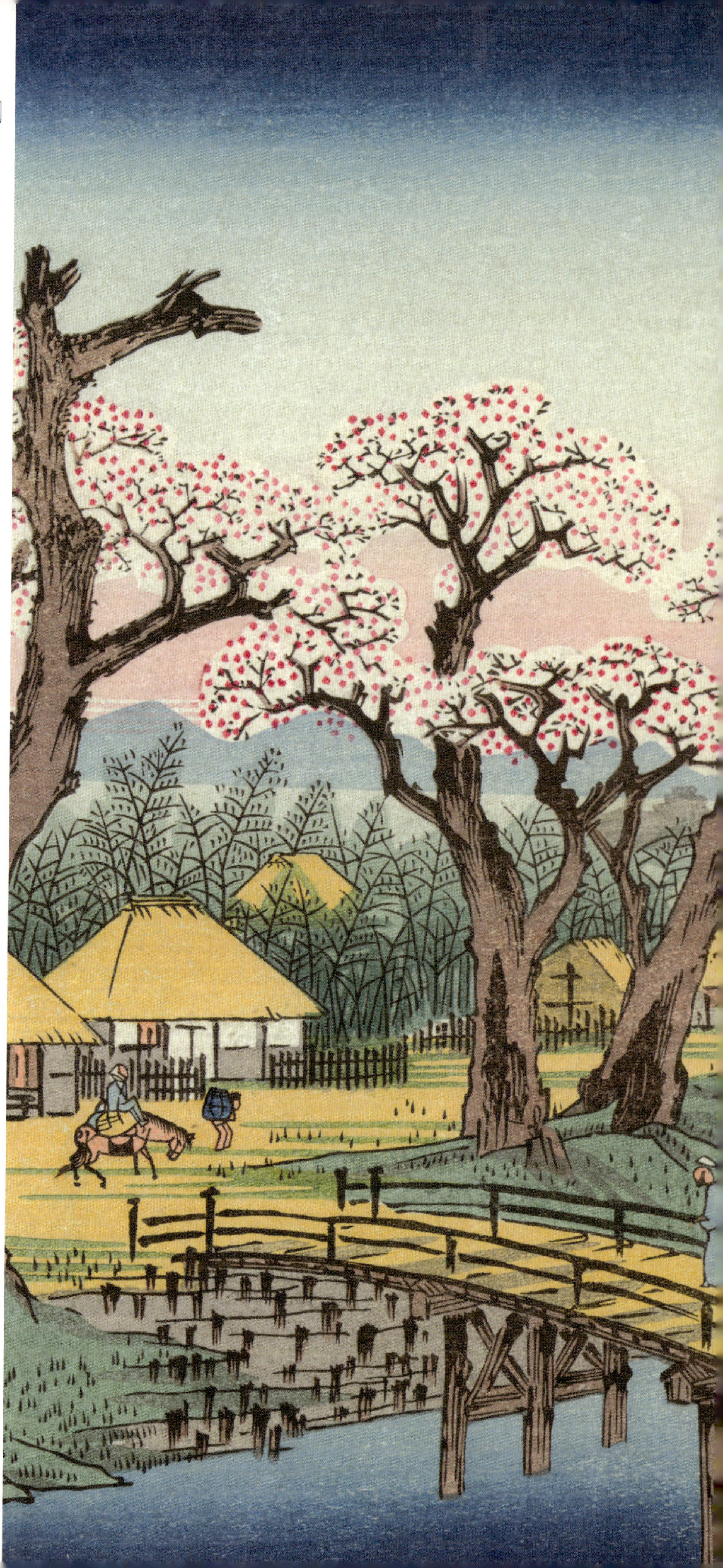

PREVIOUS PAGES Toyokuni II (Utagawa Toyoshige, *c.* 1777–1835) *A Parody of the Play 'Mount Kurama'* (1801–04)
RIGHT Utagawa Hiroshige (1797–1858) *Evening Glow at Koganei Bridge* (1838), from 'Eight Views in the Environs of Edo'

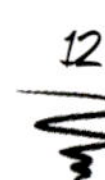

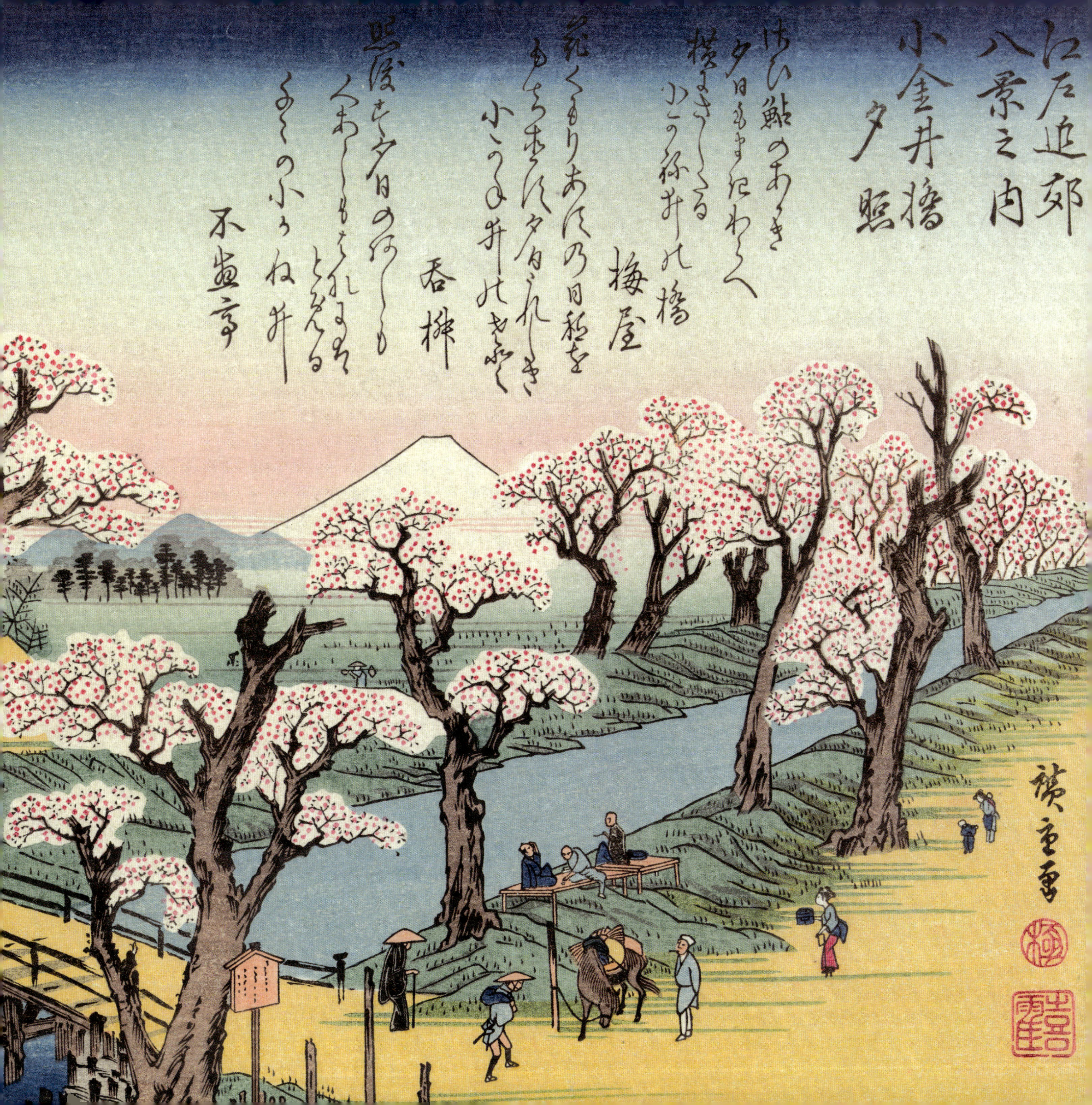
江戸近郊八景之内
小金井橋夕照
廣重画

Empire of Signs (1970). Barthes belonged to a generation of French 'structuralists' who saw language, thought and culture as being created by the relations between signs, their differences and oppositions to each other, rather than any direct connection they might have to what they signified. Seemingly divorced from a more profound past and the intrinsic 'meaning' it might have conferred on the city's scene, Tokyo to him was a festival of free-floating significance for its own sake.

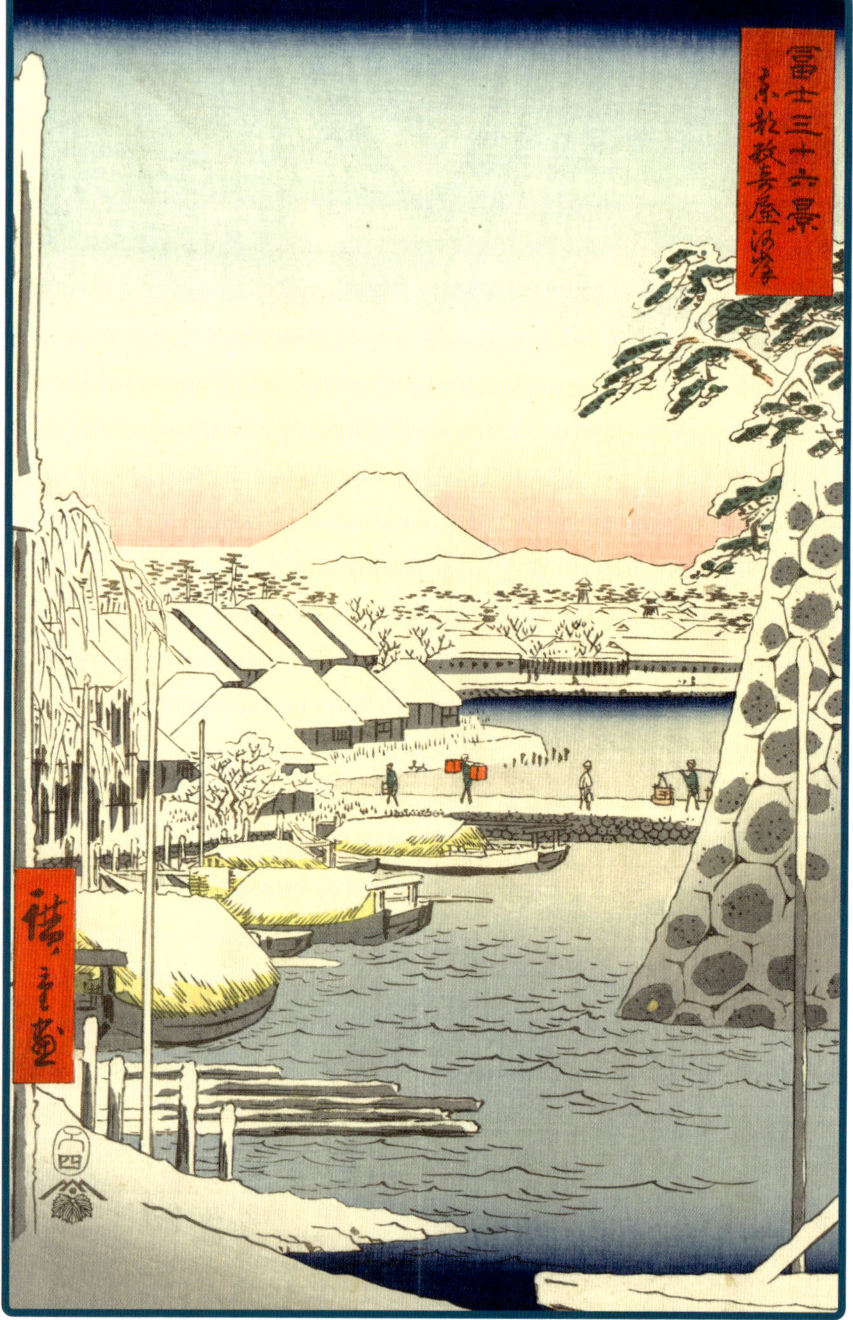

Above Utagawa Hiroshige (1797–1858) *Sukiyagashi in the Eastern Capital*, from 'Thirty-six Views of Mount Fuji' (1858)

But if Barthes enjoyed the feeling of being adrift in Japan, he did not have to live there. All the indications are that all this anarchy occasioned more uneasiness in the Japanese themselves. Hence, the continuing importance of Mount Fuji, a fixed point to which their ancestors had tied their identity for generations, and in the post-war era an anchor for a society thrown into a state of bewilderment and vertigo by unprecedentedly rapid – and frequently traumatic – change. After the devastating impact of the atom bomb had come the shock of structural transformation. A 'miracle' it might have been, but Japan's economic reconstruction had transformed it utterly. Out there, on the horizon to the far south-west, however, was Fujisan, a silent reminder that this remained Japan and that ancient values still held sway. Clear and simple in silhouette, it was a dark cone caparisoned in a cloak of dazzling snow.

Shifting Centres

This sense of an identity in flux was not in fact as new or uniquely modern as it might seem. Whilst understandable, and by no means entirely wrong, Western stereotyping of Japan as a place of static social mores and stiff ceremony, unchanged over centuries, misses the essential uncertainty around which such values evolved.

Japan's whole history might be seen as an extended search for a centre, a stable form. Prior to the second century AD, nothing so developed as a 'state' could be said to have existed in what – like other early societies – was more an anarchic collection of little chiefdoms, scattered over what was after all not just an island but an archipelago. In the later, legendary record, which was subsequently superimposed upon this period, however, the status of 'capital' was passed about between a dozen different cities.

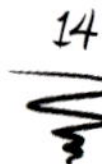

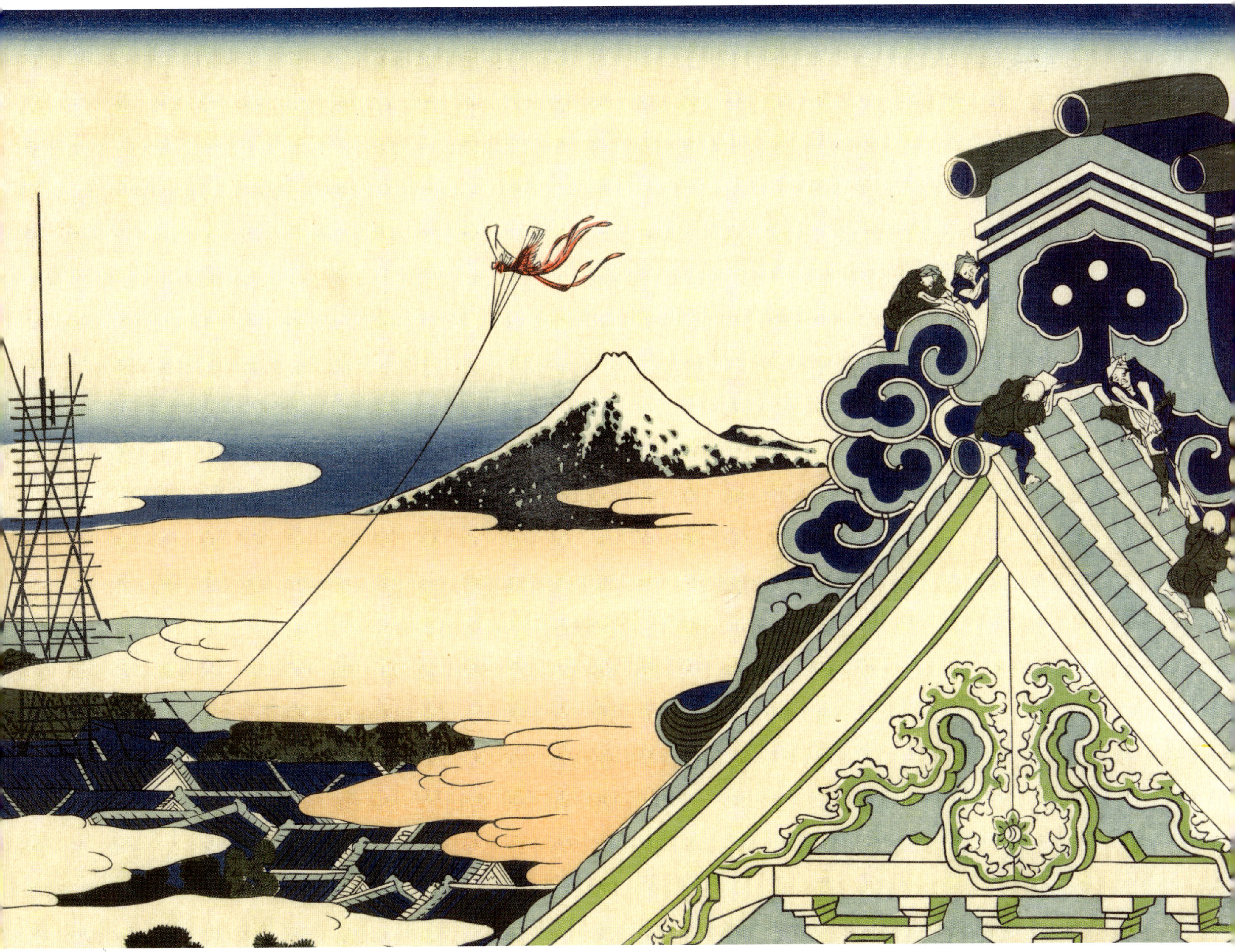

ABOVE **Katsushika Hokusai** (1760–1849) *Asakusa Hongan-ji Temple in the Eastern Capital*, from 'Thirty-six Views of Mount Fuji' (1826–33)

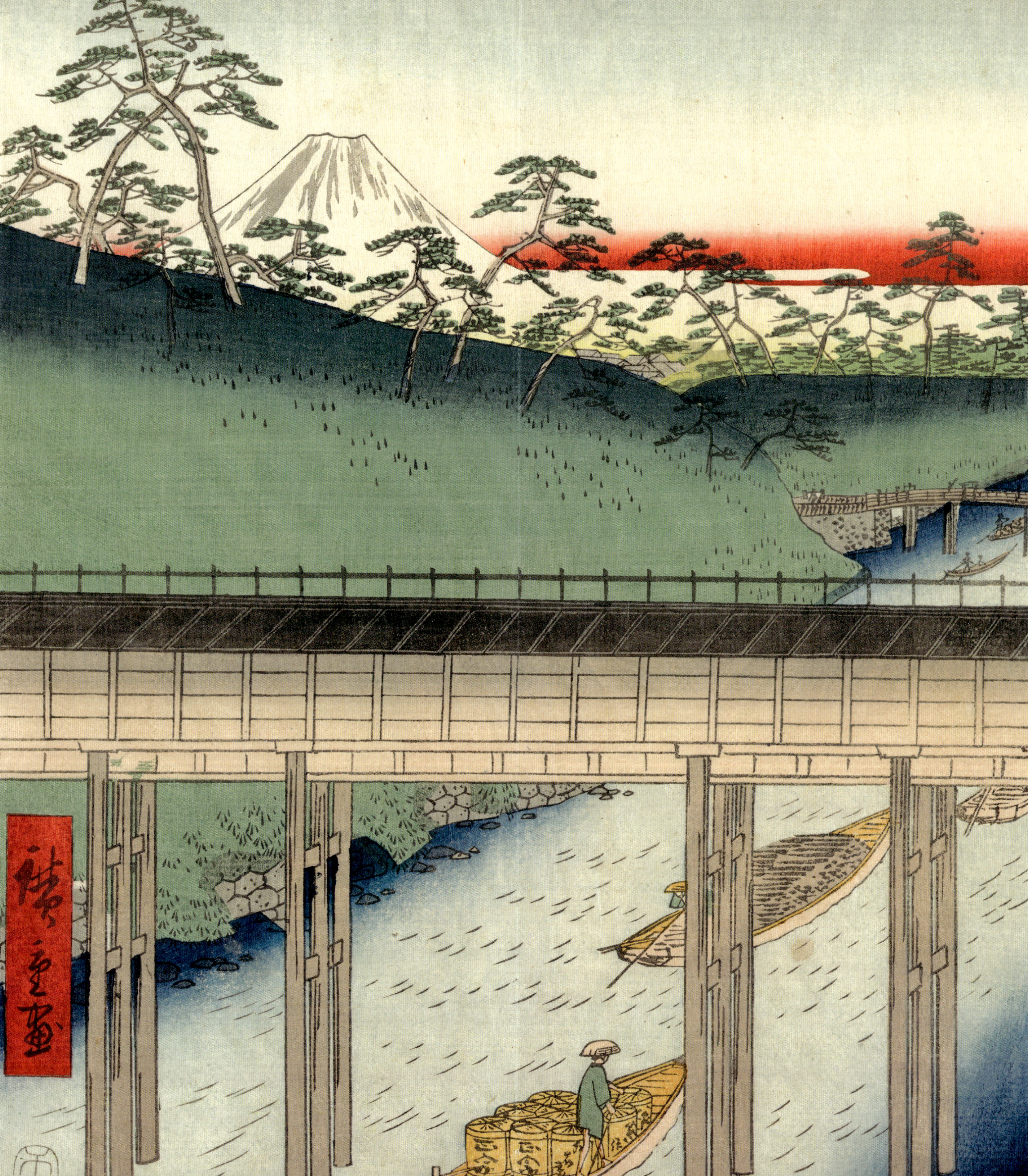
廣重画

When local warlordism did at last give way to the emergence of the first real polity, the Yamato (in what is now Nara, in central Honshu), power and governance showed the same nomadic tendencies.

Peripatetic Power

Between the fifth and the eighth centuries, the administrative centre moved back and forth between Asuka and Sakurai, with spells in Asakura, Otsu, Osaka and other cities in between. Thereafter, whilst central authority sat tight in Heian-kyo (Kyoto) for a thousand years (with just the briefest of interruptions, in 1180, when the child Emperor Antoku – 1178–85 – moved it to Kobe), political power was itself decentred, a series of *shoguns* holding sway. Though nominally ruling on the Emperor's behalf, these military strongmen had dictatorial power and held it hereditarily – alternative ruling houses, in other words.

This system – if it can be dignified with the term – was inherently unstable; power was there to be taken and rulers to be toppled. Whilst the Kamakura shogunate succeeded in holding on to power from 1192 to 1333, the ensuing Ashikaga shogunate (1336–1573) was forced to preside over mounting chaos. By the end of the fifteenth century, the so-called Sengoku Era (the Age of Warring States, 1467–1568) had begun, and the country collapsed into violent anarchy and chaos. Not until the 1580s would any sort of centralized authority be restored with the rise of Tokugawa Iesayu (1543–1616) to power; even then, it would take until 1603 for him to be acknowledged by the Emperor.

Suspended in Time

Ieyasu died in 1616, but his Tokugawa shogunate was destined to endure for 265 years. In some ways, Japan was clearly to benefit from the order it imposed – not that it could not be rough and ready in keeping that order. The idea that stability and safety could be found only in isolation was an important tenet of Tokugawa thinking from the start. It was on Ieyasu's orders that 26 Catholics – both Jesuit missionaries and Japanese converts – were crucified in Nagasaki in 1597. Thousands lost their lives during the Shimabara Rebellion of 1637–38, when Ieyasu's grandson, Tokugawa

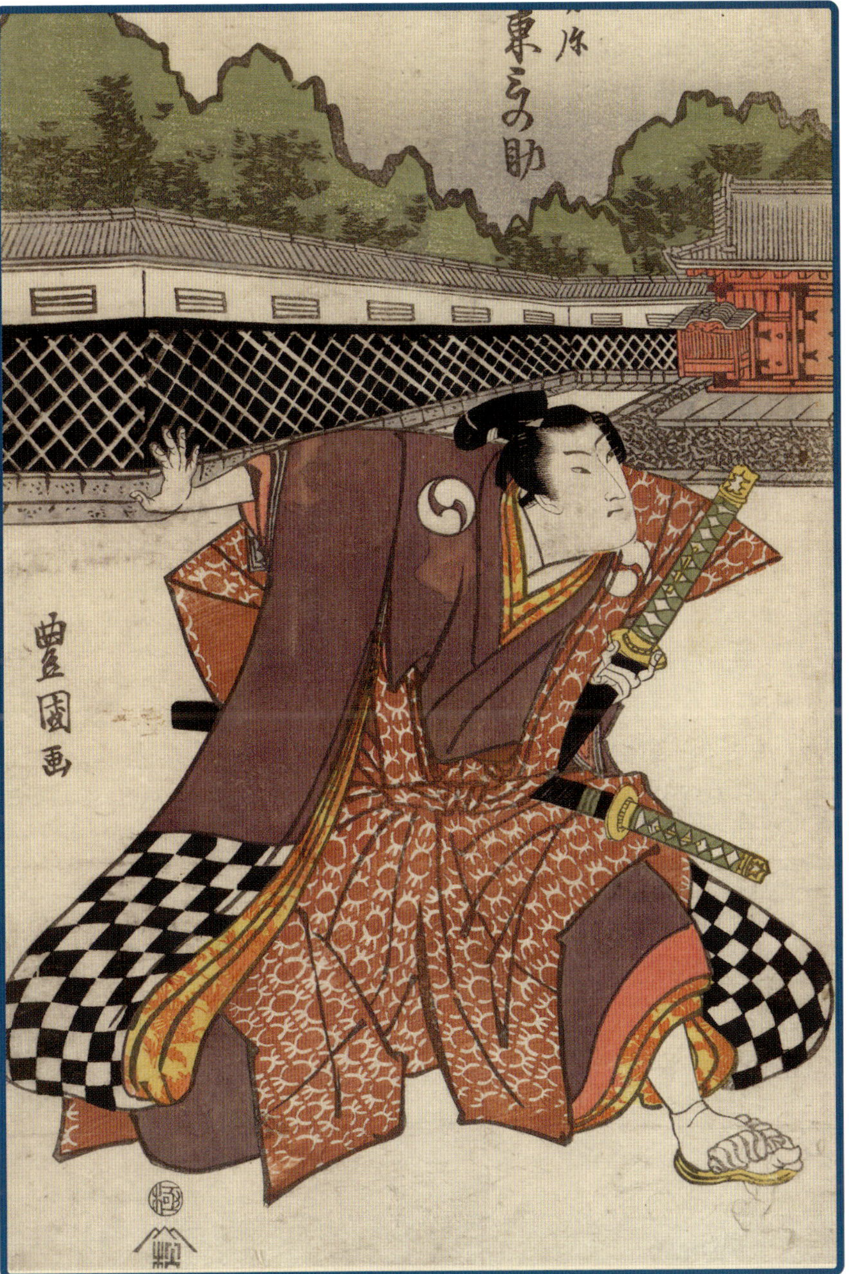

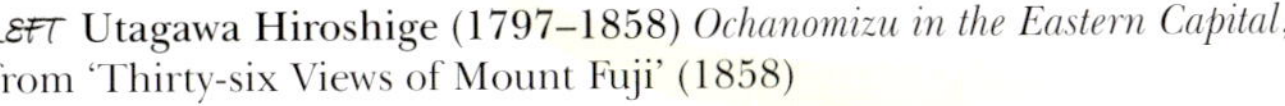
Left Utagawa Hiroshige (1797–1858) *Ochanomizu in the Eastern Capital*, from 'Thirty-six Views of Mount Fuji' (1858)

Above Toyokuni II (Utagawa Toyoshige, *c.* 1777–1835) *The Actor Bando Minosuke in the Role of Rikiya* (1801–10)

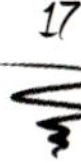

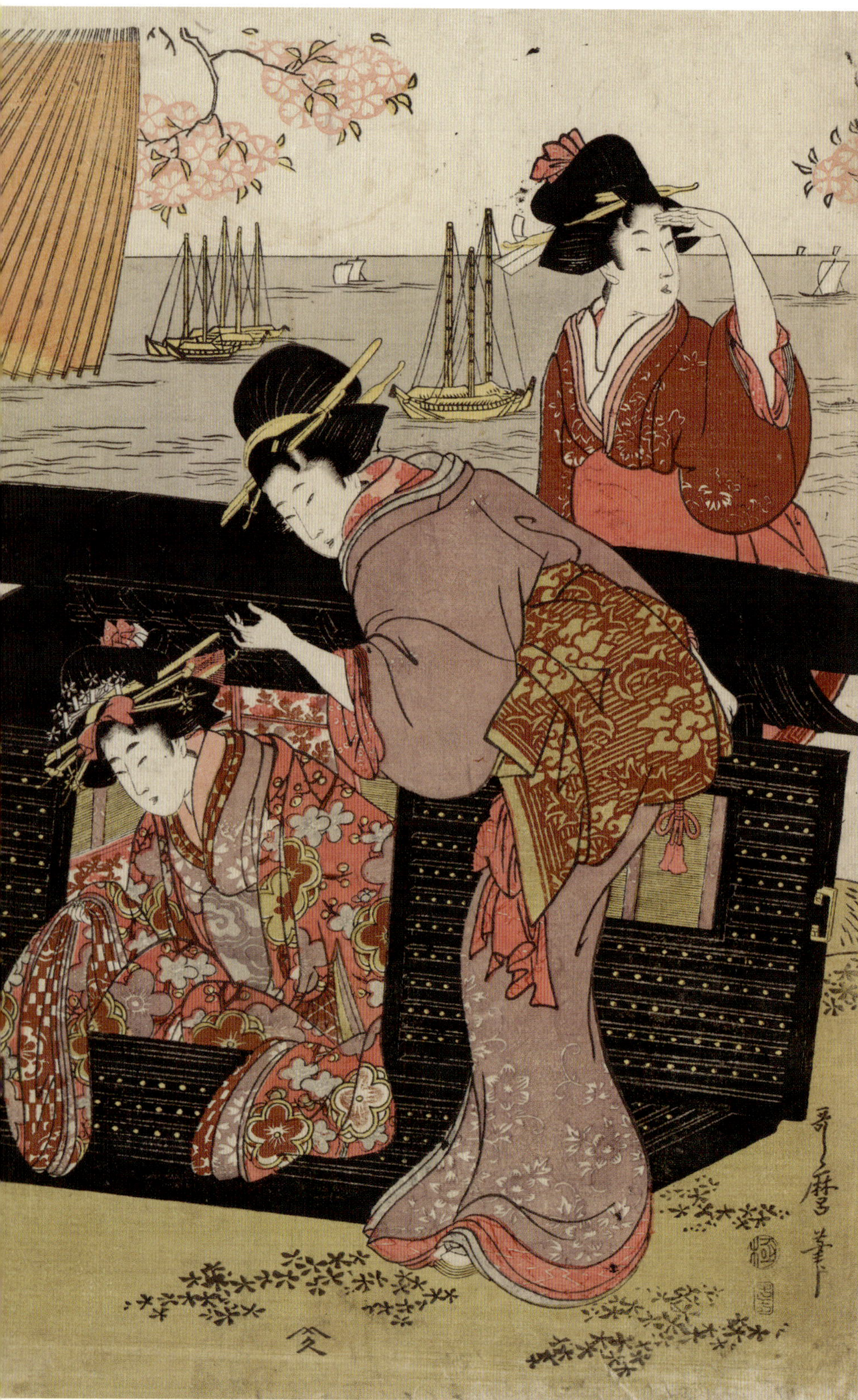

Iemitsu (1604–51), clamped down on Christian converts. Such theological objections as the shoguns may have had to the new religion appear to have been incidental to their chief concern – the preservation of the spiritual, intellectual and political status quo. Under his successors, Ieyasu's xenophobic instincts hardened into a series of legislative measures. By 1633, Iemitsu had formalized a strict *sakoku* (isolationist) policy. Japan was officially closed off: no foreigner could come in nor any native leave. Defiance of the laws was punishable by death.

Perverse it may have been, but the Tokugawa shoguns' achievement was still extraordinary. For well over two centuries, they succeeded in holding back history; stopping the march of time. In their new capital, Edo (now called Tokyo), the Tokugawa shoguns established a social order of such unshakeable solidity that it seems to have been barely possible even to imagine the idea of change. But as welcome as an end to so many generations of continuous conflict must have been, this Edo period must have been a very strange one in which to live.

A World Afloat

On the one hand, the new conditions (counterintuitively, it might be thought) fostered prosperity. In its isolation, the Japanese economy boomed. On the other hand, the *chônin* (townsmen) – the emergent class of urban artisans and merchants that this boom had enriched economically without empowering politically – were more or less condemned to waste the money that they made.

For the sons and daughters of this new wealthy class, especially, a life of leisure beckoned, with no work to do nor any real responsibilities of any kind. Affluent as they were, they could devote their lives to the pursuit of personal pleasure and social status, their only duties to look decorative and display the wealth and ease of their families. Nothing needed to constrain their conduct: their hedonism had no limits, their actions no

ABOVE Kitagawa Utamaro (*c.* 1753–1806) *Cherry-viewing at Gotenyama* (1805, printed later)

real consequences. They lived for the moment, their existence poised in place and time. If Japan had isolated itself from the wider world, this class had separated itself from Japanese society, beyond the reach of all the normal rules. Geographically, they were removed as well, spending much of their time in Yoshiwara, the Edo district officially licensed as the major centre for theatres, cafés, bars and brothels.

Unsurprisingly, these beautiful young idlers lacked apparent purpose, showing no sign of direction or seriousness of mind. To their countrymen and -women – caught between contempt and envy – they seemed adrift in their own peculiar *ukiyo* or 'Floating World'. An evocative description, whose subtle ambivalence may easily escape us, it makes wry reference to the religious realm. Buddhist mystics had long sought to attain a state of ecstatic suspension, all earthly attachments severed, all ego surrendered, the consciousness 'afloat', abandoned to the ebbs and flows of the universe.

In its seventeenth-century usage, the word was starting to suggest a more secular sort of abandonment; a rather more worldly way of letting go. The classic definition by the novelist Asai Ryoi (*c.* 1612–91), from *Ukiyo Monogotari* ('Stories from the Floating World') of 1661, makes this new meaning abundantly clear whilst looking over its shoulder at this older, more spiritual sense:

> *Let us cast aside all gloomy thoughts of our worldly wretchedness: we should rather drink sake and sing joyfully of the pleasures afforded by the snow, the moon, the flowers and the autumn leaves. Let us live out our lives like a gourd, carried downstream on the current. This is what we understand by the floating world.*

Philosophical Frivolity

Ryoi's explanation is important, illuminating as it does both the philosophical solemnity beneath the seeming heedlessness and the note

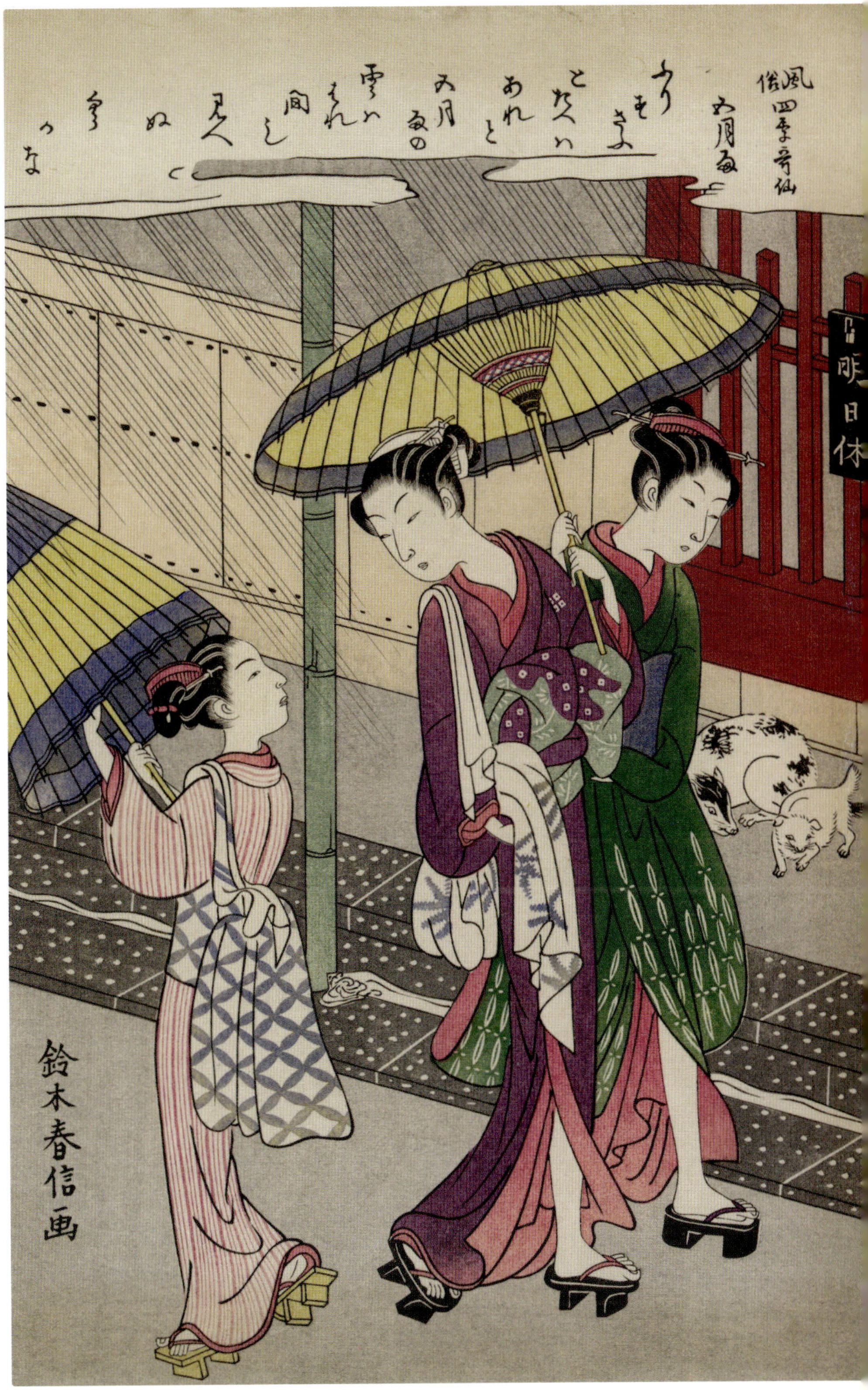

Above Suzuki Harunobo (*c.* 1725–70) *Rain in May* (1770, printed later)

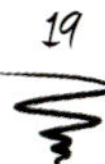

of melancholy sounding through the song of pleasure. If we wish to understand the impact of *ukiyo-e* – the art that recorded, responded to and promoted the lifestyle and activities of this 'floating world' – we have to appreciate that ambivalence to the full. The point is not that the lifestyle or the art seemed frivolous, but that they were *really* serious. The frivolity and the seriousness were both equally real and equally important, twin aspects of a single philosophical and artistic vision.

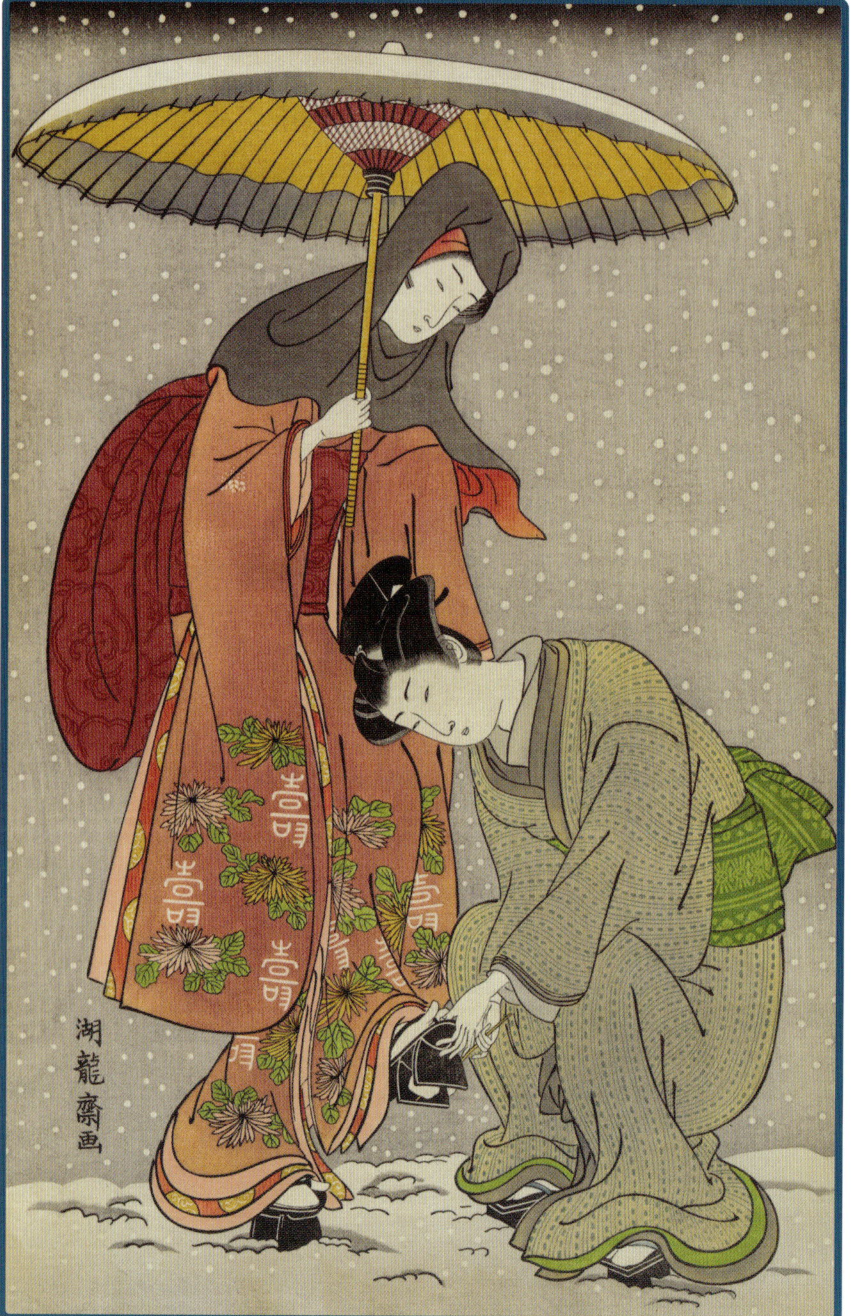

Above **Isoda Koryusai** (1735–90) *Removing Snow From One's Clogs* (1776, printed later)

For the Western reader, this paradox recalls those surrounding the ideas of the Greek philosopher of the fourth century BC, Epicurus (341–270 BC). Only the deepest soul-searching brought him to the conclusion that, in an incomprehensible universe, there is no point in our striving endlessly to fathom out deeper origins or causes; the only thing we can ultimately know is what frees us from pain. Inevitably, however, whilst his arguments for what amounted to a radical scepticism remain compelling in their integrity, the 'Epicurean' has popularly been assumed to be an amoral pleasure seeker.

Both these strands are present in the imagery of *ukiyo-e*. If there are lovely landscapes and stunning scenes from nature, there are displays of dissipation too, in the richly dressed young men and women living an empty life to the full in an endless round of parties, theatrical performances, rural excursions and river cruises. There are endless portraits of society beauties – and, in the erotic art of *shunga* (as in the homoerotic *shudo* pictures), a certain amount of pornography. The popularity of such paintings (or woodblock prints), not just in the Japan of their own time but all around the world today, can of course be accounted for in part by their sheer elegance and glamour. Who would not want to live this life – or, failing that, see it portrayed? But it is surely, too, that all this exquisiteness – suggestive as it is of the fragility of beauty and the transience of youth and joy – stirs us much more deeply than we might appreciate at our first glance.

Living Art

'One should,' Oscar Wilde (1854–1900) was to say, 'either be a work of art or wear a work of art.' The young subjects of *ukiyo-e* did both. Often they

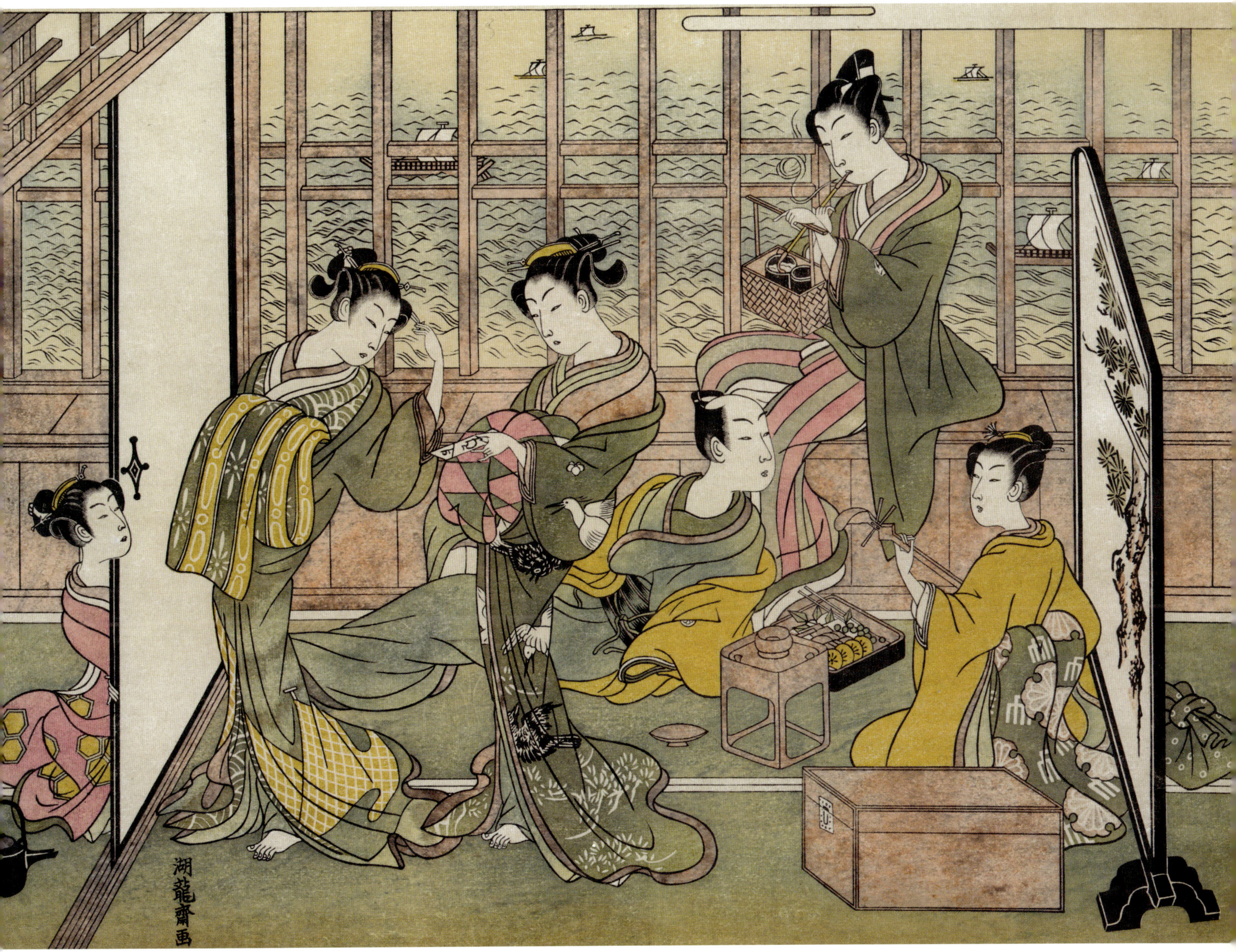

ABOVE **Isoda Koryusai (1735–90)** *A Brothel in Shinagawa* (first page of a *shunga* set) (1774, printed later)

were actors, accustomed to playing parts (in kabuki theatre some male *onnagata* specialized in representing women; whilst in some all-female companies women would have to perform male roles). Others were courtesans or *kagema* (young male prostitutes), whose working life was also already to some extent a performance, or they might be publicly

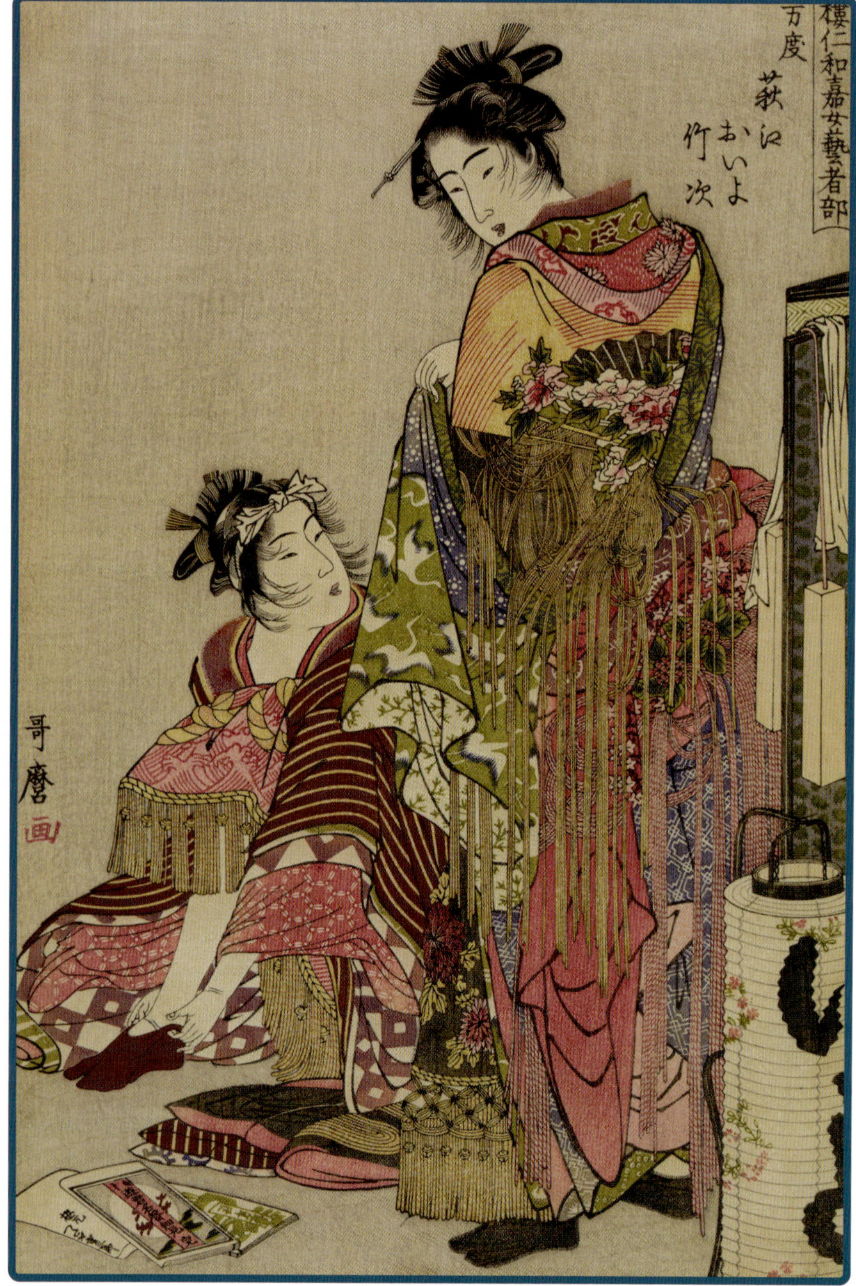

acknowledged beauties or rich young gentlemen of fashion. Pretty as pictures, with their porcelain skin and fine-brushed features, the young ladies' faces were complemented by the sumptuous colours of their stunningly cut *kosode* – not so much gowns as masterpieces of textile art. Those statuesque *shimada* hairdos completed the show with complex constructions of combs, pins, cord and frames in black, lustrous hair. Their male counterparts are scarcely less perfect in their presentation – even burly warriors are robed in luxuriantly sweeping silk, their curved swords seeming to 'rhyme' with the sinuous flexing of their mighty forms.

Not that it was just their physical appearance or personal presentation that seemed artistic – so ceremonious was their life, so stylized their activities, so artificial their customs, that they appeared to be enacting little tableaux. It can seem that way in the *ukiyo-e*, at least, as though the artist, far from having to compose his scene, simply stumbled upon his picture, ready-made. A tea ceremony; a salon; a group of friends out walking; a lovers' tryst … such occasions already seemed halfway to being art.

As for the art itself, that seemed halfway to decoration. *Ukiyo-e* ran generally to stylized, generic scenes. It was not quite that they were interchangeable, but recognizable formulas were followed in these pictures, and we have the impression that, widely bought to put up around the homes of the rapidly rising middle class in Edo and other Japanese cities, they were there to provide a splash of colour and a bit of animating energy.

Mass Culture

An important shift in media had meanwhile been taking place, the unique prestige of paintings being gradually displaced by the colour and convenience of prints. Convenient for the publisher and customer, that is: making a woodblock print was itself a long and awkward process, or

Above **Kitagawa Utamaro (*c.* 1753–1806)** Two Women Entertainers (geisha) getting dressed for a festival (1785, printed later)

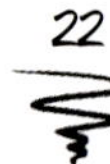

Right **Toyohara Kunichika (1835–1900)** Unnamed actor in the role of Toneri Umemaru in the play *Sugawara no michizane (Sugawar senjin ki)* (1860–66)

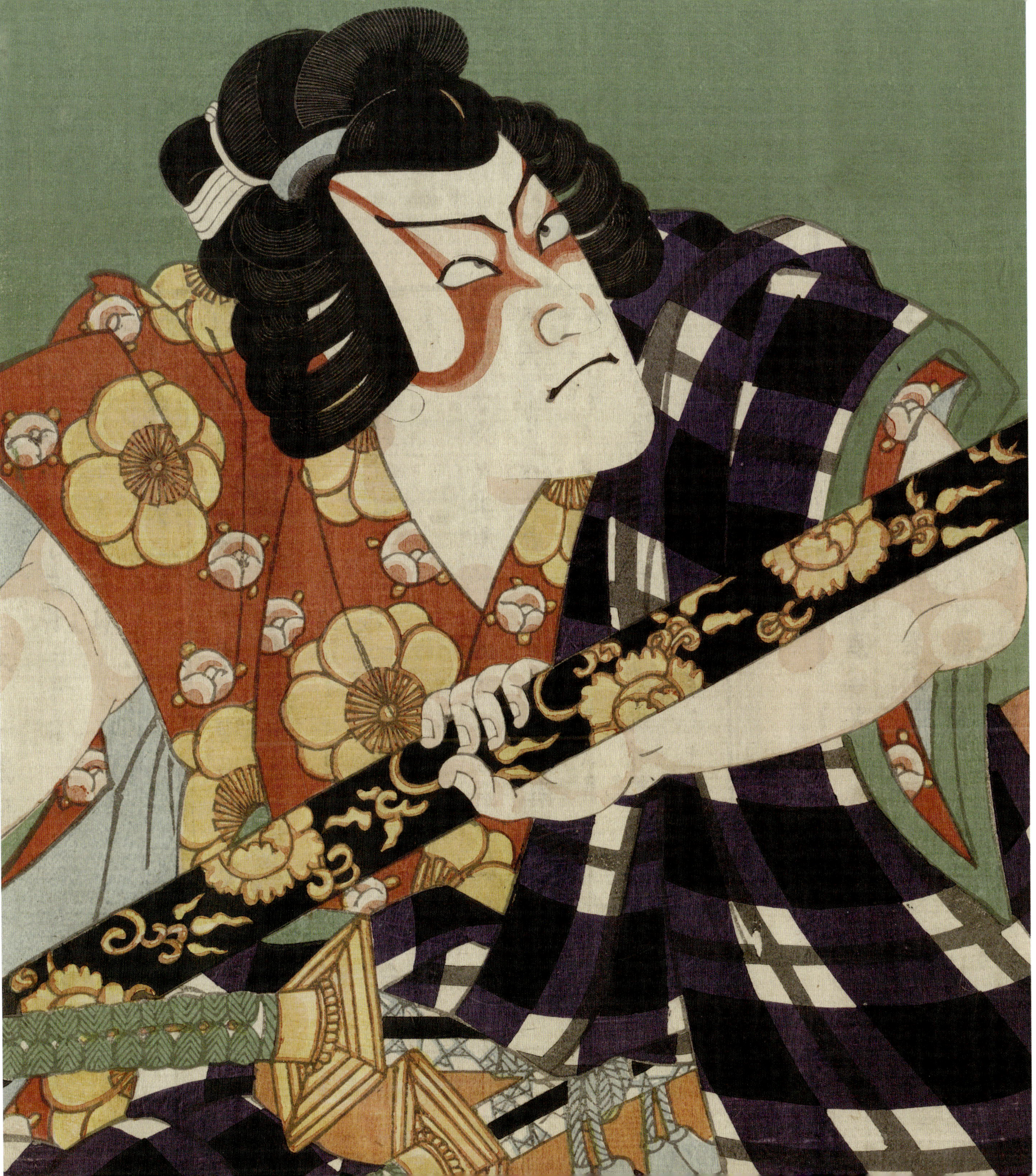

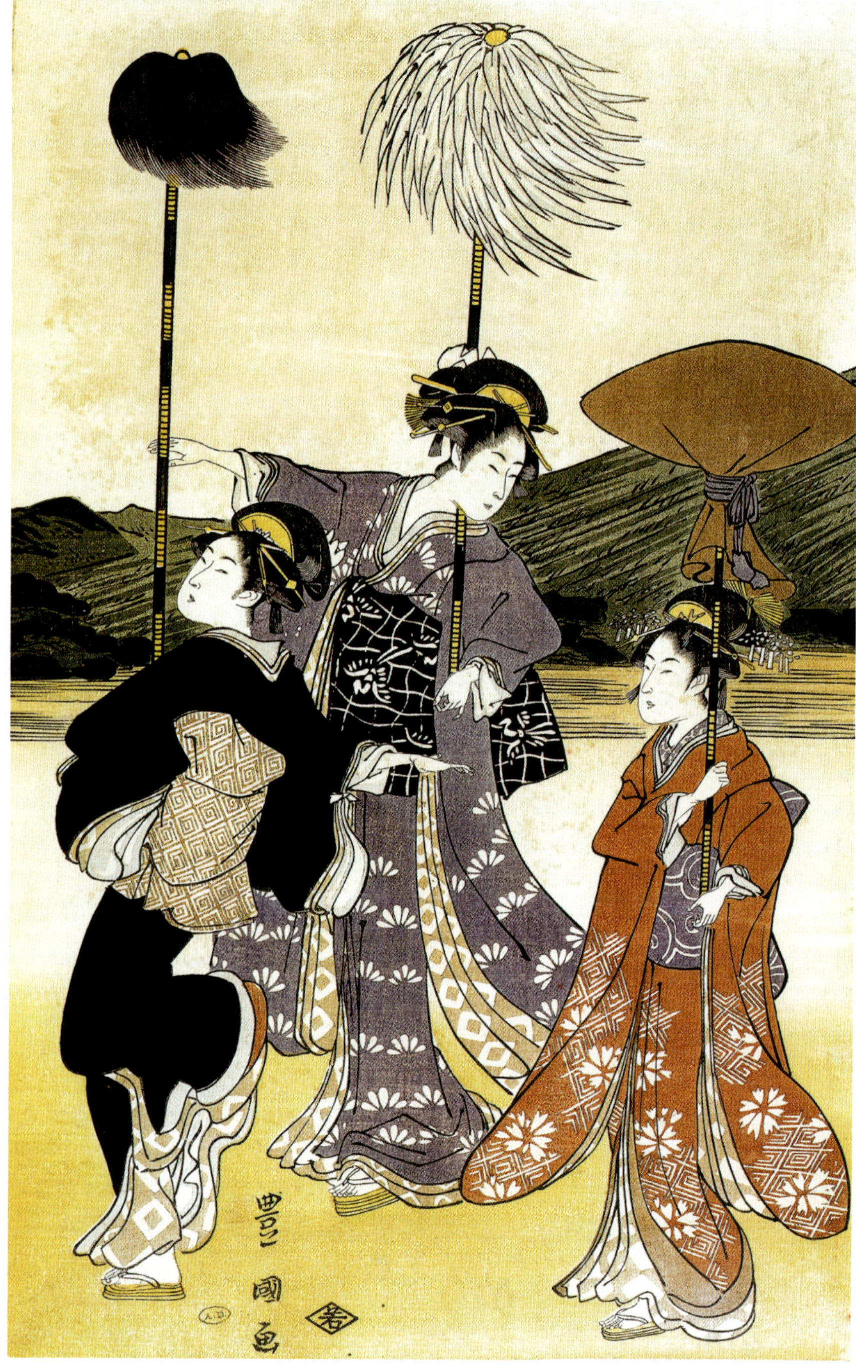

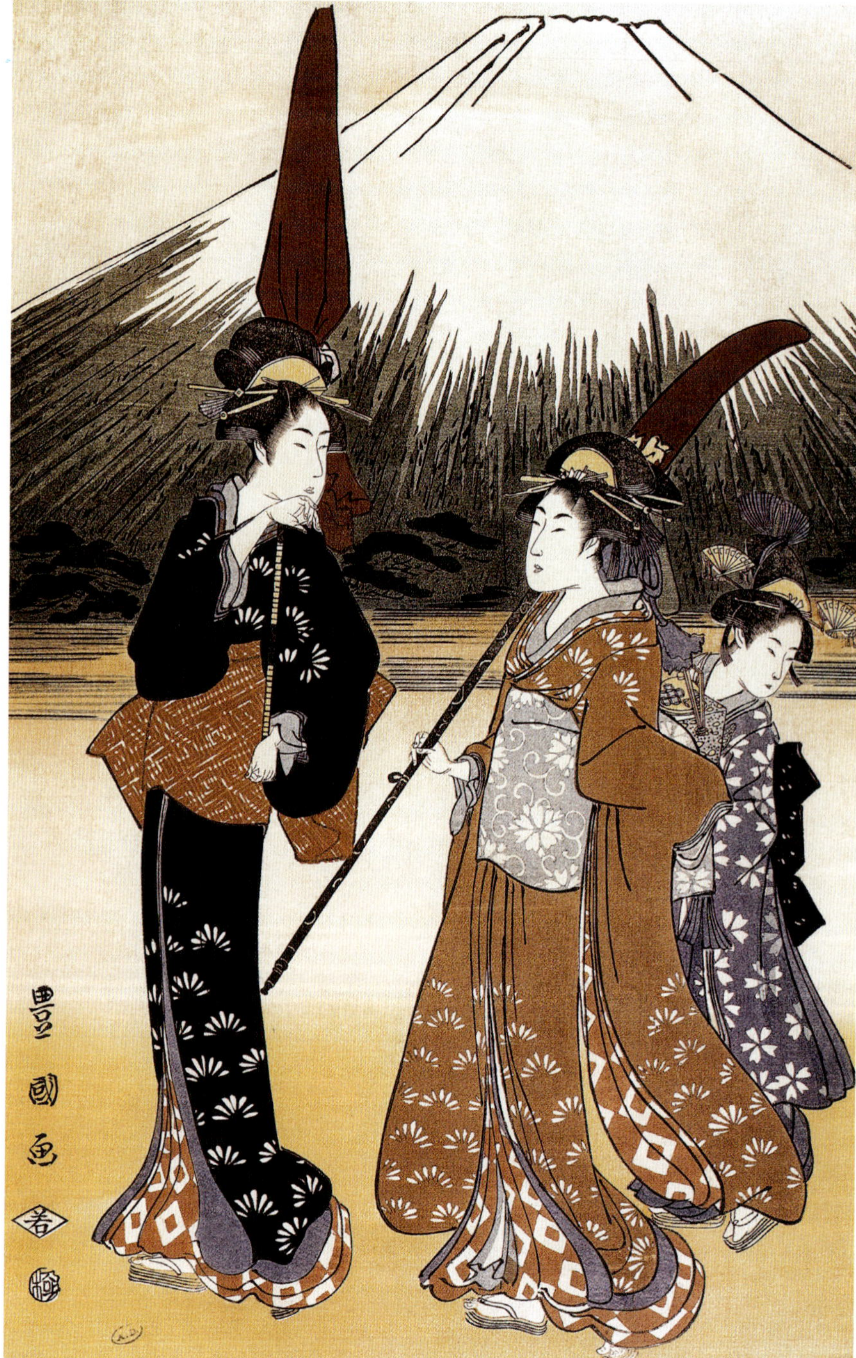

Above & Opposite Suzuki Harunobu (1725–70) *Walk towards Mount Fuji* (1765)

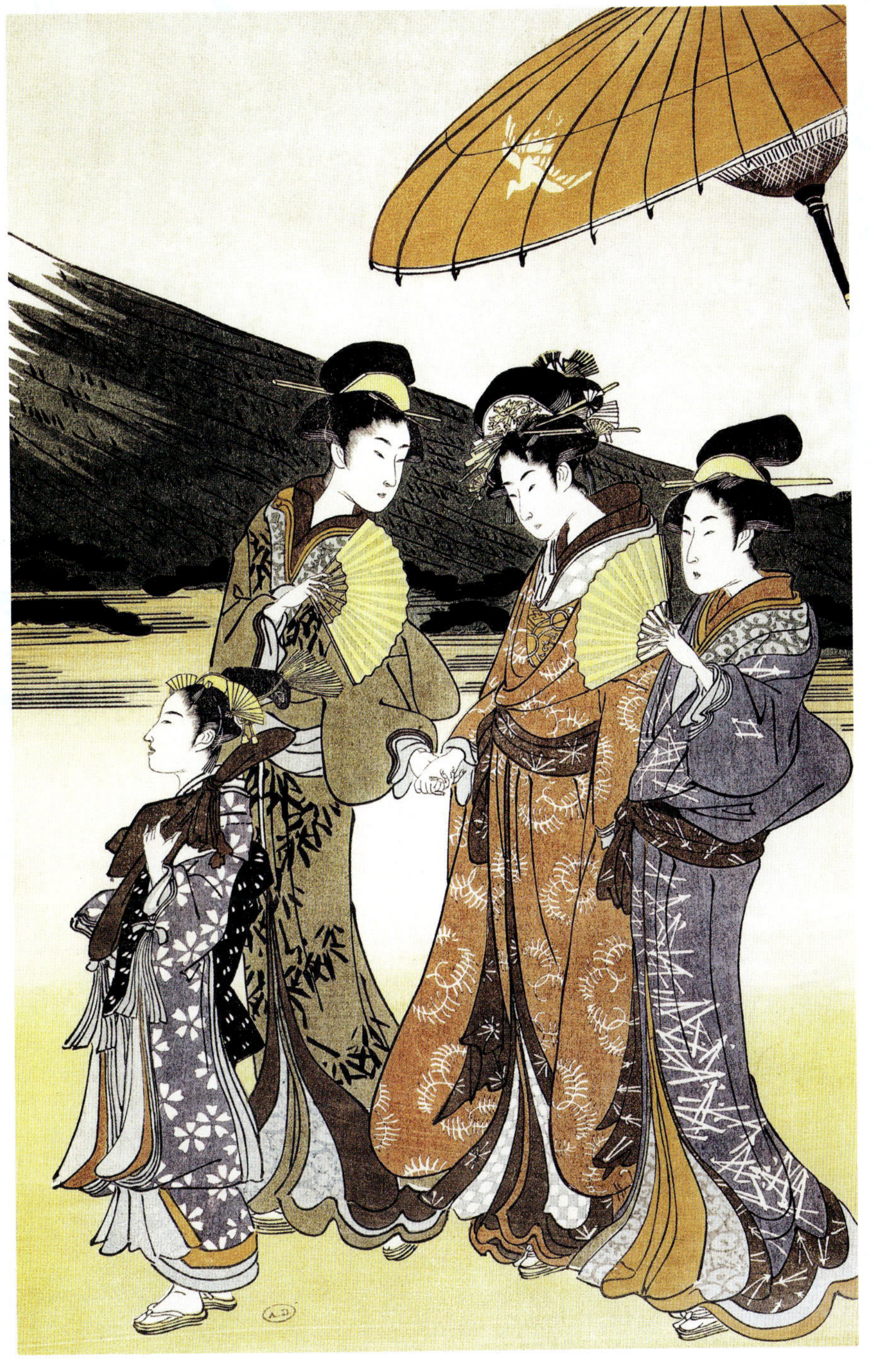

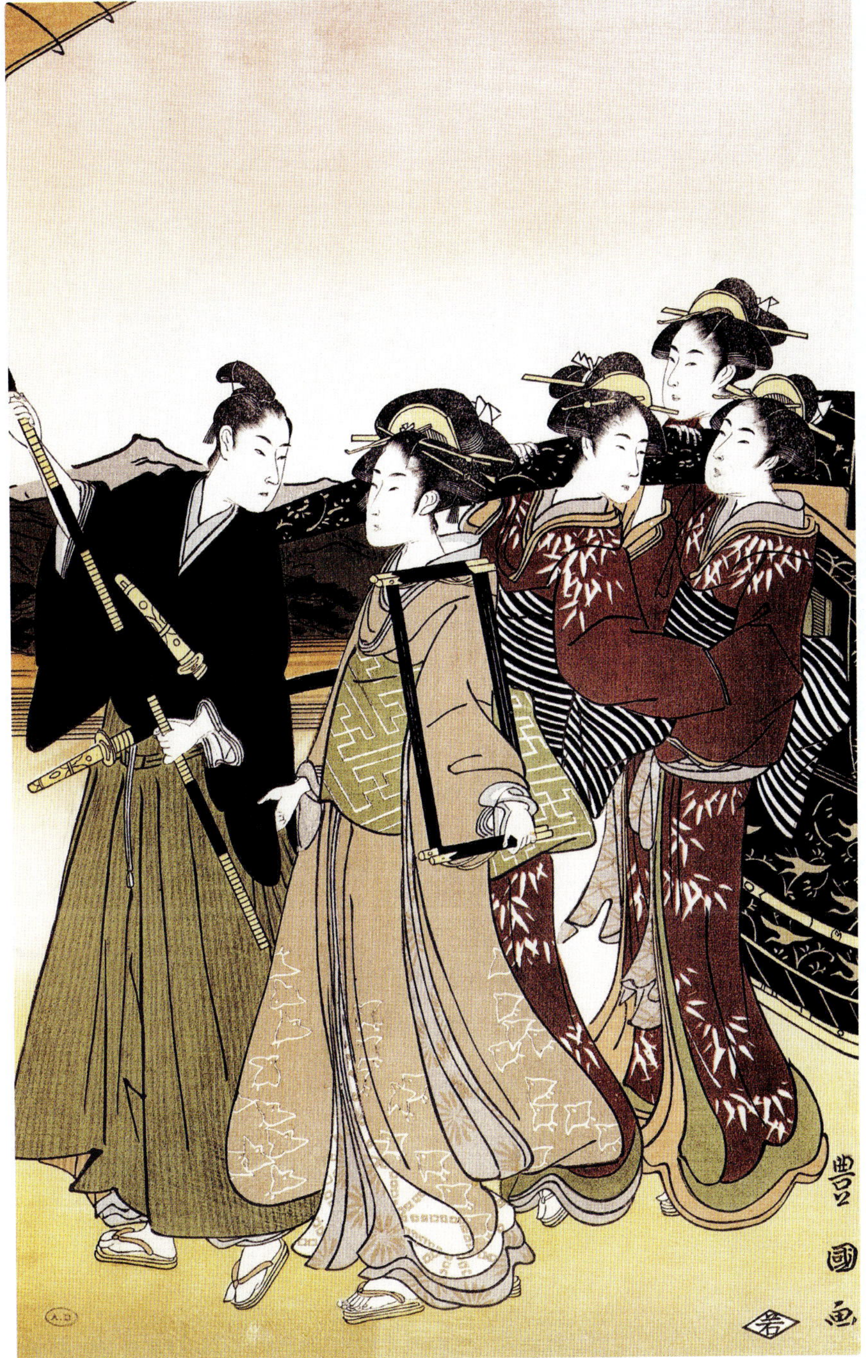

series of processes, the artistic composition – sketched with ink on *washi*, the coloured areas marked – by far the easiest of these.

A specialized craftsman, having glued the picture face down on to a convex-curving board of cherry wood, would then have slowly and meticulously scored along both sides of the drawn lines. Now a *chokoku-to* carving chisel could be used to lift away a layer of wood from inside and around the design outline, leaving the picture itself standing proud, ready for inking. A *baren* – a rounded block of compressed bamboo and leather, and faced with lacquered rice paper – was used to press down on the delicate print without causing damage. From here on, however, printing really was convenient, as hundreds of copies could be run off from a single block. Definitely a physical process, putting some considerable pressure on the cherry-wood block being used, it took its toll, so it was impossible to produce unlimited artworks from the same block. Signs of tiredness began to show (to the expert eye, at any rate) after the first couple of hundred copies – for prestige prints, the block would then be set aside.

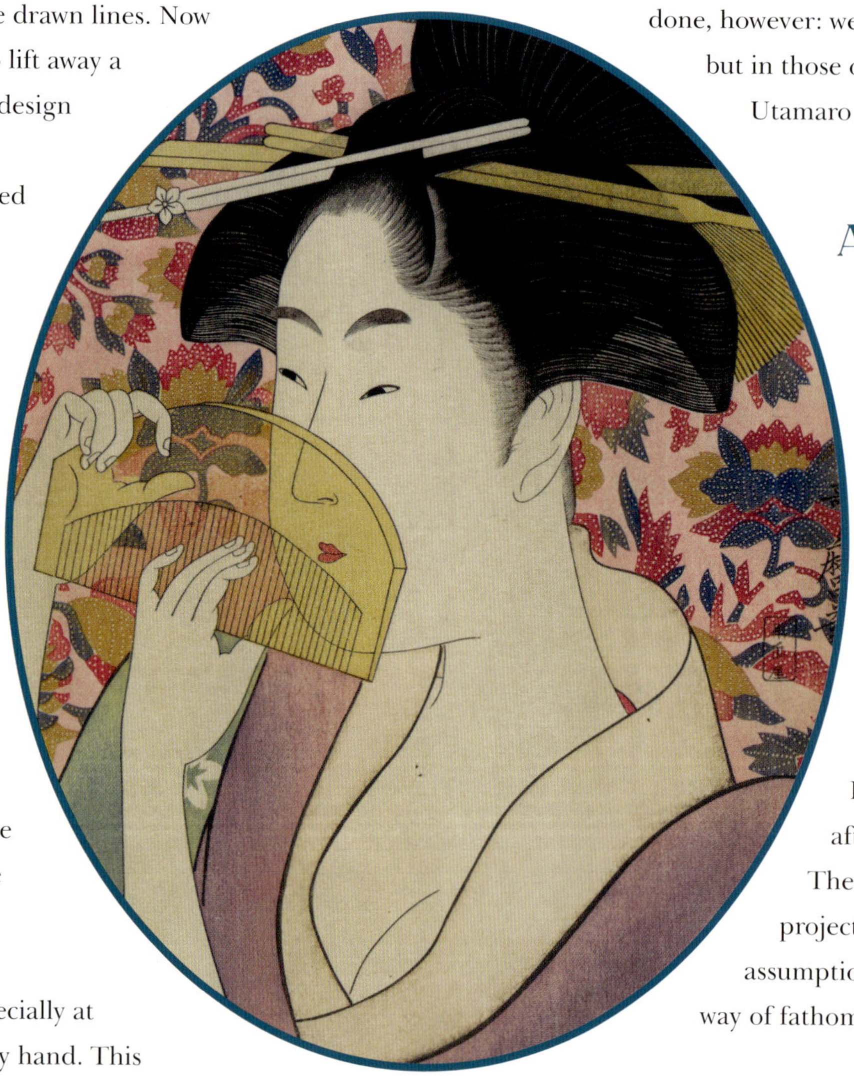

Many prints were left in monochrome, especially at first, but increasingly colours were added by hand. This involved more time and expense, but incomparable to what would be required to produce a unique painting. Or a more elaborate image might be printed by a technique using successive plates etched with different designs and inked with different colours, called *nishiki-e*. (A talismanic presence in such pictures from the first, Fuji appears in several full-colour prints by the pioneering Suzuki Harunobo, 1725–70: scenes of beauties walking before Mount Fuji are a recurring theme – *see* pages 24–25.) We can only guess at the artistic or spiritual logic which decreed that a view of feminine comeliness required the accompaniment of Mount Fuji, at the very least in a background role. It often seems to have done, however: we see this not only in Harunobo's prints, but in those of the celebrated *bijin-ga* king Kitagawa Utamaro (*c.* 1753–1806).

Another World

It's tempting to see the distant prospect of Mount Fuji in such prints as representing the spiritual purification offered by rural Nature as against the (distinctly worldly) world of urban pleasure. How else are we to interpret *Dreaming of Walking Near Fuji* (*c.* 1770, *see* right). This curious print by Isoda Koryusai (1735–90) shows what would appear to be a pair of courtesans in an Edo brothel imagining … what? An afternoon out? A vacation? A different life? There's always the risk with any 'alien' art of projecting our own cultural, social or ethical assumptions on to it. We've really no convincing way of fathoming these women's 'dream'.

The net result was, if not quite art for all, then at least art for a much greater audience than had ever had access to such creative works before, except in public places such as shrines and temples. Unsurprisingly, these prints proved popular, and the boom in their sales allowed the imagery – and, to some extent, the values – of *ukiyo* to

Above Kitagawa Utamaro (*c.* 1753–1806) *Comb* (*c.* 1780s, printed later)

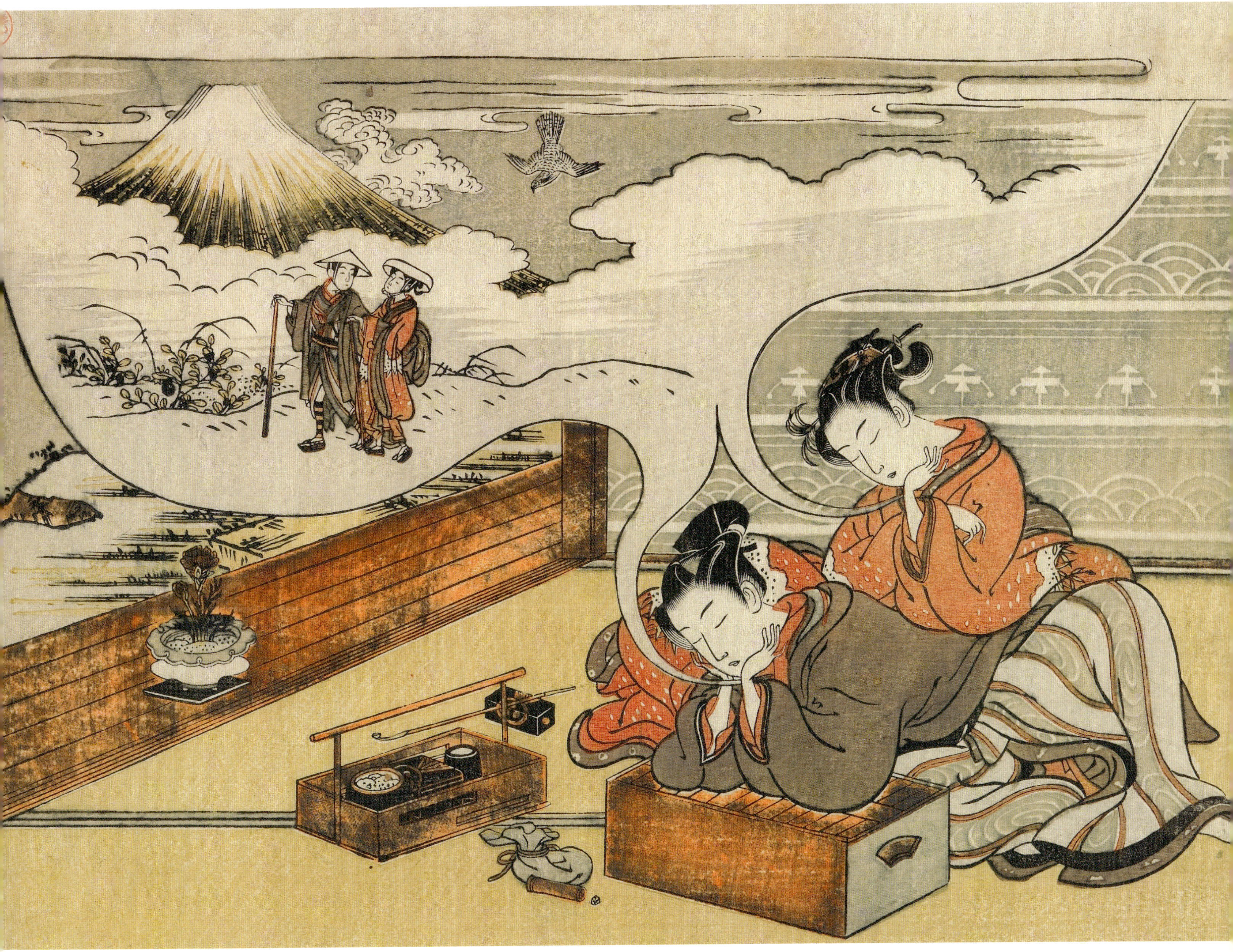

ABOVE Isoda Koryusai (1735–90) *Dreaming of Walking Near Fuji* (*c.* 1770)

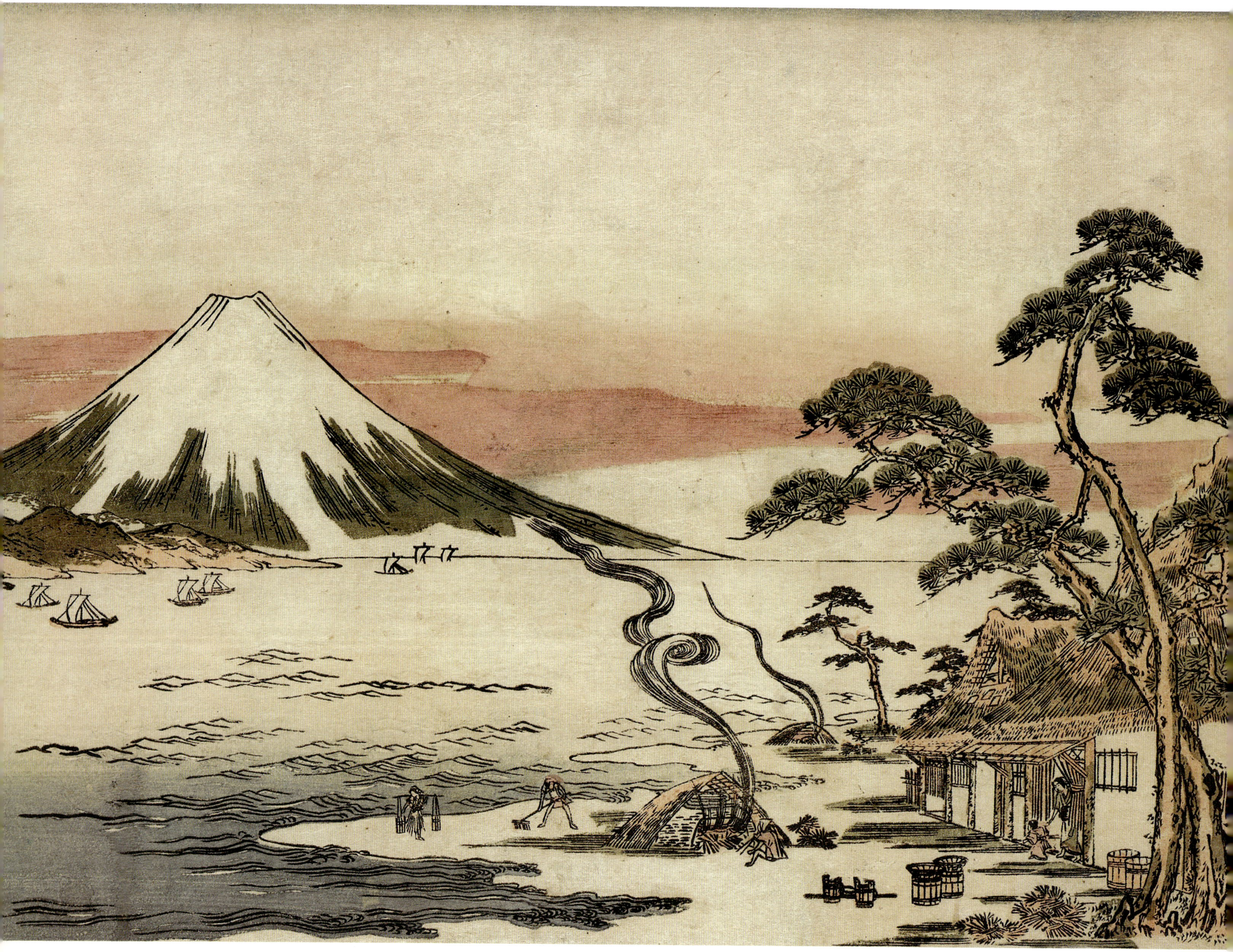

Above Utagawa Toyoharu (1735–1814) *View of Mount Fuji in Spring from Tago Bay* (date unknown)

circulate more widely in Japanese society. Those rich and privileged enough to participate in the 'floating life', as it was actually lived in Yoshiwara, of course, constituted a negligible proportion of the Japanese population as a whole. As with the 'celebrity culture' of today, however, the values and aspirations of this tiny handful to some extent 'trickled down' into echelons of society whose members were by no means obviously either privileged or free.

An Oriental Aesthetic?

Wilde's words seem especially relevant here because that paradoxically profound superficiality of his seems to resonate so well, not just with the wider values of late-nineteenth-century aestheticism in Europe but with the artistic sensibility of seventeenth-century Edo. Notoriously, in 1853, the peace and quiet of Edo was to be rudely interrupted by the appearance of Commodore Matthew Calbraith Perry (1794–1858) and his American flotilla in Tokyo Bay. Demanding commercial access – effectively at gunpoint – his arrival spelled the end of the Tokugawa shogunate.

The decades that followed saw what is generally described as the 'opening up' of Japan to the rest of the world – though that label puts an extremely upbeat spin on what amounted to colonialist coercion. Willingly or unwillingly, for better or for worse, however, Japan began trading with the Western nations; inevitably, there was cultural commerce too. It was no more than a coincidence that the first Japanese products and artefacts found a uniquely welcoming reception in Europe. Japanese art and design did not just seem new and exotic, they struck a chord.

For the continent was in the grip of Aestheticism, which in its origins owed much to Epicurus. Although it was to be presented most dramatically in England in the person of Oscar Wilde and his dandified followers, it was explored more philosophically by writers such as Walter Pater (1830–94). On the Continent, it found expression in the literary Symbolism of poets such as Charles Baudelaire (1821–67), Stéphane Mallarmé (1842–98), Paul Verlaine (1844–96) and Arthur Rimbaud (1854–91). Distrustful of established views that literature could somehow embody eternal 'truths' by the straightforward representation of external reality, these poets

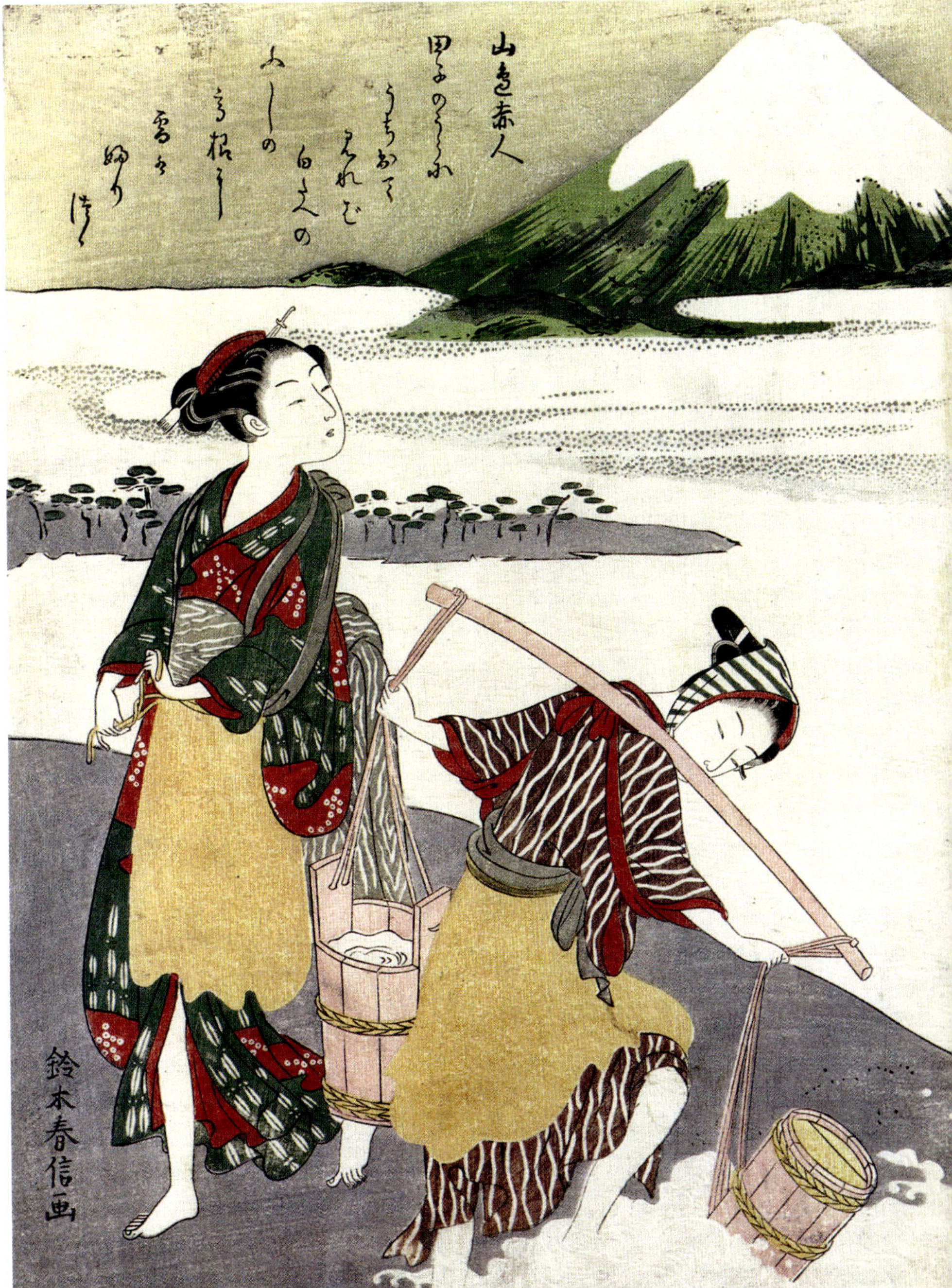

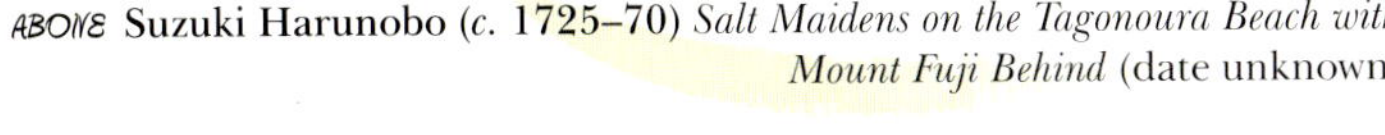
ABOVE Suzuki Harunobo (*c.* 1725–70) *Salt Maidens on the Tagonoura Beach with Mount Fuji Behind* (date unknown)

created a new kind of poetry, its beauty in its sensuality and shimmering surface, its deeper emotions displayed only in overtones and hints. Soon, painters were following where the poets led, albeit in many cases unconsciously. Impressionism, for example, conceived of itself as a

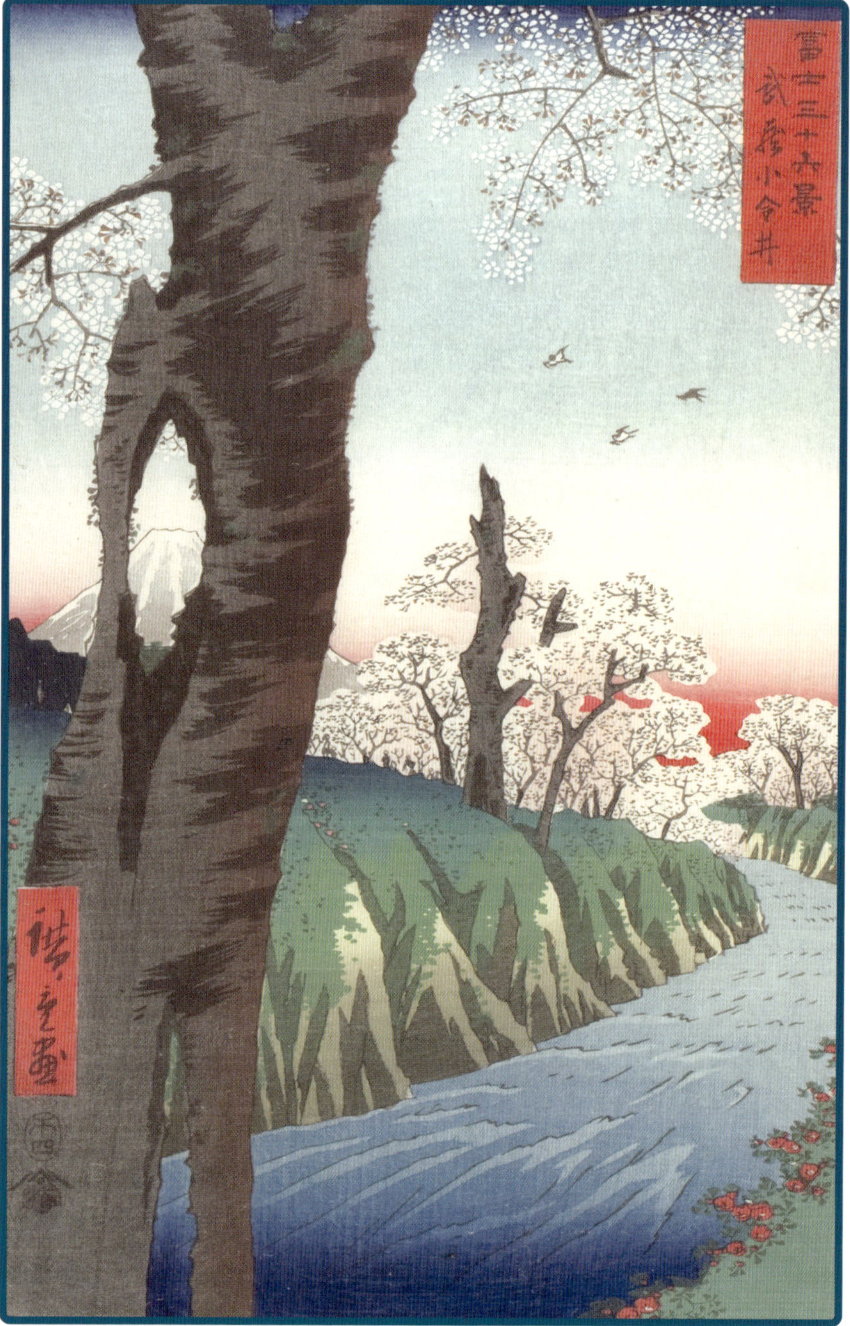

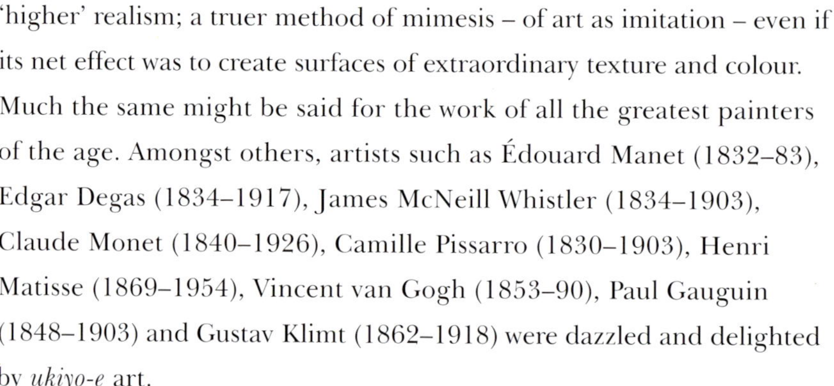

'higher' realism; a truer method of mimesis – of art as imitation – even if its net effect was to create surfaces of extraordinary texture and colour. Much the same might be said for the work of all the greatest painters of the age. Amongst others, artists such as Édouard Manet (1832–83), Edgar Degas (1834–1917), James McNeill Whistler (1834–1903), Claude Monet (1840–1926), Camille Pissarro (1830–1903), Henri Matisse (1869–1954), Vincent van Gogh (1853–90), Paul Gauguin (1848–1903) and Gustav Klimt (1862–1918) were dazzled and delighted by *ukiyo-e* art.

Into the Countryside

By this time, however, Japanese artists had themselves moved on. In a self-consciously conservative tradition, change had been slow and the continuities strong. Even so, there had been a broadening of subject matter. Landscape, and the beauties of the Japanese countryside, had been receiving increased attention ever since the great poet Matsuo Basho (1644–94) had published his *Oku no Hosomichi* (*Narrow Road to the Deep Interior*, 1694) a diary of his wanderings on foot through the wilds of northern Honshu. Rather like the Romantics of Western Europe a century later, Basho had found the empty calm of the remotest rural byways an inspiration, his experience of solitude a spur to reaching outwards to his world and to his fellow human beings.

Through the eighteenth century, accordingly, whilst scenes of city life and entertainment retained their popularity, *ukiyo-e* took a quieter, more reflective turn. Landscape, no longer an incidental background, came to the fore as a subject in its own right as artists followed – figuratively, at least – in Basho's footsteps. A mountain is a mountain, it might be thought; a wave a wave; a clump of trees a clump of trees. Yet *ukiyo-e* landscape painting was to seem every bit as alien, as strange to its first European viewers as the more obviously exotic prints of urban social life.

Above Utagawa Hiroshige (1797–1858) *Koganei in Musashi Province* from 'Thirty-six Views of Mount Fuji' (1858)

Right Utagawa Hiroshige (1797–1858) *Wild Goose Hill and the Tone River* (detail) from 'Thirty-six Views of Mount Fuji' (1858)

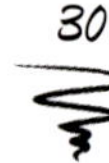

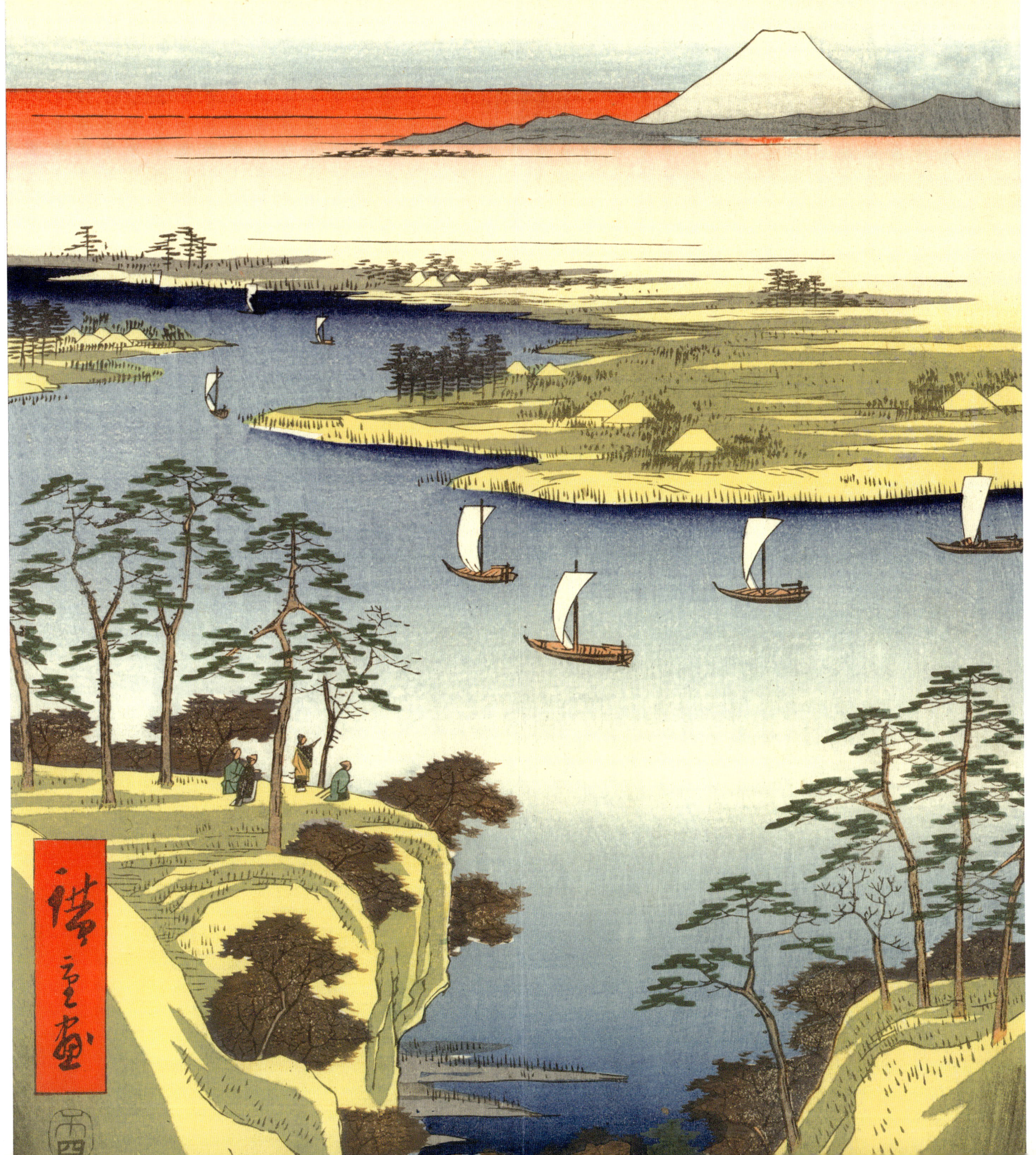
廣重画

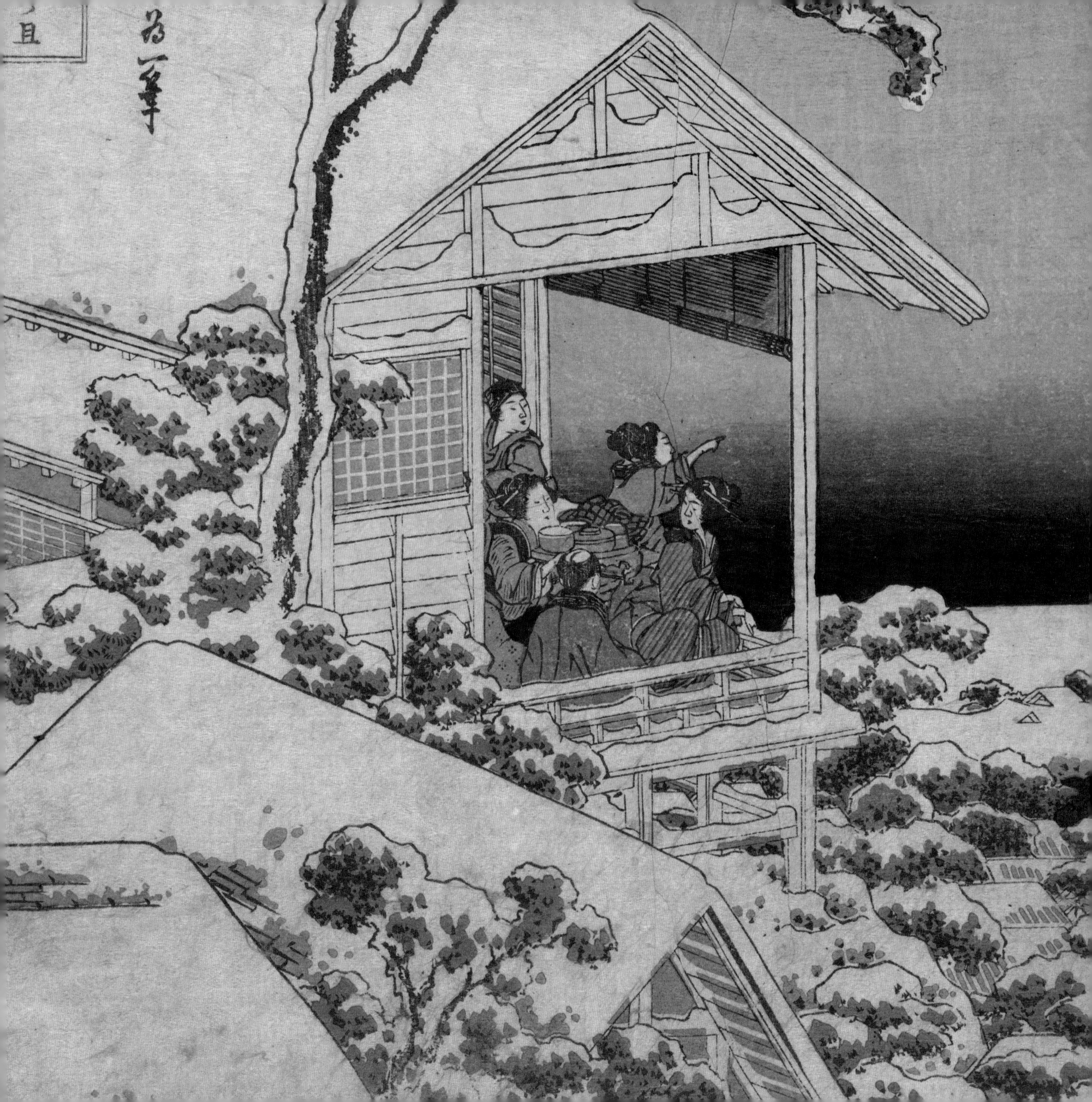
為一筆

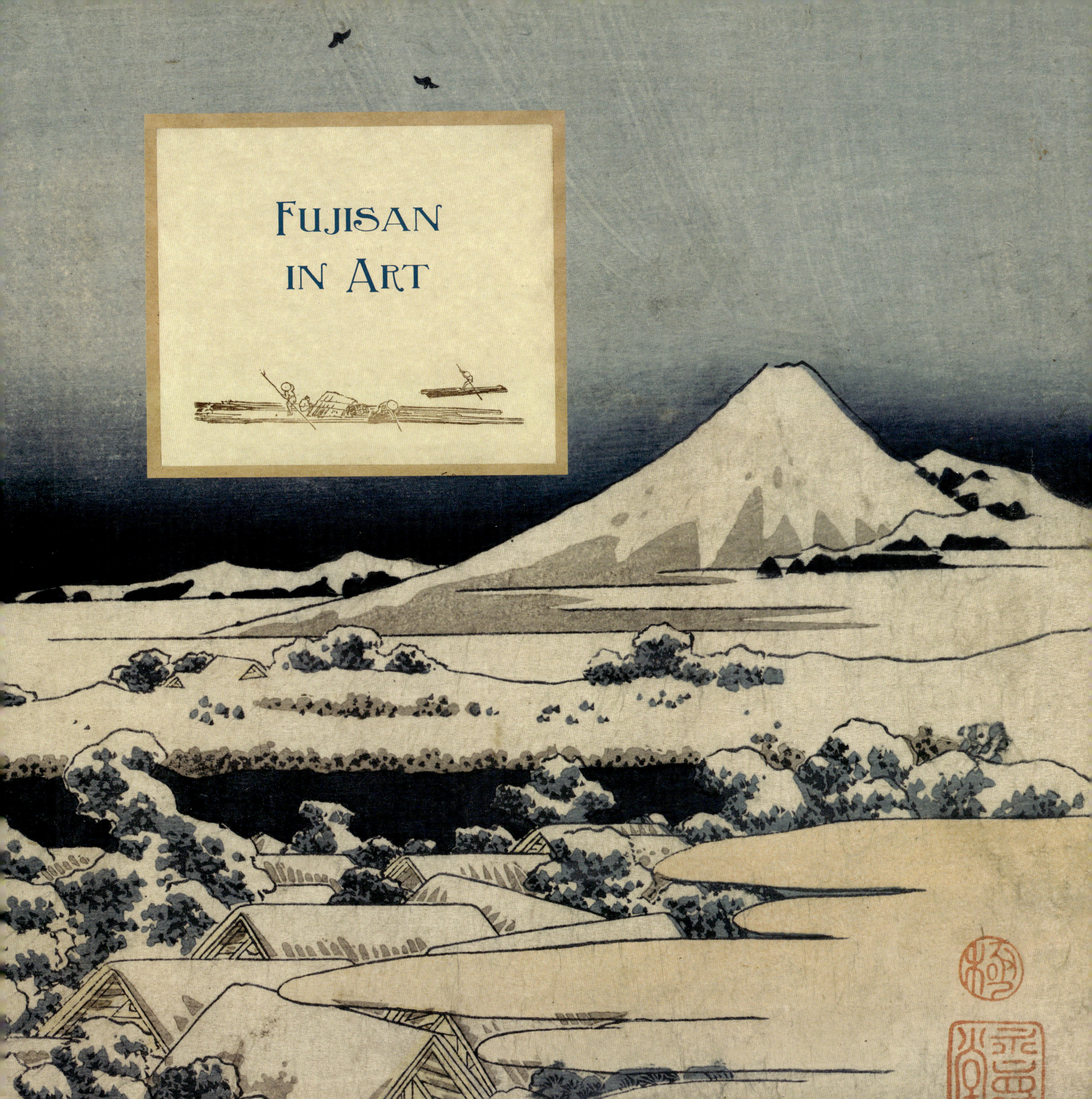
FUJISAN
IN ART

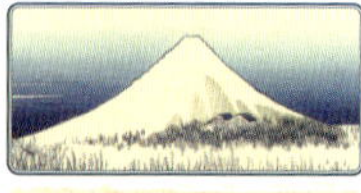

The idea of the sacred mountain is as old as the idea of sanctity itself; as ancient as the opposition between worldly earth and spiritual sky. Mythic Mount Meru towered at the cosmological centre of Indian religions, such as Hinduism, Buddhism and Jainism; their domed stupa temples mimicked its sloping form. Like Inca priests offering sacrifice amidst the Andean summits, the biblical Moses climbed Mount Sinai to receive God's Ten Commandments; Dante had to scale a mountain to pass through Purgatory to Paradise.

In a lovely Japanese landscape, Fujisan is quite literally pre-eminent, rising high above its surrounding countryside. But, as we have seen, it looms large in the country's consciousness as well. The former factor must, of course, have reinforced the latter. Its rocky sides sloping inwards, smooth and true towards a snowy summit – or concealing clouds – made the mountain an obvious emblem of spiritual aspiration.

A Natural Shrine

For a people accustomed to investing their environment with religious significance, Shinto was thus strongly rooted in the natural scene. The traditional Japanese religion had been from the first (it is believed to have begun in the early centuries of the first millennium) a state-wide schematization of what had been strictly local nature cults.

The need to reconcile the claims of grass-roots communities and the overarching state had been a deciding factor under successive emperors and shoguns for centuries, and to some extent remained so even with the Tokugawa shogunate in charge. Despite a growing sense of nationhood, Japan was still very much a collection of extended families or tribes with their own identities. The place of the *uji* or clan was still important. All had their

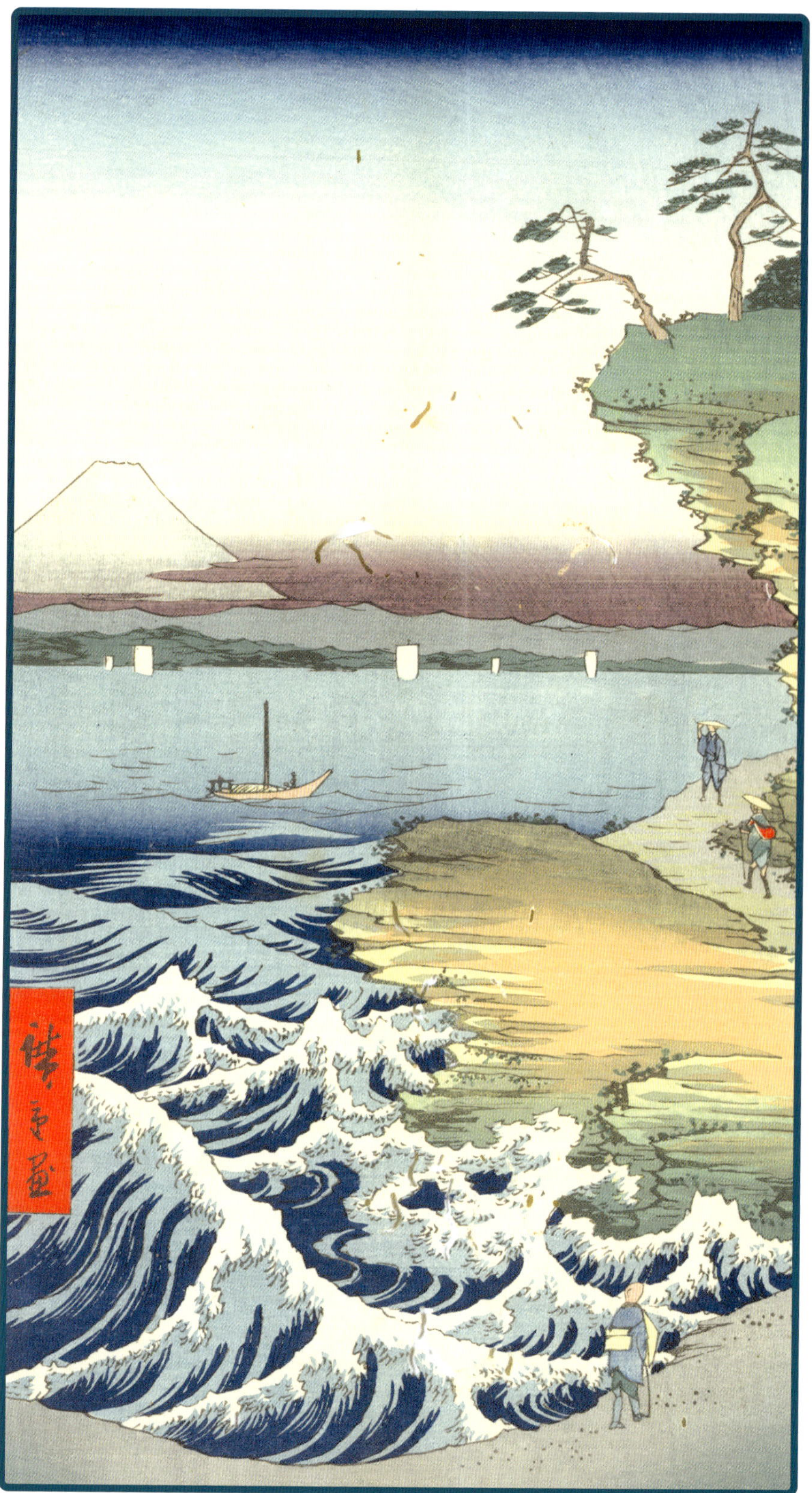

Previous pages Katsushika Hokusai (1760–1849) *Tea House at Koishikawa, the Morning After a Snowfall* (1832/33) from 'Thirty-six Views of Mount Fuji'

Above Utagawa Hiroshige (1797–1858) *The Hota Coast in Awa Province* from 'Thirty-six Views of Mount Fuji' (1858)

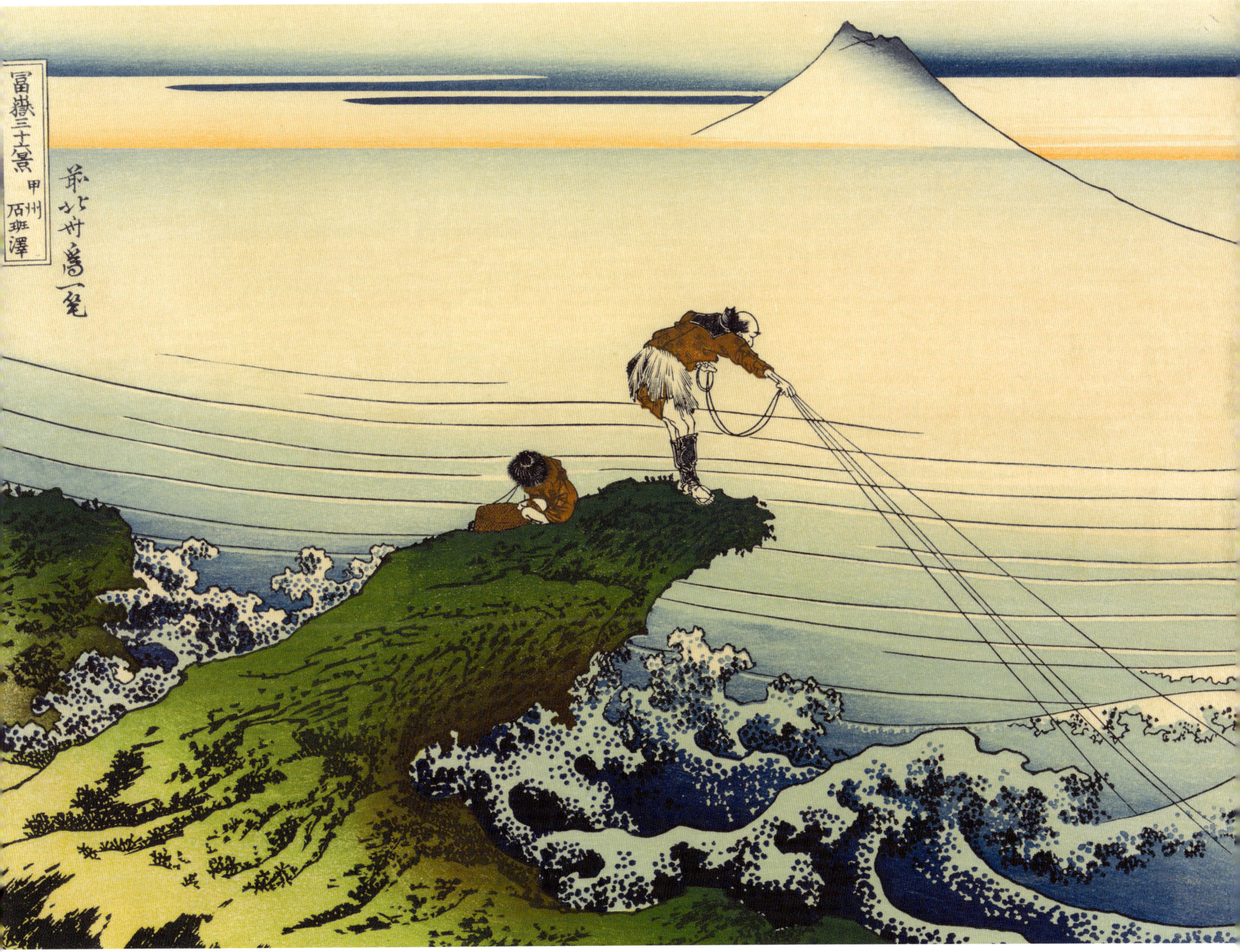

ABOVE **Katsushika Hokusai (1760–1849)** *Kajikazawa in Kai Province* from 'Thirty-six Views of Mount Fuji' (1826–33, printed later)

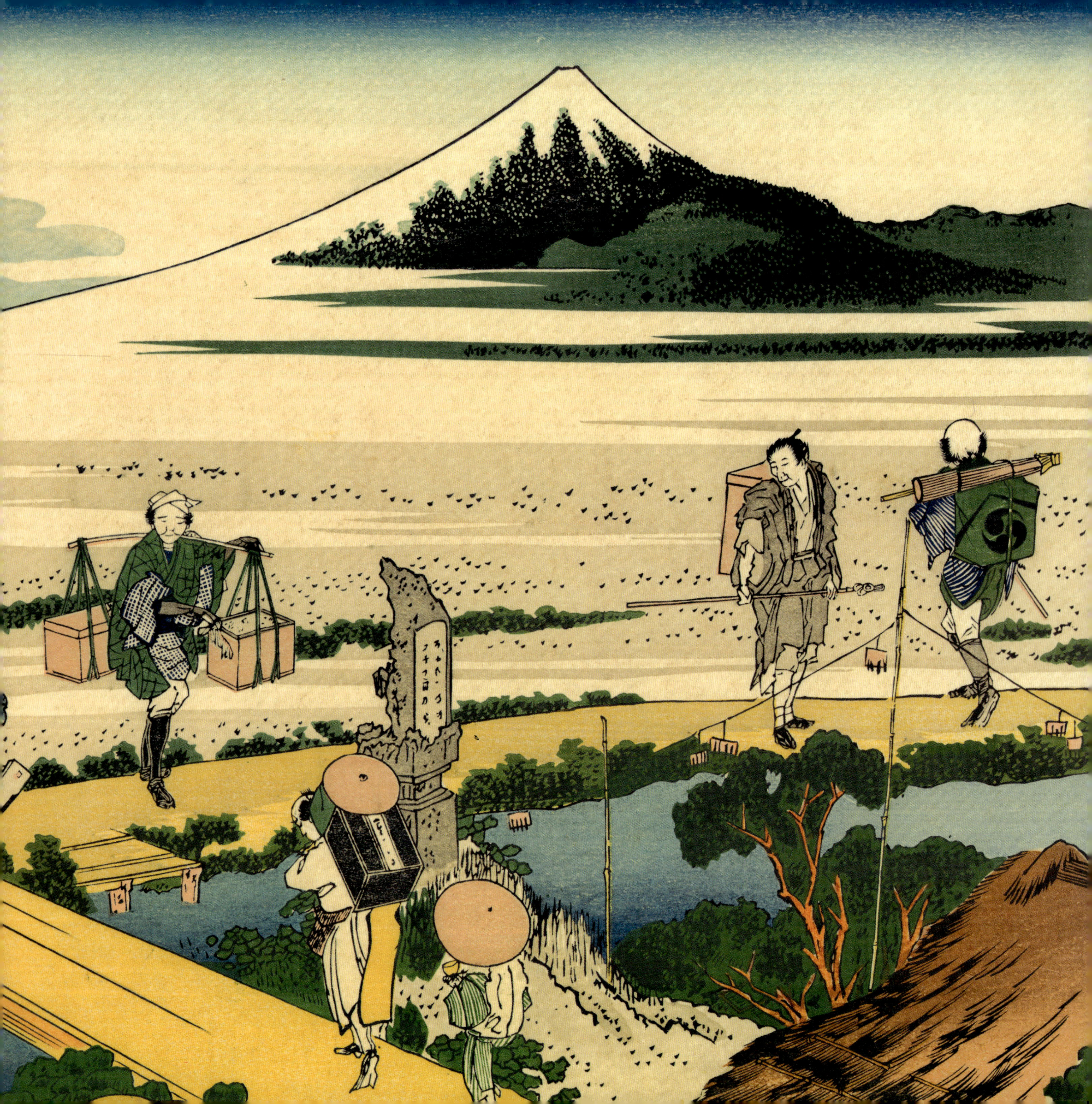

own *yorishiro*, their sacred places and features: rocks, trees, valleys, mountains, lakes, rivers, streams and waterfalls, and sometimes animals – and in certain special cases, people too. Important artefacts, such as prestigious swords and other weapons, jewellery and *gohei* (long wooden wands with trailing streamers) could all be seen as being in some way sanctified.

By tradition, there were eight million of these micro-deities (or *kami*), although this number seems little more than the vaguest gesture towards what amounted to an infinitude of sacred power. Suffice it to say that there were *kami* to be worshipped and shrines to be visited in just about every locality in every part of every island of Japan. Like charity, Shinto began at home. Every household had its *kamidana*, a little altar, on which its presiding, protective spirit was supposed to dwell. But it extended far beyond as well, making the believer's entire environment a living, resonating world of spiritual power.

The Flower and the Fury

Fujisan, unsurprisingly, had a special place in Shinto religious life: the ocean, the sun or moon apart, it is hard to think of a more imposing natural feature. So central was the mountain to this scheme, indeed, that it had its own special kind of shrine. This was the *asama*, sacred home to Konohanasakuyahime, Princess of Blossoms. Sengen-Sama, as she was also known, was the daughter of the mountain god Ohoyamatsumi. Her marriage to Ninigi, grandson of Amaterasu, the sun goddess, symbolically brought together the realms of earth and sky. Her husband had descended from the heavens to claim her hand. Their son, Jimmo Tenno, was to be Japan's first great mythic ruler; his reign from 660 BC was held to have inaugurated the whole imperial tradition.

Konohanasakuyahime had as her emblem the cherry blossom, but she was also the goddess of volcanoes, in all their sulphurous fury and their explosive power. The conjunction, eccentric to the Western mind, made perfect sense

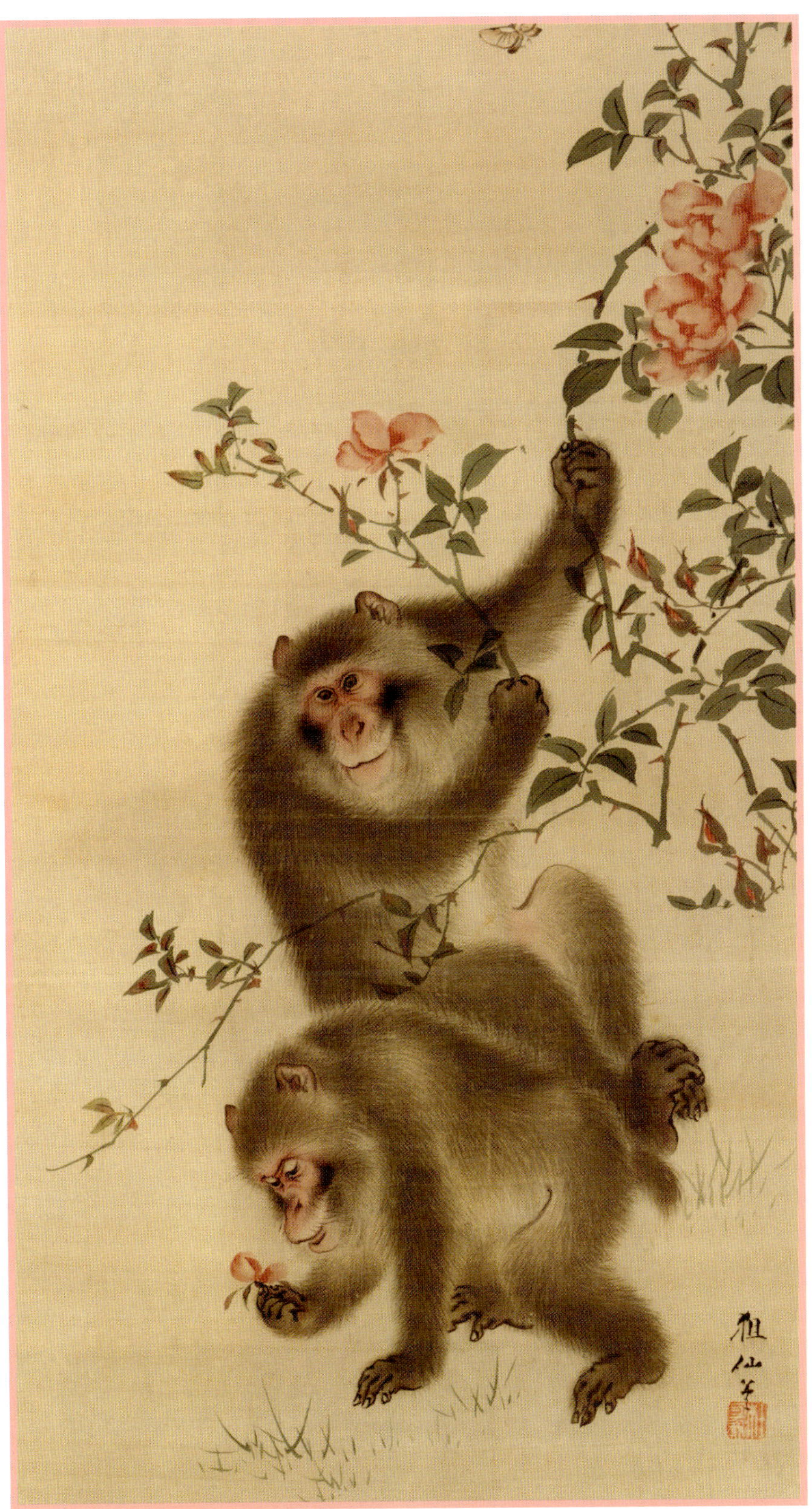

LEFT Katsushika Hokusai (1760–1849) *Nakahara in Sagami Province* from 'Thirty-six Views of Mount Fuji' (1826–33, printed later) (detail)

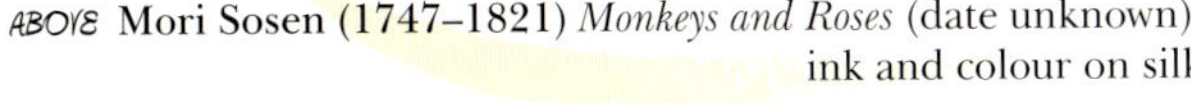

ABOVE Mori Sosen (1747–1821) *Monkeys and Roses* (date unknown), ink and colour on silk

for a Japanese culture, which saw in this flower's fragile beauty – and its dogged resilience to resisting the violence of the end-of-winter storms – an important and inspiring emblem of fortitude. Konohanasakuyahime had shown her courage when, her husband doubting her fidelity, she walked into a blazing fire to give birth to their young son. The flames, she said, would spare her and her child if he were really Ninigi's. Tried in the fire, she proved her devotion true.

Whilst there were other volcanoes in Japan, and therefore other *asama* shrines, the vast majority of shrines are within sight of Fujisan and many on the mountain slopes themselves. They are believed to have been there since at least the ninth century AD. Proudly proprietorial, Sengen-Sama is said to have trampled down the Yatsugatake Mountains of central Honshu because they threatened to overtop her Fuji home. Worshippers felt a deep devotion to her, even as they dreaded her wrath.

They had reason to feel this way, of course, as Fujisan is, after all, a big volcano and though long quiet it is certainly not extinct. Its last great outburst in 1707, known as the Hoei eruption from the Japanese name for the year in which it took place, darkened the sky and scattered ash as far as Edo.

Benignly Buddhist

But Fuji was held sacred in the Buddhist traditions of Japan as well – indeed it may have been from them that it got its name. Buddhism is believed to have been practised in Japan since 552 AD, brought to the country by Chinese missionaries invited by the Emperor Kinmei (509–71) from Korea. Monks, nuns and scholars followed a highly sophisticated reading of Buddhism and the result for Japan was an essentially elitist creed. This did, however, mean that it could coexist quite comfortably with Shinto, with aristocrats and officials becoming Buddhists while the masses remained with their ancient folk beliefs.

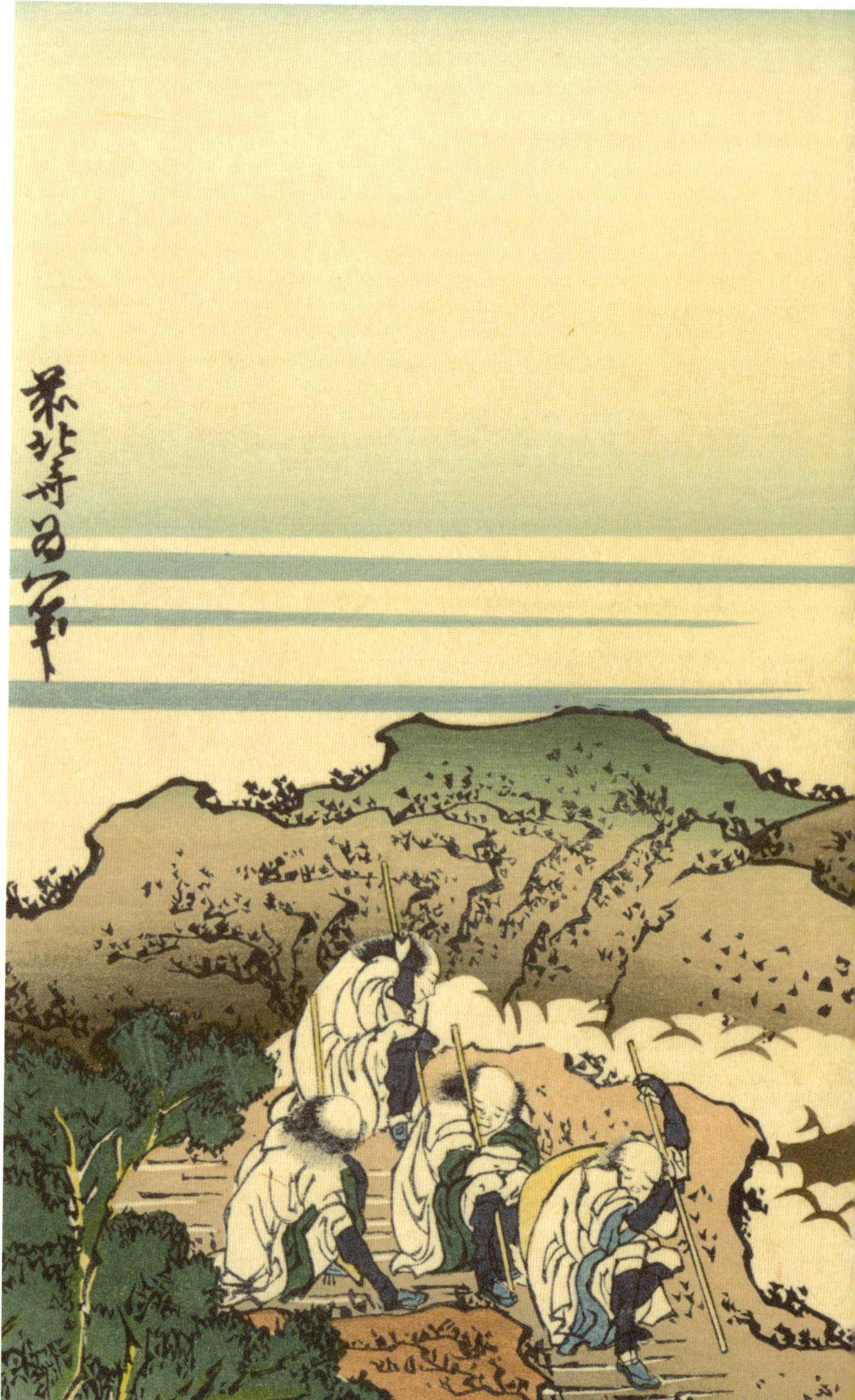

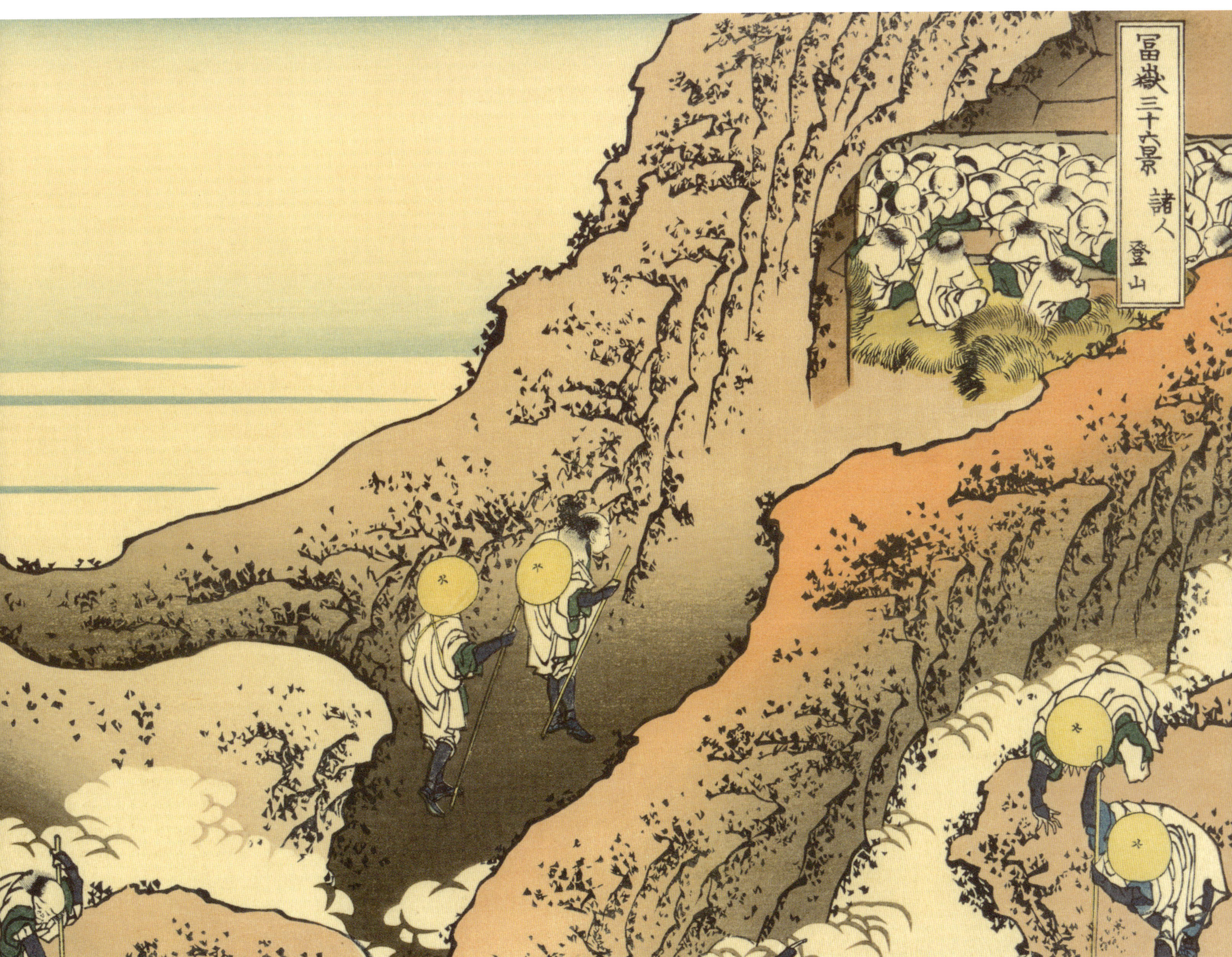

ABOVE Katsushika Hokusai (1760–1849) *Climbing on Fuji* from 'Thirty-six Views of Mount Fuji' (1826–33, printed later)

It helped that Buddhism had no gods as such; higher beings, yes, but not what we would call deities demanding attentions which might cut across the claims of the Shinto *kami*. More a code of self-transcendence, it was built around the Buddha's great injunction, 'Cease to do evil; learn to do

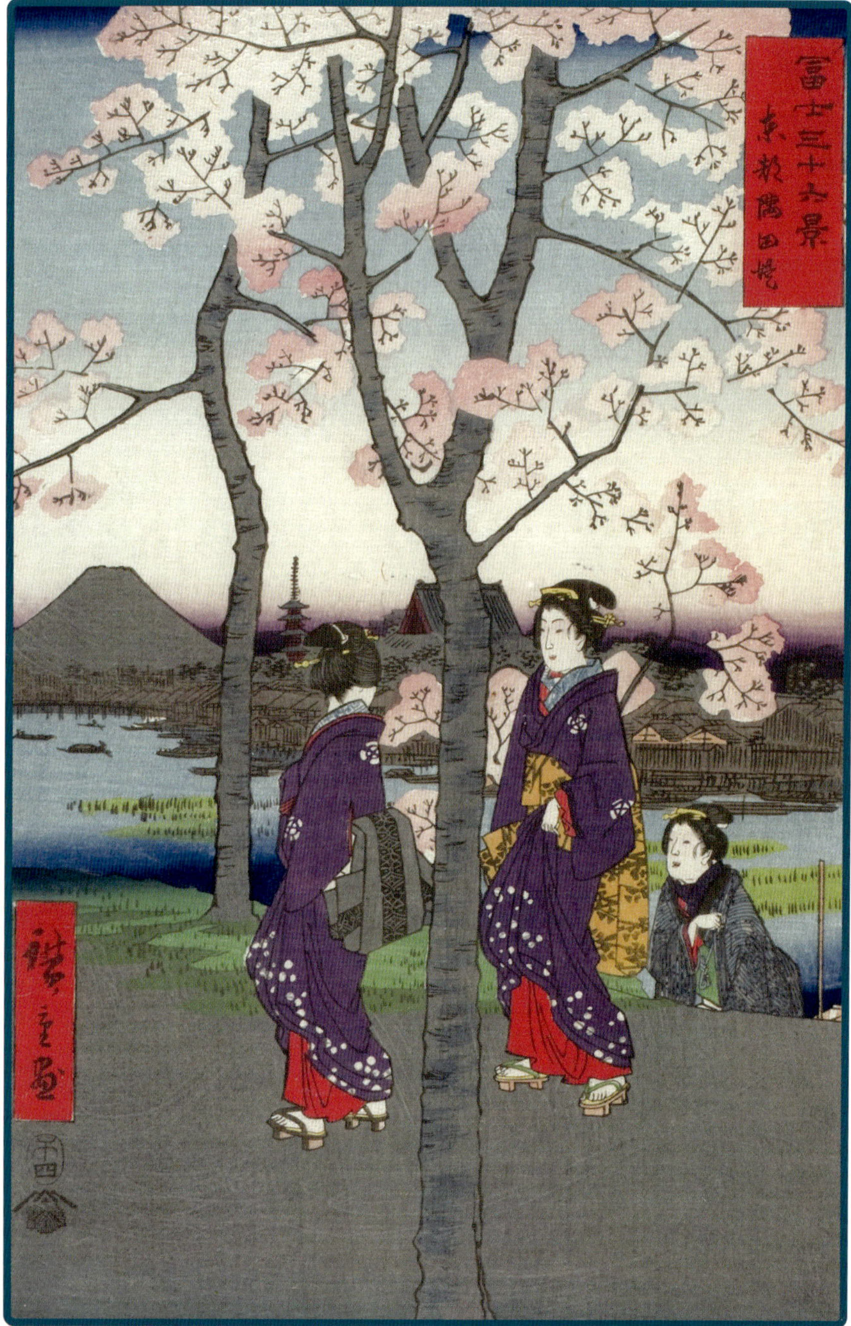

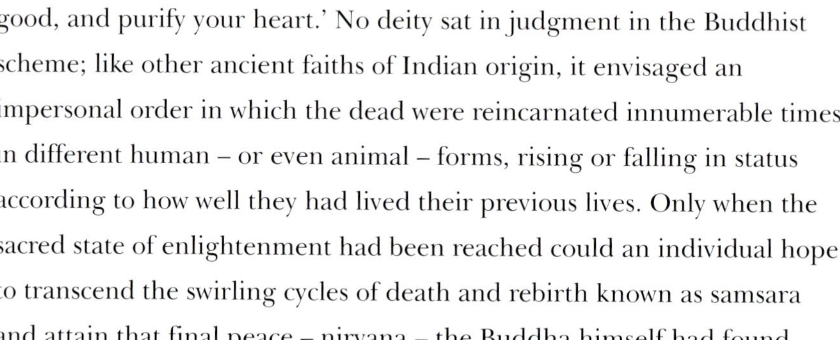

good, and purify your heart.' No deity sat in judgment in the Buddhist scheme; like other ancient faiths of Indian origin, it envisaged an impersonal order in which the dead were reincarnated innumerable times in different human – or even animal – forms, rising or falling in status according to how well they had lived their previous lives. Only when the sacred state of enlightenment had been reached could an individual hope to transcend the swirling cycles of death and rebirth known as samsara and attain that final peace – nirvana – the Buddha himself had found.

Whilst, like other Eastern religions, Buddhism was unabashed about absorbing foreign gods and goddesses into its own cosmic scheme, it saw them not as creators but as Bodhisattvas who had reached the highest level short of nirvana. So, for instance, Fuchi – after whom some scholars have suggested Mount Fuji was actually named – seems originally to have been the fire goddess of the indigenous Ainu people. She did not represent fire in its violent, volcanic, destructive manifestations, however, but in its role as provider of warmth, the kind and comforting spirit of hearth and home.

A National Talisman

Ultimately, Fujisan seems to have taken on aspects of both these traditions: an ambivalent spirit, it was at once beloved and deeply feared. Japan's most famous mountain served as a sort of *kamidana* shrine for the national household, a cosy hearth for the whole country, and as the divine destroyer who had to be placated at any cost.

No one seems to have been in any doubt of the mountain's immense importance, a significance which has endured into the present day. We cannot be sure of just how literally those who climb to the summit each year in their thousands believe in Fujisan's protective powers, but quite clearly they see it as a place of great good fortune. So too do those who, just glancing up momentarily as they go about their busy working lives in Tokyo, chance to catch a glimpse of the distant summit and cannot help

Above Utagawa Hiroshige (1797–1858) *The Sumida Embankment in the Eastern Capital* from 'Thirty-six Views of Mount Fuji' (1858)

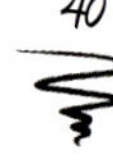

Right Utagawa Hiroshige (1797–1858) *Noge and Yokohama in Musashi Province* from 'Thirty-six Views of Mount Fuji' (1858)

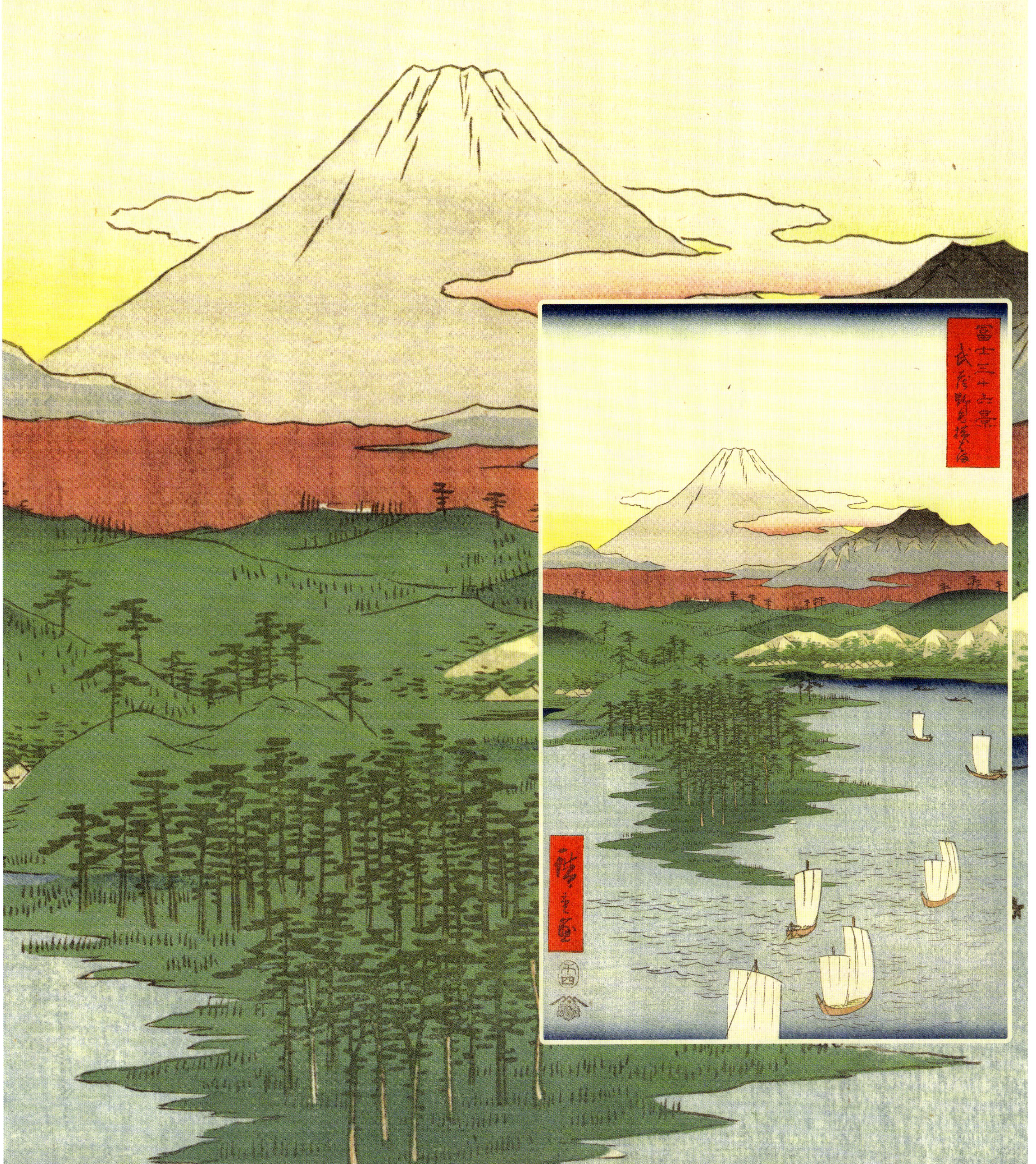
冨士三十六景
武蔵野毛横浜
廣重画

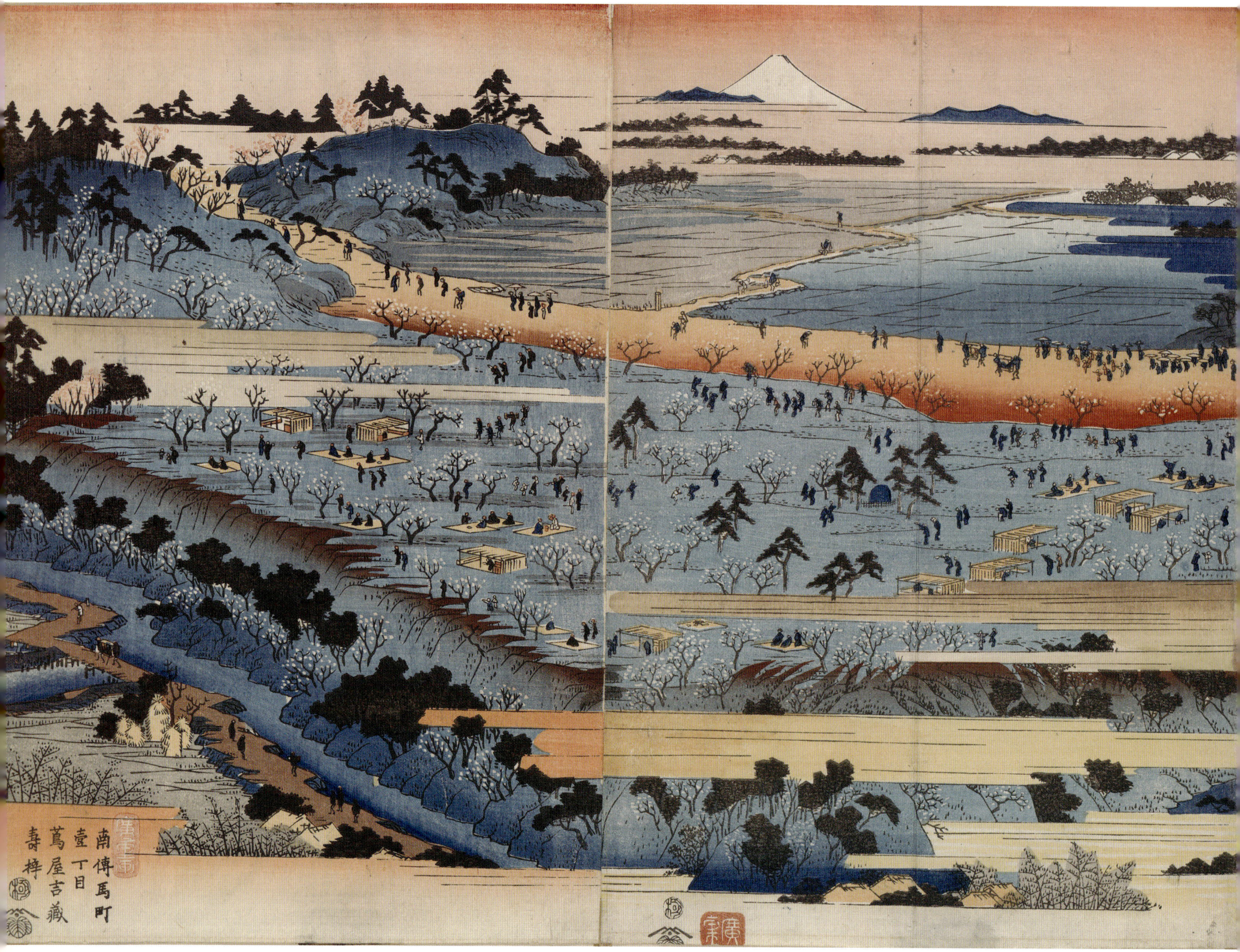

南傳馬町壹丁目 蔦屋吉藏 壽梓

Above Utagawa Hiroshige (1797–1858) *A Complete View of Asukayama* (1836–42)

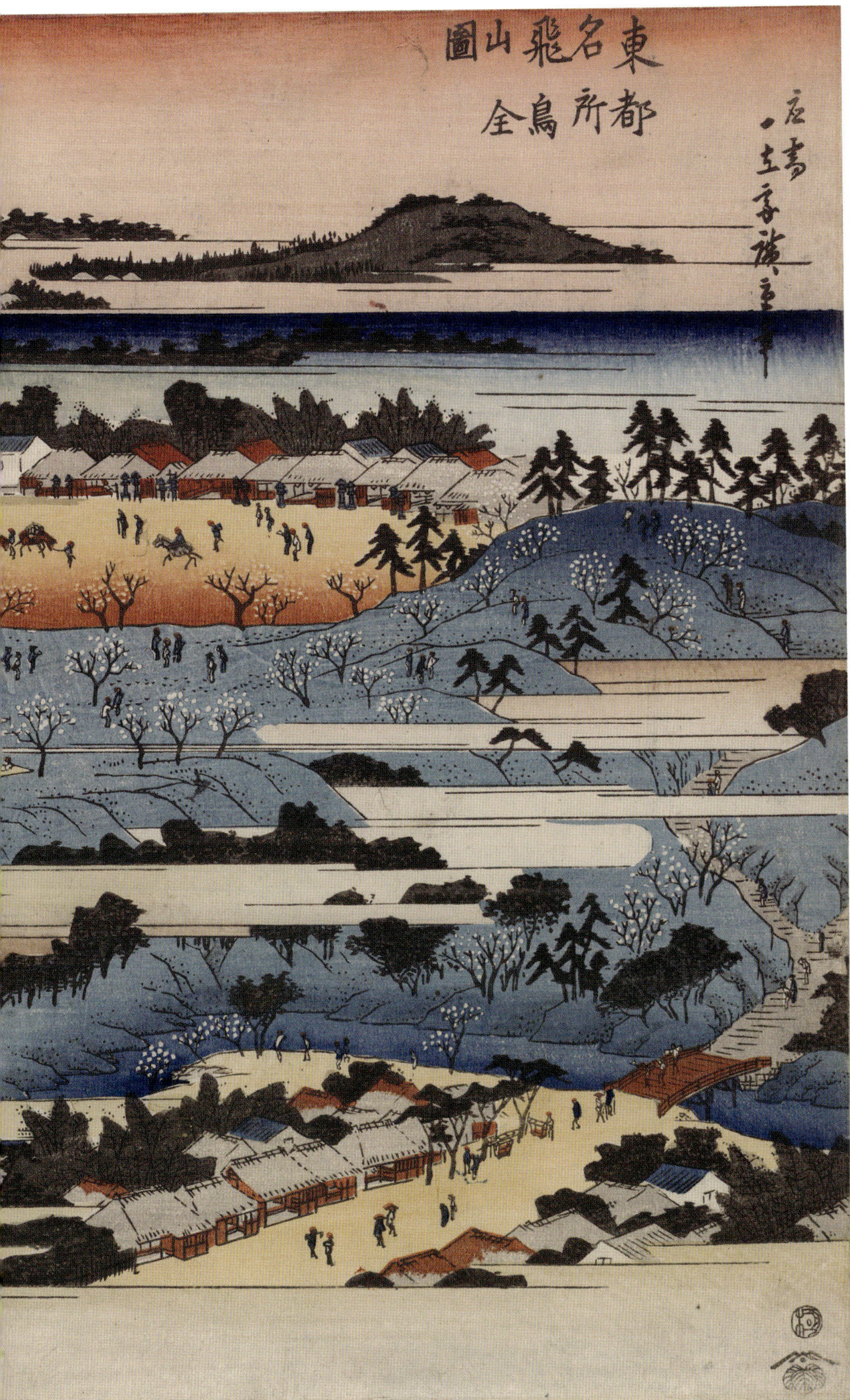

smiling. At the very least, it is a stirring sight; no one could see that iconic shape and not feel uplifted. To that extent, its mystic strength has proved enduring.

Reluctant Representation

All this being so, it is perhaps surprising to find Fujisan making its first appearance in the Japanese art tradition comparatively late – long after Akahito conjured up its image with his words. The earliest known visual representation comes in a series of painted hanging scrolls, dated 1069. The *Shotoku taishi eden* (*Life of the Prince Shotoku in Pictures*) shows the legendary sixth-century lawgiver, scholar and Bodhisattva or Buddhist 'saint' Shotoku, seemingly flying over Fujisan on his black horse.

Even here, moreover, the (oddly flattened) mountain is strictly secondary, no more than a backcloth to the figure of the flying prince. Whilst Japanese art had never had the religious taboo on representation that later Muslim (and some Christian) traditions were to have, Nature – as Shinto's source of all life and hope – was seen as sacrosanct. There was at the very least a reluctance, in early times, to make the natural landscape an artistic subject in itself. This was only gradually to give way to a more relaxed attitude (thanks at least in part, as we have seen, to Western influences). The eleventh-century artist's sketchy treatment of Fujisan, it seems, was born not out of casual heedlessness but deep respect.

The Shotoku story was frequently to be retold – some myths saw him as the man who had brought Buddhism to Japan in the first place – so more paintings of this sort were to come in the centuries that followed. Fujisan itself, in its conical perfection, was seen as a stand-in for Meru, mystic mountain of the cosmos. As such, it became an important subject for mandalas, the sacred diagrams illustrating the organizing principles of Buddhist existence. Even so, it was shown in severely stylized, rather than realistic, form. Generally speaking, its snow-covered peak was presented in triplicate. This way, Fujisan could clearly embody the 'Three Marks of Existence' Buddhism acknowledged: the transience, the unsatisfactory nature and the non-selfhood of all things. (The last of these requires a little glossing: an elusive concept, in the original Indian Pali word *anatta*,

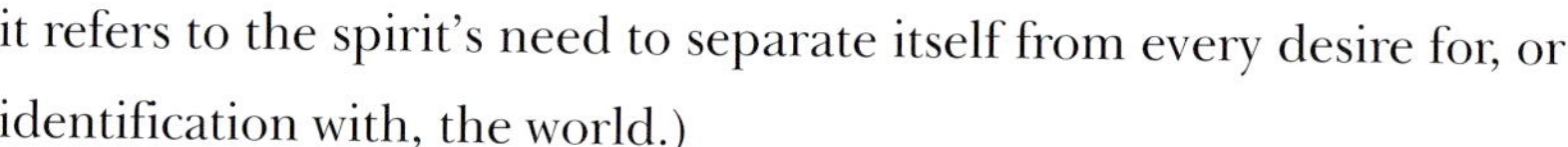

it refers to the spirit's need to separate itself from every desire for, or identification with, the world.)

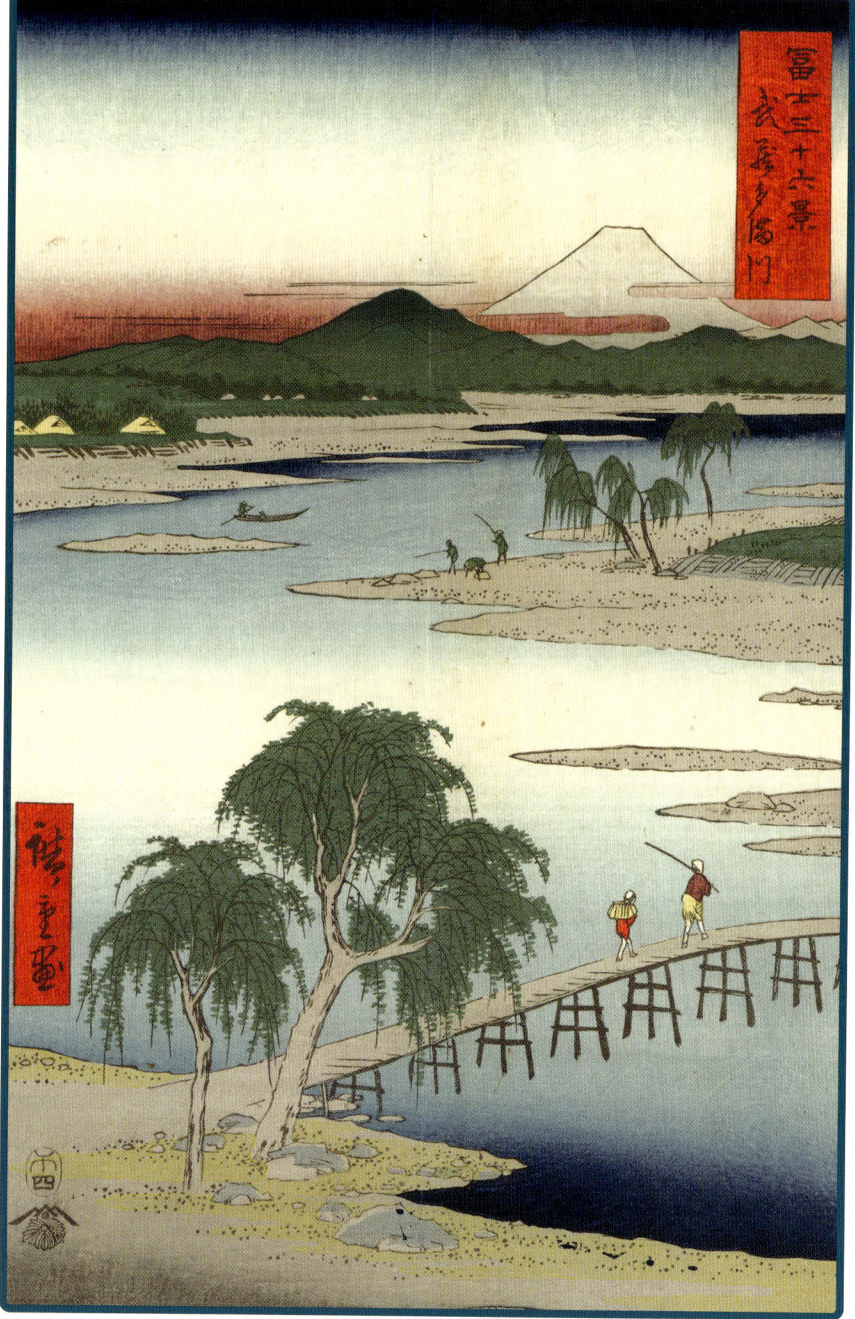

ABOVE **Utagawa Hiroshige (1797–1858)** *The Tama River in Musashi Province* from 'Thirty-six Views of Mount Fuji' (1858)

Japan's artists at this time were generally less interested in depicting landscape than the 'Pure Land' of Buddhist doctrine: those spiritual abodes in which Bodhisattvas could hope to find themselves. Only gradually would the features of these essentially allegorical scenes, as in the *Shotoku taishi eden*, come in any way to resemble the real contours of the countryside. In the Muromachi period (1392–1573), China's commercial support was important and its cultural influence strongly apparent in Japan. Artists enthusiastically embraced the aesthetics and techniques of the Chinese academic artists (or 'literati', as they have come to be known to Western scholars), who made stunning landscape sketches using just brushes and black ink on *washi* paper.

Climbing to Enlightenment

If mountains have loomed large in religious tradition, they have also been of immense importance in the secular imagination – or, at least, in that mysterious realm where artistic sensibility and spiritual feeling meet. Hence, in the Western tradition, the start of the Renaissance has often been dated to the moment when the Italian poet Petrarch went up Provence's Mont Ventoux in 1336. No one before, he insisted, had ever climbed a mountain just for the experience. (An intriguing, if obviously unverifiable, claim.) What he saw from the summit might have been a familiar landscape, but his sentiments were new as he sat down and opened his copy of the *Confessions* of St Augustine (*c.* 380). 'People,' he read, 'are moved to wonder by mountain peaks, by vast waves of the sea, by broad waterfalls on rivers, by the all-embracing extent of the ocean, by the revolutions of the stars. But in themselves they are uninterested.'

What the Renaissance writer could see, which the great pre-medieval theologian had not been able to, was that looking out at the world and

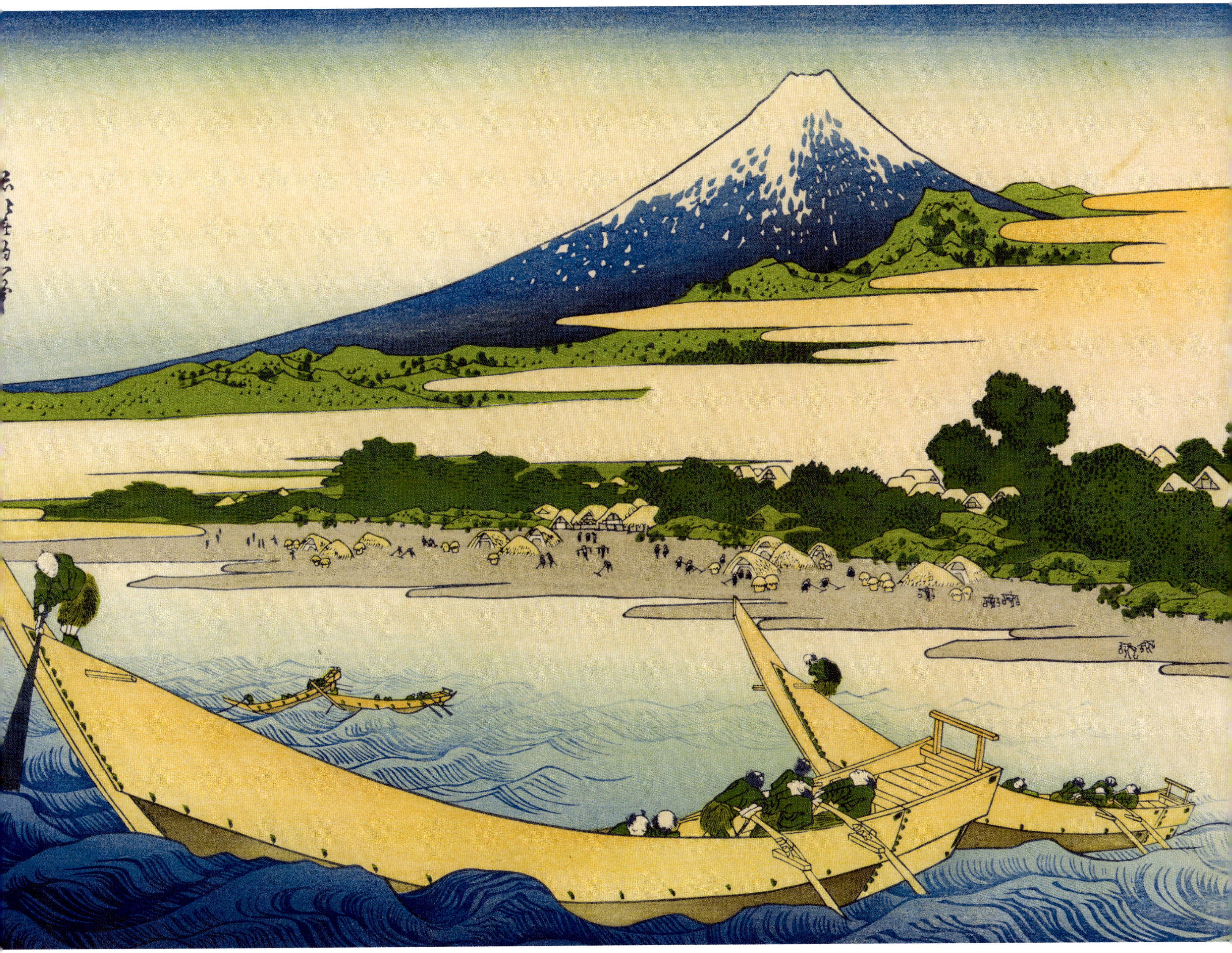

ABOVE Katsushika Hokusai (1760–1849) *Shore of Tago Bay, Ejiri at Tokaido* from 'Thirty-six Views of Mount Fuji' (1826–33, printed later)

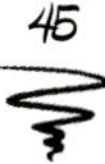

looking inward were not mutually exclusive. It was precisely because he read St Augustine's praise of introspection in this mountain summit setting that Petrarch could fully appreciate its import. 'Going out, I found, was really going in,' John Muir (1838–1914) was later to write. The Scottish Sage of the Sierras was one of the fathers of the environmental movement in the United States, but he believed that nature had to be conserved as much for our sake as for its own.

Insight Outdoors

Like the Romantic poet William Wordsworth (1770–1850), Muir saw a walk amidst the wonders of nature as a way of opening himself up to the 'wisdom and spirit of the universe'. Even for Wordsworth though, inseparably associated as he is with the external beauties of north-western England's Lake District – its hills, its rivers and its daffodils – the ultimate purpose of being on one's own with Nature was the insights it could give us into human consciousness:

One impulse from a vernal wood
May teach you more of man,
Of moral evil and of good,
Than all the sages can.

It is clear that Matsuo Basho had understood this too. The 'deep interior' to which his 'narrow road' through the countryside took him was not just that of Honshu, but that of his own – and of humanity's – mind and spirit. So too, increasingly, did the Japanese painters who, inspired by his example, were turning their attentions to the world of Nature.

The painter-poet Yosa Buson (1716–84) started out his creative life by retracing Matsuo Basho's walk into the interior of Honshu, making it the model for his own journey of inspiration. His friend Ike no Taiga (1723–

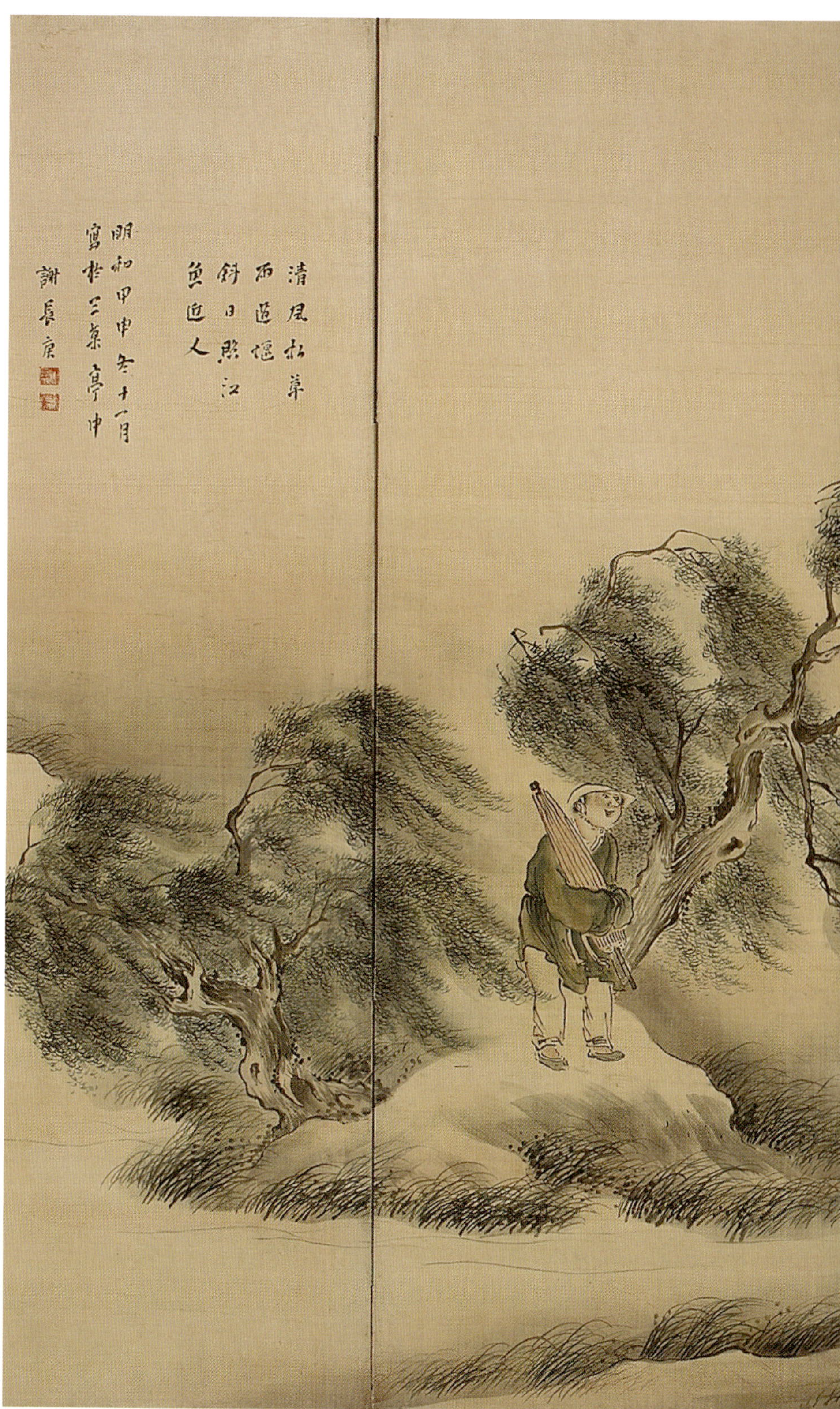

Right Yosa Buson (1716–84) *Fishing on a River after Rain* (date unknown)

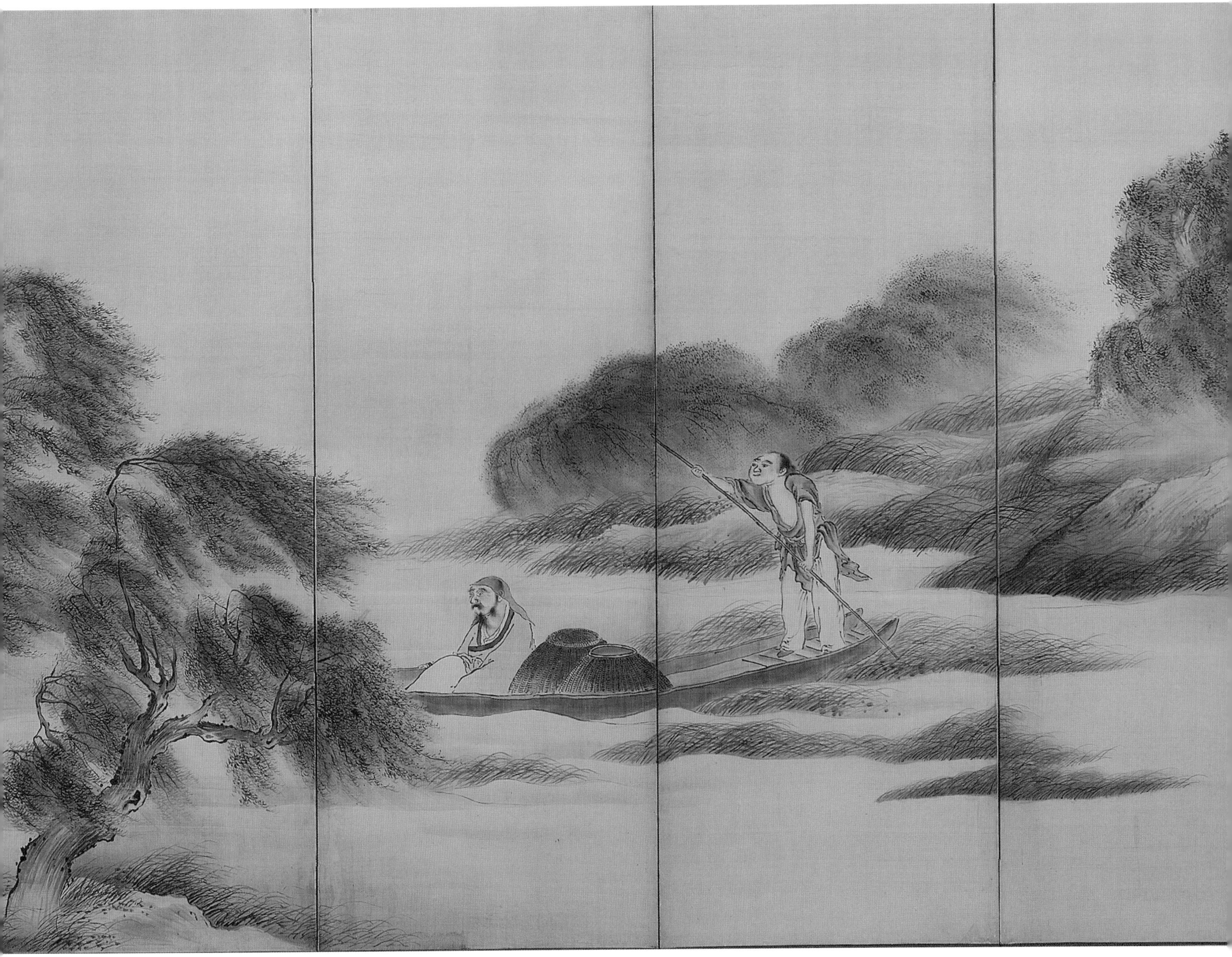

76), another solitary wanderer in the countryside, created landscape art of almost lyrical expressiveness. With artists such as these at work over the decades that followed, there would certainly be no shortage of 'mountain peaks … waves of the sea … waterfalls … rivers' and the rest in the Japanese art of the eighteenth century. The 'mountain peaks' would mostly be Mount Fuji.

A Change of Scene

This shift in sensibility is striking; so too are its parallels with a European culture in which landscape painting had also been moving into the artistic foreground. The Frenchman Claude Lorrain (*c.* 1604–82) is believed by many to have made this a serious field of artistic endeavour, his most famous canvases showing scenes from myth or scripture, or depicting the Italian countryside. Dutch masters, such as Rubens (1577–1640) and Rembrandt (1606–69), had found inspiration on what might have seemed an unpromising Netherlandish scene.

Originally Flemish, Anthony van Dyck (1599–1641) took the taste for landscape art with him when he went to England. It quickly caught on, with Thomas Gainsborough (1727–88) making the genre really fashionable by the middle of the eighteenth century. This was long before the same sort of Romanticism which inspired Wordsworth's Nature verse had found visual expression in the works of artists such as John Constable (1776–1837) and J.M.W. Turner (1775–1851).

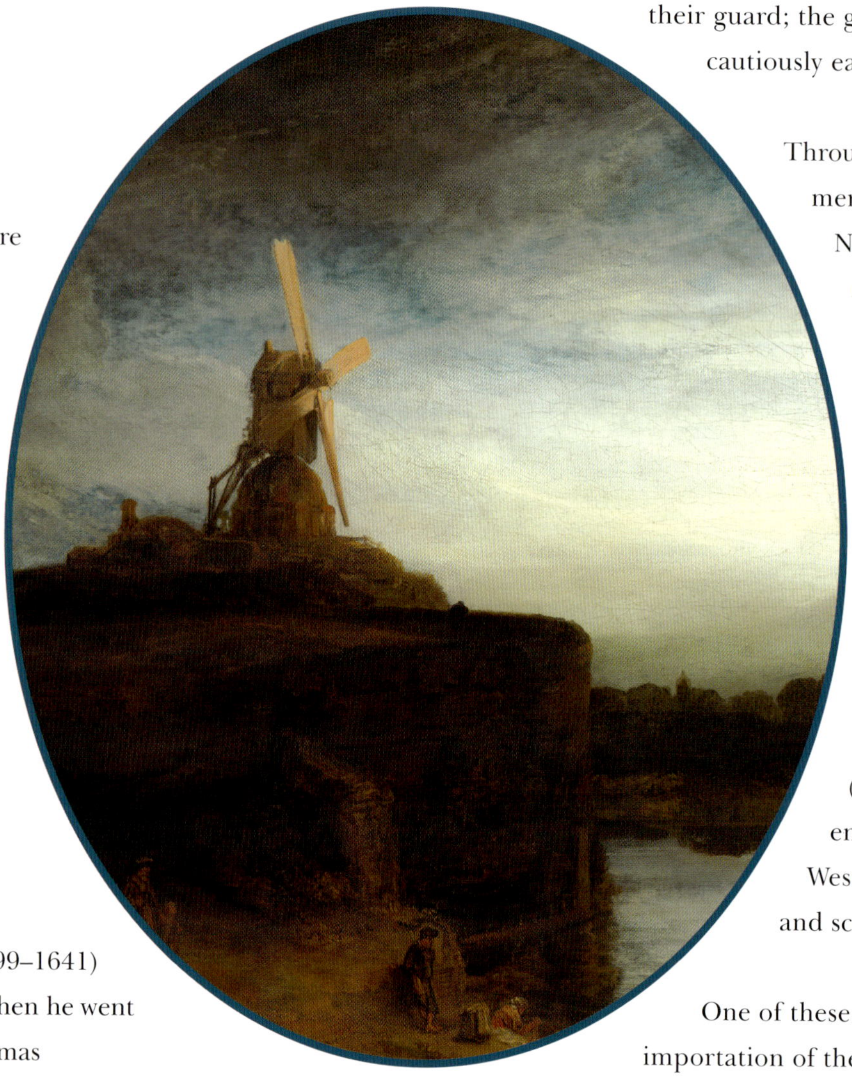

New Perspectives

By the 1780s, in fact, it becomes possible to detect the start of a certain limited convergence between *ukiyo-e* and European art. Successive shoguns were slowly, warily, beginning to drop their guard; the great *sakoku* shut-out was being cautiously eased.

Throughout the Edo period, Dutch merchants had been allowed a toehold in Nagasaki Bay, on Dejima, an artificial island through which the regime could trade for items it could not otherwise secure. For the best part of 200 years, this trading post had been kept all but hermetically sealed off; now, however, there were signs of a relaxation of vigilance. So much so that scholars like Hiraga Gennai (1728–80) were soon devoting themselves to the new academic discipline of *rangaku* ('Dutch Learning'), which encompassed everything from Western literature to technology and science.

One of these 'Dutch' innovations was the importation of the first 'Prussian Blue' – an artificial pigment known to chemists as Ferric ferrocyanide. Prior to this, Japanese painters hoping to work in a rich, deep blue (*see* right for example) had been compelled to use an ultramarine made from powdered lapis lazuli, which was prohibitively expensive. The lack of an alternative had been a major handicap.

ABOVE Rembrandt van Rijn (1606–69) *The Mill* (1645/48), oil on canvas

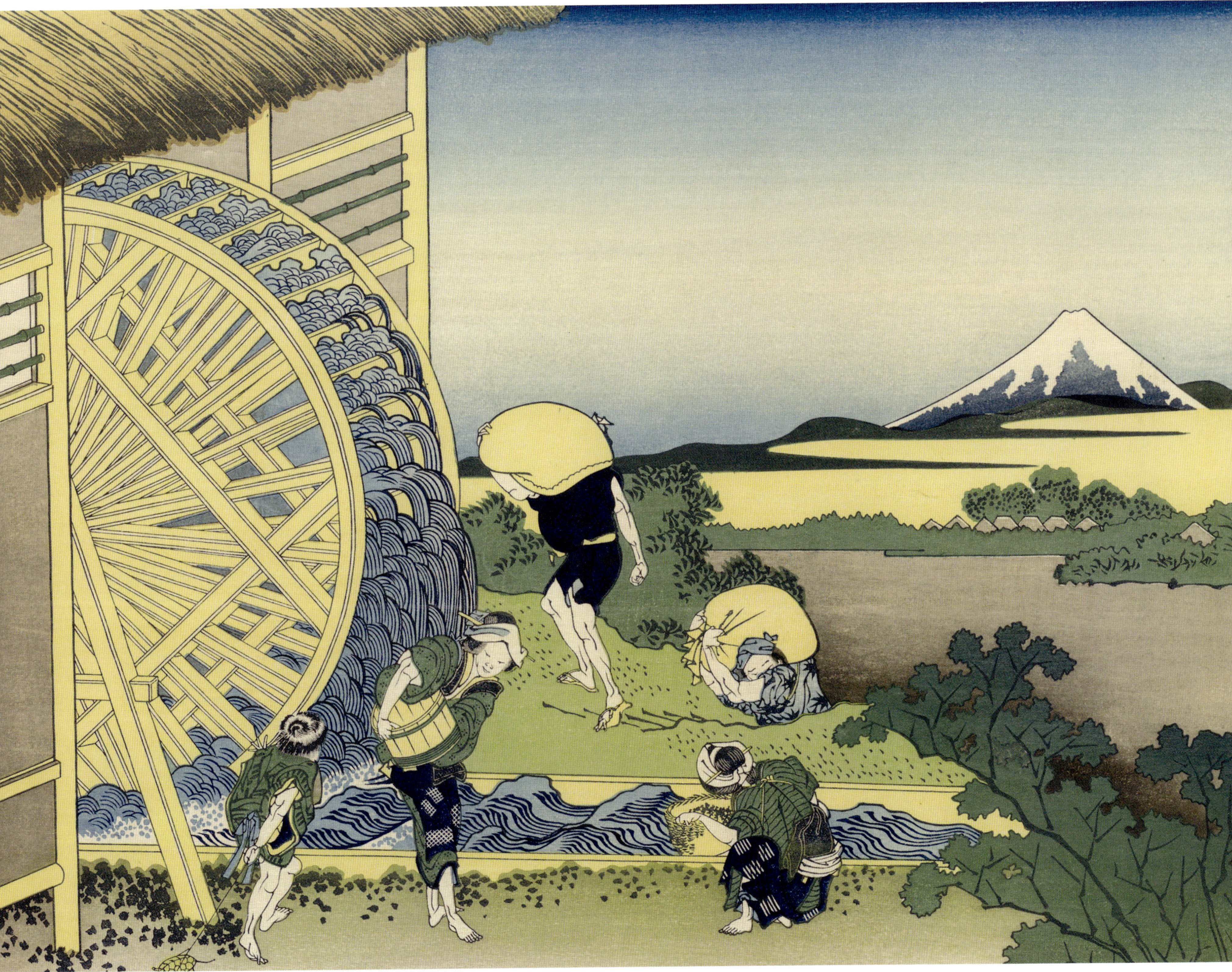

Above **Katsushika Hokusai (1760–1849)** *Watermill at Onden* from 'Thirty-six Views of Mount Fuji' (1826–33, printed later)

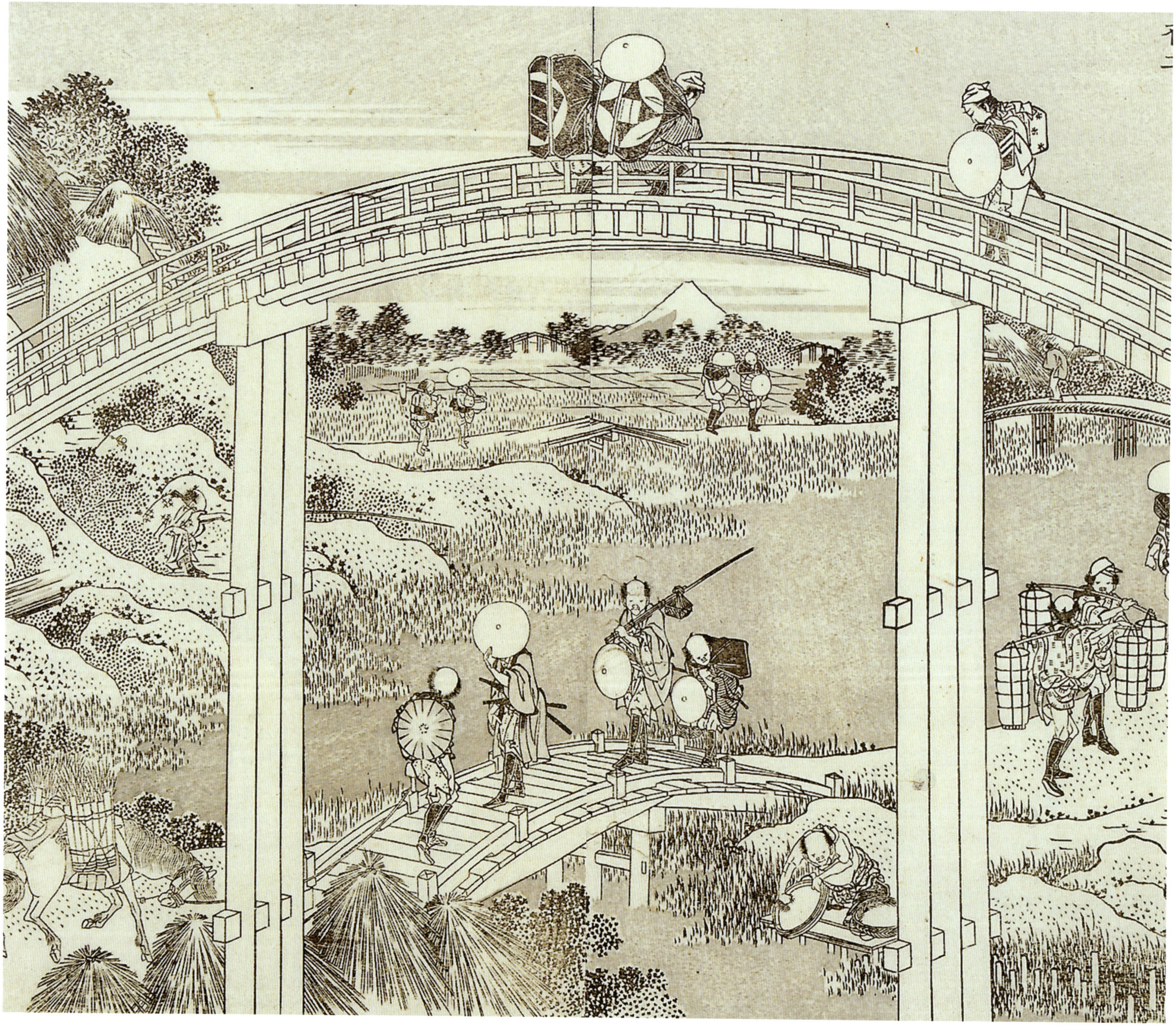

ABOVE Katsushika Hokusai (1760–1849) *A Look at Fuji with Seven Bridges* from Vol. 2 of 'One Hundred Views of Fuji' (1835)

Another import appears to have been the understanding of perspective, the Western way, which begins to feature in *ukiyo-e* landscapes at about this time. So a certain seepage of European influence into Japanese art had already taken place before Commodore Perry blew the country open with his threats of force. There is reason to think that Ike no Taiga and Yosa Buson both got the chance to study Western paintings and to incorporate some of their techniques into their own work, but the influence is most apparent in the work of the Kyoto school, and especially in that of Maruyama Okyo (1733–95), who had made something like a scientific study of perspective after a boyhood job in a toyshop which sold imported stereoscopes. These simple devices showed slightly different versions of the same object or scene to left and right eye respectively; the viewer then saw it seemingly in three dimensions.

Best of Both Worlds?

But Okyo's mania for Western-style realism struck some of his students as excessive. European art may have been compositionally striking, and the possibilities of perspective certainly exciting, but they were in no hurry to ditch their creative heritage. Chinese and Japanese artists had been skilled in establishing a sense of distance and space for centuries: why replace their understanding with a game of geometry?

Matsumura Goshun (1752–1811) was particularly perturbed. Although a devoted disciple of Okyo, he also had deep admiration for Yosa Buson and Ike no Taiga, both of whom had been able to learn from 'Dutch' examples without giving up either their Japanese identity or the individual personality of their art. Happy as he was to learn what he could from external sources, Matsumura wanted his art to make an inward journey, both into Japanese tradition and into his own consciousness. The Shijo school – named for the Kyoto street on which its members lived and worked – tried to reconcile the new European techniques with more obviously Eastern Chinese and Japanese styles. The animal paintings of Mori Sosen (1747–1821, *see* page 37 and below), self-consciously though they clearly recall the conventions of earlier oriental art, show great mastery in their use of shadowing and of scientific perspective.

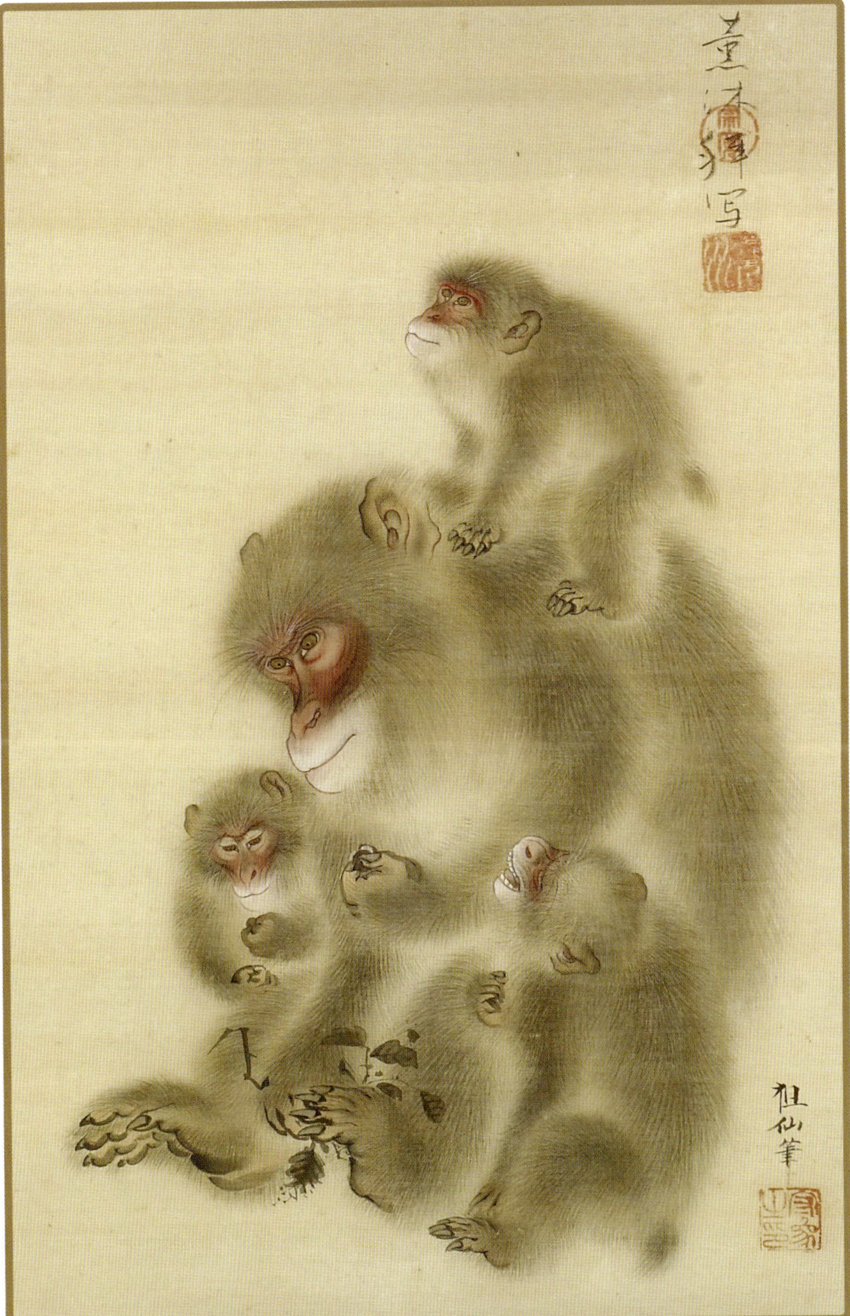

Above Mori Sosen (1747–1821) *Monkeys* (1787), ink and colour on silk

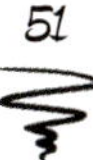

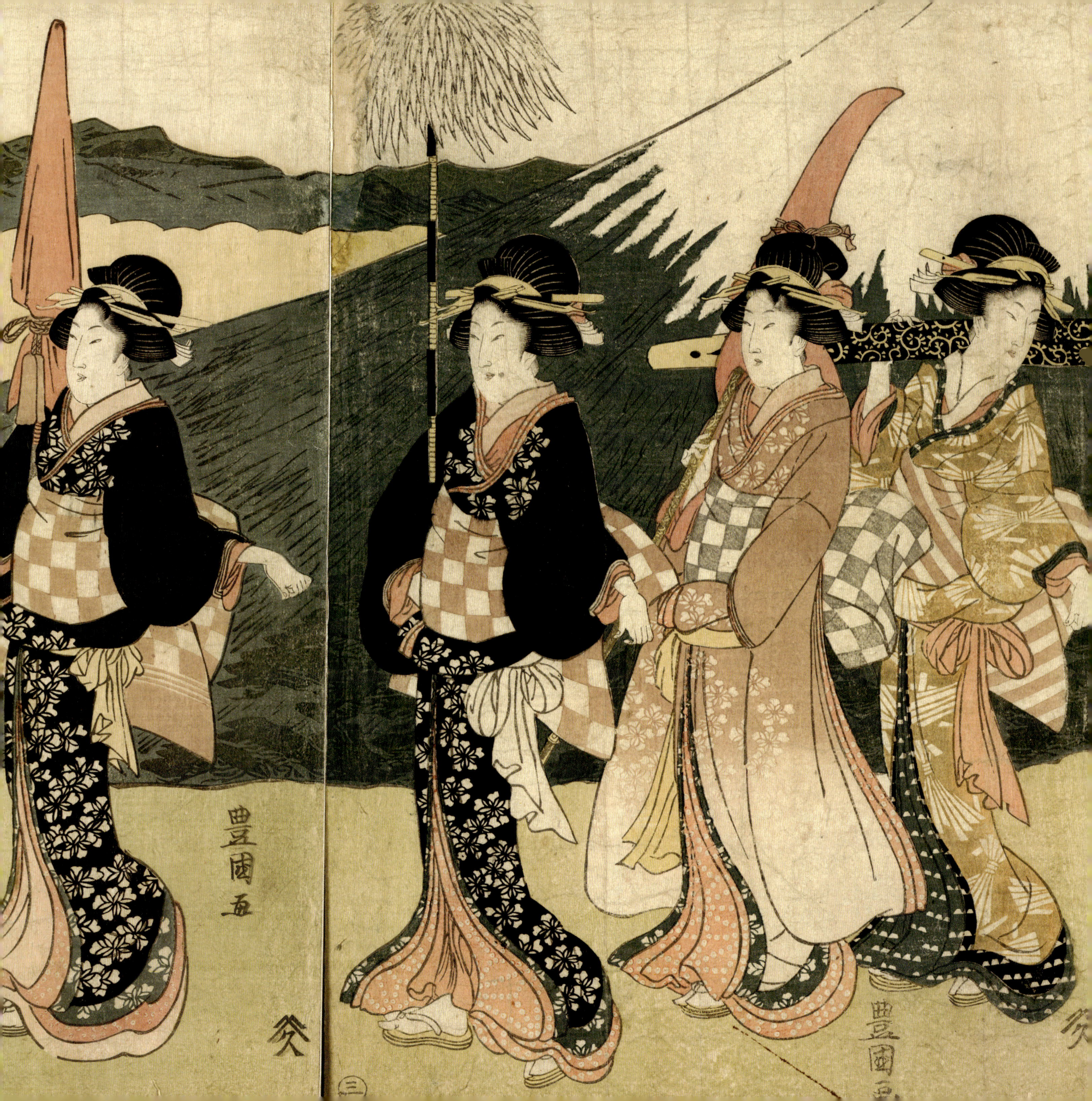
豊国画
三
豊国画

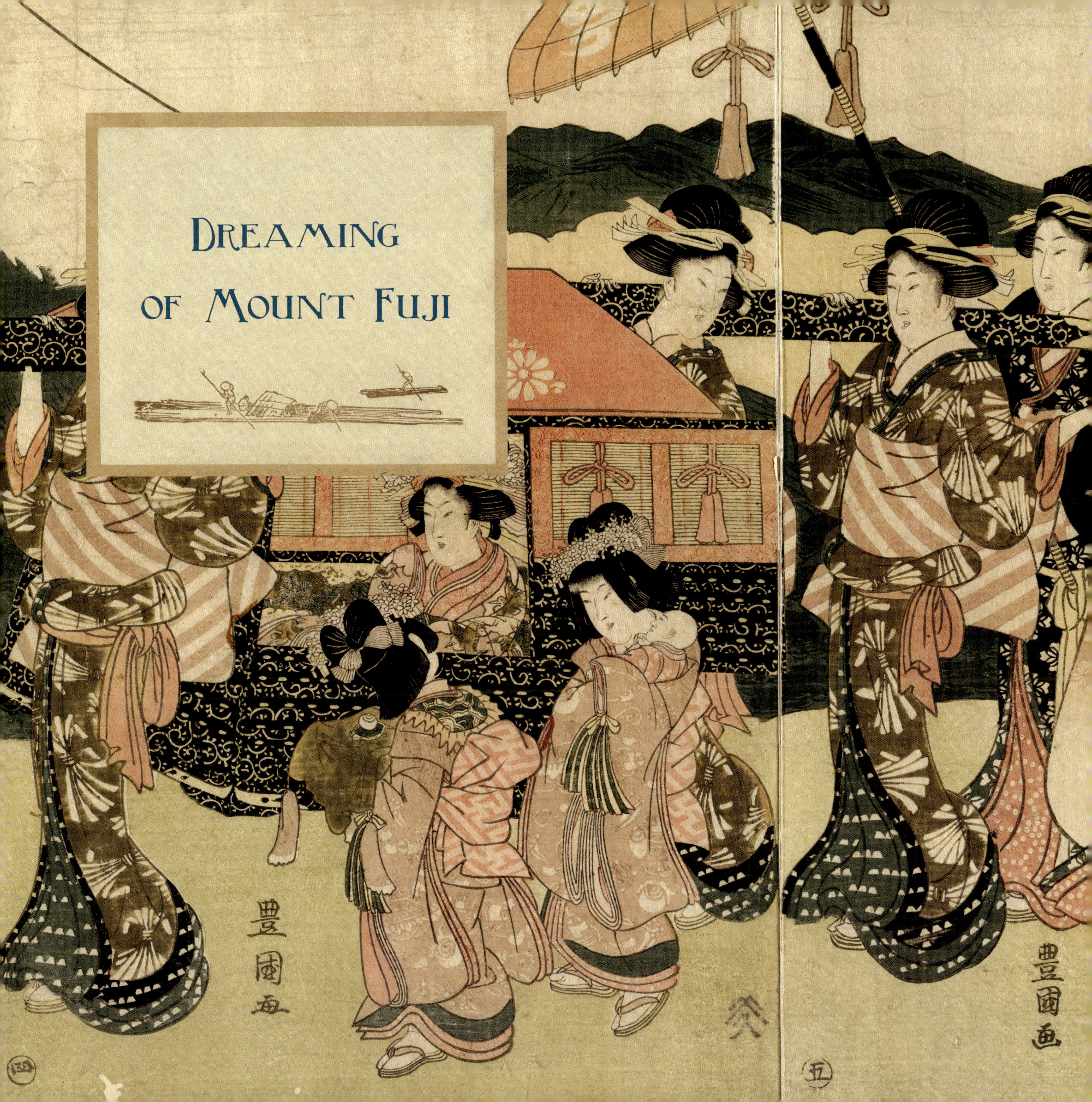
DREAMING
OF MOUNT FUJI
豊國画
豊國画

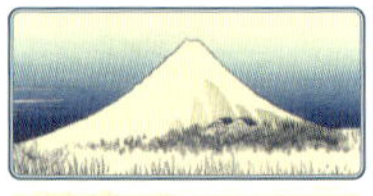

About 10,000 miles, ten years and an almost infinite distance in culture and consciousness separate Italy's Gulf of La Spezia, in the July of 1822, and the waters off Kanagawa, outside Edo, in the late 1820s to early 1830s. However, the two connect imaginatively, the former being the scene of the death-by-drowning of the English poet Percy Bysshe Shelley (1792–1822) in a sudden and violent tempest and the latter the location of the most celebrated storm in world art history.

Katsushika Hokusai's creation, *The Great Wave off Kanagawa* (*see* opposite), has become, for better or for worse, the *Mona Lisa* of the East, its sheer fame easily eclipsing its artistic character. Down the face of the wave in Hokusai's picture scud a couple of boats of the *oshiokuri-bune* type – small, fast cargo vessels. We see a third skiff surging on the swell in the middle distance. Their cowering crews could hardly represent more plainly humanity's helplessness in the face of an overwhelming Nature – Shelley must have felt the same in his final moments. Down in the left foreground, meanwhile, a much smaller wave rises upwards, triangular in profile; it rhymes almost exactly with the cone of Mount Fuji on the far horizon. Framed by the curve of the great wave itself, the mountain's blue-stone slopes with their crown of winter snow match the foam-topped crests of the ocean waves.

Never the Twain

Despite this connection, the two cases clearly also illustrate important differences between the ways Western Romanticism and Japanese *ukiyo-e* saw the world. 'Thou for whose path the Atlantic's level powers / Cleave themselves into chasms,' Shelley had importuned in 'Ode to the West Wind' just three years before his death: 'O! lift me as a wave, a leaf, a cloud!' Its unsettling intimations of his eventual end apart, the line is striking chiefly for the exhilaration it evidently finds in Nature's violence; its ecstatic thought of an overwhelming force before which the spirit can let itself go.

The idea of the ocean's cleaving itself into 'chasms' has a visual echo in Hokusai's picture – but the thrill-seeking sense of rapture is nowhere to be found. On the contrary, much of the mystique of this celebrated image must surely lie in the way it presents the power of the sea as being at the same time almost unthinkably anarchic and destructive, and perfectly poised, beautifully stylized – strangely sedate, indeed.

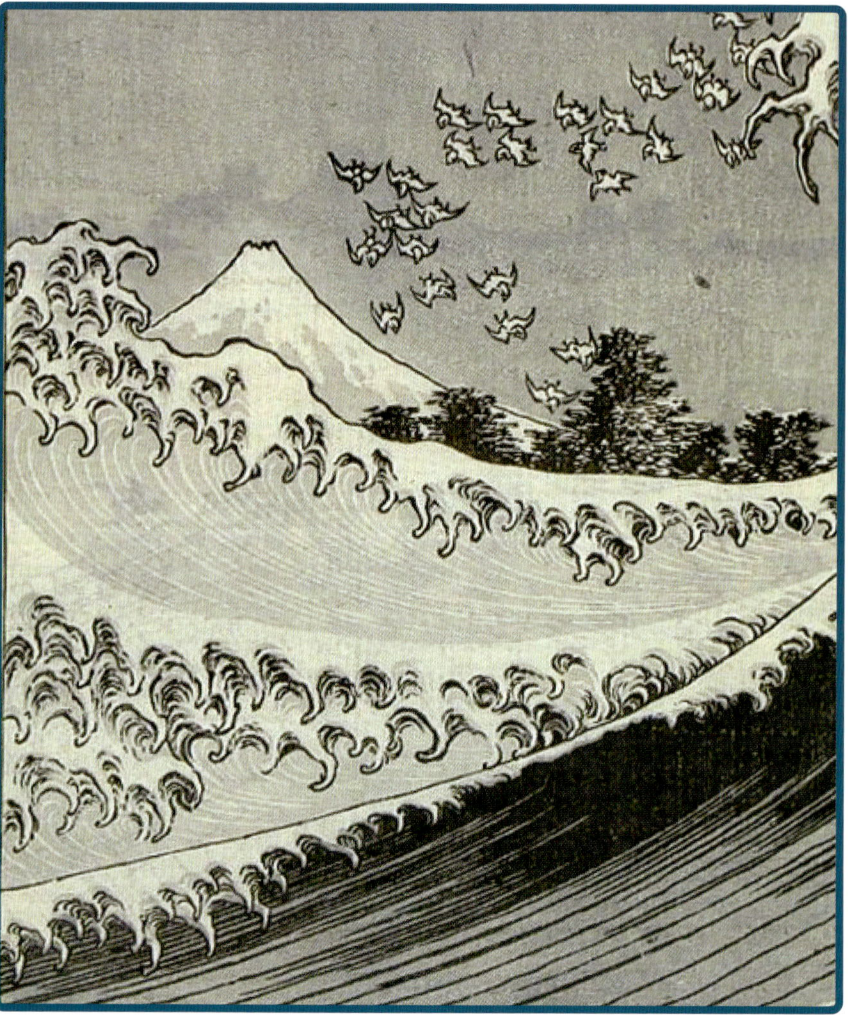

Previous pages Utagawa Toyokuni (1769–1825) *A Procession of Flowers Before Mount Fuji* (1804–18)

Above Katsushika Hokusai (1760–1849) *Mount Fuji in the Sea* from Vol. 2 of 'One Hundred Views of Fuji' (1835)

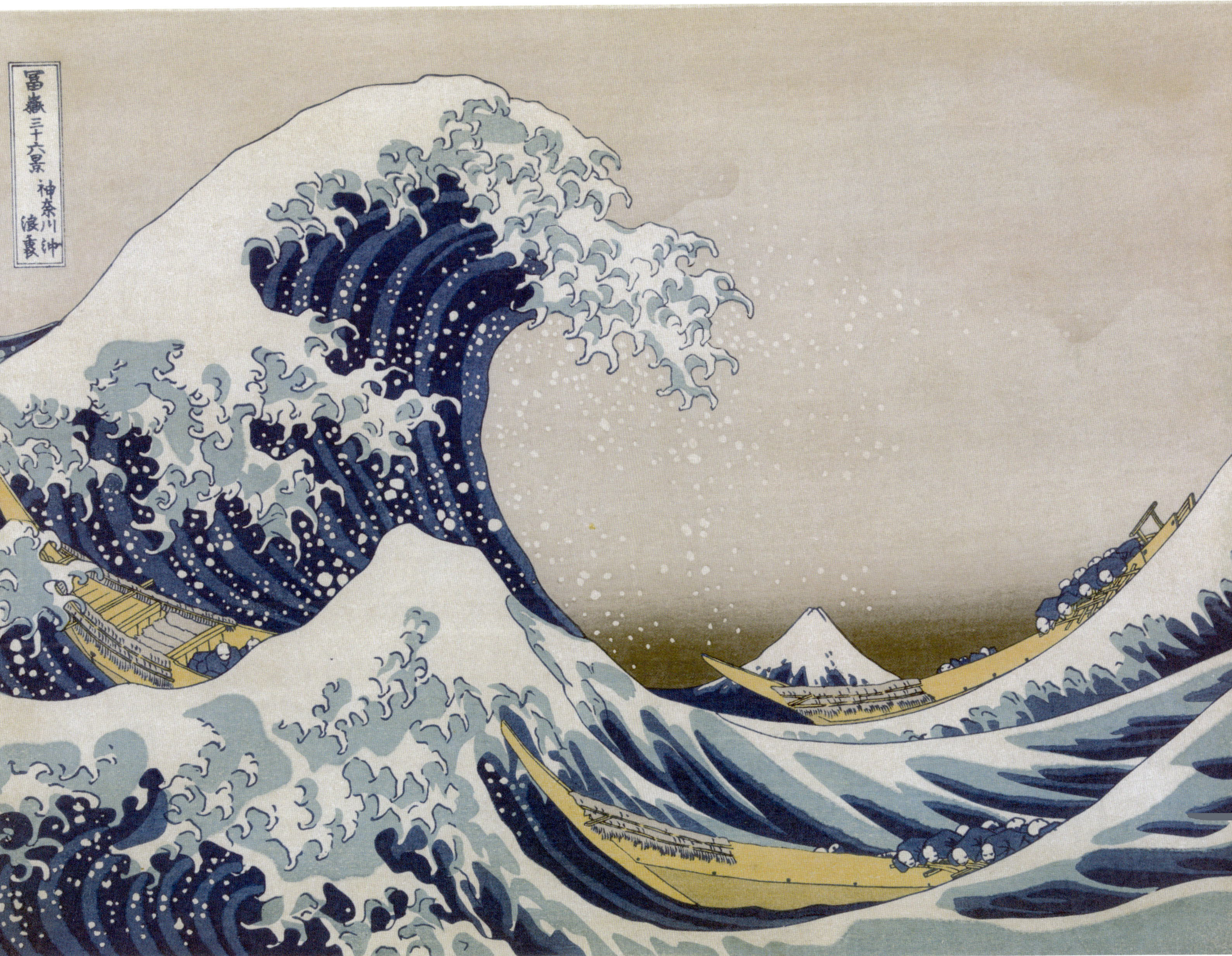

Above Katsushika Hokusai (1760–1849) *The Great Wave off Kanagawa* from 'Thirty-six Views of Mount Fuji' (1826–33, printed later)

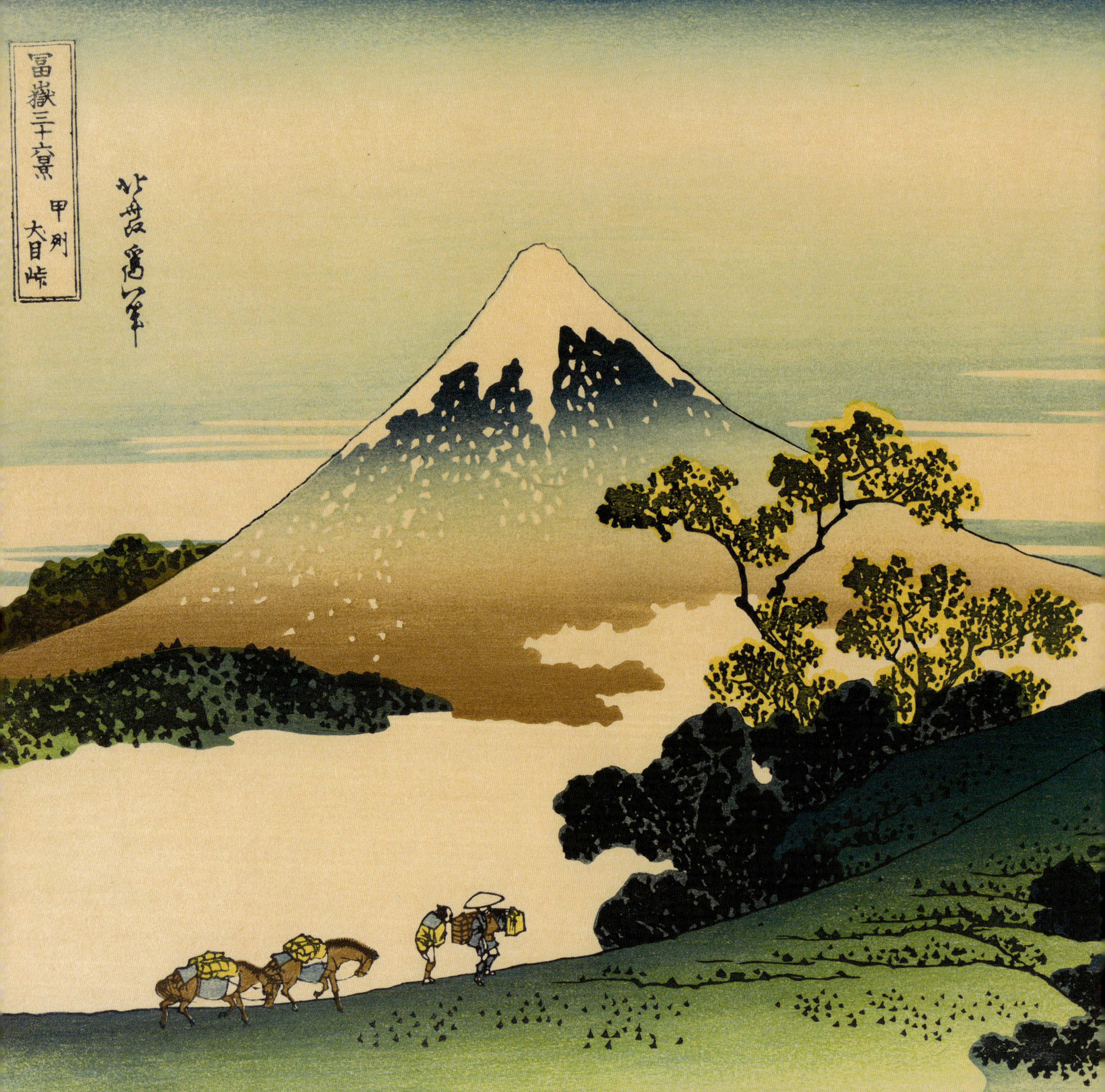
冨嶽三十六景
甲州
犬目峠

While Shelley rejoices in the destructiveness of the storm, Hokusai's delight appears to be in the balancing out of opposing principles; as violent as his image is, it is utterly controlled.

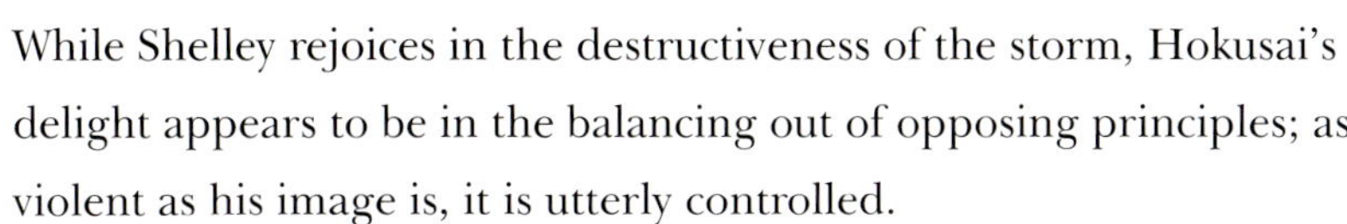

Self–Improvement

Of course, Shelley had been young – only in his twenties – when he wrote this ode; Hokusai was in his seventies by the time he created his most famous work. Moreover, he had a vision of his art that saw it as the accrual of age, experience and wisdom. That control, poise and balance had been hard won.

Unlike Shelley, a Romantic individualist who wrote often and earnestly of his philosophical and poetic vision, Hokusai left few thoughts on his attitude to art or his own development as an artist. He did, however, write a personal postscript to a collection of his prints just a few years later:

> *From the time I was six, I had a knack for copying the forms of things; my pictures were often published from my fifties. Not till I was about seventy, though, did anything I do have any real merit. By the age of seventy-three, I was starting to get some sense of plants and trees and how they grew, and of how birds, animals, insects and fish were put together. By the time I'm eighty, then, I hope I'll have improved further; by the time I'm ninety I hope I'll really be beginning to comprehend the principles underlying the way things are, so that by the time I reach my century I'm producing work of divine perfection. Even then I hope I'll be able to get better: when I'm a hundred and ten, I trust, every little line and dot will seem to sing with life. Any of you who live long enough will be able to look at the work I do then and see if I've managed to deliver on this commitment!*

What starts out as seeming self-deprecation ends in a hyperbolic promise: it would plainly be wrong to say that Hokusai is simply being modest. It is nevertheless striking that, rather than hinting at any inner genius, he dismisses his early talent as no more than a 'knack'.

LEFT Katsushika Hokusai (1760–1849) *Inume Pass, Koshu* from 'Thirty-six Views of Mount Fuji' (1826–33, printed later)

And a knack for 'copying' at that. Whilst classical artists in the West had certainly suggested that the basis for all art was *mimesis* (the Greek for 'imitation'), few would have written off the artist as no more than a sort of visual scribe, especially in the Romantic period of the early nineteenth century when the important input into artistic creativity was believed to come from within the painter or poet – from inspiration – rather than from external forms.

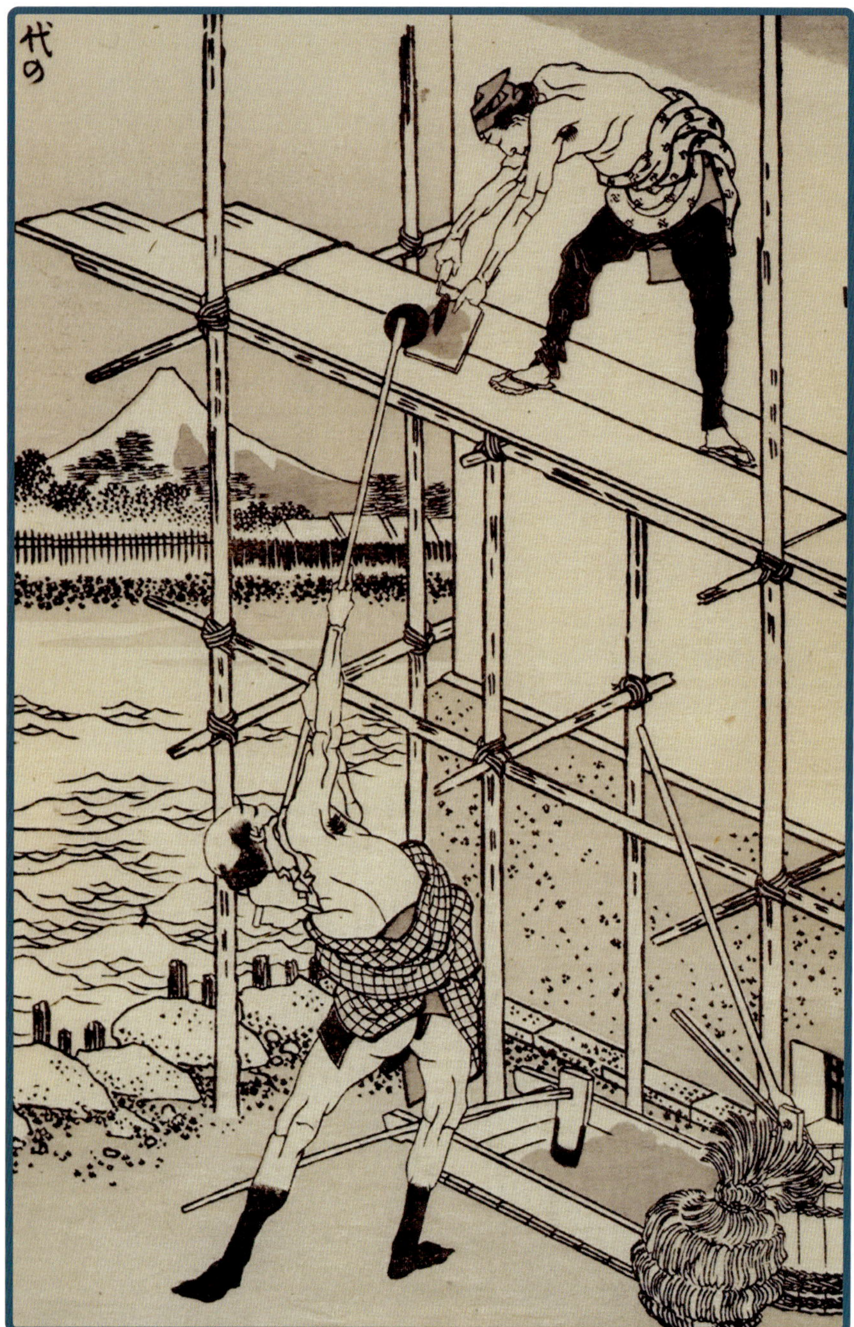

Above Katsushika Hokusai (1760–1849) *A Scene of Two Builders with Mount Fuji in the Background* from Vol. 3 of 'One Hundred Views of Mount Fuji' (1840s)

Youth and Age

And whilst Hokusai's pretensions to 'divine perfection' would not have surprised the Western Romantic, they would have wondered at his hoping to get there by this dogged, practice-makes-perfect route. Artistic beauty was not something that could be worked at. Shelley had made the point in his eloquent *Defence of Poetry* (1821):

> *The mind in creation is as a fading coal, which some invisible influence, like an inconstant wind, awakens to transitory brightness; this power arises from within, like the colour of a flower which fades and changes as it is developed, and the conscious portions of our natures are unprophetic either of its approach or its departure.*

It was not just the 'mind in creation' that was a fading coal but, to some extent, the creative mind. Originality, freshness and spontaneity: these were the roots of Romantic inspiration and none of them came with experience or age. The Romantic life was stereotypically short – like that of Shelley himself, who did not reach the age of 30. His friend John Keats (1795–1821) had not even lived that long. No great overarching destiny but sheer happenstance carried both these talents off before their time, of course, but their older contemporary William Wordsworth, who died at the age of 80, would generally be felt to have 'passed on' as a poet 40 years earlier.

Romanticism was a young man's movement: Johann Wolfgang von Goethe (1749–1832), who had arguably helped establish the whole new sensibility with his works of *Sturm und Drang* ('Storm and Stress', late 1760s–early 1780s), had in so doing also helped establish the cult of

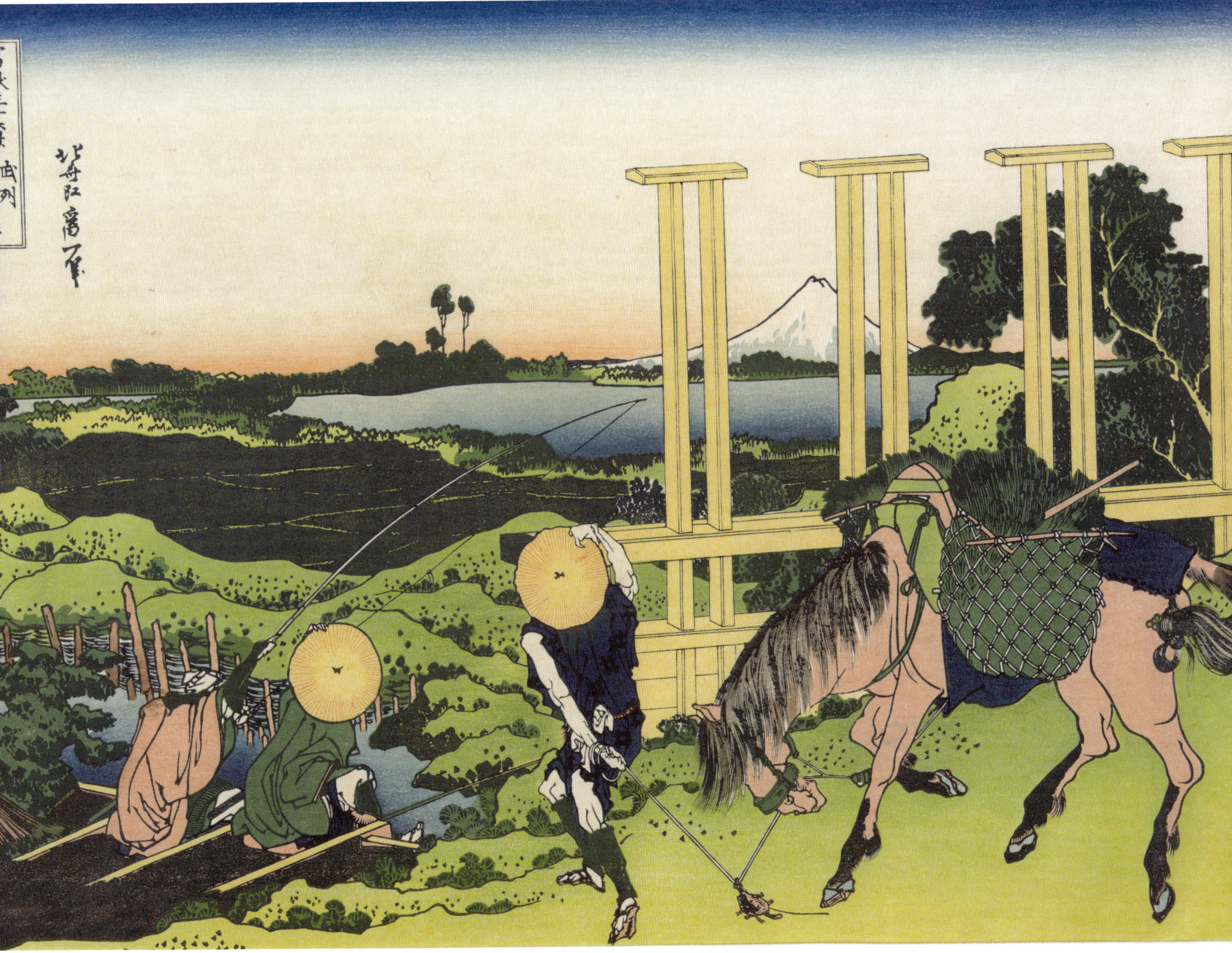

ABOVE Katsushika Hokusai (1760–1849) *Senju, Musashi Province* from 'Thirty-six Views of Mount Fuji' (1826–33, printed later)

youth. When – himself still only in his twenties – he had written his fantastically successful novel *The Sorrows of Young Werther* (1774), he had created the prototype of the Romantic protagonist as a passionate but tormented – and essentially *youthful* – soul.

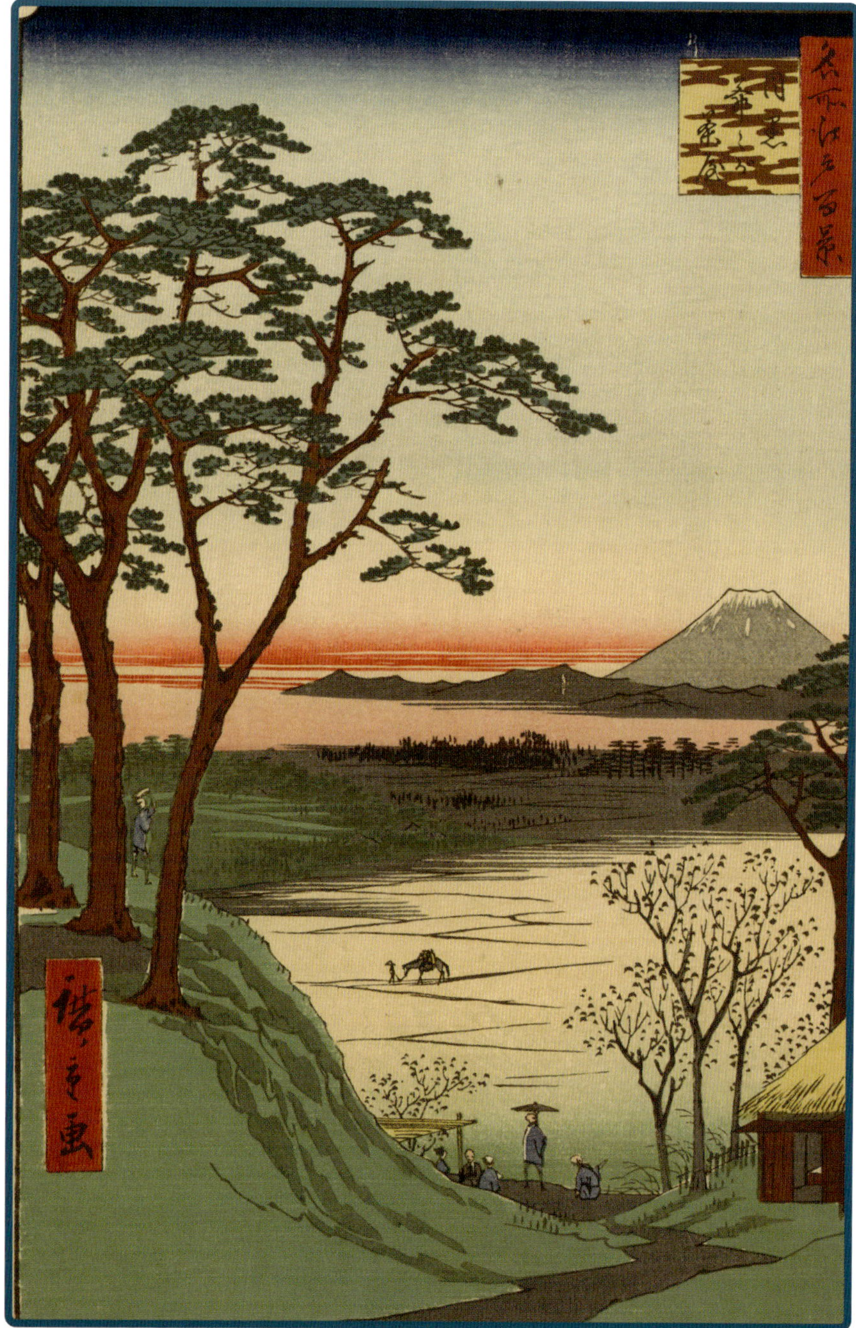

ABOVE Utagawa Hiroshige (1797–1858) *Grandpa's Teahouse in Meguro* from 'One Hundred Famous Views of Edo' (1856–58)

As its title suggests, the hero of Goethe's novel is young – and the brevity of his life, which he cuts short by suicide, is at the heart both of his inspiration and his pain. Hokusai, by contrast, clearly saw his path to inspiration as a quasi-Buddhist process of personal purification; a gradual ascent, through decades of discipline, to artistic enlightenment. From a standpoint such as this, the 'inspiration' of the flamboyant young genius would not seem interesting or admirable; artistic achievement was something to be patiently perfected over many years.

Opposites Attract?

As intriguing as the parallels may be between *ukiyo-e* and European Romanticism in their relation to the landscape, the distance that divides them is still vast. The apparent resemblances might even be the result as much of contrariety as of kinship. Where, for Romanticism, the walk in the wilderness was a way of venturing inward, to find the self in solitude, for Japanese Buddhists it was emblematic of the long, slow journey to enlightenment in which layers of the self were progressively sloughed off.

Is it no more than a grand coincidence, then, that so many Westerners respond so immediately and with such pleasure to Japanese landscape art? Does the West see something that really is not there? The question is an unsettling one and by no means self-evidently misconceived. Fortunately, it does not have to be resolved.

The Long Haul

In any case, in his own way Hokusai was clearly every bit as self-conscious as any European Romantic could be; his sense of artistic destiny just as strong. That does suggest a degree of determination on his part, a desire to be taken seriously and a resolve not to let himself be passed over with

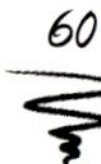

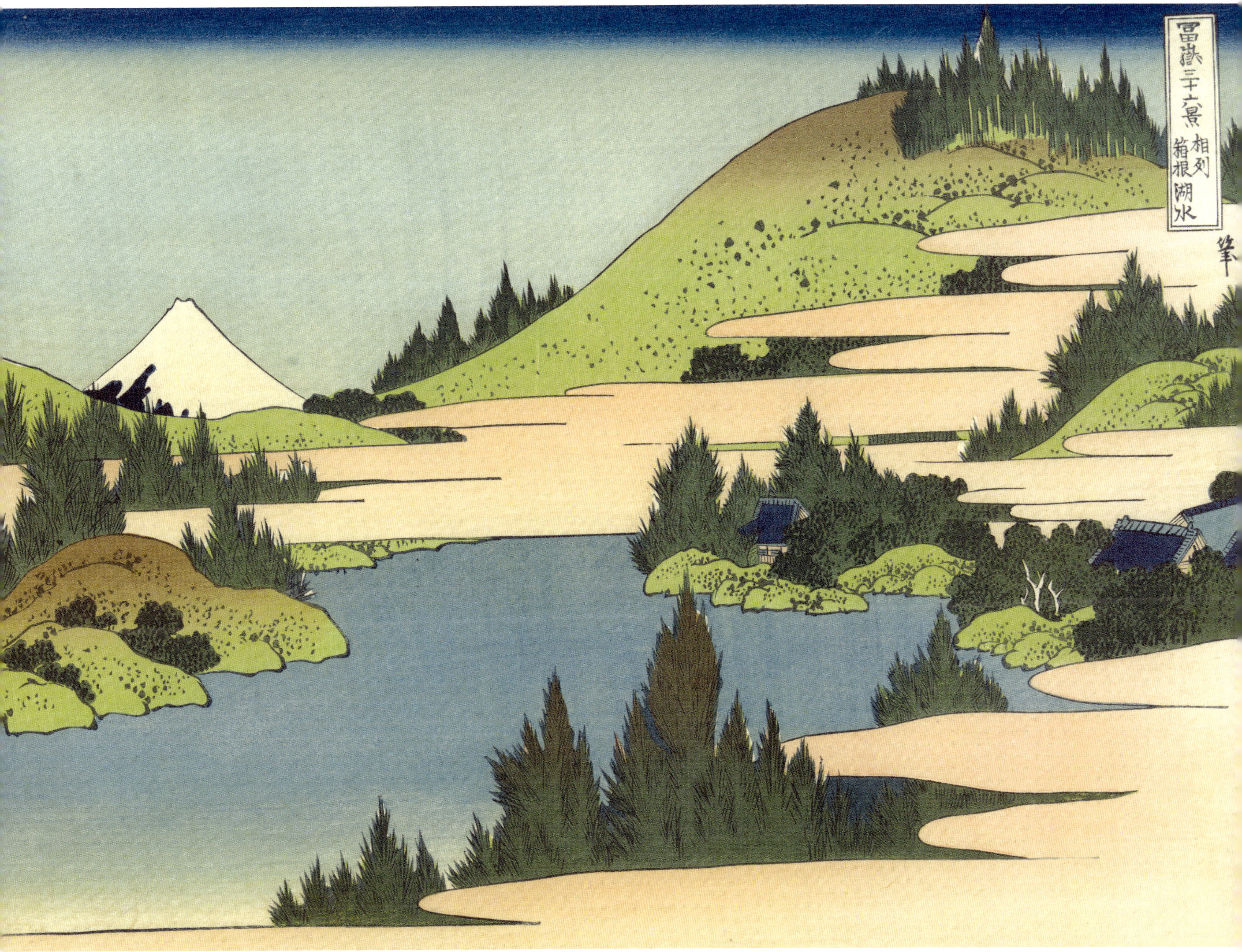

ABOVE Katsushika Hokusai (1760–1849) *The Lake of Hakone in Sagami Province* from 'Thirty-six Views of Mount Fuji' (1826–33, printed later)

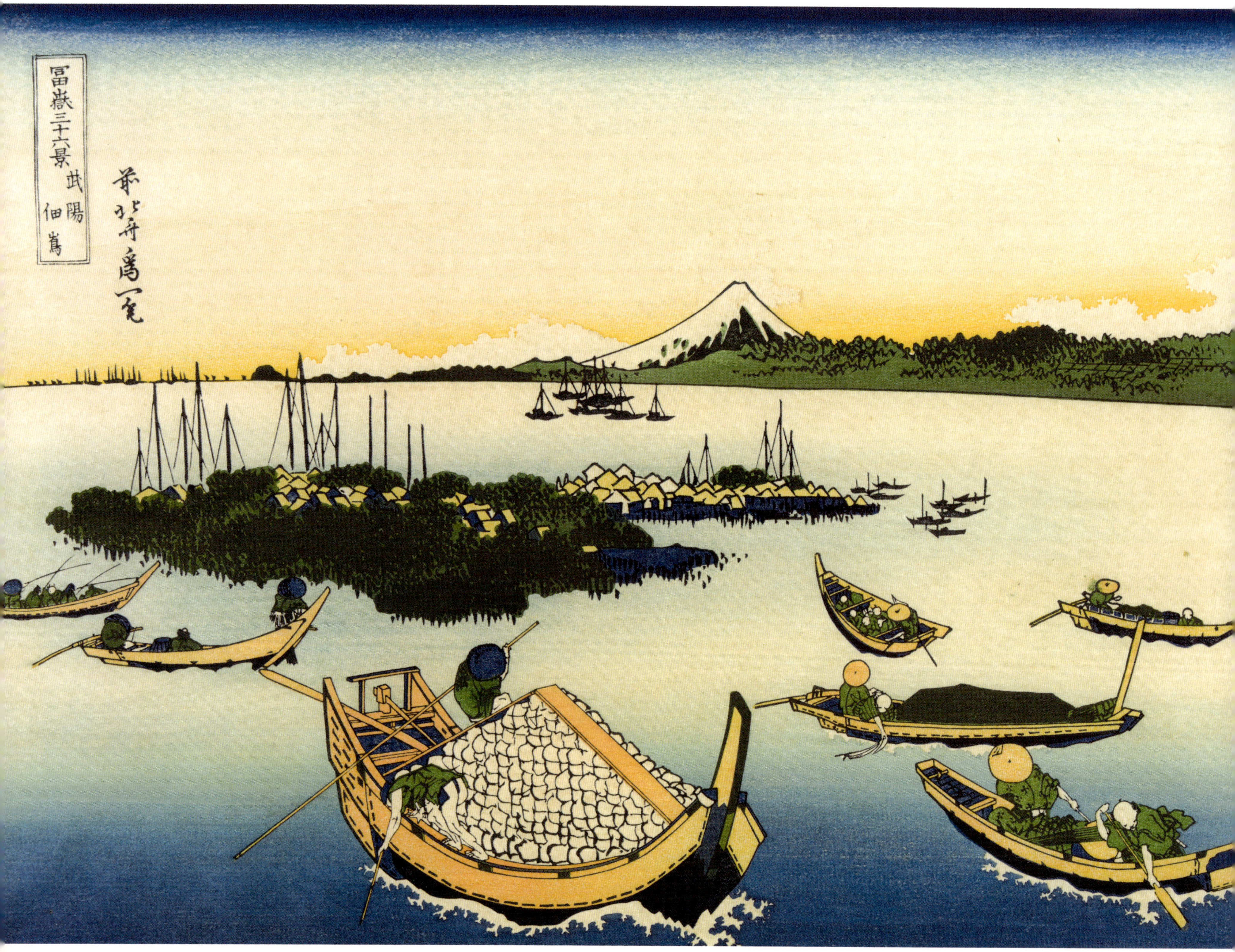

ABOVE **Katsushika Hokusai** (1760–1849) *Tsukuda Island in Musashi Province* from 'Thirty-six Views of Mount Fuji' (1826–33, printed later)

disdain. For, as of 1830, there was no particular sign that he was marked out for great distinction – although, as we have seen, he was entering his seventies.

Until now, in truth, he could not really be characterized as anything much more than a jobbing artist. Nor had his background marked him out for any special glory. His origins were comparatively obscure: born Tokitaro (his childhood name), he had been brought up in the household of the Edo mirror-maker Nakajima. We have no way of knowing if he was this prosperous craftsman's legitimate son or, for that matter, his child at all, as Nakajima certainly did not seem to have made the boy his heir.

If Tokitaro's career in the world of print media started early, it also started at the bottom, with a boyhood job delivering printed and illustrated books around the city. At 14, he began an apprenticeship with a woodblock carver, in which (highly skilled and specialized) work he now spent several years: he could hardly be accused of not knowing the ins and outs of his chosen trade.

New Job, New Name

By the time he was 18, Tokitaro had enlisted in the service of an actual artist, Katsukawa Shunsho (1726–92). Having come to the capital as a poet and painter, Shunsho had stayed to build up a business as a printmaker. Whilst his *bijin-ga* (beautiful people) pictures, showing glamorous women, were held in high regard, he had cornered the market in the *yakusha-e* prints that showed celebrated kabuki actors.

This was a specialized and in many ways exacting line of artistic work to have fallen into. Rather like the paparazzi of today, Tokitaro would have had to go out and about to the restaurants, bars and theatres to find and draw his subjects. He would have had to take direction, too, over which personalities were 'in' and how they should be presented; he would have needed to keep his wits about him so as to have a sense of what a fast-moving market might call for at any given time and he would have had to be ready to adapt and compromise.

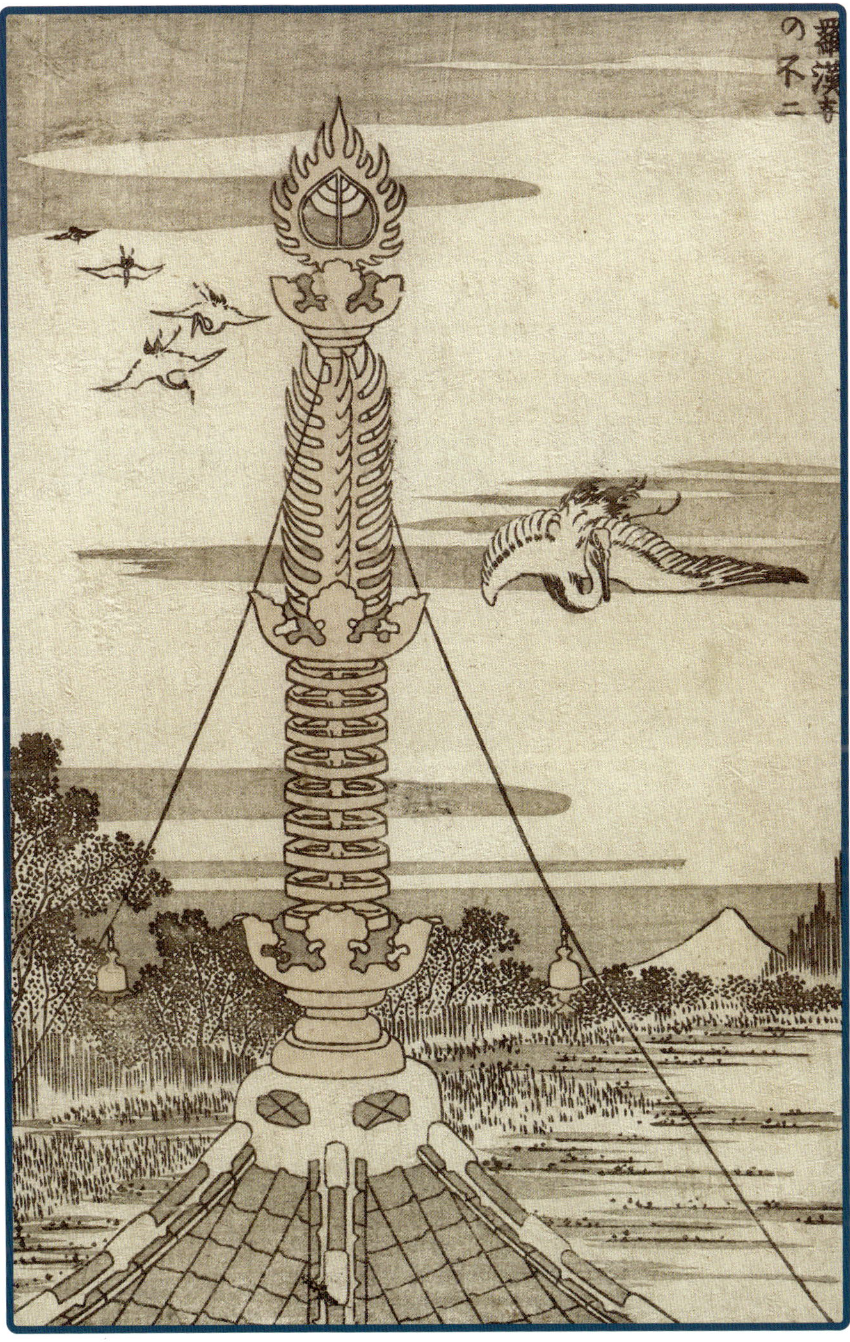

Above Katsushika Hokusai (1760–1849) *Mount Fuji Viewed from Rakan Temple* from Vol. 3 of 'One Hundred Views of Mount Fuji' (1840s)

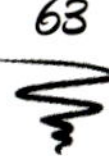

This was a rigorous training in its way, if obviously a far cry from the quiet calm of Fuji and the spiritual landscapes of Hokusai's later years. Even so, the young man appears to have acquitted himself well, if not spectacularly – well enough, at least, for his new master to give him a version of his own name. If the *yakusha-e* pictures perhaps underwhelm, his other works as 'Shunro' (mainly monochrome scenes from fashionable Edo life) frequently show real energy and flair.

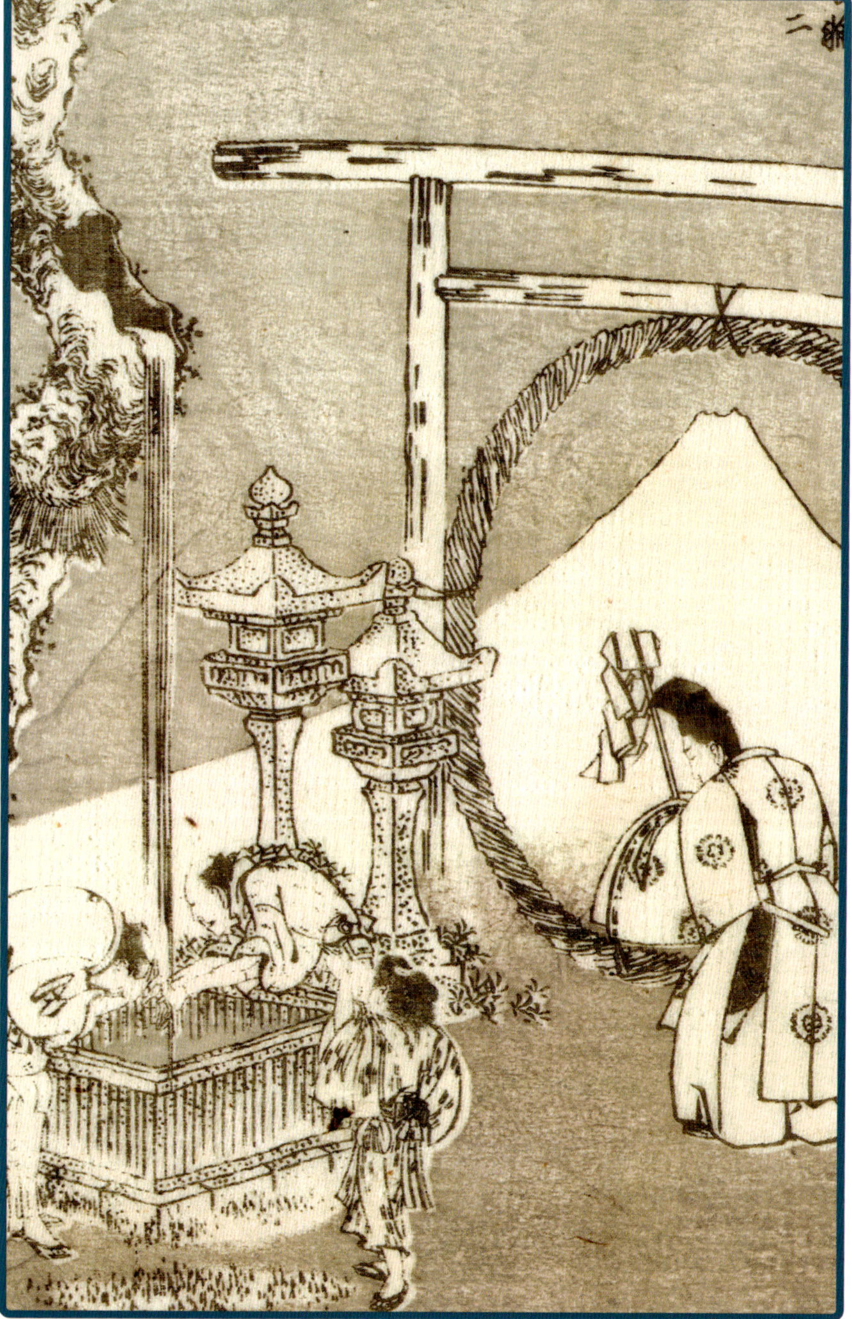

Above Katsushika Hokusai (1760–1849) *Chinowa No Fuji, Mount Fuji Framed by a Fire Circle* from Vol. 3 of 'One Hundred Views of Mount Fuji' (1840s)

In 1793, 15 years into his service, his master Shunsho died. 'Shunro' should have been secure in his place in his workshop, and very likely was. His duty as apprentice was over though, so Shunro was free to leave – and two years later it appears he did. We do not know whether he was pushed out (there does seem to have been some fairly toxic workshop politics among Shunsho's sons and apprentices), whether he chose to leave in order to escape a poisoned atmosphere or whether he simply left to broaden his skills.

From Shunro to Sori

Shunro certainly did develop his art. In the years that followed, loosely attached to the Tawaraya School, he worked under the name of 'Tawaraya Sori'. Despite his affiliation with what had been one of Japanese art's historic schools, he was effectively working as a sort of freelance. As he practised and studied in several different fields, this eclecticism must, at least in part, have been forced upon him by necessity: it seems to have been slow-going sometimes, and difficult on his family (a first wife having died in 1794, he remarried three years later; of his four children, daughter Katsushika Oi (*c.* 1800–66) became an artist).

But Sori does appear to have been motivated too by a desire to broaden his understanding and his skills. He seems to have been especially concerned to trace Japanese art back to its pre-print roots in painting. Workmanlike as he was in his approach, both through economic necessity and a down-to-earth attitude, he undoubtedly had a sense of a higher vocation as well. Despite his struggles, he was successful enough by the second half of the 1790s for his 'Sori Style' to be recognized and respected throughout the Edo art world.

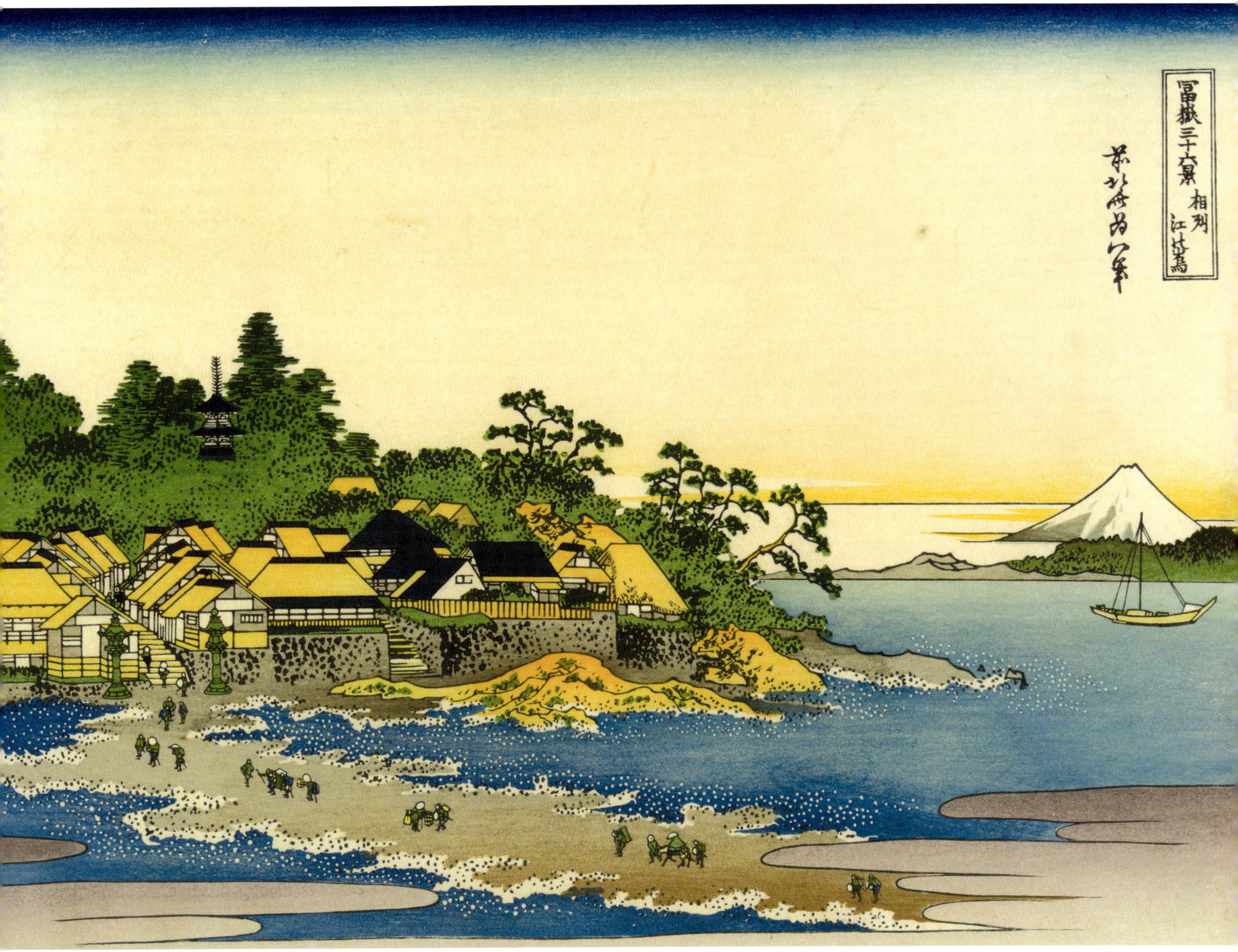

ABOVE **Katsushika Hokusai (1760–1849)** *Enoshima in Sagami Province* from 'Thirty-six Views of Mount Fuji' (1826–33, printed later)

Hokusai Himself

In 1797, the artist formerly known as Tokitaro, Shunro and Sori bequeathed this last name to a favoured student and in turn became Hokusai. Able to pick and choose his work to some extent by now, he devoted much of his time to the privately commissioned, limited-run *surimono* small-format prints. Prestige objects, often literary in theme, and aimed at a self-consciously sophisticated elitist audience, they could be a little more adventurous artistically than the more conventional commercial prints.

The meticulous precision of his workmanship suited the *surimono*, but Hokusai did not see why he could not work in the same fine detail over larger areas. Hence his increased production of 'long-*surimono*', which – as the name suggests – were stretched out sideways, into an elongated landscape format.

Views and Verses

This transition in turn led naturally to ventures into landscape art, which by 1799 had become a favourite genre for Hokusai. In 1800, he brought out a book of *Views of Edo*, and another of *Sights of the Eastern Capital*. Other books of the same sort followed, such as *Views of Both Banks of the Sumida River* (*c.* 1804). Sometimes these books of views included poems, with *Mountain Upon Mountain* (1804) being one of these. And vice versa: with so many poems of the period addressing the wonders of nature and the beauties of the countryside, books of verse often afforded opportunities for landscape art.

Hokusai had for some time already been hard at work producing illustrations for the little poetry anthologies popular among the more educated echelons of Edo society – again, their small format suited the way he worked. Among these collections had been titles such as *Verses of the Four Seasons* (1798), an anthology of haiku (exquisite short lyrics of just 17 syllables). But Hokusai also contributed (often elaborate, and elaborately witty) illustrations to collections of *kyoka* ('mad song' satirical poems). These too, despite their comic tone, often dealt with the beauties

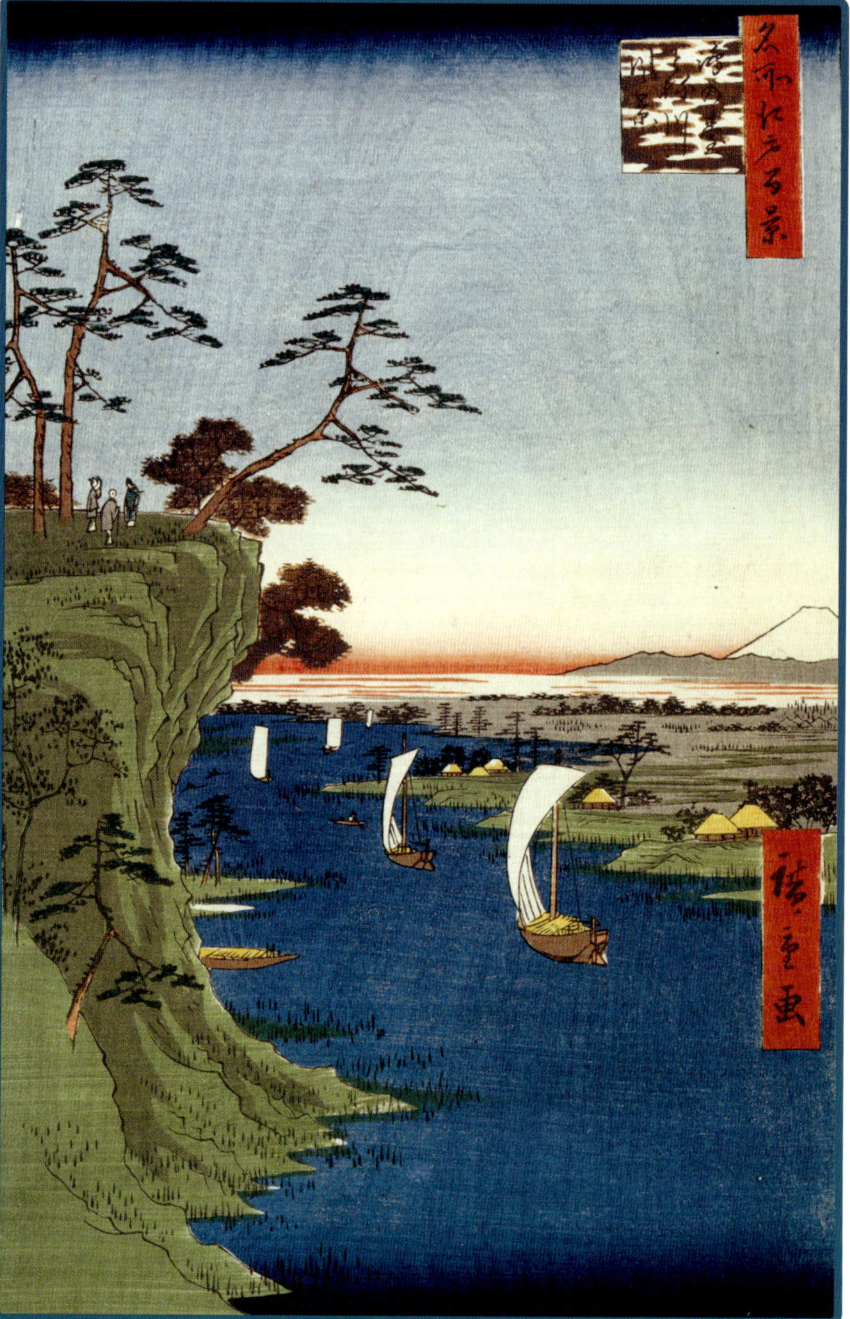

Above Utagawa Hiroshige (1797–1858) *View of Konodai and the Tone River* from 'One Hundred Famous Views of Edo' (1856–58)

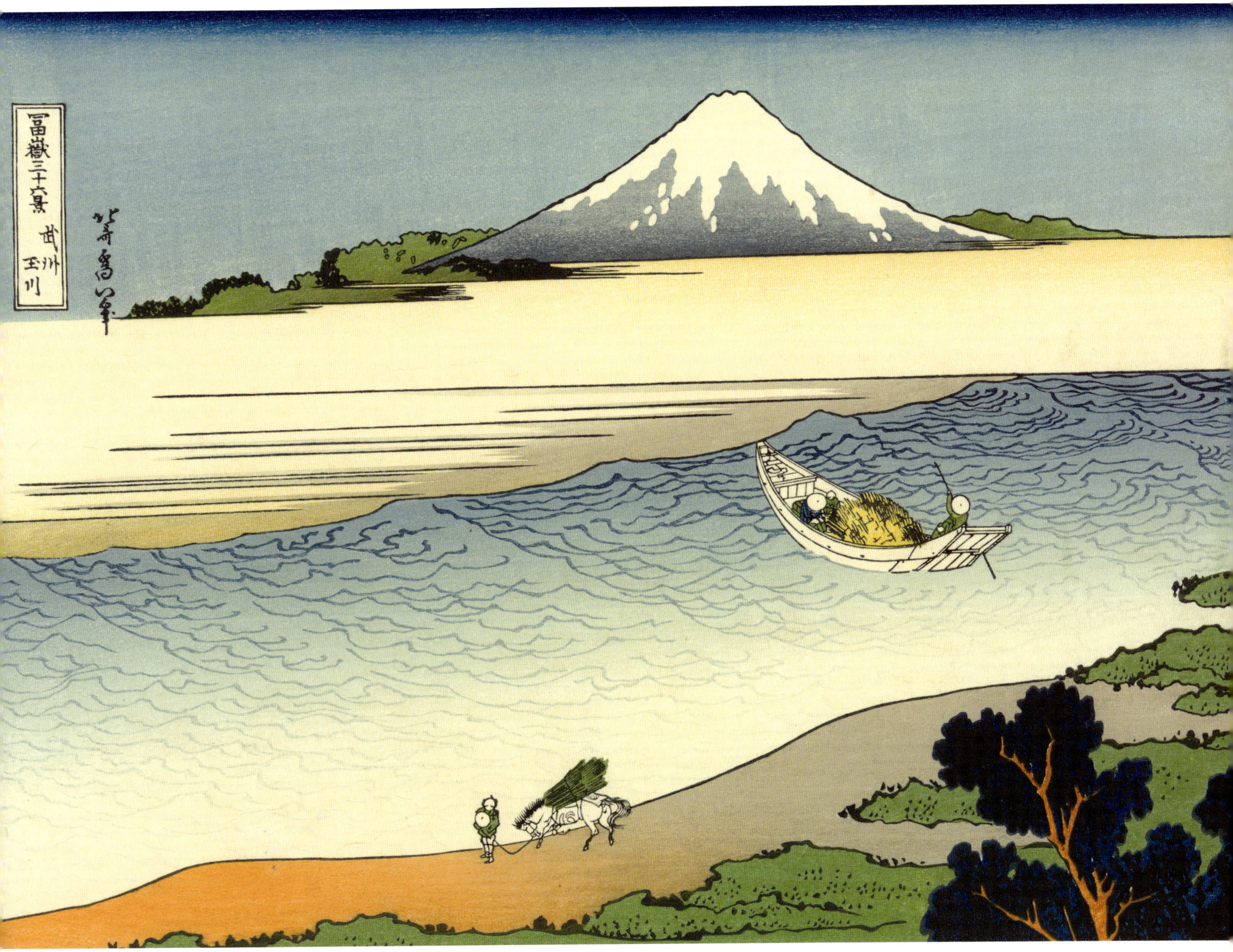

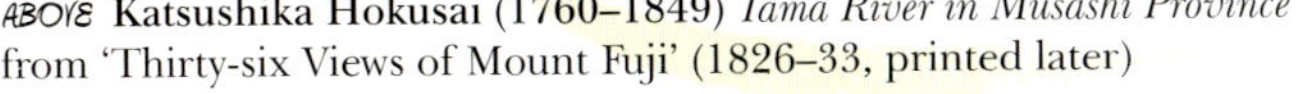

Above Katsushika Hokusai (1760–1849) *Tama River in Musashi Province* from 'Thirty-six Views of Mount Fuji' (1826–33, printed later)

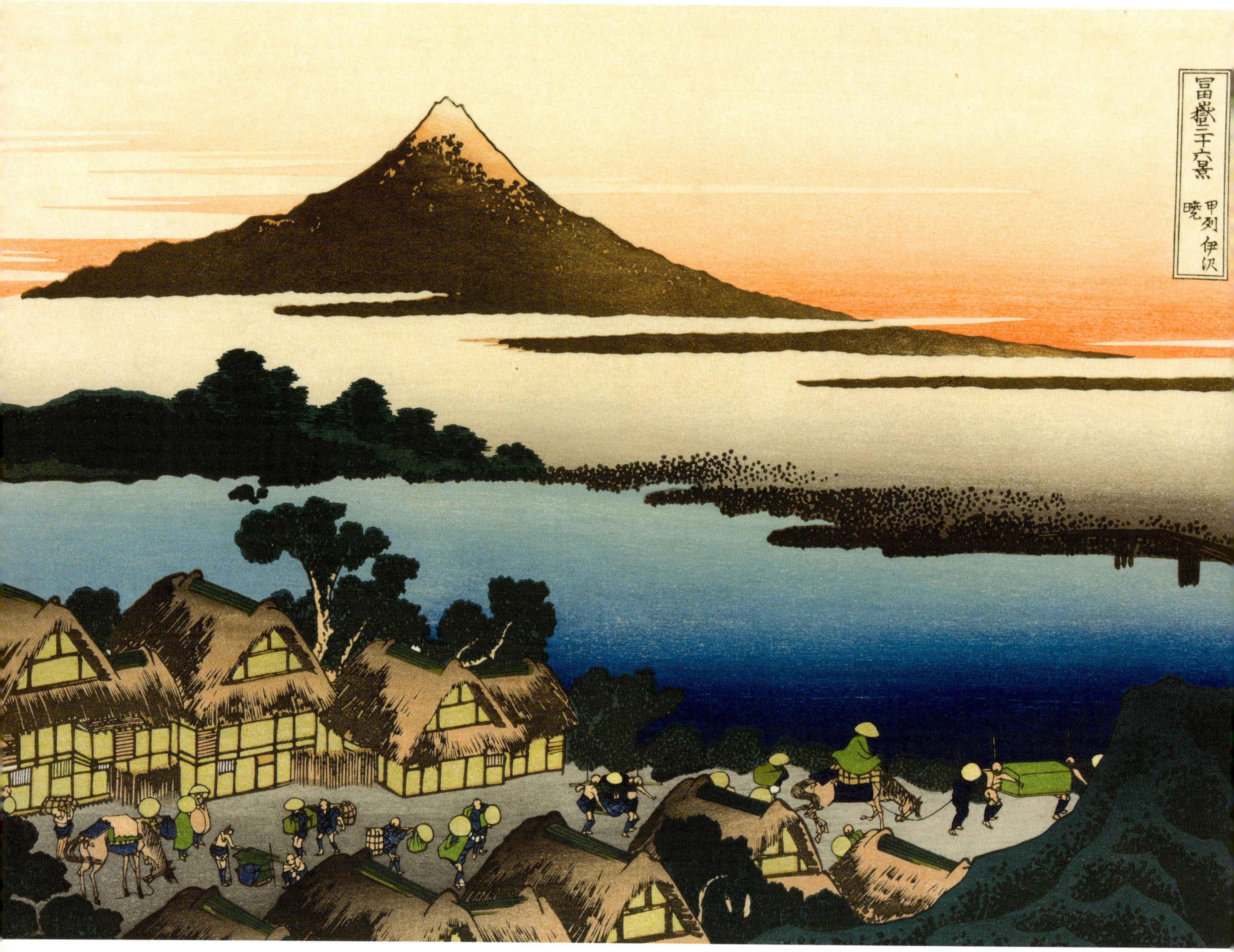

ABOVE Katsushika Hokusai (1760–1849) *Dawn at Isawa in Kai Province* from 'Thirty-six Views of Mount Fuji' (1826–33, printed later)

of nature, as is indicated by the titles of some of those Hokusai illustrated – such as 'Elegance of Spring' (*c.* 1798), 'Snow on the Branches' (1799) and 'The First Moon' (1803). Hokusai's *kyoka* anthologies of 1803 also included 'Fuji in Spring' and 'On Viewing Mount Fuji'.

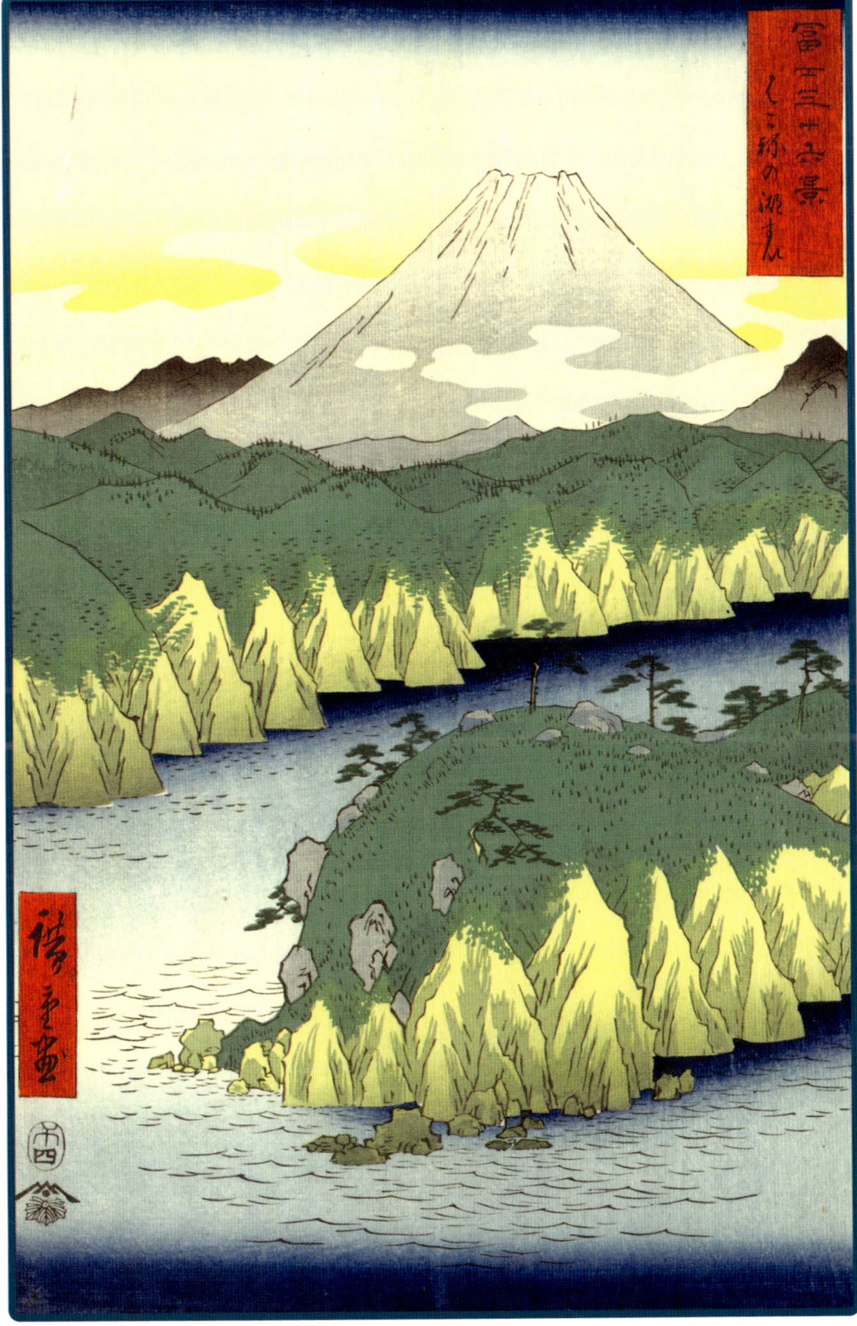

ABOVE Utagawa Hiroshige (1797–1858) *Lake at Hakone* from 'Thirty-six Views of Mount Fuji' (1858)

Hokusai the Hero

As Hokusai's work became better known, respect turned into renown before edging over into celebrity. Mindful, perhaps, of earlier struggles, he was quick to build on this popularity. In 1804, it is said that during a ceremony at the Gokokuji Temple, on the edge of Edo, he stood before a large crowd with a broom and a bucket of black ink, painting a portrait of the famous Bodhisattva, Daruma, 180 m (590½ ft) long. At what point does an act of reverence become a stunt? In 1817, Hokusai repeated this achievement at the temple of Nagoya – this time Daruma's face filled 240 sq m (2583⅓ sq ft) of paper.

Whether because he hoped to 'cash in' on this celebrity or wanted to share his gifts we cannot be sure, but in 1810 and 1812 Hokusai brought out two drawing manuals. The second, the *Quick Guide to Drawing*, proved popular not just on publication but for the rest of the century, testimony to Hokusai's lasting fame but also to the book's intrinsic worth. However cynical its conception, it makes fascinating browsing now, not least for its insights into how Hokusai composed and created his more famous pictures. In particular, it shows how he liked to pile up geometric forms – including circles, squares and triangles – to build up a sense of three-dimensional space and depth.

An Erotic Turn

It was during this period too that Hokusai produced his most notorious books of *shunga* (erotic art). His plates are often stunningly done, though they can be controversial now in their overtones of violence (or quite blatant acts of rape) and sometimes simply perplexing, as they can be more sculptural than sexual in their complex intertwining of limbs and loosened gowns. They are invariably alien in their cultural and historical remoteness: should the (in)famous picture of a pair of octopuses pleasuring a naked diving girl (1814) arouse us with its eroticism, outrage us as a licence to bestiality or simply amuse us with its wit?

How are we to take them now? Just what would we consider porn? Something more explicit than that or simply something different? As in a modern porn movie, a fairly minimal storyline would provide the narrative framework for a succession of vividly imagined sex scenes. But these books had much more cultural cachet than the average porn flick; lavishly produced, with sometimes sumptuous colour pictures, they were clearly designed as collectibles, for self-consciously discerning (and distinctly well-heeled) 'readers'.

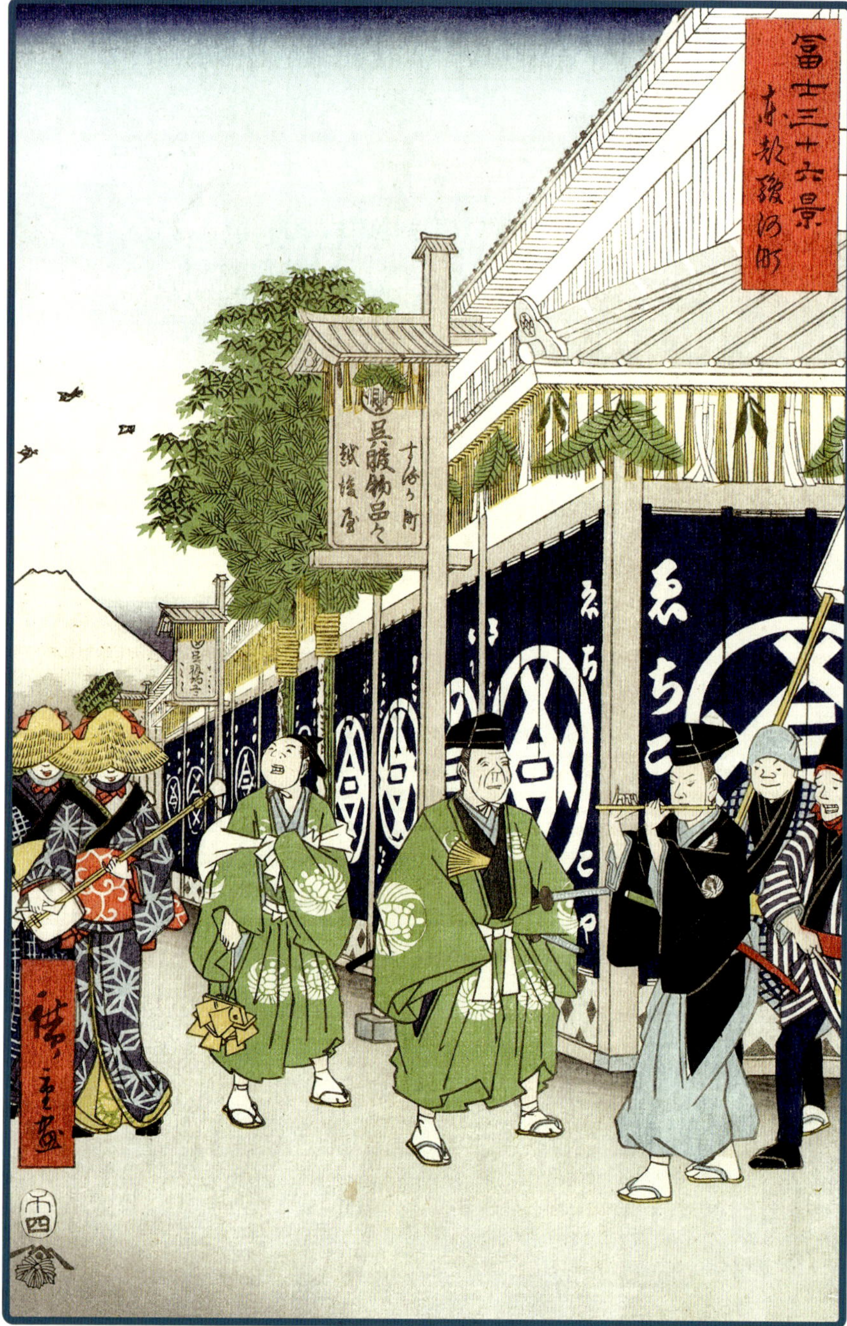

ABOVE **Utagawa Hiroshige (1797–1858)** *The Suruga District in the Eastern Capital* from 'Thirty-six Views of Mount Fuji' (1858)

Points of View

Books of *shunga* seem to have served another function as well, one that makes no sense at all from a modern standpoint and that tends to make questions of morality or objectification seem rather moot. For reasons we really cannot begin to fathom, the Edo culture set value on these books as talismanic objects (hence in part, perhaps, their extravagant production values). That copies would be handed to brides, as good-luck tokens, might seem understandable – if not, perhaps, what we would do now. It did not stop there, however. The evidence is that both men and women of the upper classes liked to carry books like this about with them, apparently as protective charms against fire and death.

The importance of point-of-view has to be borne in mind when we try to appreciate the point of Hokusai's views – in particular, perhaps, those of his most famous work, the 'Thirty-six Views of Mount Fuji' series of 1826–33 (*see* all thirty-six here, on pages 71–73). Quite simply, whilst his first audience evidently found this book every bit as stunning as we do now, they clearly cannot have seen these views in the same way as we do. To take one possibly trivial (but maybe much more important) example, whilst – as we have already seen – *The Great Wave off Kanagawa* is full of interest, excitement and mysterious portent for us, we can never hope to experience the shock Hokusai's first customers must have felt at simply seeing such a symphony in blue.

'Prussian blue' – probably known as 'Dutch blue ' to the Japanese, of course – was still comparatively new and rare (*see* page 48). Opening their new book (note: the Japanese read from right to left, and thus from 'back'

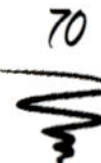

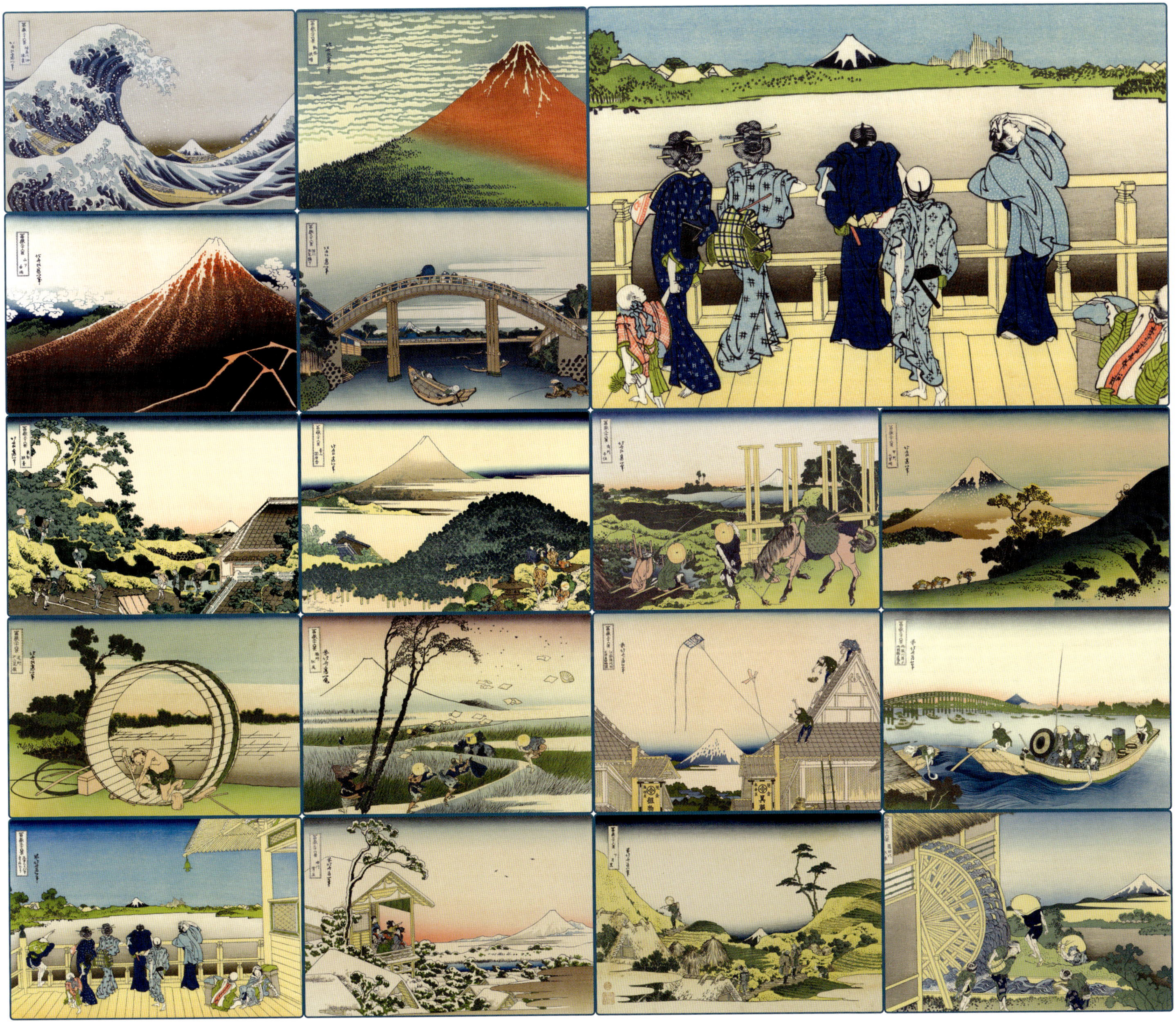

Above **Katsushika Hokusai** (1760–1849) prints 1–16 from 'Thirty-six Views of Mount Fuji' (1826–33, mostly printed later), with extra detail of print 13

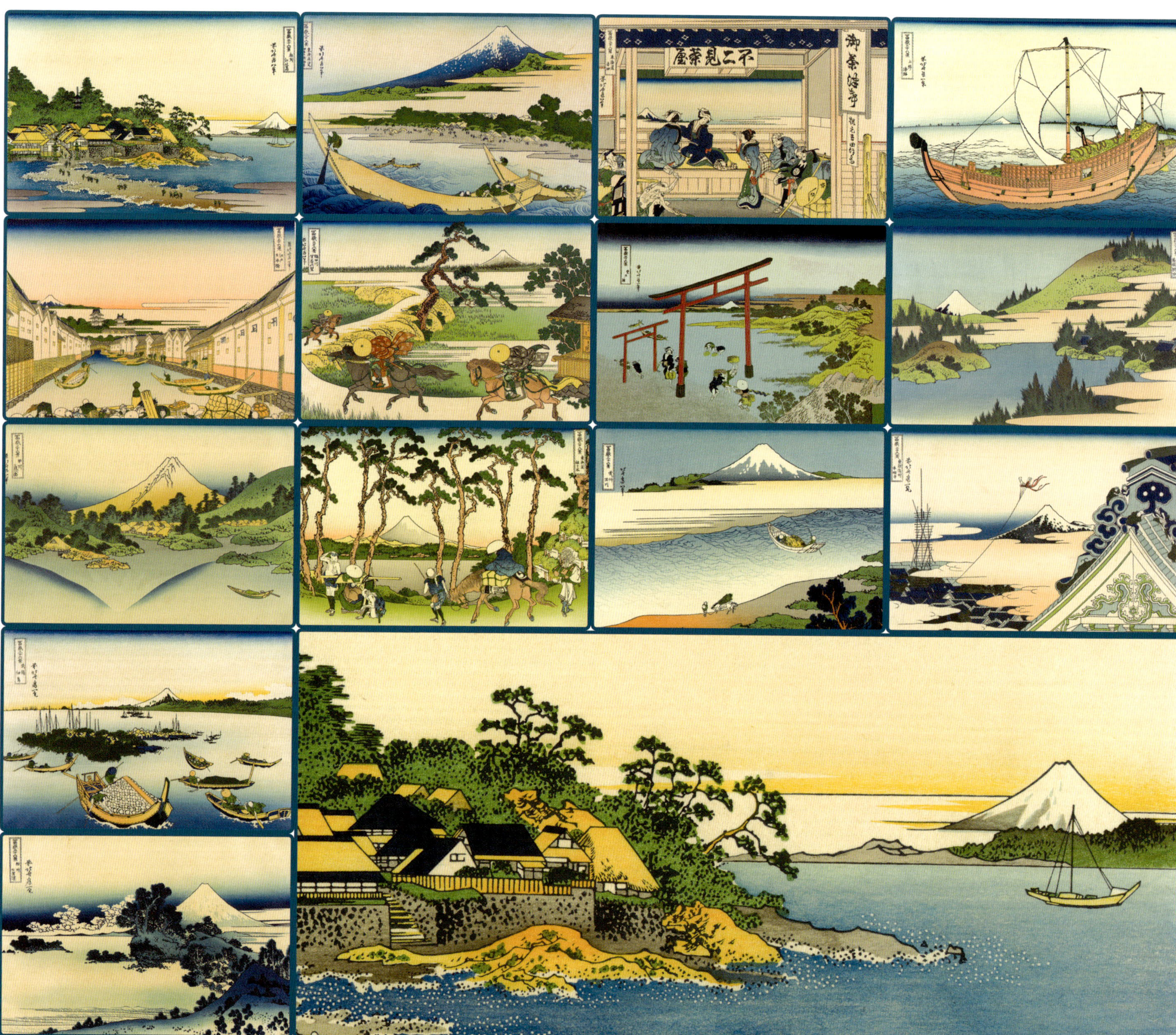

ABOVE **Katsushika Hokusai** (1760–1849) prints 17–30 from 'Thirty-six Views of Mount Fuji' (1826–33, mostly printed later), with extra detail of print 17

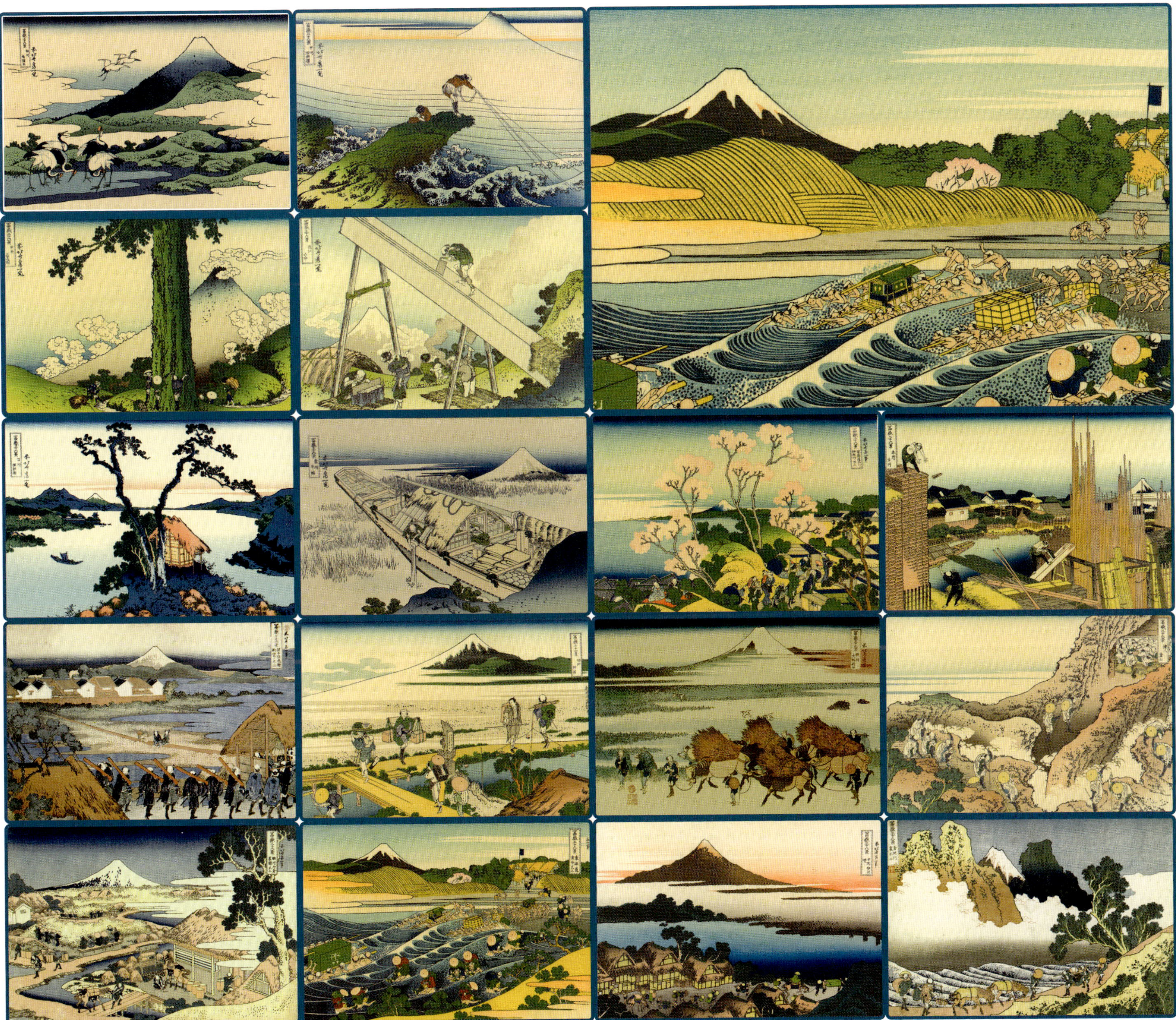

Above **Katsushika Hokusai** (1760–1849) prints 31–36 from 'Thirty-six Views of Mount Fuji', plus the additional 10 prints (1826–33, mostly printed later), with extra detail of print 44

to 'front' according to the Western scheme), the first element which would have confronted the browser here was this blue sea, its colour as deep and mysterious as the ocean waters. Only then could they have begun to appreciate the geometric tricks, the visual puns (the waves mimicking mountains; the is-it-foam-from-the-waves-or-is-it-snow?) – or the dreadful human drama taking place amongst it all.

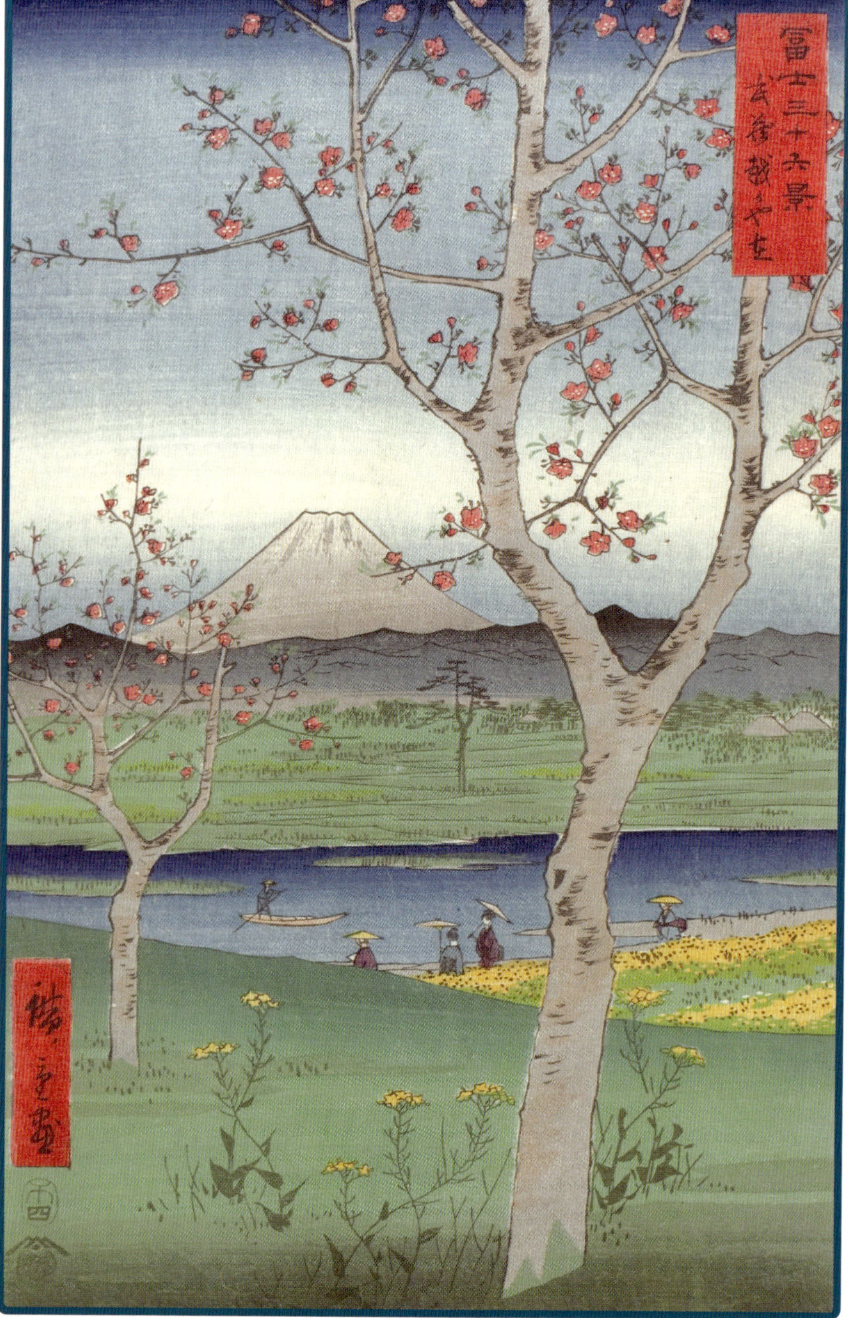

Above Utagawa Hiroshige (1797–1858) *Koshigaya in Musashi Province* from 'Thirty-six Views of Mount Fuji' (1858)

More generally, and more important, we can only really wonder what Hokusai can have meant by his conception of his series as a whole. No one seriously believes that it should be seen as a reel of random snapshots or collection of picture postcards. Acknowledging Fujisan's religious importance for Hokusai, Western scholars have tended vaguely to assume that he intended to capture his beloved Fujisan in all its facets, from every side, in every season and in all its moods. This view of the series as what might be called a 'spiritual survey' is at least respectful (in assigning a higher purpose than pure representation), but it does not tell us too much and arguably raises more questions than it answers. Many of them will very likely never be answered, but being aware of the difficulties cannot hurt.

Simplicity Itself

In the second print (*see* right), the same quality of blue – now sky, not sea – is upstaged by the rich red earth of Fuji's cone, with only light striations of snow on its upper reaches. A dark woodland stubble crowds the mountain's base. In between, however, the main mass of the mountain is an open plane of pure colour; that Hokusai does not feel compelled to fill this space, that he dares to do nothing, is testimony to his confidence. This picture is quite astounding in its assurance.

Despite the plate's traditional title, *South Wind, Clear Sky*, the sky's bright blue is broken up by innumerable streaks of cirrocumulus cloud. But there is nothing remotely dull about this day. The purity of the colours and the clarity of their demarcation are a tribute to the quality of the *nishiki-e* overprinting process Hokusai used. If Fujisan was a distant presence in the previous print, here it takes the foreground, slightly off-centre, giving an ironic twist to its symmetry.

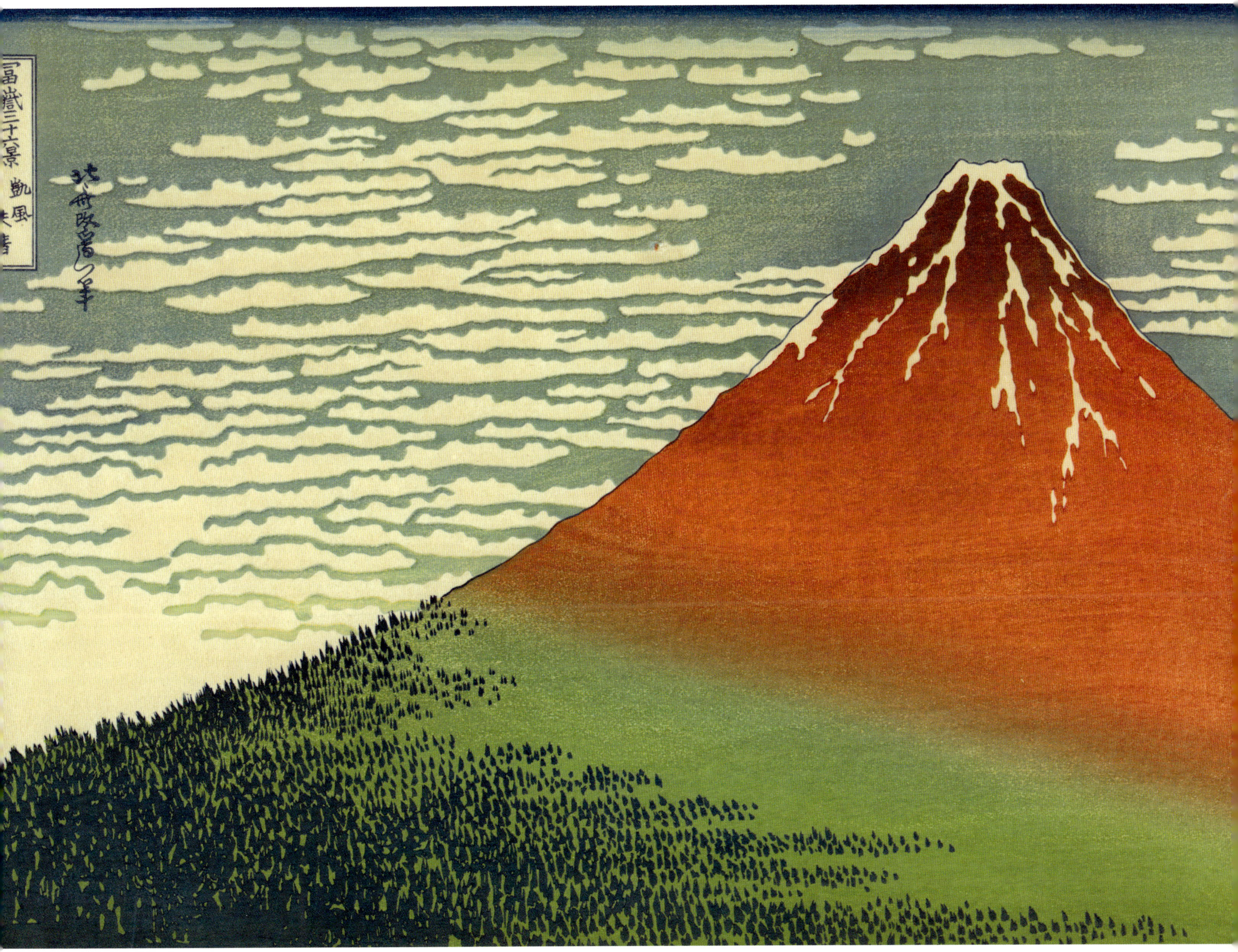

Above Katsushika Hokusai (1760–1849) *South Wind, Clear Sky* (also known as *Red Fuji*) from 'Thirty-six Views of Mount Fuji' (1826–33, printed later)

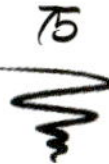

More is Less?

Rainstorm Beneath the Summit (*see* right) is almost as simple, though the bold contrasts are softened here by a brown-black mottled mountainside,

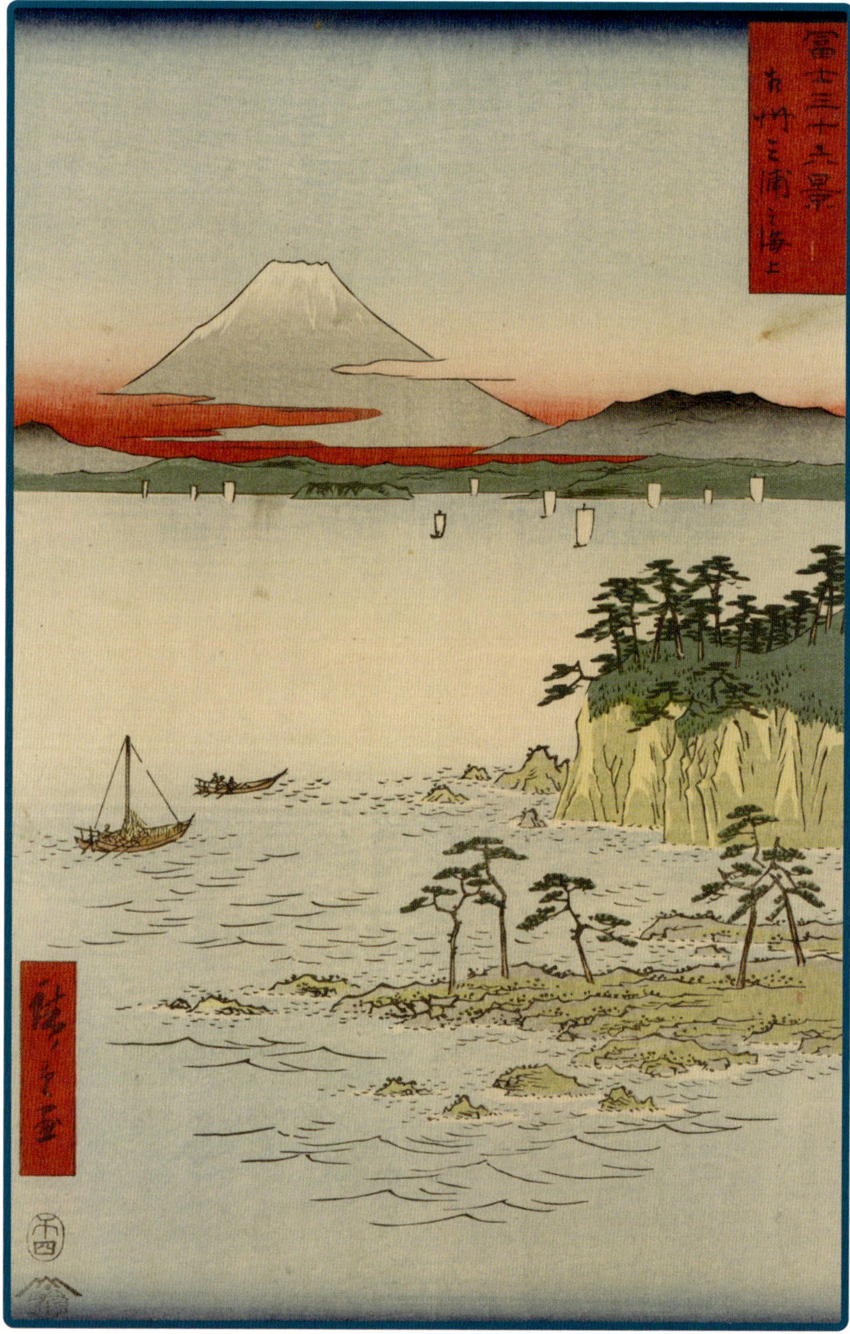

ABOVE **Utagawa Hiroshige (1797–1858)** *The Sea off the Miura Peninsula in Sagami Province* from 'Thirty-six Views of Mount Fuji' (1858)

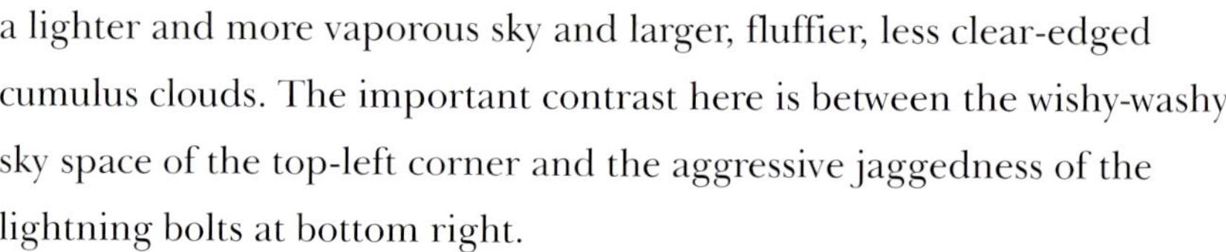

a lighter and more vaporous sky and larger, fluffier, less clear-edged cumulus clouds. The important contrast here is between the wishy-washy sky space of the top-left corner and the aggressive jaggedness of the lightning bolts at bottom right.

This print has not captured the Western imagination in quite the way the two companion pieces we have looked at, but its importance to Hokusai is underlined by the fact that he made several studies of the same view. Are they successive stabs at a vision that never quite came off, formal theme and variations deliberately different and yet the same, or artistic meditation on a visual mantra?

That to most of us, in all honesty, *Rainstorm…* does not rise to the Fuji-like heights of *South Wind, Clear Sky* may just be evidence that even the great artist cannot make a masterpiece every time. Or it may raise once again the question of point-of-view. Granted, Hokusai's 'greatest' works may chime with Western tastes formed by the colourful boldness of Manet, Matisse and Picasso, but do we see Hokusai clearly when we view him through a modernist prism?

The Human Factor

South Wind… and *Rainstorm…* both show us Nature in a pure, unpeopled state, but this is far from typical of Hokusai's landscape art. However spiritual his aspirations for his series, the artist for the most part does not abstract his subject from its surroundings – not just in the wider countryside but in the scheme of Japanese life. Even when he shows us Nature at its wildest and most dramatic, then, he mostly includes people – even if they are reduced to insignificance, like the trembling mariners in *The Great Wave…*

By the same token, most of the 'Thirty-six Views…' show a more conscious human conception at work than these more impressionistic pages. They

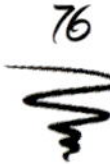

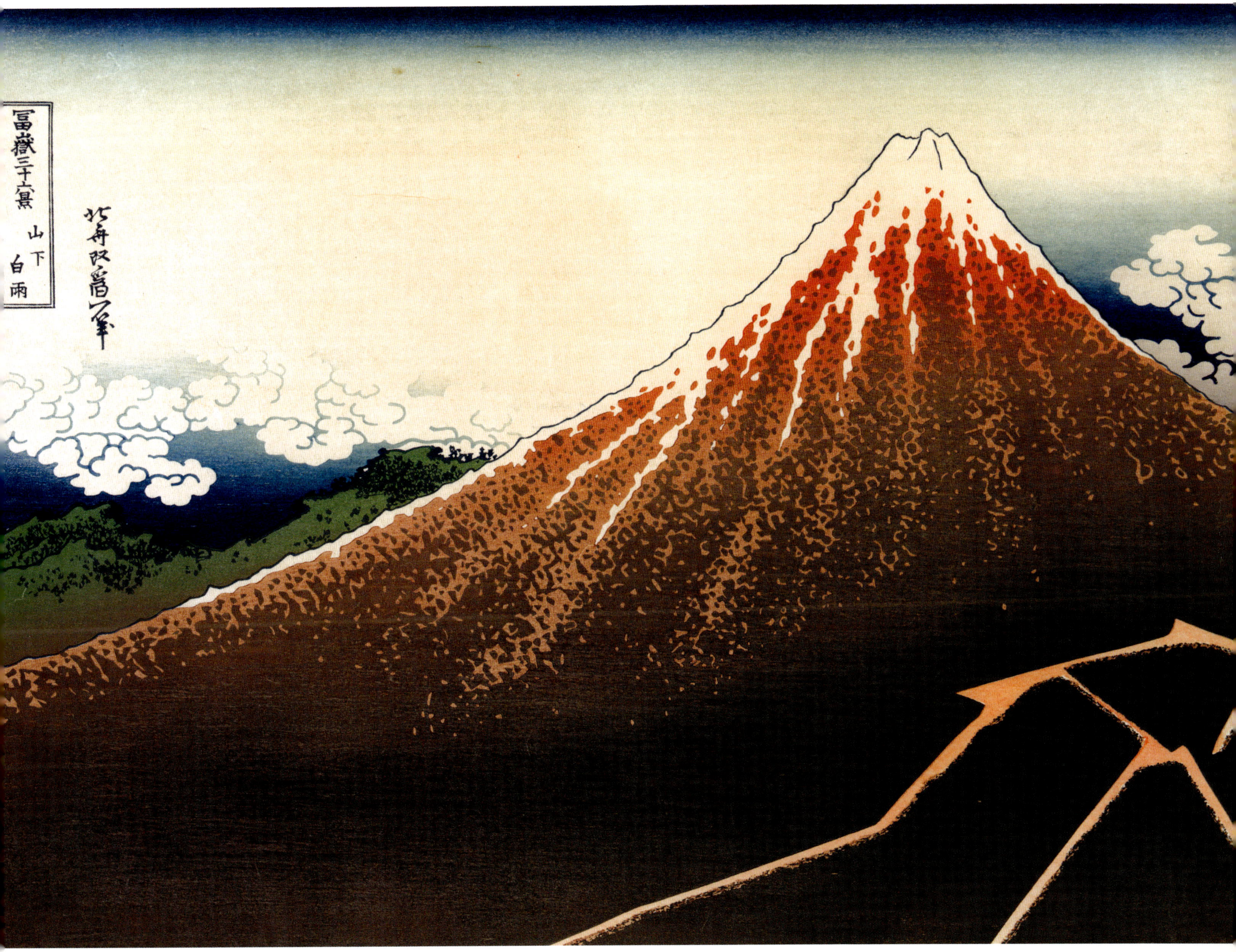

Above Katsushika Hokusai (1760–1849) *Rainstorm Beneath the Summit* from 'Thirty-six Views of Mount Fuji' (1826–33, printed later)

are less painterly, more obviously drawn. In *Under Mannen Bridge at Fukagawa* (*see* page 59), the famous mountain is once more relegated (or promoted) to the far horizon, to a picture-within-a-picture, framed and focused by the arch and pilings of the bridge. Again, it is very obviously designed and drawn, the starkness of its outlines standing out against a thin and watery sky.

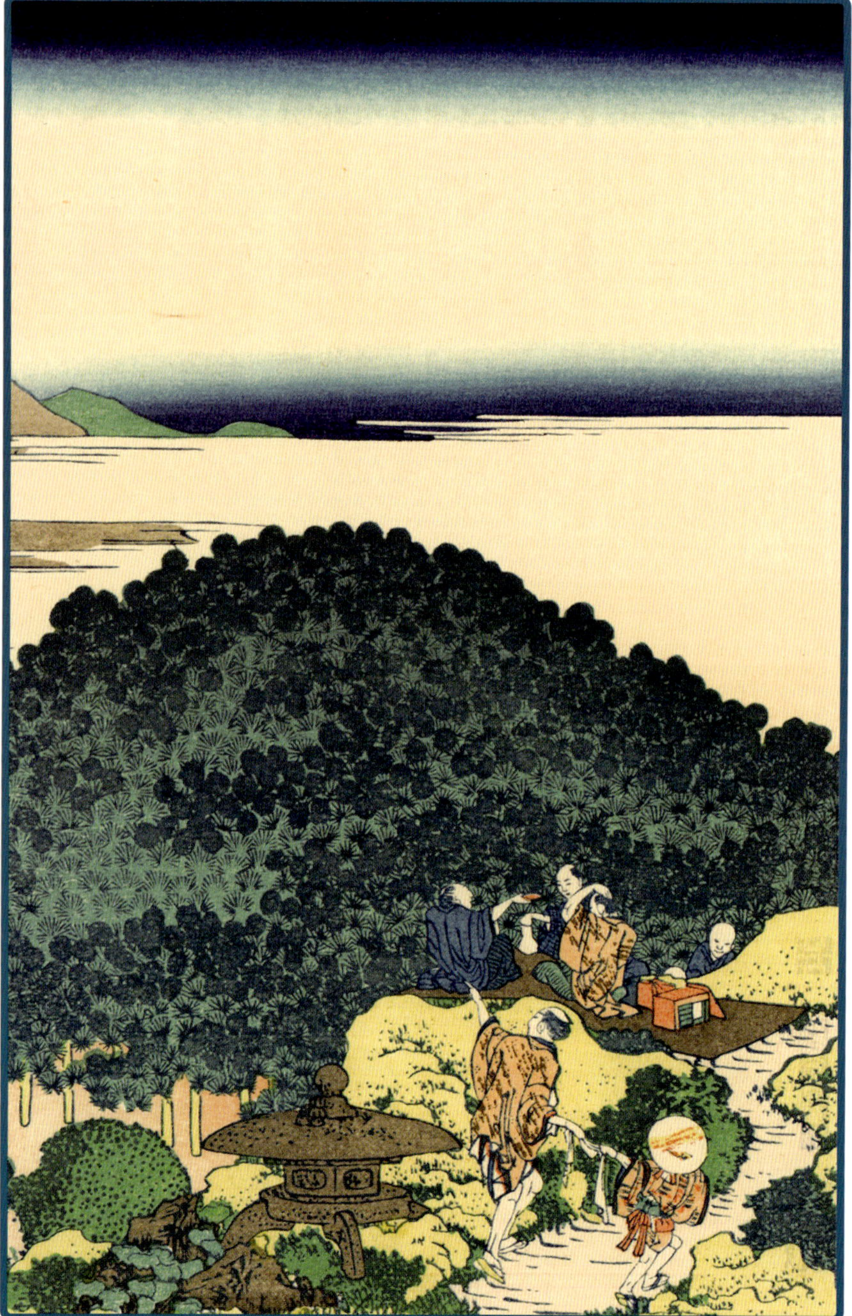

ABOVE Katsushika Hokusai (1760–1849) *Cushion Pine at Aoyama* (detail) from 'Thirty-six Views of Mount Fuji' (1826–33)

Men and Mountains

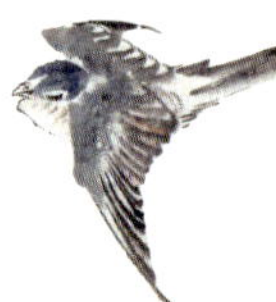

The work is also packed with the sort of geometric forms which featured in the 1812 *Quick Guide to Drawing*; indeed it is the counterpointing of these shapes that makes the picture. The gentle concavity of Fuji's slopes contrasts with the sweeping arch of the bridge above, as do the curvilinear forms of the boats below. The interplay is complicated by the arcing rods and *sugegesa* (coolie hats) of the fishermen and the bright blue parasol atop the bridge.

People are well to the fore in *Sundai, Edo* (*see* right), the roofs of the village of Sundai, just outside Edo, rising high above the distant peak in the perspective we have here. Peasants and pedlars come and go along a busy mountain road beneath the shadow of a spreading pine tree. Though the scene is quieter – and the form of Fujisan even more abstract in conception – there are travellers too, in *Cushion Pine at Aoyama* (*see* left). One man points across a valley floor fluffy with pine-tree tops at the prospect of the mountain in what Keats called 'wild surmise', inviting us to share his sense of the sheer sublimity of this view.

In *Senju, Musashi Province* (*see* page 59), Fujisan can barely be seen across the expanse of rice paddies extending away into the distance, the vista being interrupted by what appears to be the wooden framework of a sluice gate. This structure rises high above the river, beside which a pair of fishermen sit quietly. In the immediate foreground, a man leads a horse, its rein weighted down by the turtle he has attached to it – presumably for carrying convenience. Again, games of geometry are being played. The triangle of Fuji in the far distance is mirrored by the foreleg of the horse, its hanging rein and the man who is holding it. It may seem surprising, given the cruelty with which we see it suspended

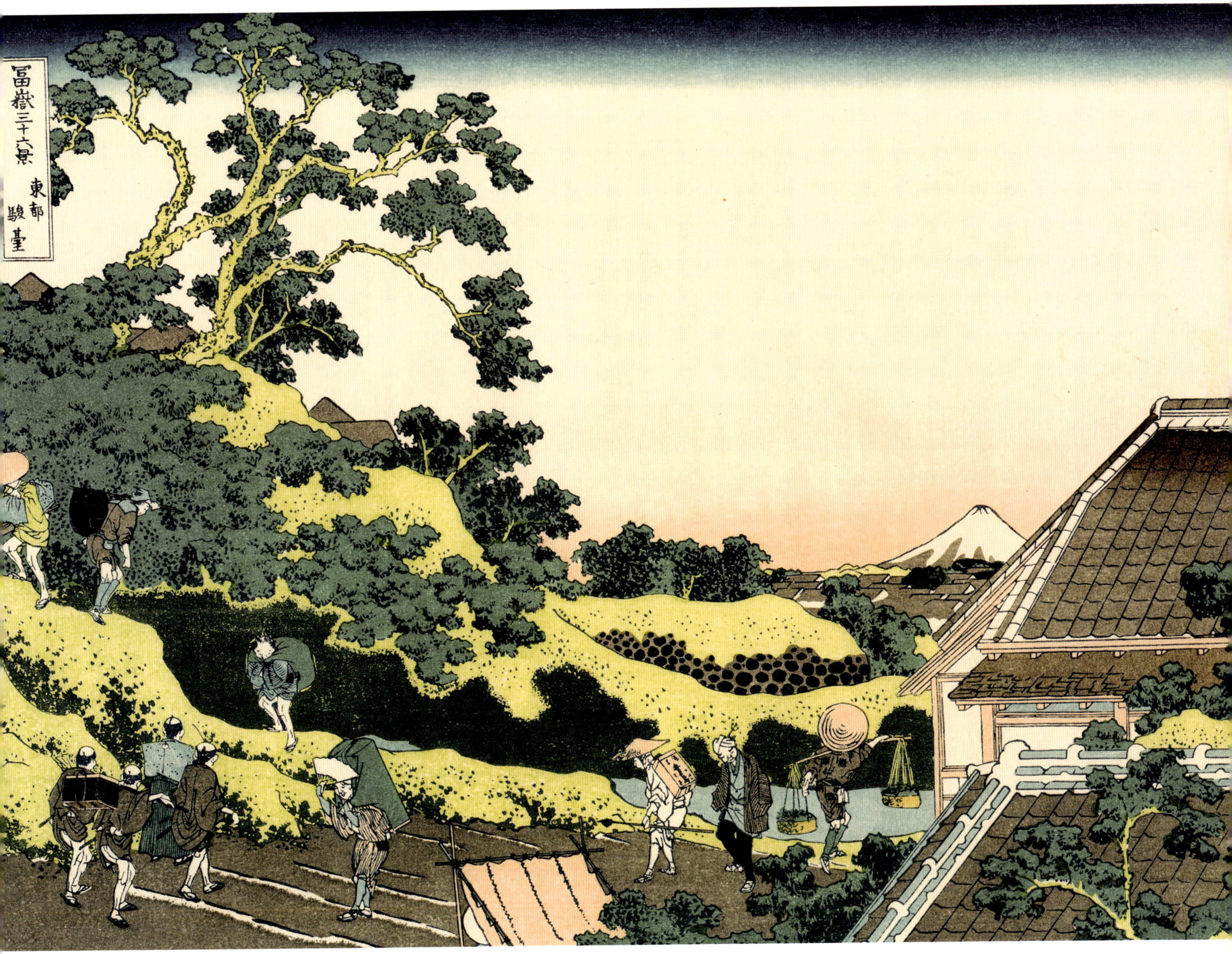

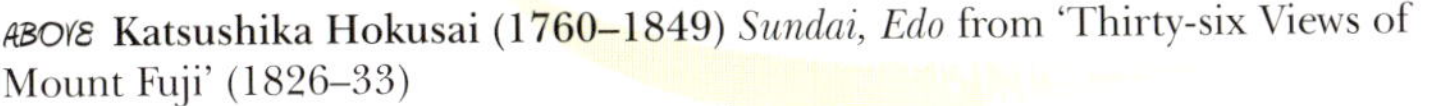

ABOVE Katsushika Hokusai (1760–1849) *Sundai, Edo* from 'Thirty-six Views of Mount Fuji' (1826–33)

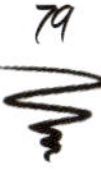

here (and again, *see* page 149), to find that the turtle was held in reverence in Japan. Its well-known longevity, as well as the similarity perceived between its sloping shell and the dome of Mount Meru – or, of course, the cone of Fujisan – made it a powerful emblem of long life.

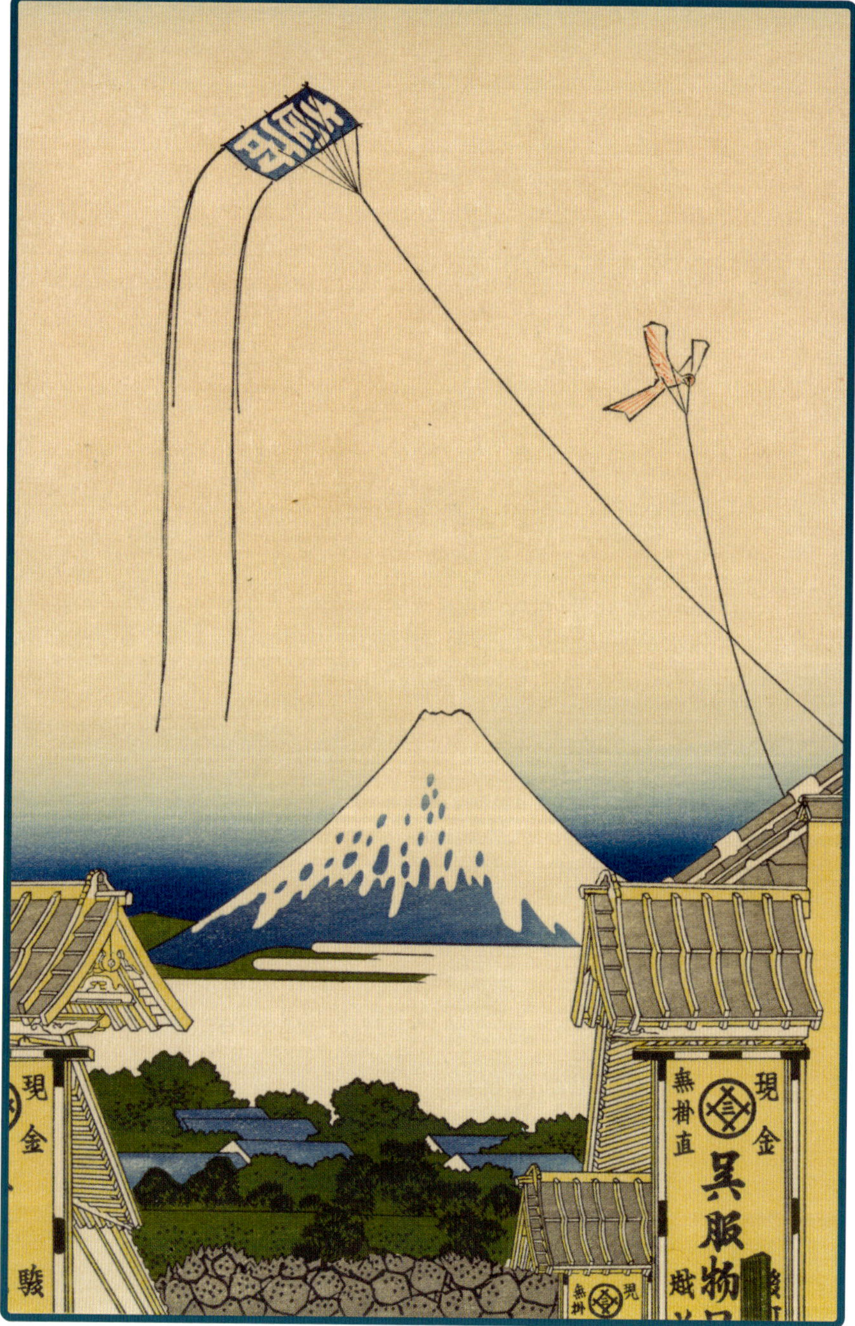

ABOVE Katsushika Hokusai (1760–1849) *A Sketch of the Mitsui Shop in Suruga in Edo* (detail) from 'Thirty-six Views of Mount Fuji' (1826–33, printed later)

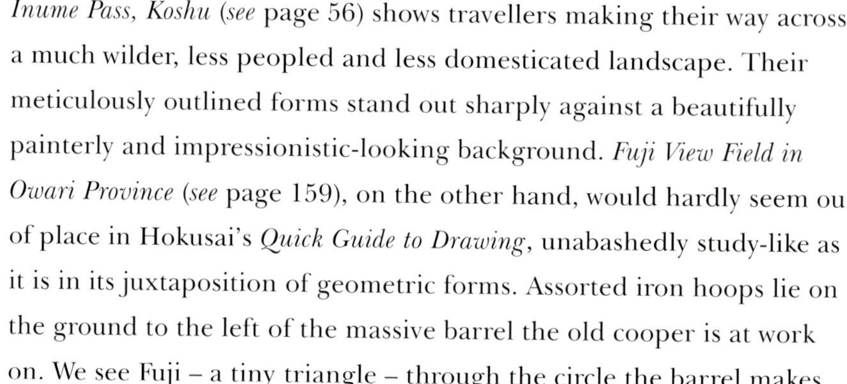

Inume Pass, Koshu (*see* page 56) shows travellers making their way across a much wilder, less peopled and less domesticated landscape. Their meticulously outlined forms stand out sharply against a beautifully painterly and impressionistic-looking background. *Fuji View Field in Owari Province* (*see* page 159), on the other hand, would hardly seem out of place in Hokusai's *Quick Guide to Drawing*, unabashedly study-like as it is in its juxtaposition of geometric forms. Assorted iron hoops lie on the ground to the left of the massive barrel the old cooper is at work on. We see Fuji – a tiny triangle – through the circle the barrel makes.

Dynamic Duo

In *Ejiri in Suruga Province* (*see* right), we find a different sort of counterpointing – not so much of shape as of energy, or life force – *ki*, as it still is called. The contrast here is between the eternal stillness of the mountain – in the background and yet looming large (edged forward by the range of blue hills visible behind it) – and the dynamism of the gale that persecutes the passers-by in the picture's foreground. While most of those we see manage just to hold on to hats, parasols and other items, one wayfarer has to bid his hat farewell and another loses the battle to keep hold of the papers he has been carrying. Away into the sky they fly, joining the crowd of leaves streaming free from the storm-whipped trees – like those fleeing 'like ghosts from an enchanter' in Shelley's 'Ode to the West Wind'. Even the swirling path seems to have been blown off course by the rushing wind.

We see the same sort of thing done more subtly in the print that follows, *A Sketch of the Mitsui Shop in Suruga in Edo* (*see* detail, left). At first glance, it feels as though an uncanny stillness reigns. The buildings in the foreground (the shop itself and its immediate neighbour) seem as firmly rooted as the peak of Fuji far behind them, with whose form their gabled rooftops clearly rhyme. Again, however, there is a tension between these static topographic fixtures and the

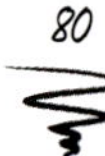

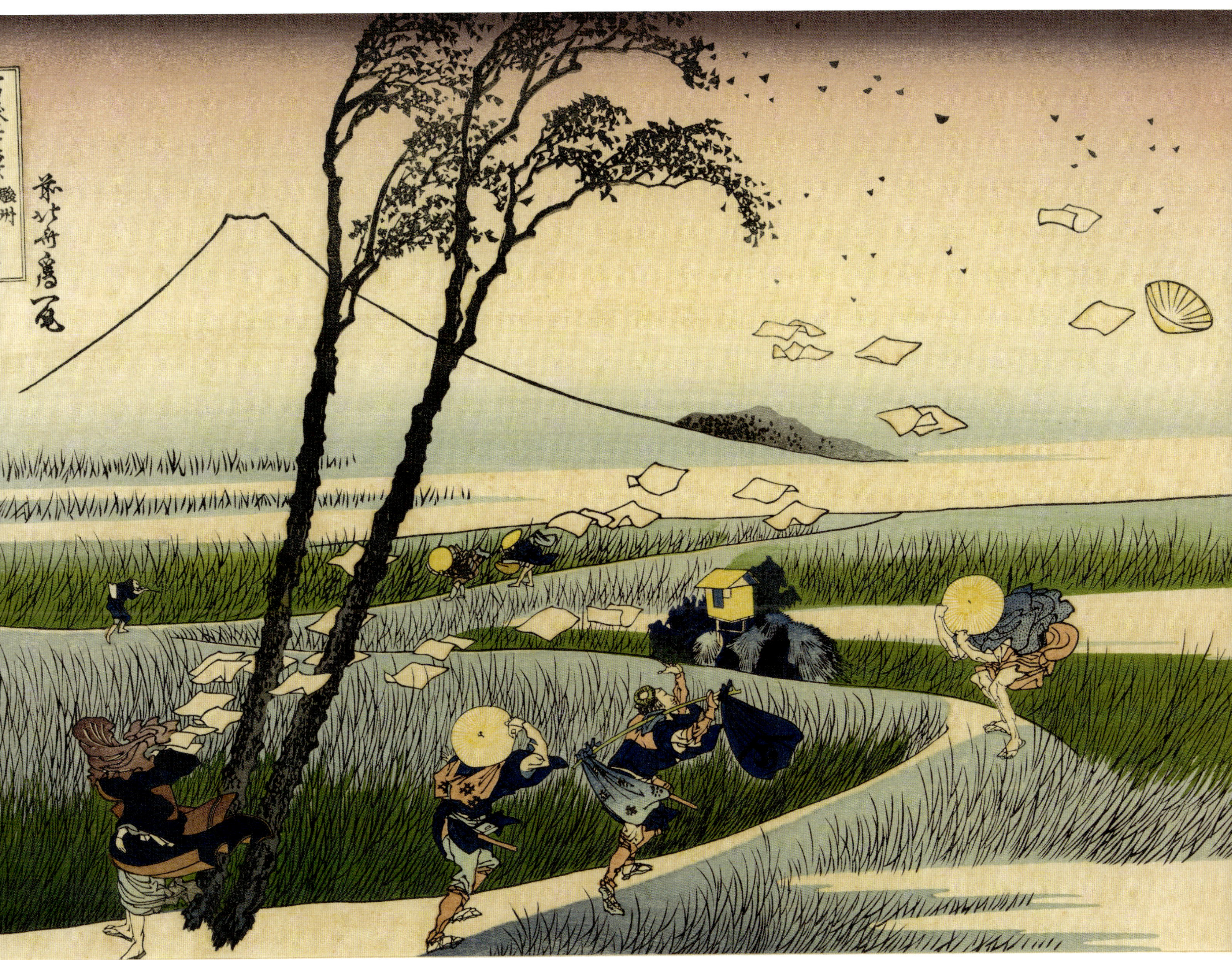

ABOVE Katsushika Hokusai (1760–1849) *Ejiri in Suruga Province* from 'Thirty-six Views of Mount Fuji' (1826–33, printed later)

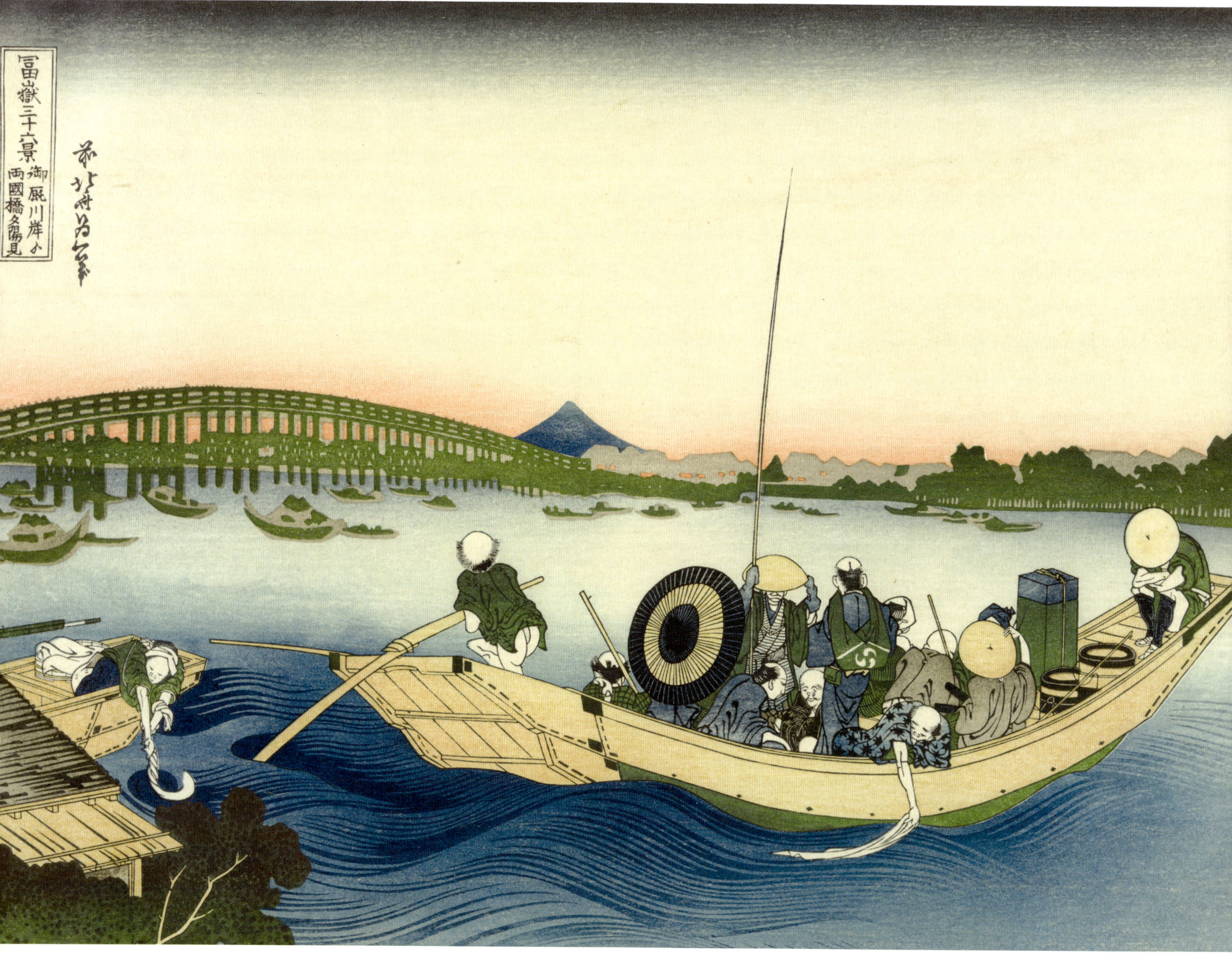

ABOVE **Katsushika Hokusai (1760–1849)** *Sunset across the Ryogoku Bridge from the Bank of the Sumida River at Onmayagashi* from 'Thirty-six Views of Mount Fuji' (1826–33, printed later)

flexibility and dynamism detectable between. Whilst two kites hang still, their very presence implies the pull of a breeze, while a tile is flying through the air, thrown by a roofer.

Line and Space

Tensions are also evident in *Sunset Across the Ryogoku Bridge from the Bank of the Sumida River at Onmayagashi* (*see* left). If there is a realistic air about the bridge in the middle distance, it looks utterly washed-out in the evening twilight as compared with the vibrancy of the trippers setting out in the immediate foreground. Whilst the gentle arch of the bridge is reflected by the downward curve of the ferryman's overgrown gondola, the open water between is barely there at all.

In this, the composition clearly brings together the techniques of 'Dutch'-style perspective and the more arbitrary spacing used by oriental artists for centuries. Meanwhile Mount Fuji, on the far horizon, is little more than a blue triangle. If, in the intensity of its colour, it matches the water we see directly before us, its angled lines contrast with the stylized undulation of the river's waves.

Excitement by Proxy

The next print shows a group of beautifully turned-out visitors looking out from a lakeside balcony at the *Sazai Hall – Temple of Five Hundred Rakan* (*see* right and page 71). This shrine at Kawagoe, in Saitama Prefecture, east of Edo, takes its name from its 500 statues of rakan – what the Japanese called their *arhats* or Buddhist saints. The bright colours of the costumes contrast vividly with the grey-brown expanse of water, which in its turn brings out the blue of Fujisan. Again, as in *Sunset Across Ryogoku Bridge*… there is a real audacity in Hokusai's readiness to compose his picture around so seemingly uninspiring an empty space. Of course, there is any amount of life in the foreground: the excitement of the visitors as they look across at Fuji is palpable (and also reflects our own) even though we mostly only see them from behind.

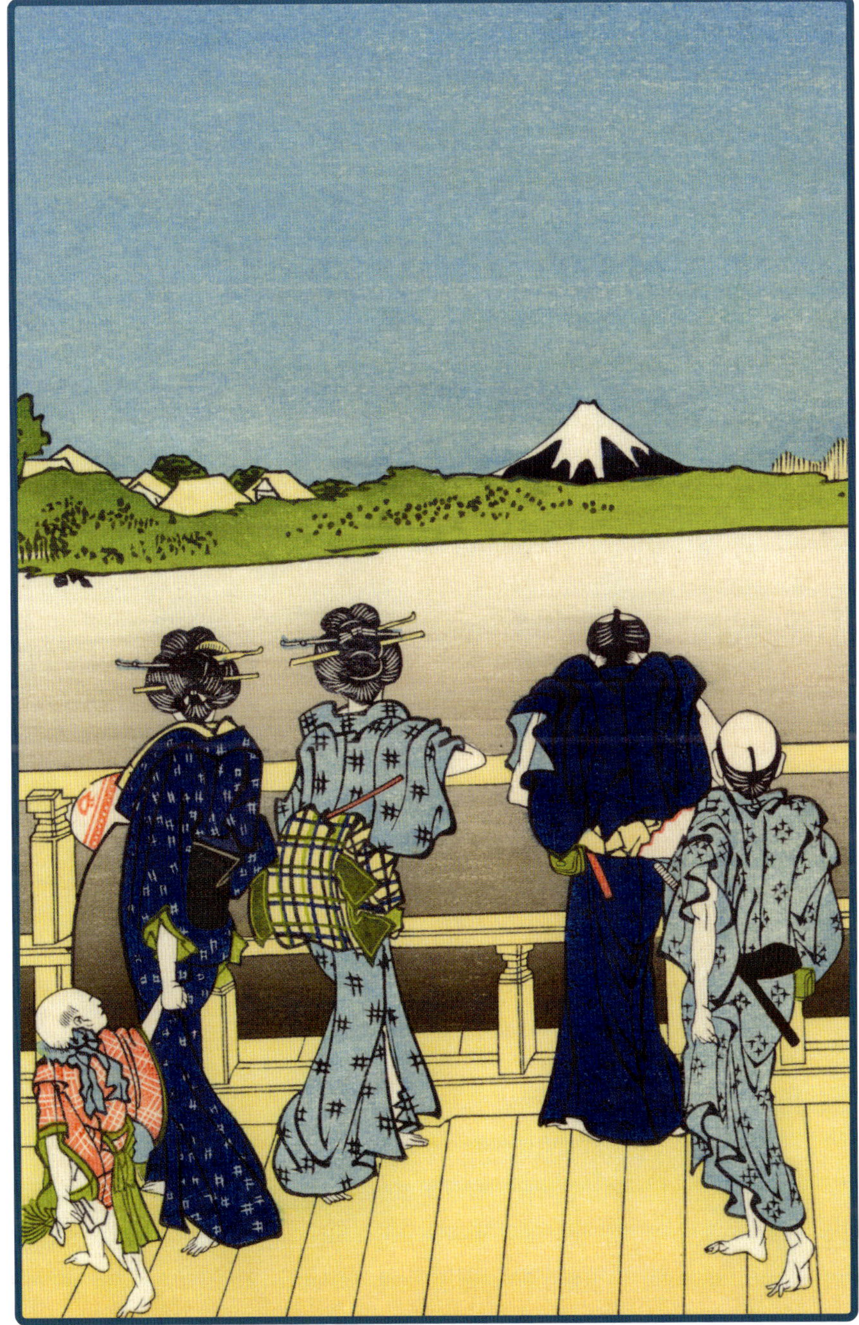

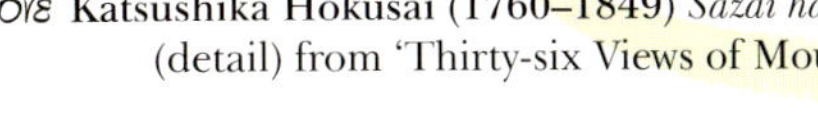

ABOVE Katsushika Hokusai (1760–1849) *Sazai hall – Temple of Five Hundred Rakan* (detail) from 'Thirty-six Views of Mount Fuji' (1826–33, printed later)

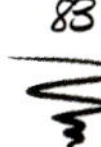

More excited sightseers stand in for us, staring and pointing gleefully at Fuji from the *Tea House at Koishikawa* (*see* opposite). It is (we might surmise even if the subtitle did not tell us) the morning after a snowfall. The botanical gardens at Koishikawa, in Tokyo's Bunkyo district, were originally opened in the 1680s and remain popular with visitors to this day.

The Summit as Spectator

The only snow to be seen at *Below Meguro* (*see* right and page 71) cloaks Mount Fuji's distant summit. The nearer hillsides here are covered instead with terraced fields. A labourer carries his hoe as he makes his way along a lane through Meguro's productive fields, whilst a pair of falconers talk to a villager squatting by the roadside at centre-right; at the bottom of the picture, a harassed woman tries to coax her child to put on a hat. A warm and cheerful scene, there is a certain enjoyable bathos in the way this village's thatched roofs and haystacks provide a mundane match for the towering form of Fujisan. (The outsized figure of the farmworker walking on the road above perhaps underlines the extent to which, in this particular setting, the force of Nature has been tamed, domesticated – just as the diminutive forms of the mariners in *The Great Wave off Kanagawa* showed the reverse.)

More seriously, perhaps, after *Sazai Hall…* and *Tea House…*, in this next little group of pictures it is Fujisan that is the spectator, standing as a silent but supportive witness to the country's life. That certainly seems to be what's happening in *Watermill at Onden* (*see* page 49). As with *Fuji View Field…* earlier (*see* page 159), there is an obvious contrast between Mount Fuji's distant cone and a striking circle in the foreground. This time, however, the wheel is hard at work, the water rushing through it while the peasants bring it rice for grinding. In the background, beyond the village, even the rice fields are still and quiet.

Enoshima, in Sagami Province, was an important place of pilgrimage. There are caves here with important Buddha statues. As in medieval Europe, these mass excursions could be as much about recreation as piety – indeed, in modern times, with a rail connection to its seacoast site, Enoshima started

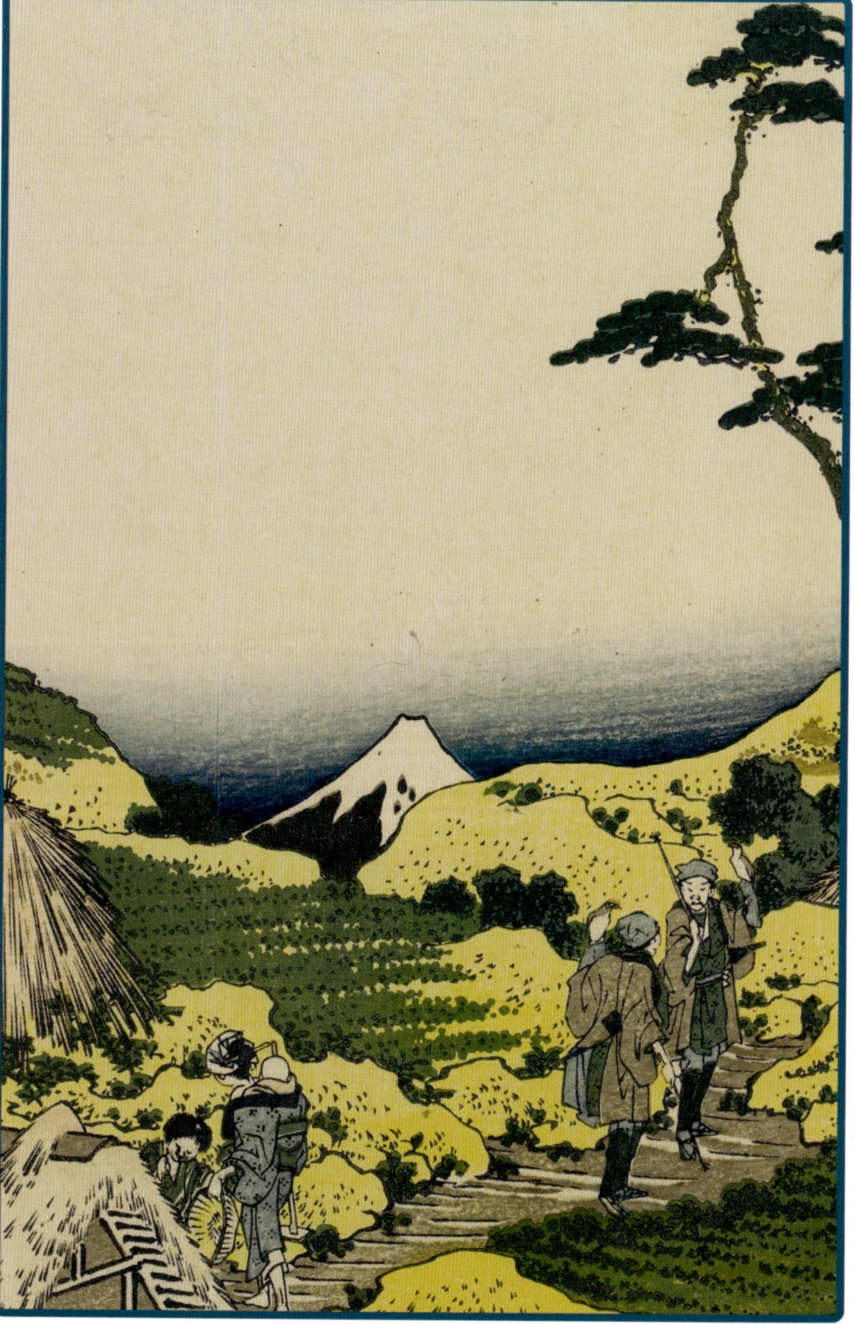

ABOVE Katsushika Hokusai (1760–1849) *Below Meguro* (detail) from 'Thirty-six Views of Mount Fuji' (*c.* 1830–35)

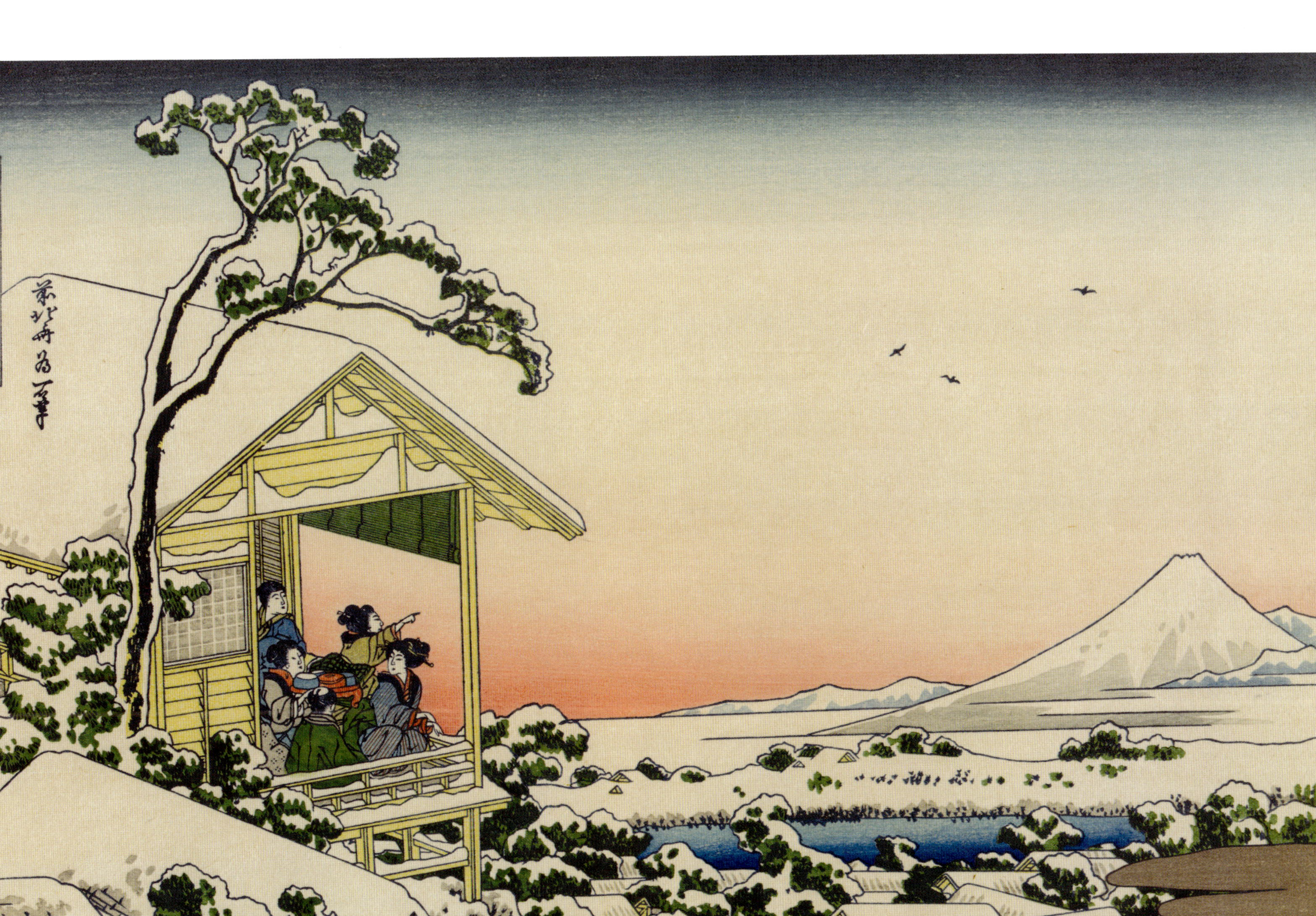

ABOVE Katsushika Hokusai (1760–1849) *Tea House at Koishikawa, the Morning after a Snowfall* from 'Thirty-six Views of Mount Fuji' (1826–33, printed later)

shading imperceptibly into a beach resort. In Hokusai's *Enoshima in Sagami Province* (*see* page 65), this is still very much a religious site, although the energy about the shrine is clearly apparent and thrown into relief by the distant stillness of Mount Fuji. (We get a clearer picture of the Enoshima complex, with its elaborately ordered outer and inner shrines, in *Clearing Weather, Enoshima*, from 'Eight Views of Famous Places', *c.* 1833, by Hokusai's younger contemporary Toyokuni II, 1777–1835 – *see below*.)

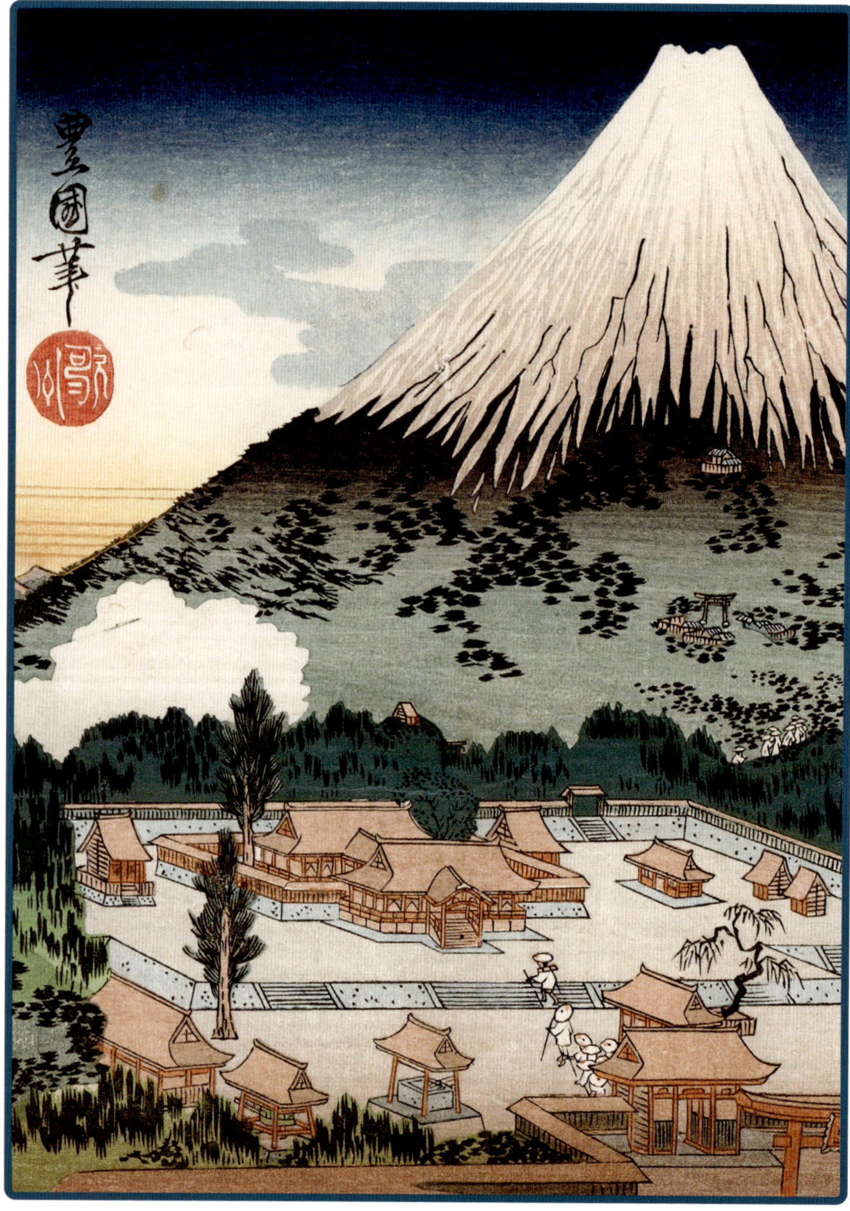

ABOVE Utagawa Toyokuni II (*c.* 1777–1835) *Clearing Weather, Enoshima* (*c.* 1833), from 'Eight Views of Famous Places'

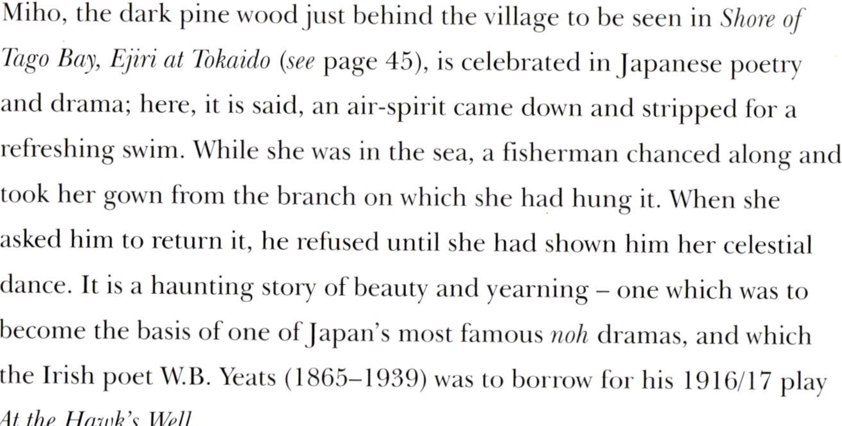

Miho, the dark pine wood just behind the village to be seen in *Shore of Tago Bay, Ejiri at Tokaido* (*see* page 45), is celebrated in Japanese poetry and drama; here, it is said, an air-spirit came down and stripped for a refreshing swim. While she was in the sea, a fisherman chanced along and took her gown from the branch on which she had hung it. When she asked him to return it, he refused until she had shown him her celestial dance. It is a haunting story of beauty and yearning – one which was to become the basis of one of Japan's most famous *noh* dramas, and which the Irish poet W.B. Yeats (1865–1939) was to borrow for his 1916/17 play *At the Hawk's Well*.

As Hokusai saw it, however, this was a real place where real, poor people lived, in a grinding cycle of well-nigh ceaseless work. The strain on the face of the man pulling up the net at the prow of the nearer boat is unmistakeable and the effort of the rowers amidships only too palpable. Back on the beach, meanwhile, villagers toil over the saltpans so important to the local economy. (Compare Hokusai's realism here with the glamorizing vision of an earlier artist like Suzuki Harunobo, whose image of *Salt Maidens on the Tagonoura Beach* – *see* page 29 – delightful as it is, offers only the frothiest fantasy of hard work.)

On the Move

The Tokaido, or East Sea Road, ran from Edo to Kyoto along the coast. It was almost as popular for tourism as it was for trade. In *Yoshida at Tokaido* (*see* right), we see a group of travellers at a wayside tea house in the town of Yoshida being shown the view of Fuji by a servant girl. She has put down her tray of tea on the bench to point out the prospect. The younger ladies appear appropriately amazed, but their elders are less impressed. This scene cuts across class boundaries: in the left foreground a pair of porters rest, barely dressed, despite the clearly cold conditions. The closer of the two, seemingly footsore from his days of walking on the road, attempts to soften a straw sandal with a hammer.

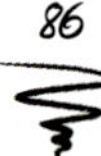

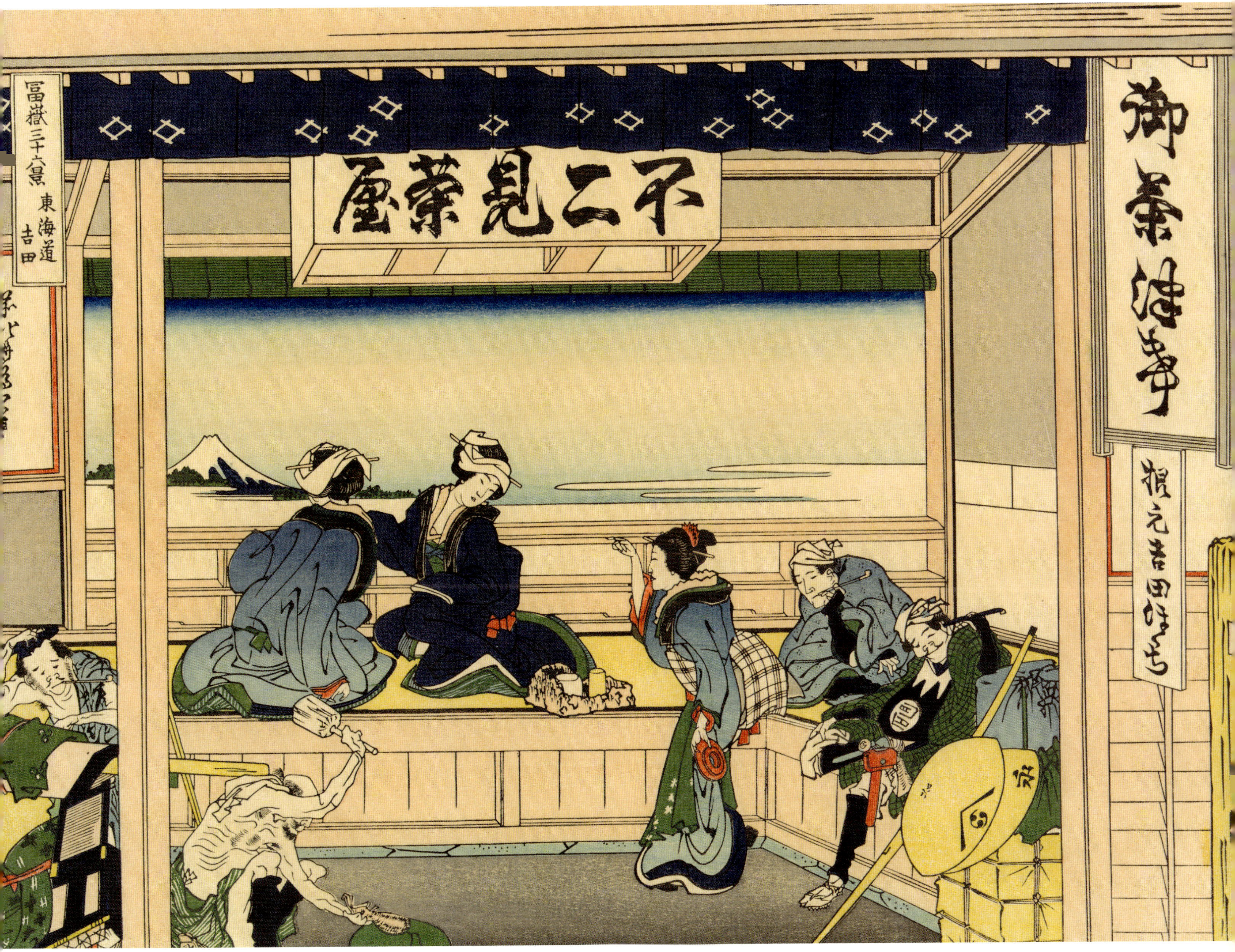

ABOVE Katsushika Hokusai (1760–1849) *Yoshida at Tokaido* from 'Thirty-six Views of Mount Fuji' (1826–33, printed later)

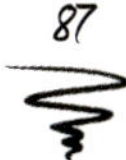

The Kazusa sea route led across Edo Bay, around the southern tip of the Boso Peninsula, to the port of Kazusa, on the Pacific side. *The Kazusa Province Sea Route* (*see* page 72, top right) shows a pair of junks making their way across these waters, well out to sea, with Mount Fuji barely showing above the horizon. And almost forgotten in the picture's scheme, those faces we see peering from a porthole on the nearer vessel are of course looking out to the seaward side. Even so, Hokusai seems to suggest that Fujisan offers a psychic anchorage in the far distance.

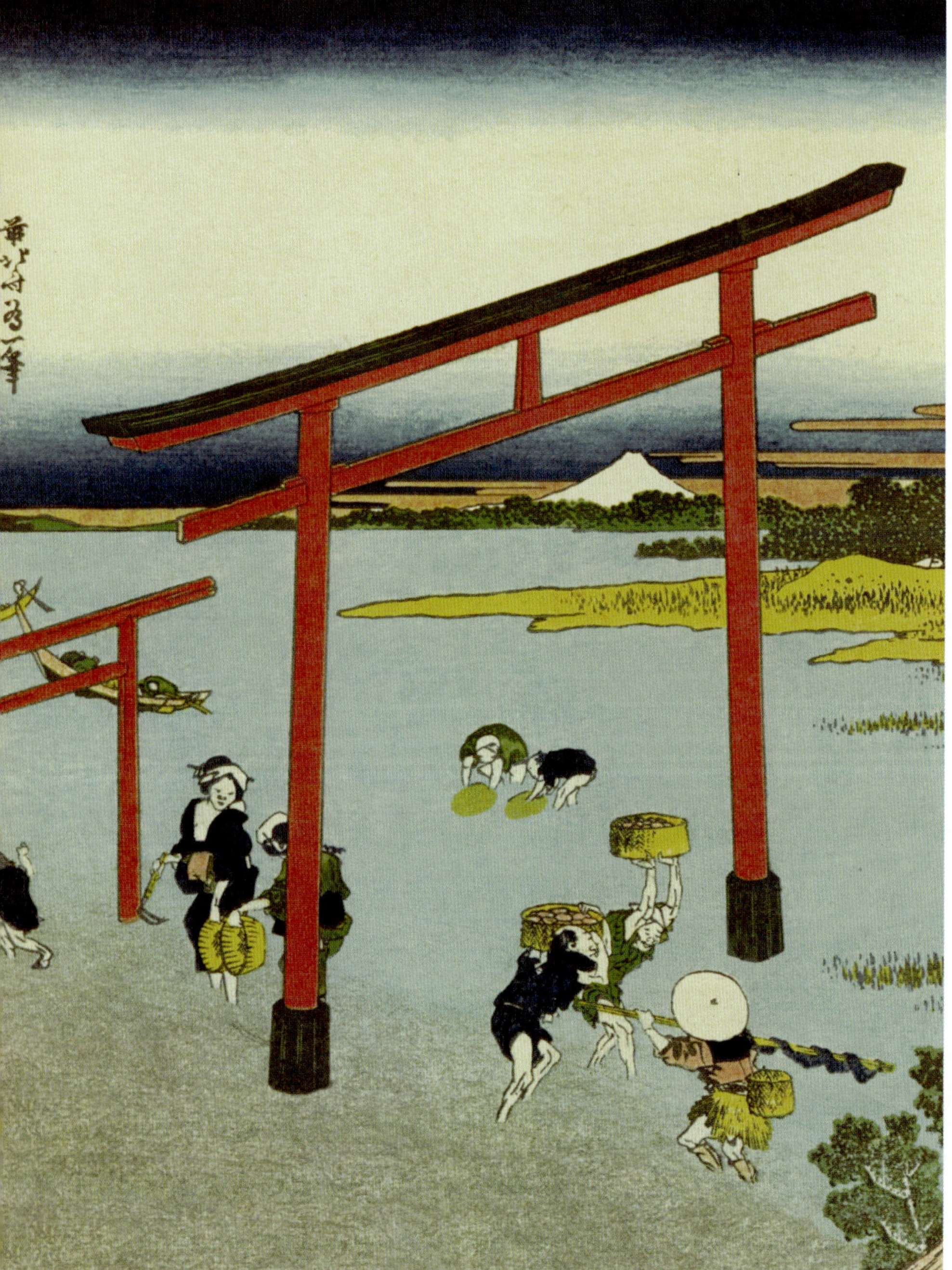

ABOVE **Katsushika Hokusai (1760–1849)** *Bay of Noboto* (detail) from 'Thirty-six Views of Mount Fuji' (1826–33)

The view from *The Nihonbashi Bridge in Edo* (*see* page 156) takes full advantage of Hokusai's familiarity with Western perspective, whilst still creating an unmistakeably oriental atmosphere. Here we look across a crowd of toiling, jostling, shoving porters to see the warehouses arrayed on either side of the Nihonbashi River. Much of Edo's trade came through this bustling commercial centre. There had been a bridge and a market here since the seventeenth century, and the district remains abustle to this day.

The mail must get through, and it is clearly at a gallop that these samurai couriers ride across the Arakawa Dam with what are evidently important missives. Their headlong haste in *Sekiya Village on the Sumida River* (*see* right) is in obvious contrast to the unruffled stillness of Mount Fuji. The wooden structures we see in the waters of the *Bay of Noboto* (*see* left, and in full on page 72) are *torii*, the stylized 'gates' that advertise the presence of a Shinto shrine. Villagers gather shellfish in the shallows here. Fuji, framed by the *torii* in the foreground, is also echoed in the thatched rooftops of the village and counterpointed by the rolling sand dunes along this coast.

Mystic Lakes

Hakone is hallowed: there has been a Shinto shrine here, it is said, since the middle of the eighth century AD. *The Lake of Hakone in Sagami Province* (*see* page 61) captures the eerie atmosphere of the place. If there is something faintly naïve and childlike about the impenetrable banks of pink-brown mist Hokusai has drifting across the lake, there is an undoubted strangeness they bestow on this mysterious and completely unpeopled scene.

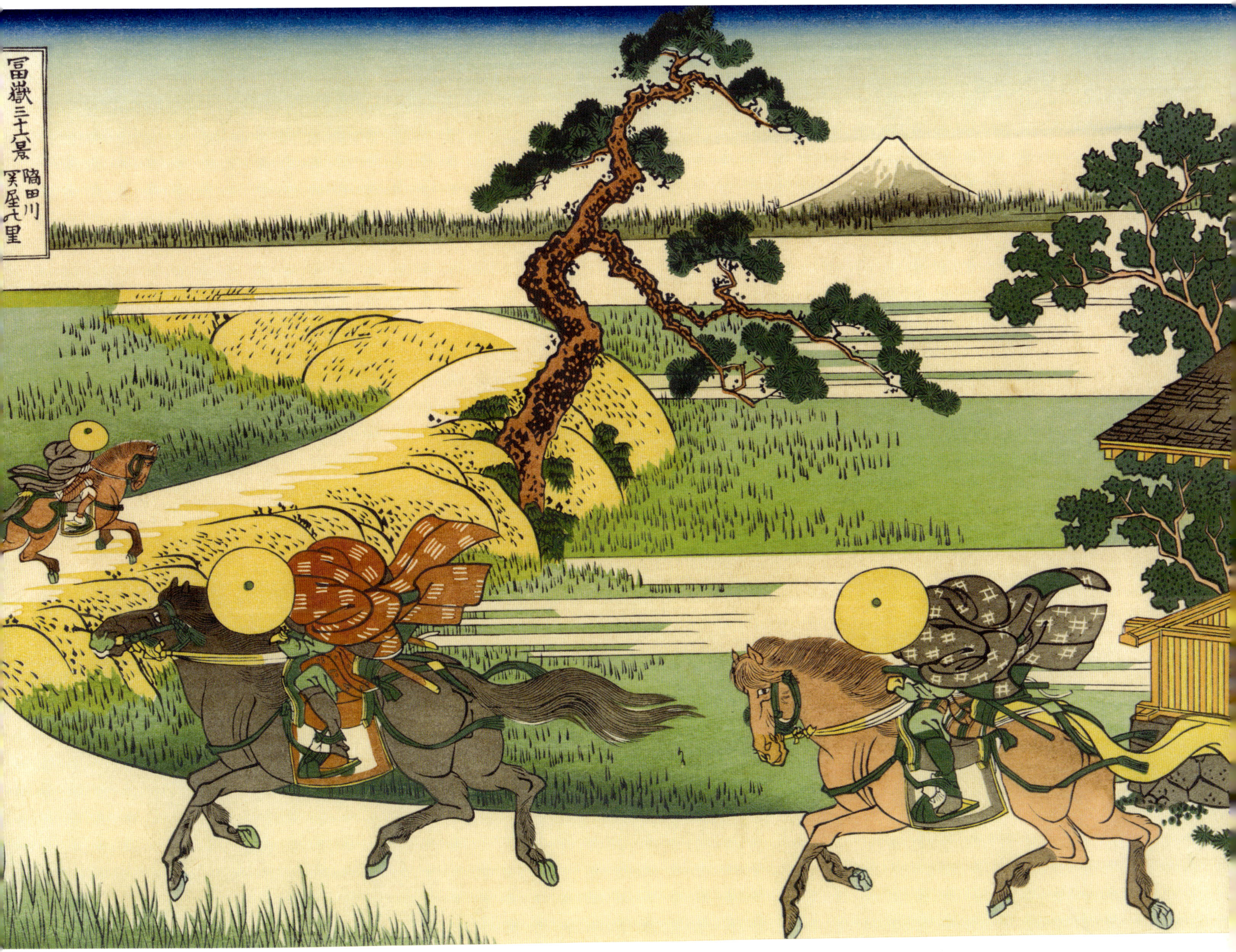

Above Katsushika Hokusai (1760–1849) *Sekiya Village on the Sumida River* from 'Thirty-six Views of Mount Fuji' (1826–33, printed later)

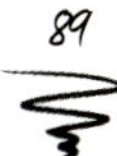

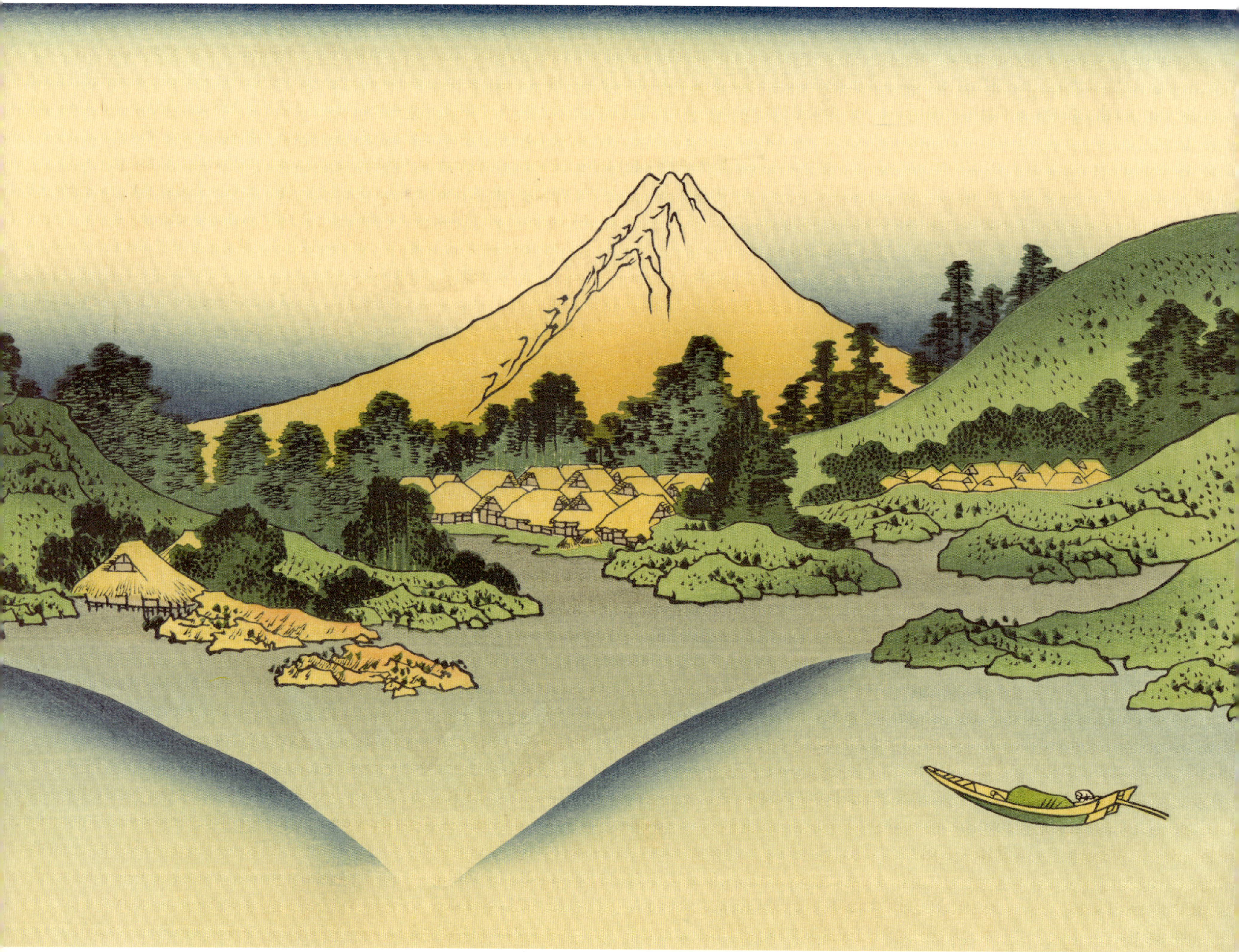

ABOVE **Katsushika Hokusai** (1760–1849) *Mount Fuji Reflects in Lake Kawaguchi, Seen from the Misaka Pass in Kai Province* from 'Thirty-six Views of Mount Fuji' (1826–33, printed later)

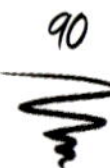

Everything is out of kilter in *Mount Fuji Reflects in Lake Kawaguchi, Seen from the Misaka Pass in Kai Province* (*see* left), starting with the reflection itself, which strikes us as skewed, and not just in its orientation, odd as this is, but in the fact that it reveals a wintry, snow-capped mountain while the real thing is summer-bare. Could this be a summit for all seasons? The two triangles slot together to form a vaguely trapezoidal shape, which must have meant something to Hokusai, though it is hard even to imagine what this might be.

Life's Realities

In *Hodogaya on the Tokaido* (*see* right and in full on page 72), two porters take a break, setting down the sedan chair in which they have been carrying their mistress. Coming up behind them, another servant leads his master's horse. While he glances up to see Fuji through a knot of twisted pines, his master hides beneath his hat, apparently oblivious.

Heading off in the opposite direction, meanwhile, we see a *komuso*, a Buddhist monk who lived by begging on the roads of Japan. Supposed to envelop his head completely, to symbolize the suppression of his earthly desires and ambitions, his woven straw hat is instead tipped back so he can see clearly. The *komuso's* anonymity made them a vital tool of the shogunate who were known to use these 'holy men' as spies.

Atmospherics

The pink mist of morning slowly clears in one of Hokusai's most captivating Fuji views, *Tama River in Musashi Province* (*see* page 67). A pedlar halts with his horse to gaze up in wonder at the sacred mountain rising in the distance, whilst a ferryman heads directly into a bank of fog. There is not a hard edge or outline here; the figures seem to float, suspended effortlessly, an advantage of the use of traditional Chinese-style spacing instead of 'Dutch' perspective to confer depth.

Hokusai's use of mist is striking, and strange, perhaps, in an artist who clearly does not shy from creating atmospheric effects. Where Western artists have tended to be drawn by its diaphanous, translucent quality, Hokusai is often content to have it spill across his scenes in a cartoonish

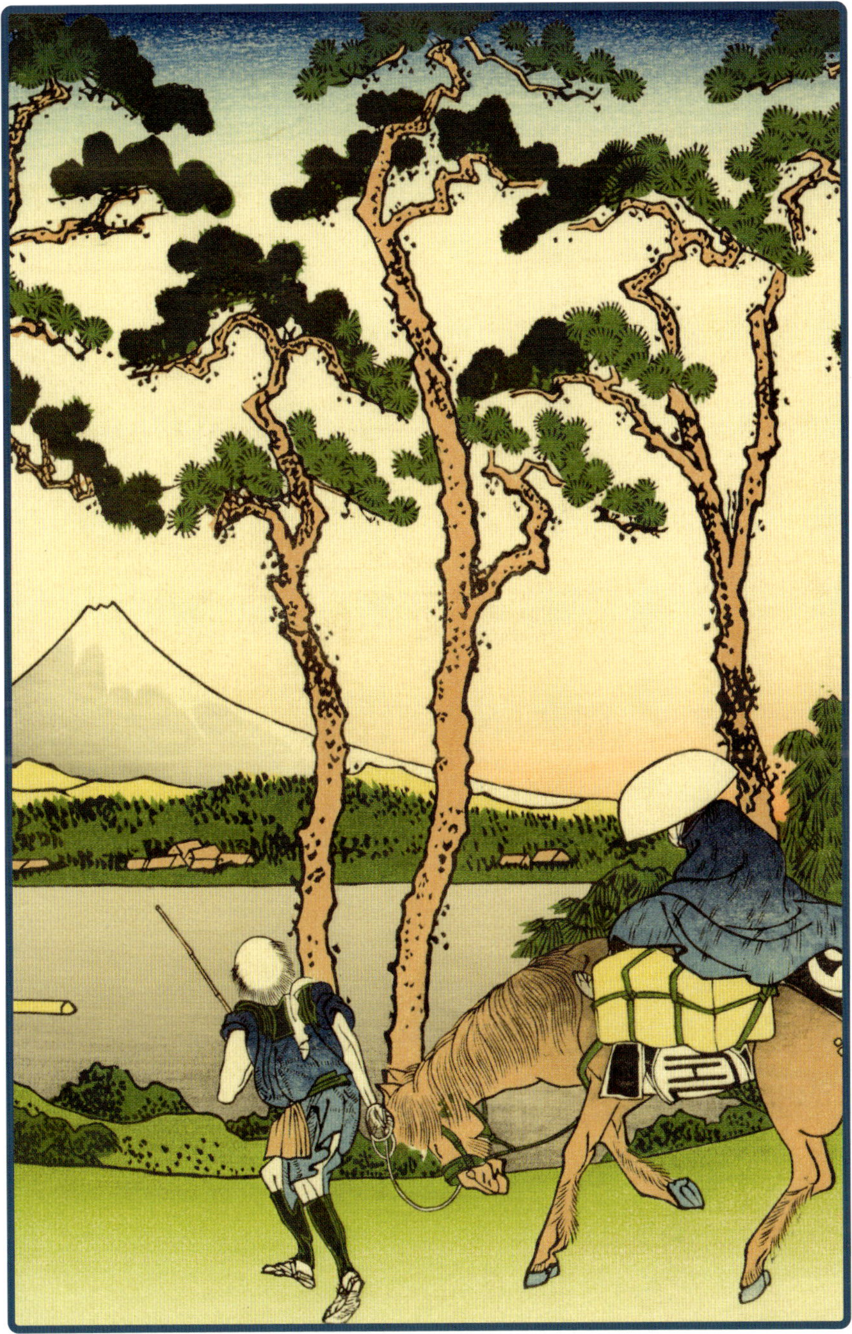

Above Katsushika Hokusai (1760–1849) *Hodogaya on the Tokaido* (detail) from 'Thirty-six Views of Mount Fuji' (1826–33, printed later)

blob. This is certainly a function of his medium, as woodblock printing does not really lend itself to wraithlike uncertainties. But then why include mist and fog so often in his works?

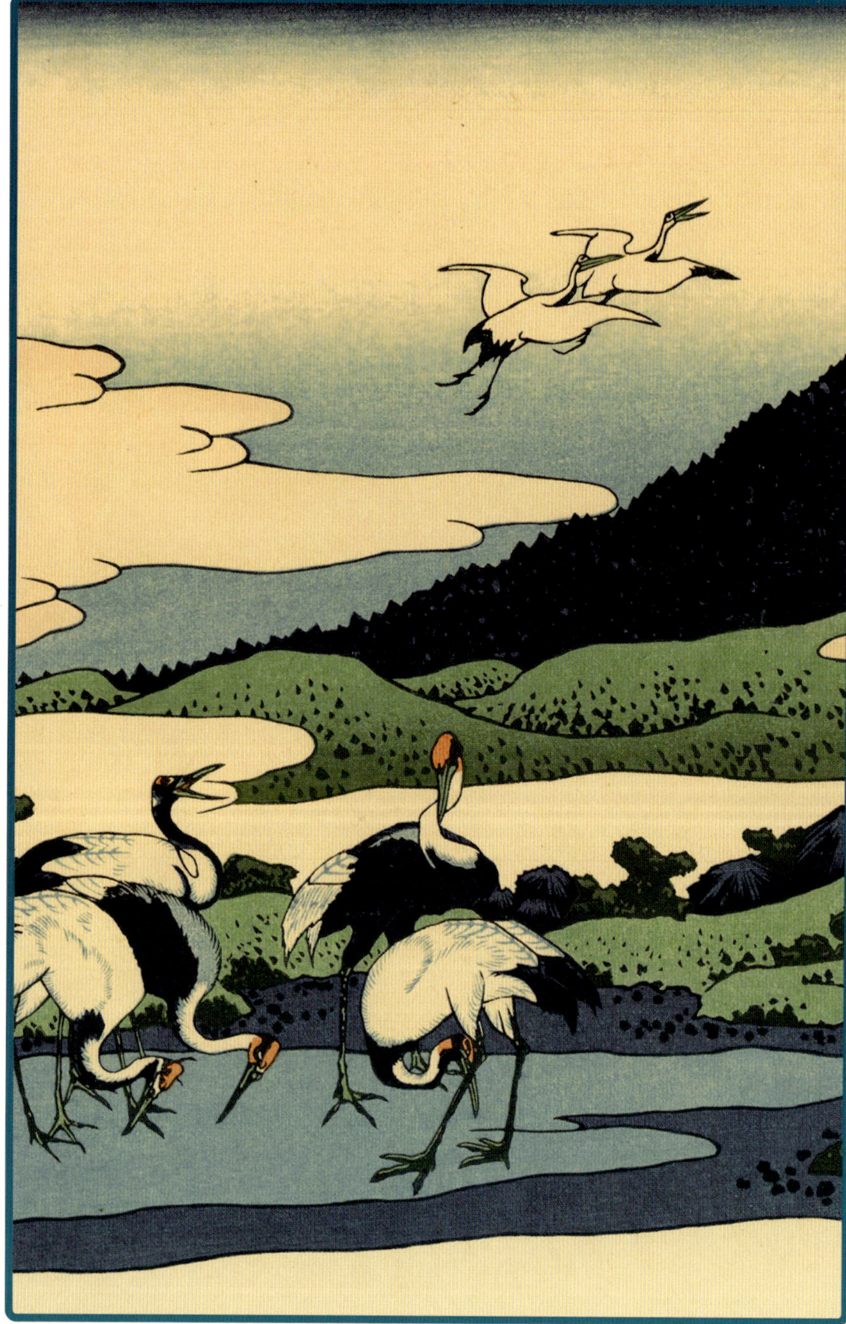

ABOVE Katsushika Hokusai (1760–1849) *Umezawa in Sagami Province* (detail) from 'Thirty-six Views of Mount Fuji' (1826–33)

Clouding the Issue

Low clouds largely obliterate our view of what would in fact have been a bustling *Asakusa Hongan-ji Temple in the Eastern Capital* (*see* page 15). Asakusa was a religious centre, with some of Edo's most important Buddhist and Shinto shrines, which in turn made it a major centre for trade and commerce. This rooftop view cuts out the bustle of the streets below: here the human figures serve only to lend emphasis to the sheer size (and, hence, the spiritual significance) of the Hongan-ji Temple. Built in 1657, it rises clear above the clouds in this representation, making Mount Fuji, on the far horizon, look quite small.

In *Tsukuda Island in Musashi Province* (*see* page 62), white cumulus clouds on the horizon flank Fujisan on either side, as though its snowy heights were just one summit in a cloudy mountain range. In the foreground, fishing boats and cargo craft flock around this artificial island, an important centre at the mouth of the Sumida River. Clouds steal the show in Hokusai's representation of *Shichiri Beach in Sagami Province* (*see* right) as well, although, again, they are in what should be the background of this work. This time towering stratocumulus, they do not rhyme only with Fuji but also with the gnarled and irregular forms of the rock formations and the pine trees at the picture's centre and the scrubby bushes in the foreground. Clouds appear to encroach from either side of *Umezawa in Sagami Province* (*see* left and page 73), their pure white billows matching the colour of a knot of cranes.

An uncharacteristically nebulous mist shrouds much of the scene in *Kajikazawa in Kai Province* (*see* page 35). It is hard to know where the swirling atmospherics end and the snow-capped Fujisan begins. In the foreground, a fisherman casts his nets from an overhanging promontory whose angled point provides a subtle parallel not just to the distant line of Fuji, but to the curling crests of the angry waves beneath. Their fury, and the jaggedness of the coastal rocks, offset the soothing blandness of the bank of mist that, higher up, is tinged with the delicate blush of dawn or twilight. The overall effect is quite simply breathtaking in its beauty.

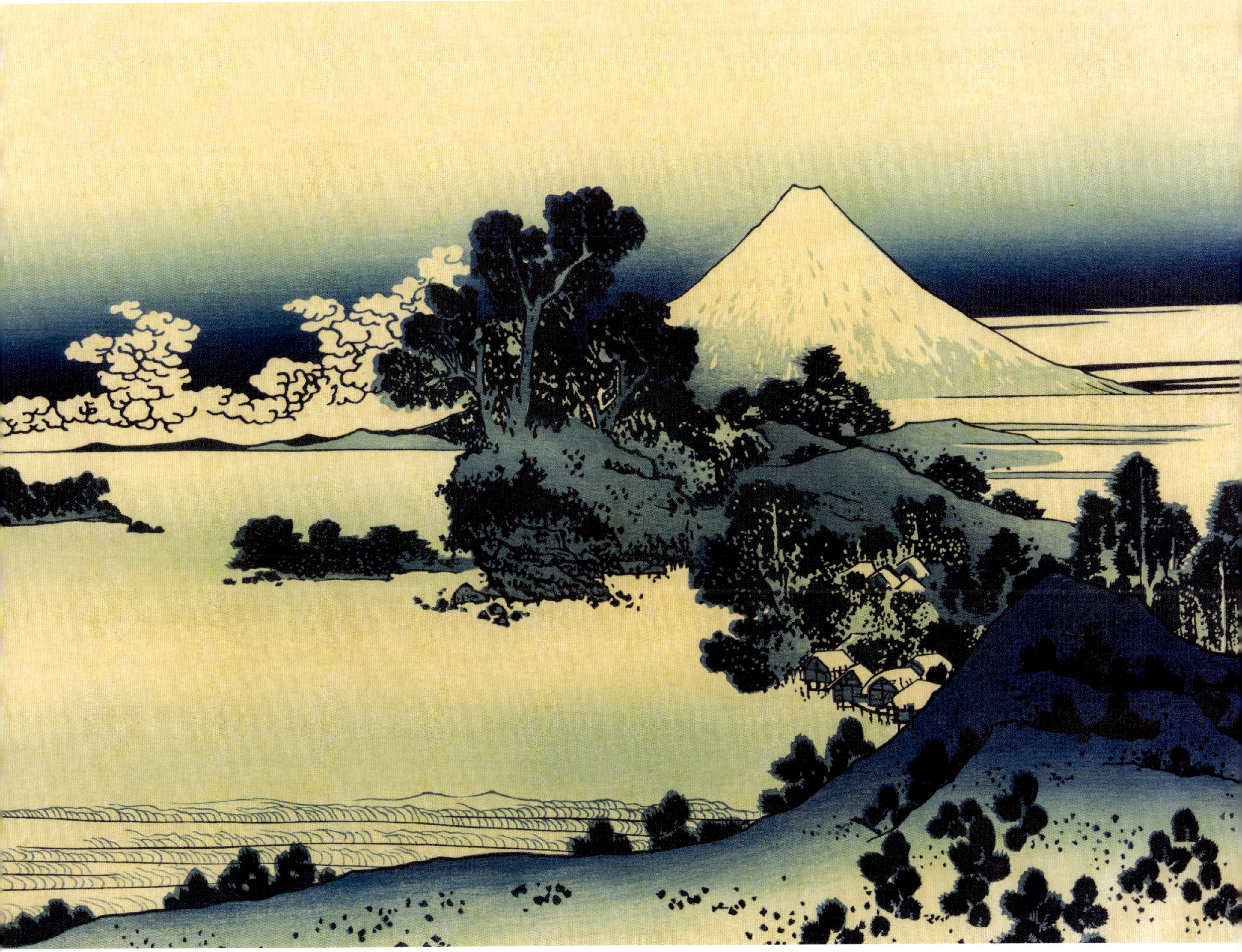

ABOVE **Katsushika Hokusai** (1760–1849) *Shichiri Beach in Sagami Province* from 'Thirty-six Views of Mount Fuji' (1826–33, printed later)

Balancing Humankind and Nature

A distinctive kind of cloud which wraps itself around Fujisan's summit is known as a *kasagumo* (umbrella cloud). One appears here in the *Mishima Pass in Kai Province* (*see* right), the veiled Fujisan striking a dramatic contrast with the gigantic pine tree that rises from its centre foreground and, uncontainable, soars straight through the top of Hokusai's picture. Below, it, a group of travellers, seemingly staggered by its enormous size, join hands around its base to measure it.

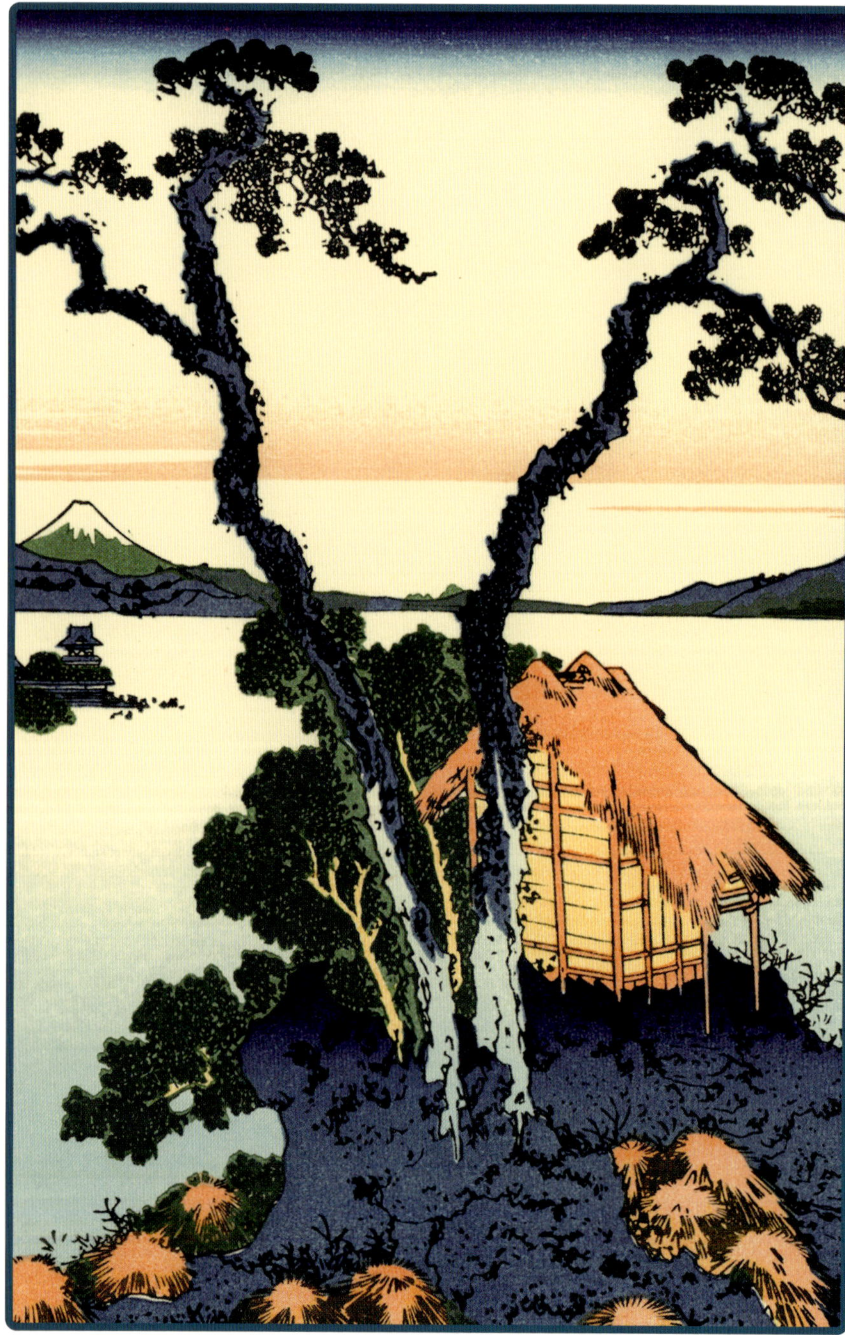

Above **Katsushika Hokusai (1760–1849)** *Lake Suwa in Shinano Province* (detail) from 'Thirty-six Views of Mount Fuji' (1826–33)

If *Mishima Pass…* is a reminder of how the great works of Nature dwarf the human scale, *Mount Fuji from the Mountains of Totomi* (*see* pages 97 and 73) reverses these proportions. Here, the trestle on which loggers saw into planks what was clearly until recently a mighty pine tree, seems to frame (and contain) the distant form of Fujisan. Symbolically, of course, the workers are subjugating Nature. The wood they are cutting will be used in constructions that mark the Japanese landscape as the property of humankind.

Lake Suwa in Shinano Province (*see* left) shows humanity and Nature in near-perfect balance, the hut at centre foreground symbolically surrounded by a tree before and the lake behind. The building is a work of compromise, its crooked frame and its ragged thatch partaking both of natural anarchy and human-imposed order. And then, of course, there is the way the 'V' of the cloven tree picks up the wedged rim of the left-hand crater and the pagoda-like towers of the temple below, all subtly mirroring the rises of Mount Fuji and the man-made roof. A stunning scene, yet wonderfully soothing, it represents to perfection the harmony that can reign in a scene in which humanity has made its peace with the natural world. In *Ushibori in Hitachi Province* (*see* page 96), the balance is between the bow of the long boat projecting upwards towards the top left of the picture and the form of Fuji rising to the right between the mountain's snowy slopes and the pallid waters of the lake-edge marshes.

A Fujisan for all Seasons

Why 36 views? We cannot be sure. If there were once some numerological significance to the figure, it has been long since lost in historical and cultural

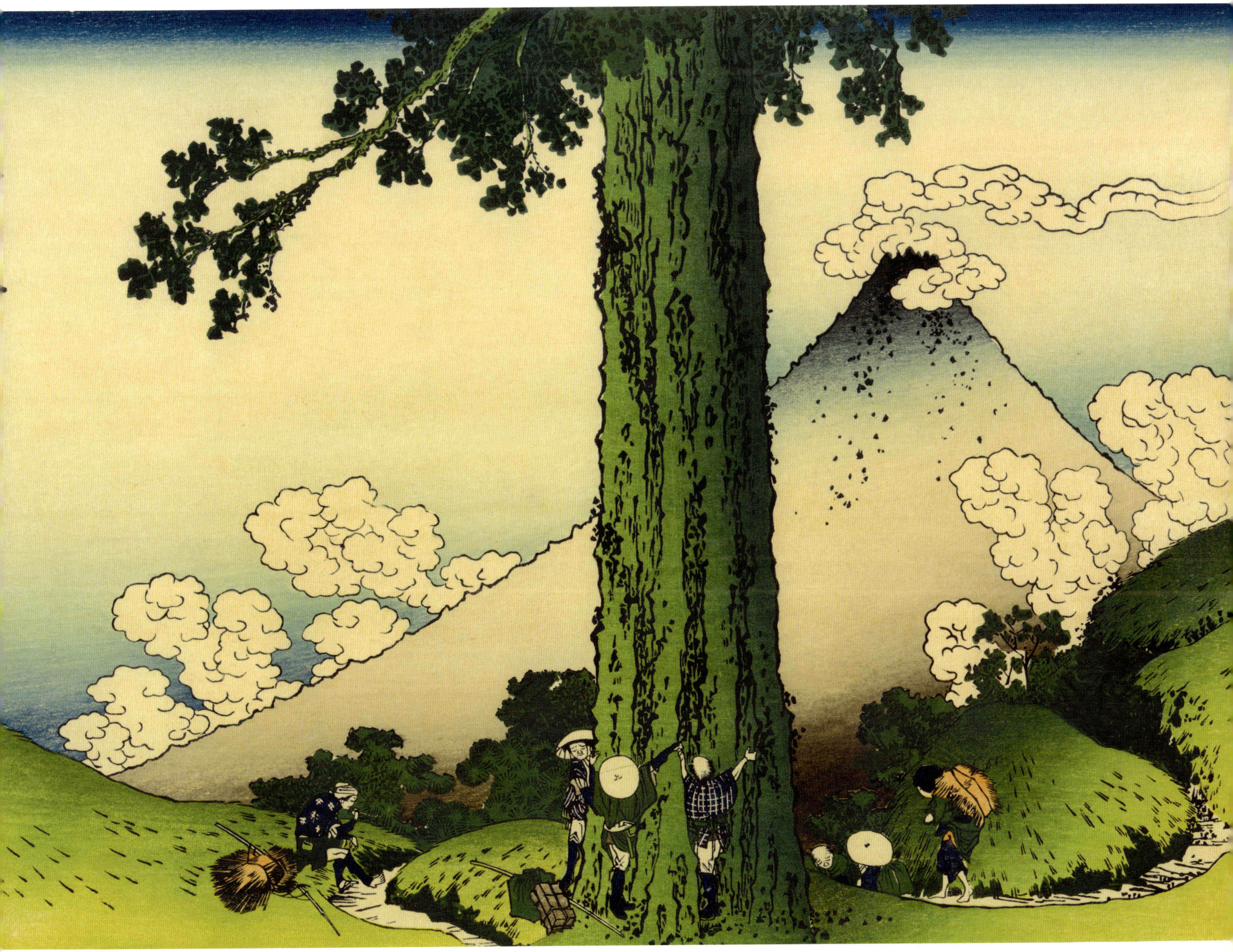

ABOVE **Katsushika Hokusai** (1760–1849) *Mishima Pass in Kai Province* from 'Thirty-six Views of Mount Fuji' (1826–33, printed later)

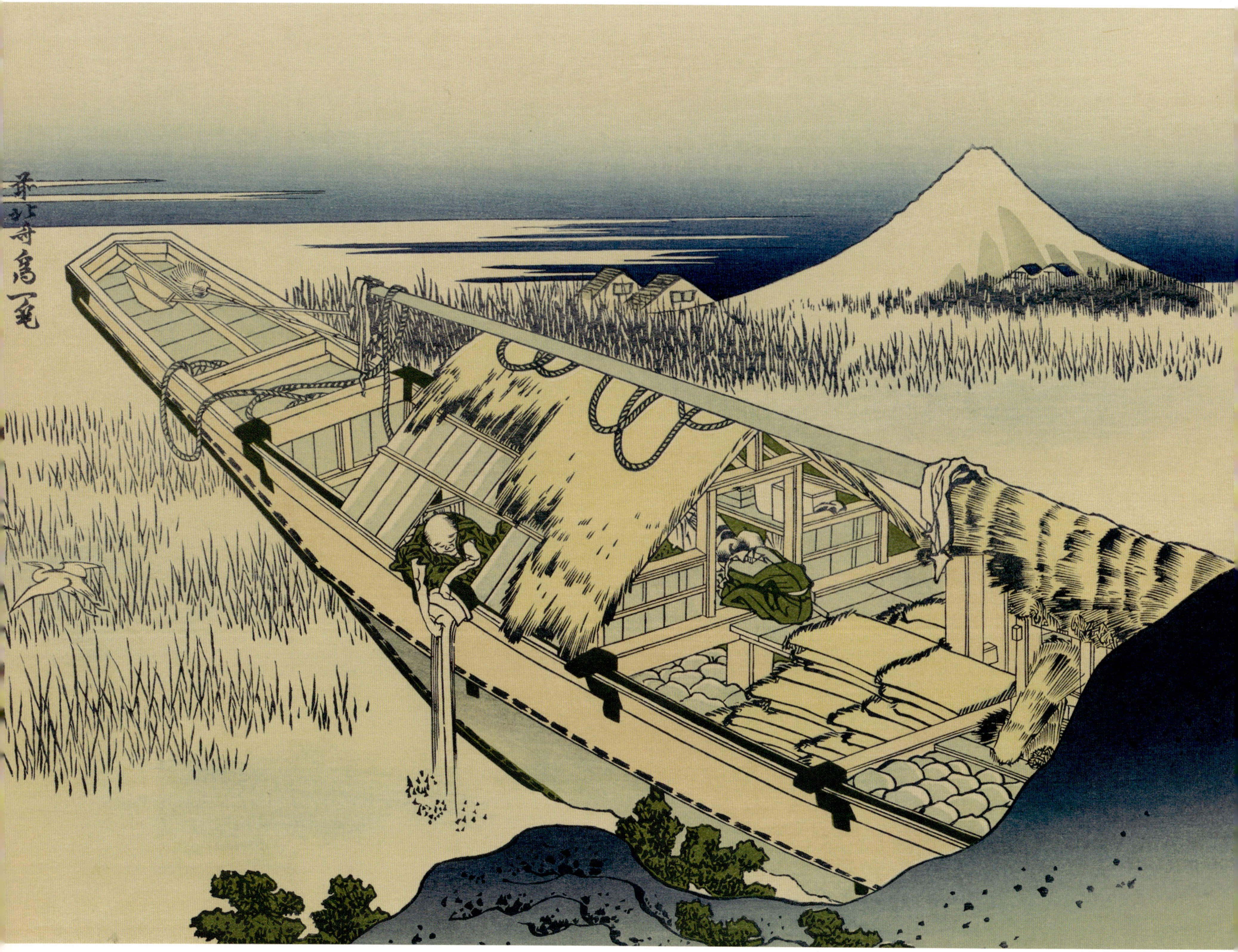

Above **Katsushika Hokusai** (1760–1849) *Ushibori in Hitachi Province* from 'Thirty-six Views of Mount Fuji' (1826–33, printed later)

confusion. In any case, there is evidence that Hokusai's publisher was hoping for a hundred prints in all. Like any Western artist of his day (or since, for that matter), the Japanese master was a working professional who had to balance his own artistic instincts with those of his paying patrons. That does not nullify the aesthetic integrity of the 'Thirty-six Views…', or its clear spiritual overtones: it does, however, have to be borne in mind before we speculate too ambitiously over Hokusai's artistic intentions.

In the end, we can only hope to guess at those – and not just with regard to any meaning inherent in their number, but in almost every other respect as well. What we *can* do is try to identify some of the values and significance that *we* find in the work. If there really are no certainties, it nevertheless does not seem too unlikely that Hokusai might have shared some of these.

It does seem that in this stunning series he gives us a Fujisan for All Seasons, a mountain that, seen from every conceivable direction, offers a sort of centre not just for the geography but for the wider social and cultural life of Japan. Whether it takes centre stage as an artistic or spiritual focus for our gaze or plays a more attendant role, just there in the background to a scene of everyday bustle, work or fun, his Mount Fuji is a constant (and presumably protective) presence.

Fuji Revisited

Certainly, if there were reasons for Hokusai's deciding on 36 images for his first series of views, they were not compelling enough to prevent his providing another 10 when his delighted publisher pressed him. These were reportedly to show *Ura-Fuji* – Fuji's 'farther side'.

His publisher's upbeat mood seems to have communicated itself to the artist, who begins this supplementary collection in festive mood. In *Goten-yama Hill, Shinagawa on the Tokaido* (*see* page 99), between the mild and gentle blues of Edo Bay and of a kindly sky above, the central and most striking impression is that made by the trees and branches festooned in cherry blossom. Goten-yama-hill was a popular beauty spot, both for its trees and for its view of Fuji. The happy party arriving in the foreground adds considerably to the colour of this scene.

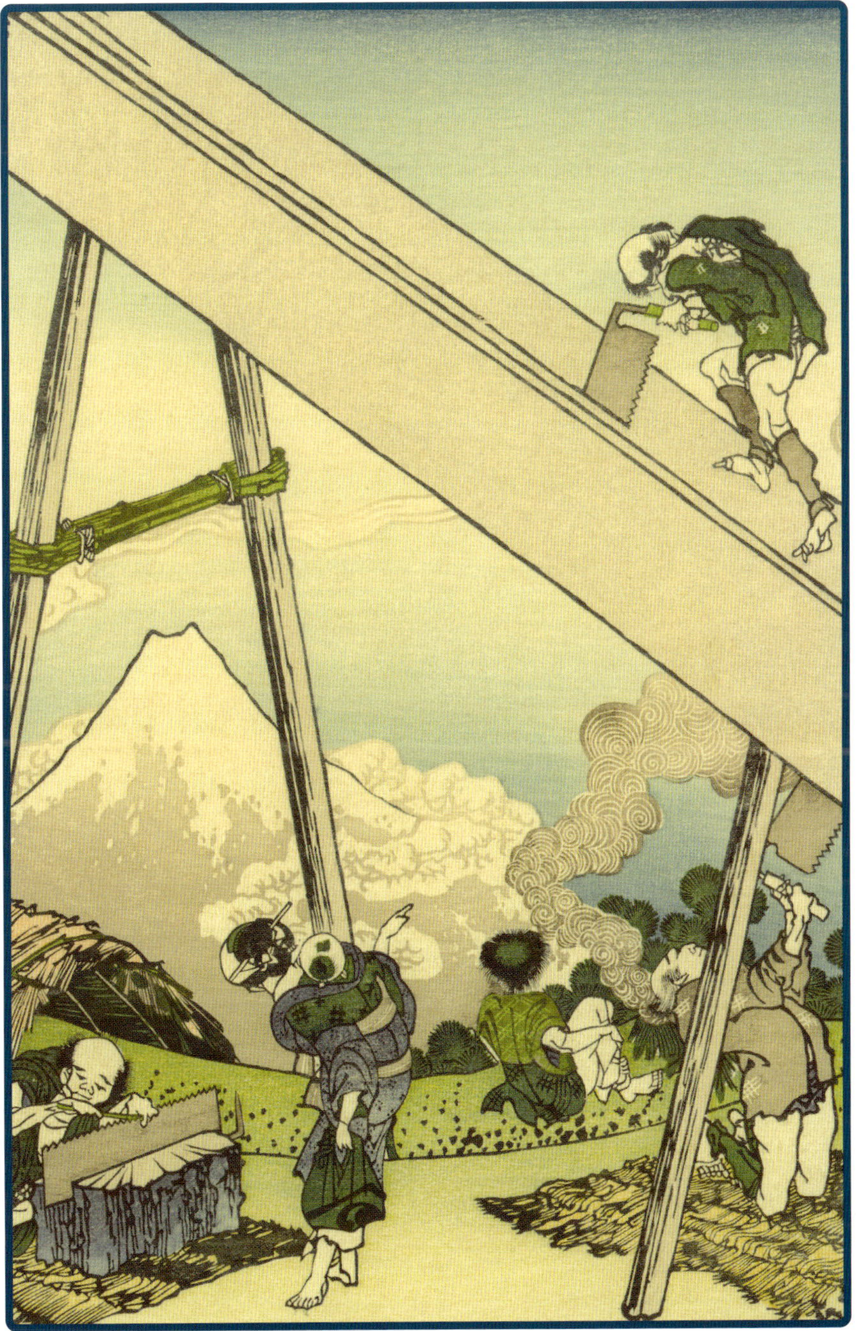

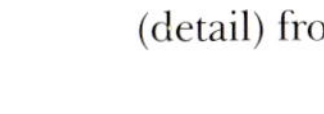
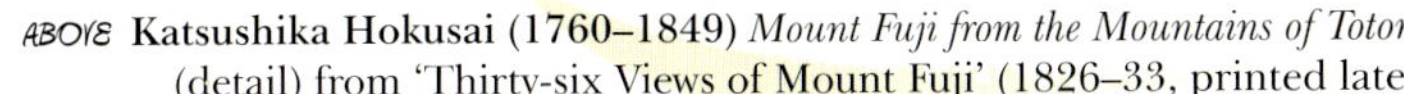
Above Katsushika Hokusai (1760–1849) *Mount Fuji from the Mountains of Totomi* (detail) from 'Thirty-six Views of Mount Fuji' (1826–33, printed later)

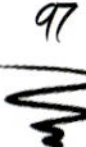

There is a certain continuity of colour between this scene and that of *Honjo Tatekawa, The Timberyard at Honjo* (*see* below), the pink of the blossom being replaced here by the rosy tinge of a dawn or evening sky

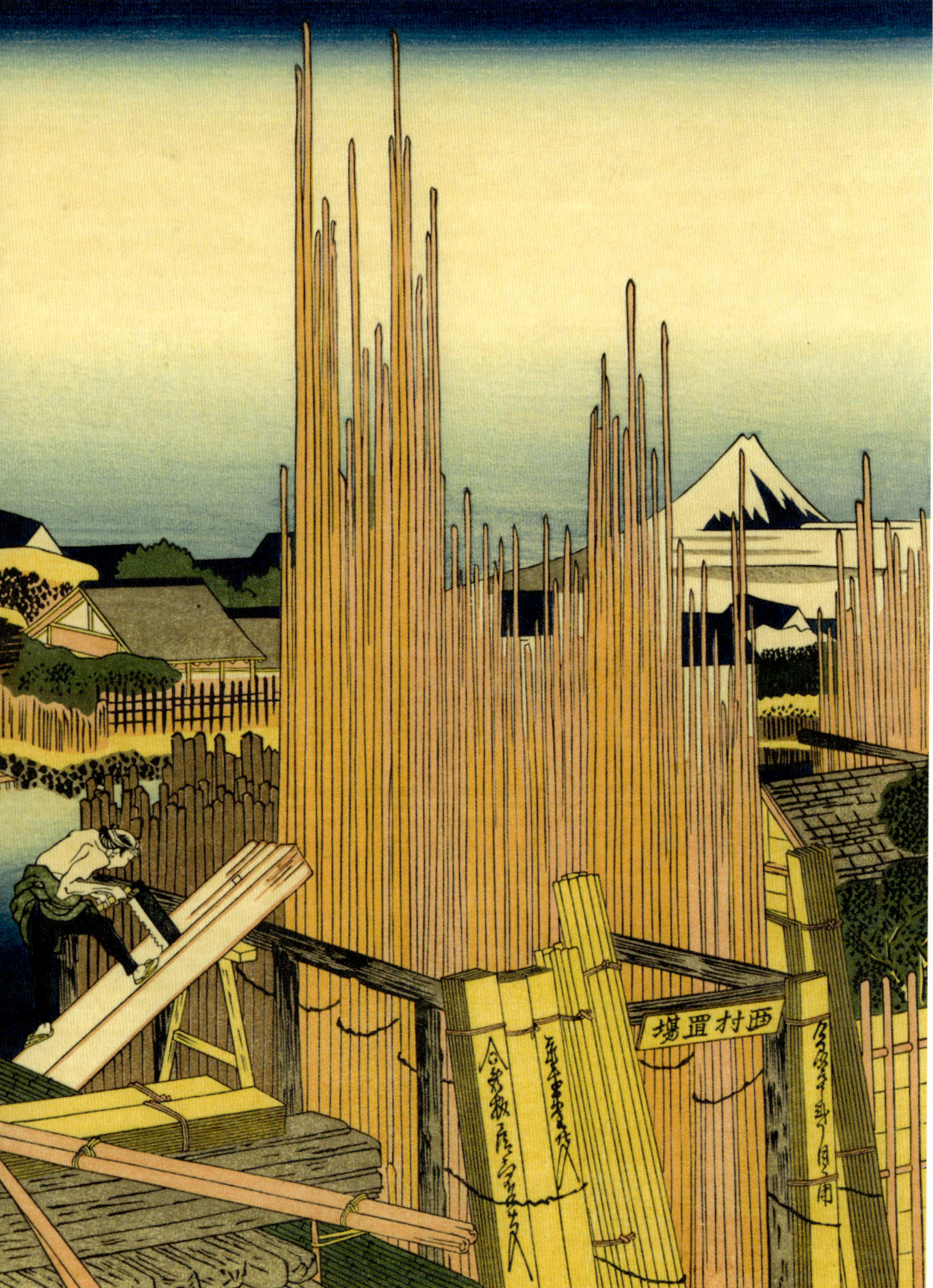

ABOVE **Katsushika Hokusai (1760–1849)** *Honjo Tatekawa, the Timberyard at Honjo* (detail) from 'Thirty-six Views of Mount Fuji' (1826–33, printed later)

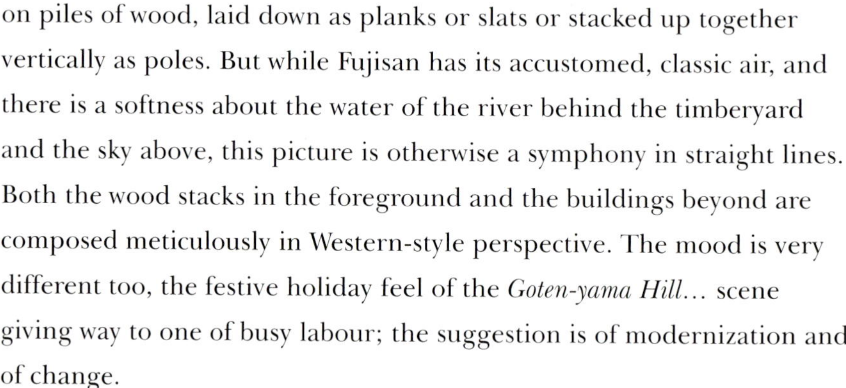

on piles of wood, laid down as planks or slats or stacked up together vertically as poles. But while Fujisan has its accustomed, classic air, and there is a softness about the water of the river behind the timberyard and the sky above, this picture is otherwise a symphony in straight lines. Both the wood stacks in the foreground and the buildings beyond are composed meticulously in Western-style perspective. The mood is very different too, the festive holiday feel of the *Goten-yama Hill…* scene giving way to one of busy labour; the suggestion is of modernization and of change.

In the foreground of *Mount Fuji Seen from the Senju Pleasure Quarter* (*see* page 73, fourth row, left), a column of soldiers march, their muskets swathed in brown cloth over their shoulders. A couple look up in the direction of the mountain; two women rest together beside the road. There is not much sign of pleasure here. Senju, a privately administered quarter, home at its height to no fewer than 38 brothels, stands in the background of the picture, stockaded away from view.

Greens and blues behind and browns and pinks towards the foreground balance out the scene from *Nakahara in Sagami Province* (*see* page 36). Framed by the diamond made by Fuji above and by the footbridge and the roof edge nearer to us below, this scene contrasts the quiet and empty space of Nature with the crowded hurry of human life. (The thatched roof would appear to belong to a shrine, given the carved stone idol we see standing before it by the stream.) We have the sense here of a little rush hour unfolding before us in this charming, yet clearly realistic, village scene.

Their oxen all but overwhelmed by the size of the bundles of cut reeds they are carrying, a group of villagers heads home in *Rice Paddies at Ono in Suruga Province* (*see* pages 154–55), after what has clearly been a hard day's work. Herons fly in a straggling line behind them, while beyond, the snowy slopes of Fuji rise, far across these marshes where pallid mist and water meet.

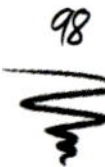

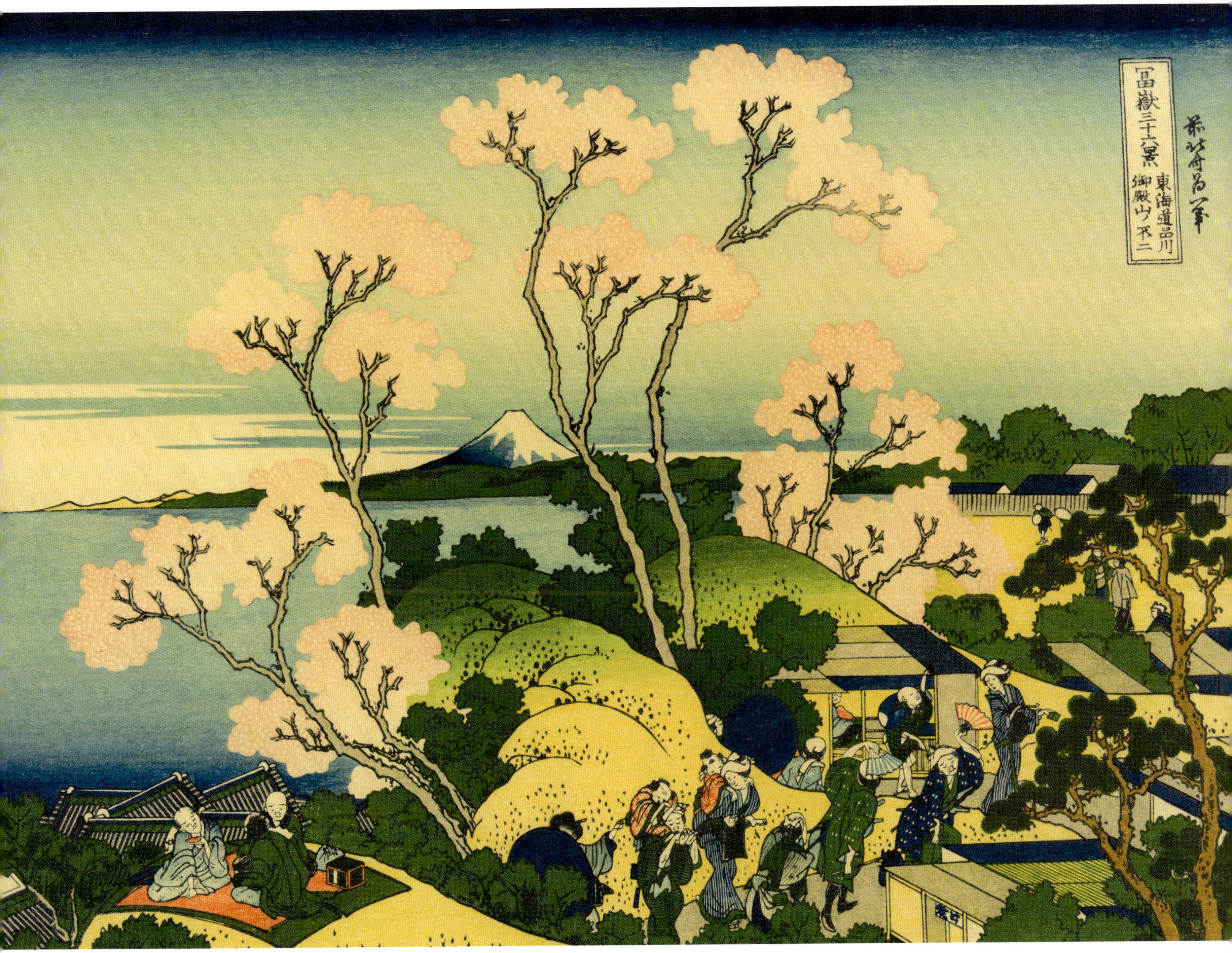

ABOVE **Katsushika Hokusai (1760–1849)** *Goten-yama Hill, Shinagawa on the Tokaido* from 'Thirty-six Views of Mount Fuji' (1826–33, printed later)

Up Close and Mineral

Climbing on Fuji (*see* pages 38–39) brings us into close proximity for the first time with what until now has been invariably a more or less distant subject. It feels as though we could almost touch the rough, red stone of the rugged mountainside up which a line of pilgrims slowly and painstakingly makes its way. Or, rather, up and down which, seen up close, those smoothly tapering sides we have grown used to are so chaotically uneven that those ascending have to follow a ridiculously complex route, dipping this way and that along labyrinthine pathways, wreathed by wisps of cloud, to reach the top. The group here have some way to go; their immediate object would appear to be the little *asama* shrine in which a considerable company of worshippers is already assembled.

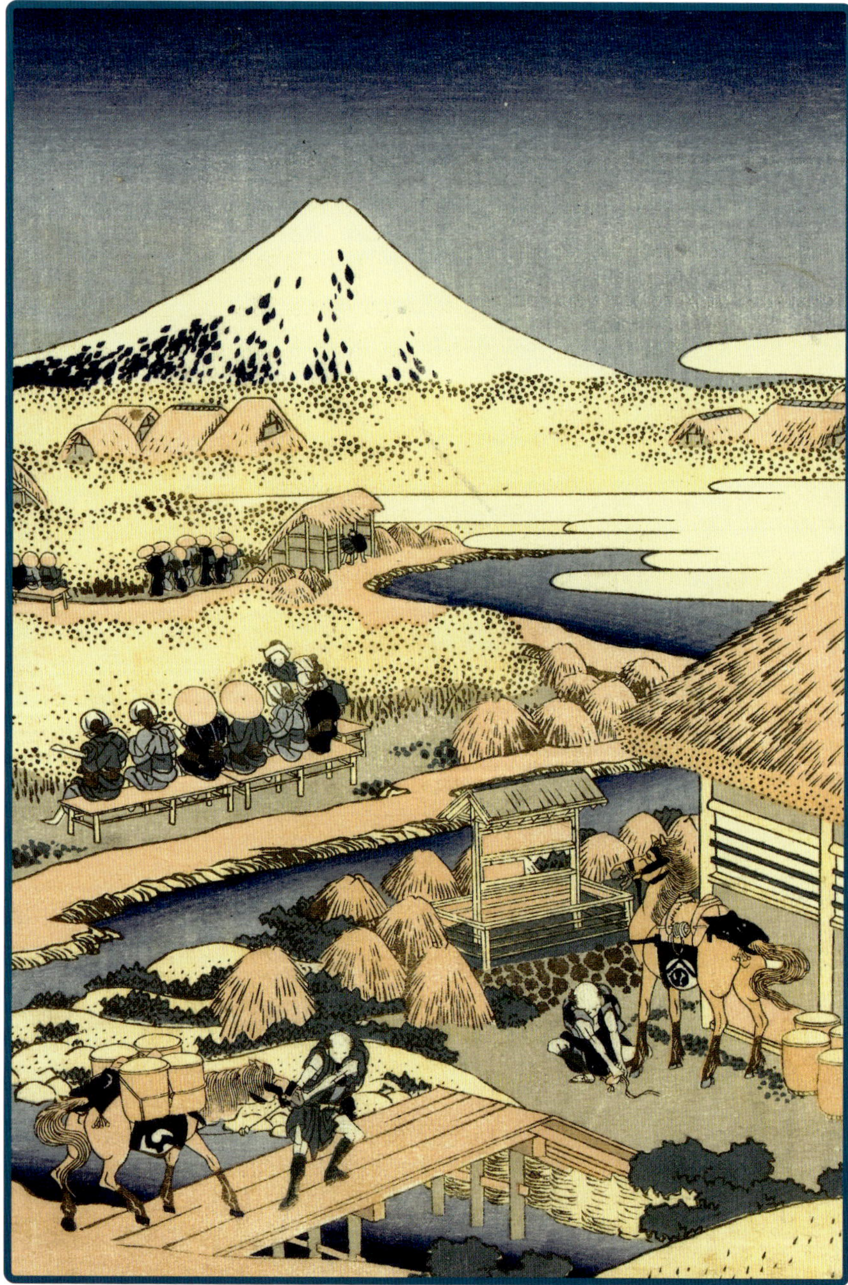

ABOVE **Katsushika Hokusai (1760–1849)** *The Tea Plantation of Katakura in Suruga Province* (detail) from 'Thirty-six Views of Mount Fuji' (1826–33)

Land of the Rising Sun

The morning mists have yet to clear over *The Tea Plantation of Katakura in Suruga Province* (*see* left and in full on page 73), but the place is already buzzing. Women in wide hats and with baskets on their backs are hard at work picking the precious leaves, whilst another team takes a rest, off to one side. In the left foreground, a couple of porters carry big chests of tea towards the main plantation building, before which we see a worker carefully checking a horse's shoe.

The Oi River was a major impediment to communications in the area to the east of Edo Bay well into modern times. In *Fuji from Kanaya on the Tokaido* (*see* right), we see intrepid travellers braving the ford at Kanaya (now Shimada) – left deliberately unbridged through the centuries of civil conflict as part of the outer defences of Edo. It is morning here as well. There is an enamelled quality about the waves in a foreground Hokusai has pretty much flooded with Prussian blue, as there is about the form of Fuji, its black silhouette crowned with dazzling white snow tinged pink by the sun of barely broken dawn. Travellers pass through a break in the striated slopes of the dike, intended to protect the town from flooding; this striped appearance reflects its construction, built up with bamboo baskets filled with gravel.

Another early sun touches the scene in *Dawn at Isawa in Kai Province* (*see* page 68 and 103). At first, looking down at a steep angle, we barely register life

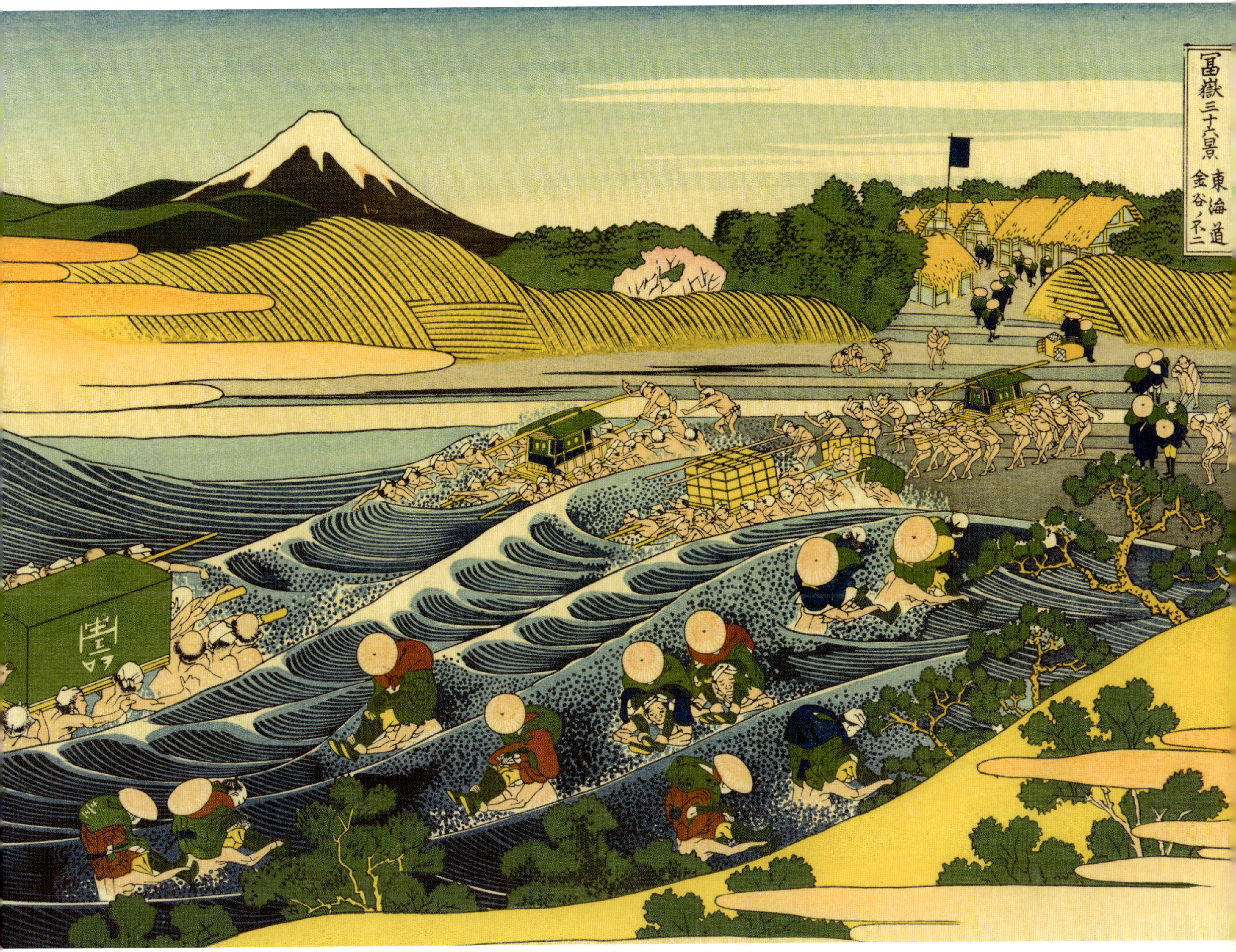

ABOVE **Katsushika Hokusai** (1760–1849) *Fuji from Kanaya on the Tokaido* from 'Thirty-six Views of Mount Fuji' (1826–33, printed later)

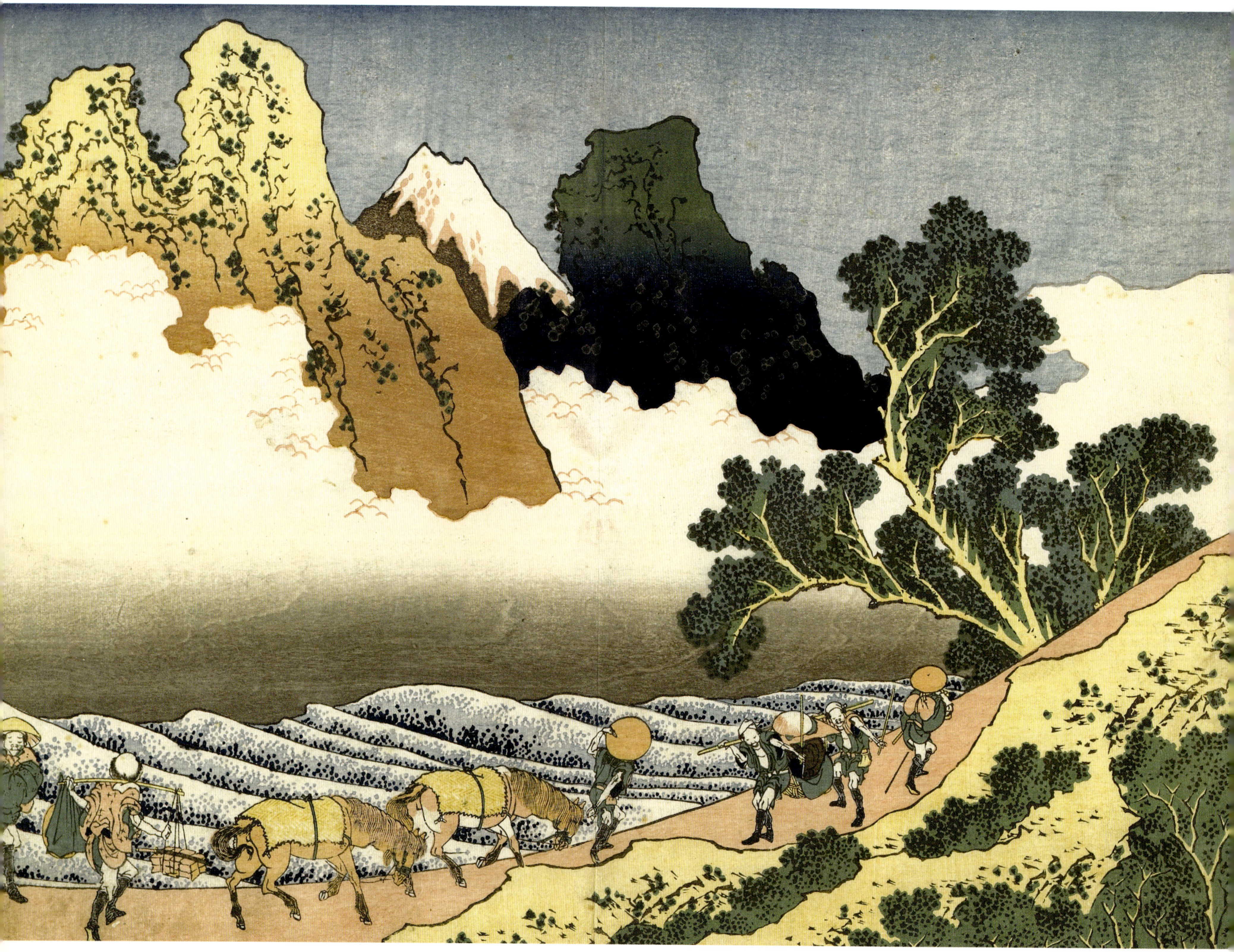

ABOVE Katsushika Hokusai (1760–1849) *The Back of Fuji from the Minobu River* from 'Thirty-six Views of Mount Fuji' (1826–33)

going on in the village street below. Instead, the view is dominated by the shape of Fujisan, rising above the mist as though above a sea. Barely visible between more jagged and much closer mountains, Fujisan still stands out in *The Back of Fuji from the Minobu River* (*see* left), transfigured as it is by the touch of daybreak. The pinkish tinge of its snowy peak picks up the roseate clouds encircling the cliffs we see, just across the rushing torrent of the Minobu. On the near bank, before us, the daily traffic of peasants, porters and other travellers passes, with one wayfarer important enough to be carried in a litter.

46. And Counting…

This, the closing image of the whole 36 + 10 sequence, seems to be saying that even when seen to greatest disadvantage, Mount Fuji's magic and mystique remain as strong as ever.

Its hold over Hokusai was certainly undiminished. Far from having got his Fujisan interest (or obsession) out of his system with this sequence, he almost immediately embarked on another collection. By 1834 he was bringing out the first of the three volumes of what was to be his 'One Hundred Views of Mount Fuji' (*see* pages 104–09).

Monochrome Miracle

This work has remained comparatively unfamiliar in the West. Just as the other 35 of the 'Thirty-six Views…', with all their beauty, have suffered from being in the shadow of *The Great Wave off Kanagawa*, the 'One Hundred Views…' have suffered by comparison with the 'Thirty-six Views…'.

The difference in reception is as understandable as it is unjust. Where the 'Thirty-six Views…' were stand-alone prints in expansive format and (often blazing) colour, this collection took the form of a trio of little books, their prints in monochrome. Inevitably, then, it has been overshadowed. In Japan though, among artists and connoisseurs (as, indeed, it would appear to have been in Hokusai's own creative mind), it is the 'One Hundred Views…' that is held to be the masterwork.

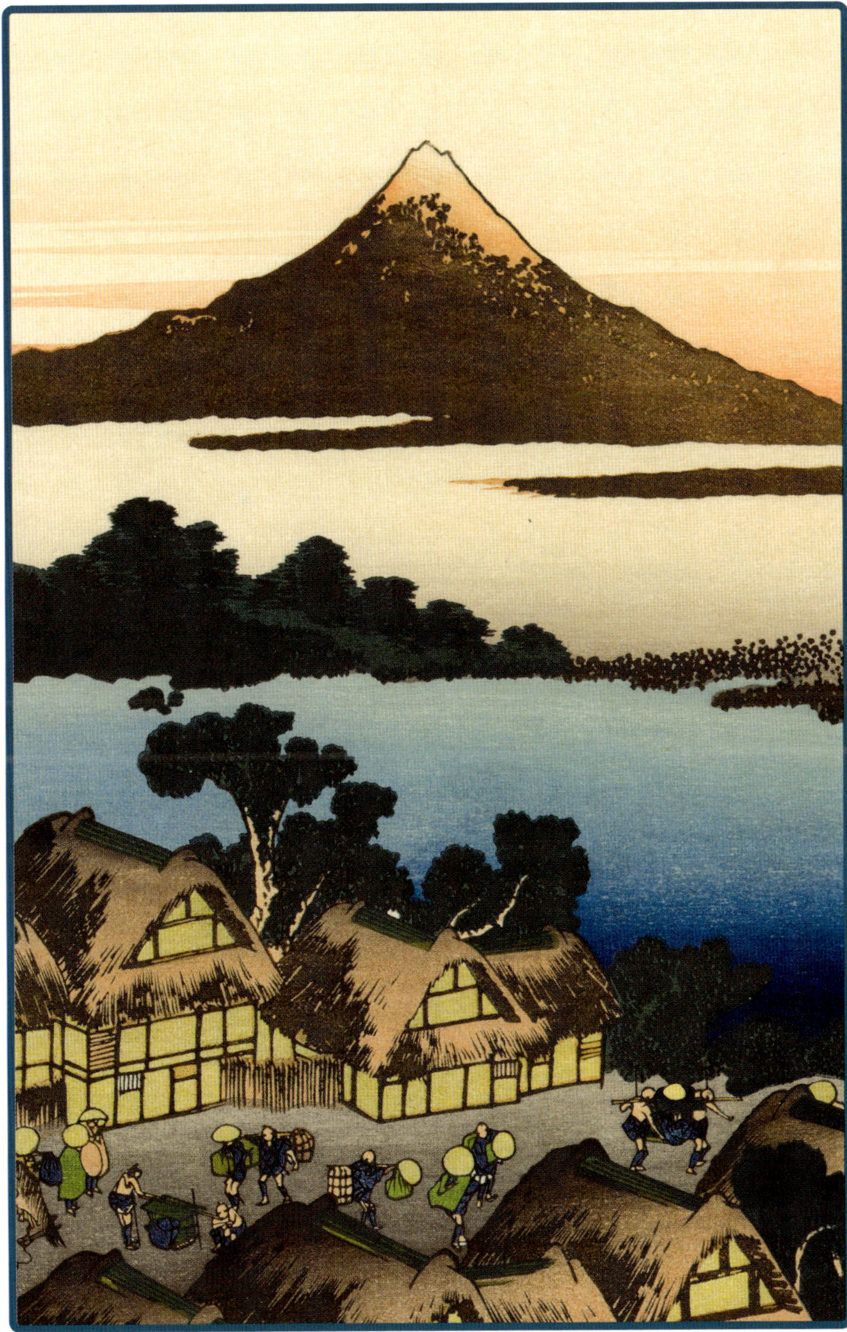

ABOVE Katsushika Hokusai (1760–1849) *Dawn at Isawa in Kai Province* from 'Thirty-six Views of Mount Fuji' (1826–33, printed later)

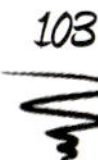

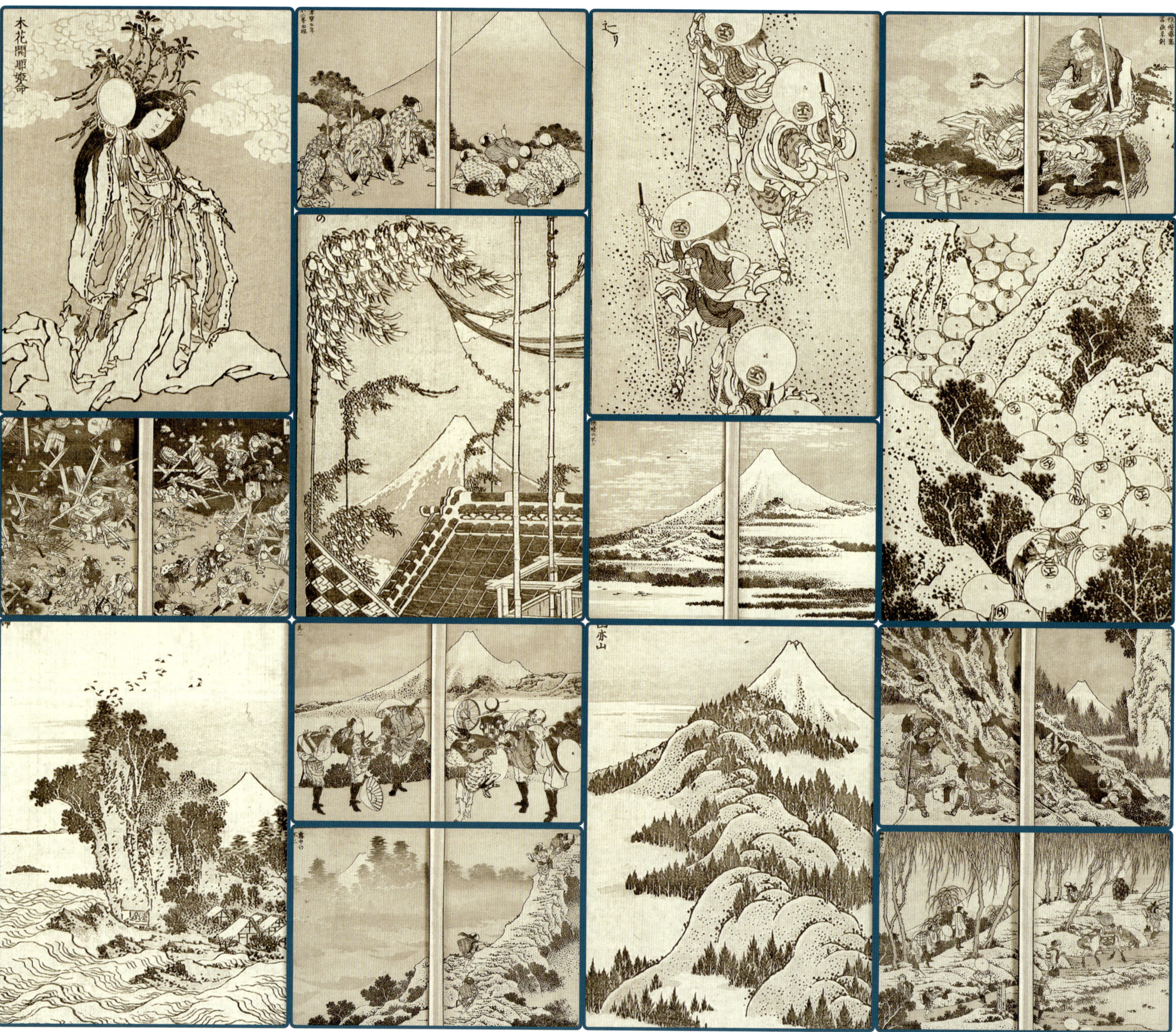

Above Katsushika Hokusai (1760–1849) 'One Hundred Views of Mount Fuji', Volume 1 (1834)

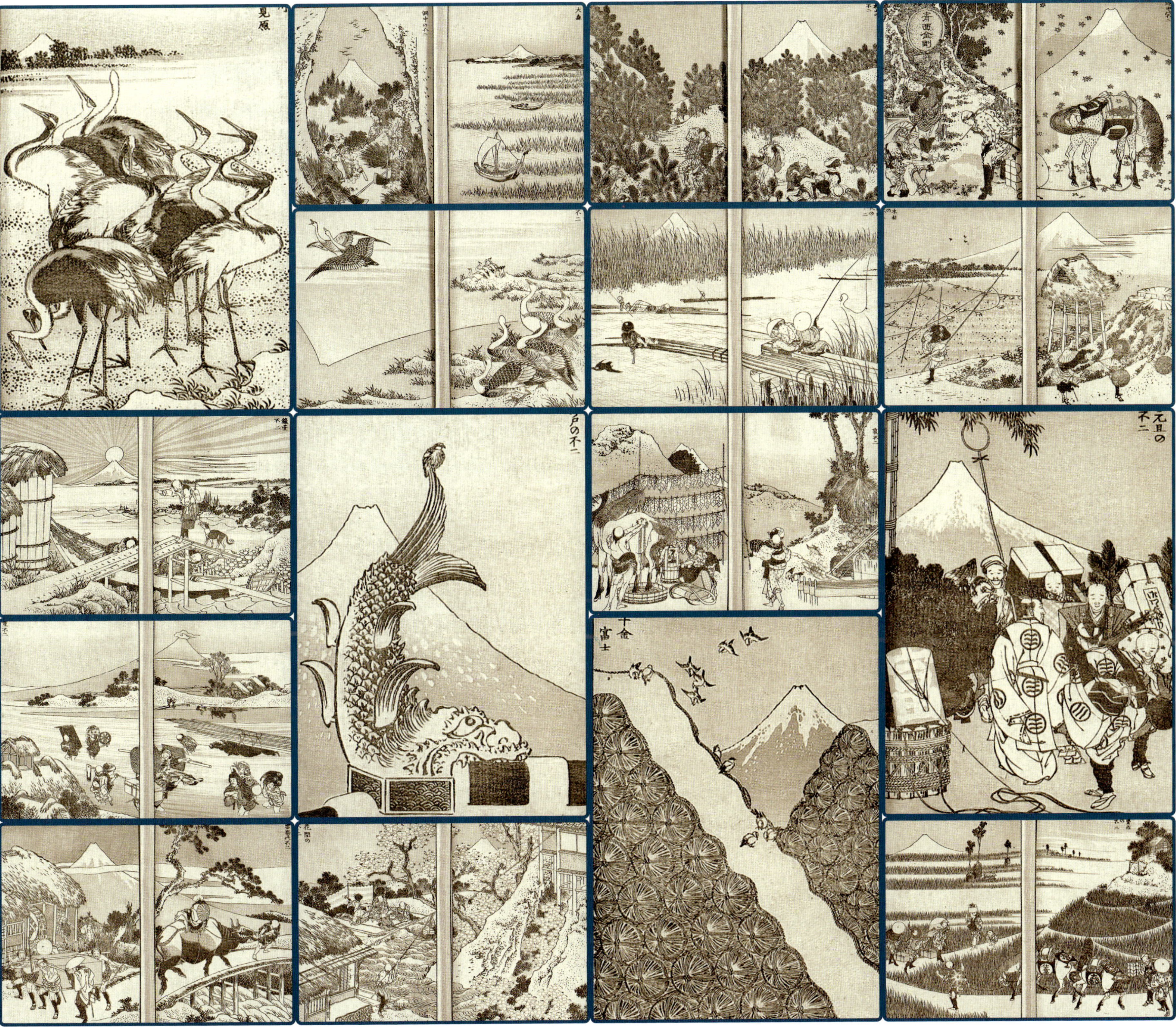

ABOVE Katsushika Hokusai (1760–1849) 'One Hundred Views of Mount Fuji', Volume 1 (1834)

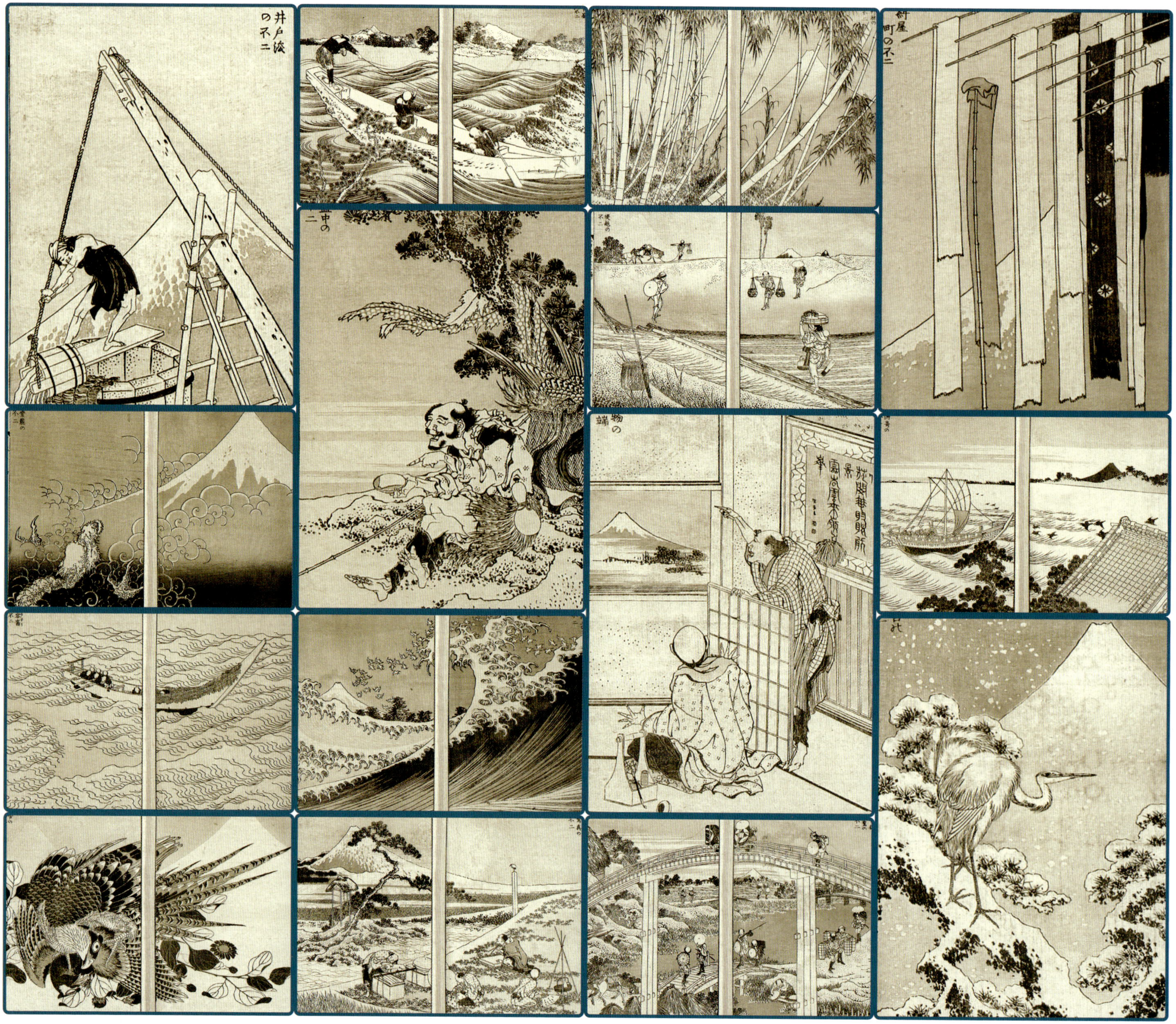

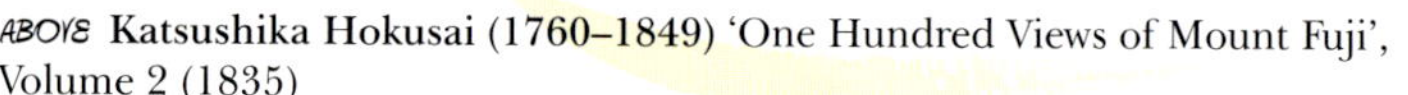

Above **Katsushika Hokusai** (1760–1849) 'One Hundred Views of Mount Fuji', Volume 2 (1835)

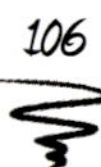

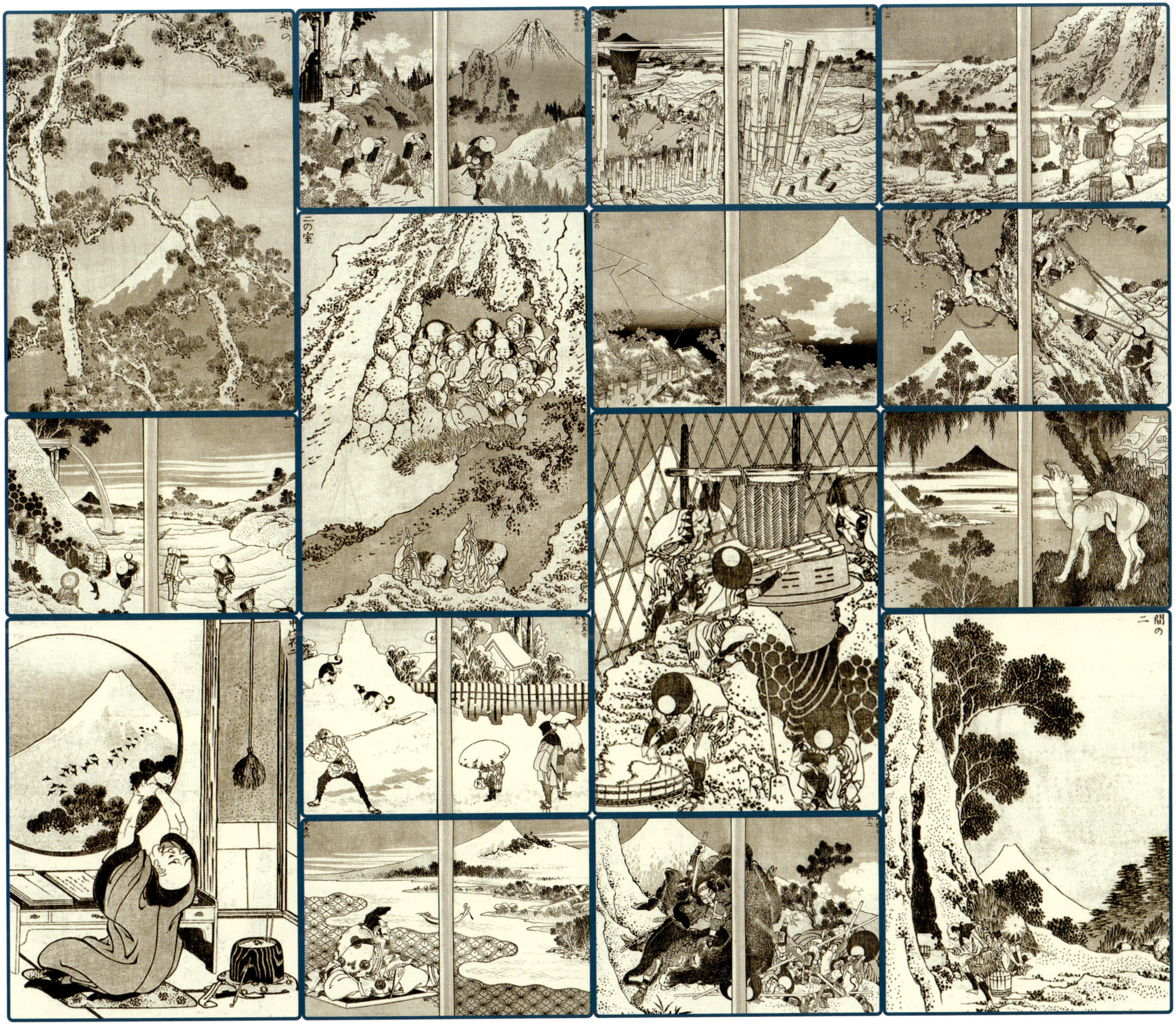

Above **Katsushika Hokusai (1760–1849)** 'One Hundred Views of Mount Fuji', Volume 2 (1835)

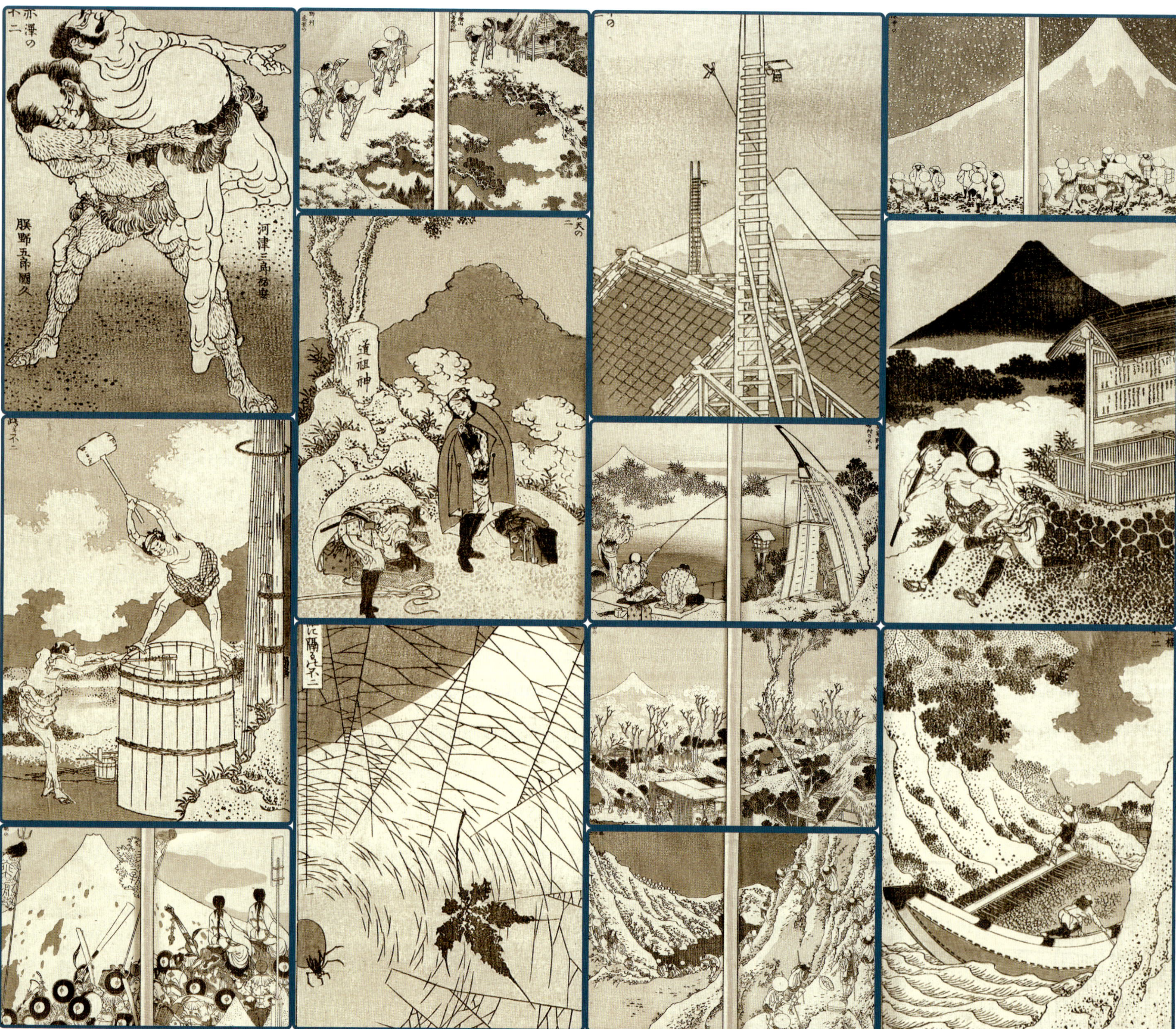

Above Katsushika Hokusai (1760–1849) 'One Hundred Views of Mount Fuji', Volume 3 (1849)

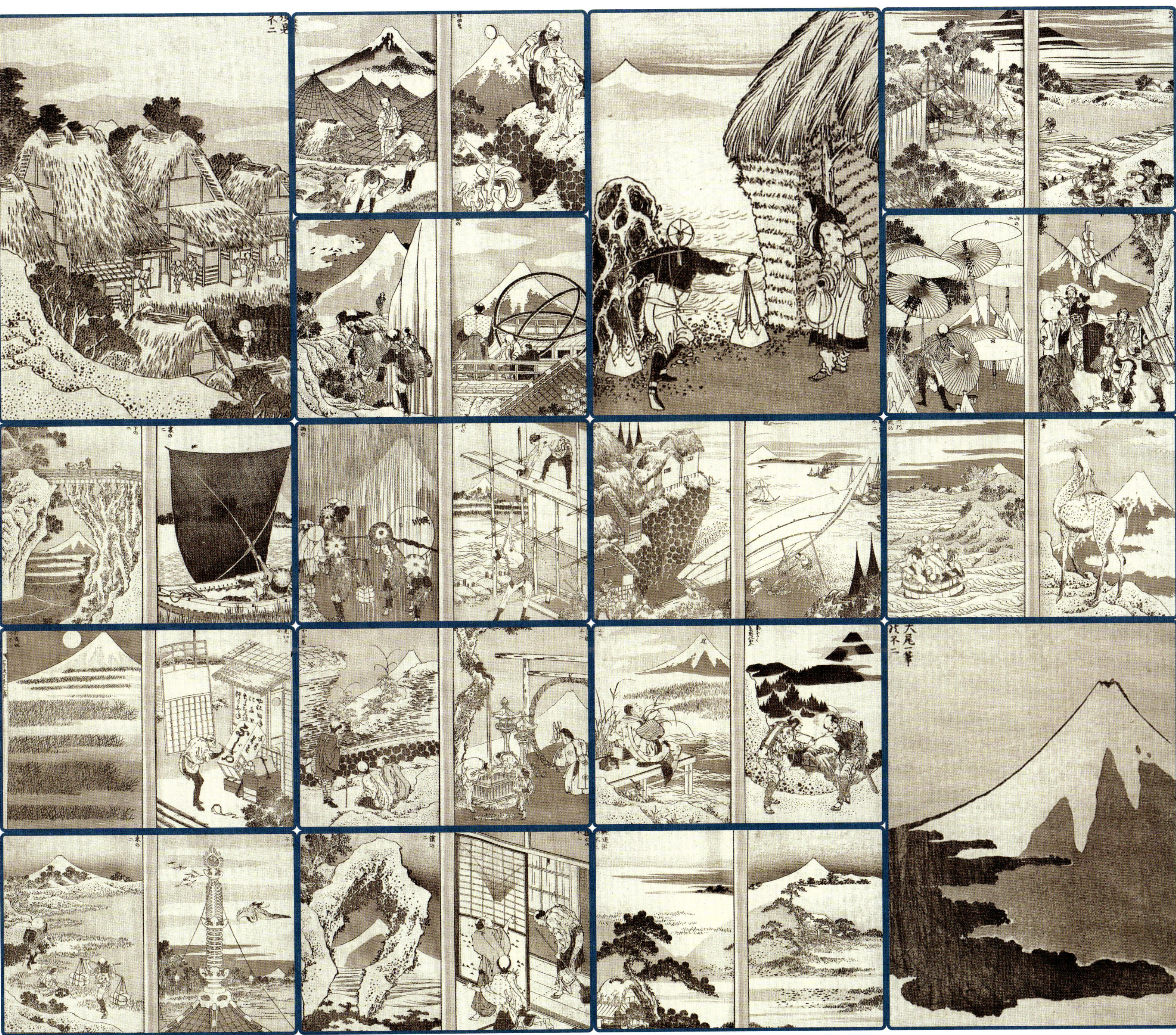

Above Katsushika Hokusai (1760–1849) 'One Hundred Views of Mount Fuji', Volume 3 (1849)

Undoubtedly, it makes more demands on its viewer/reader. Black and white prints, however accomplished, cannot realistically hope to match the direct assault that Hokusai's colours can make on the eyes and mind. But the artist himself appears to have trusted the medium more on this account. Like the modern movie *auteur* who wants his or her films to be in black and white for greater purity and integrity, he saw this work as representing himself in a way his more popular collection never had.

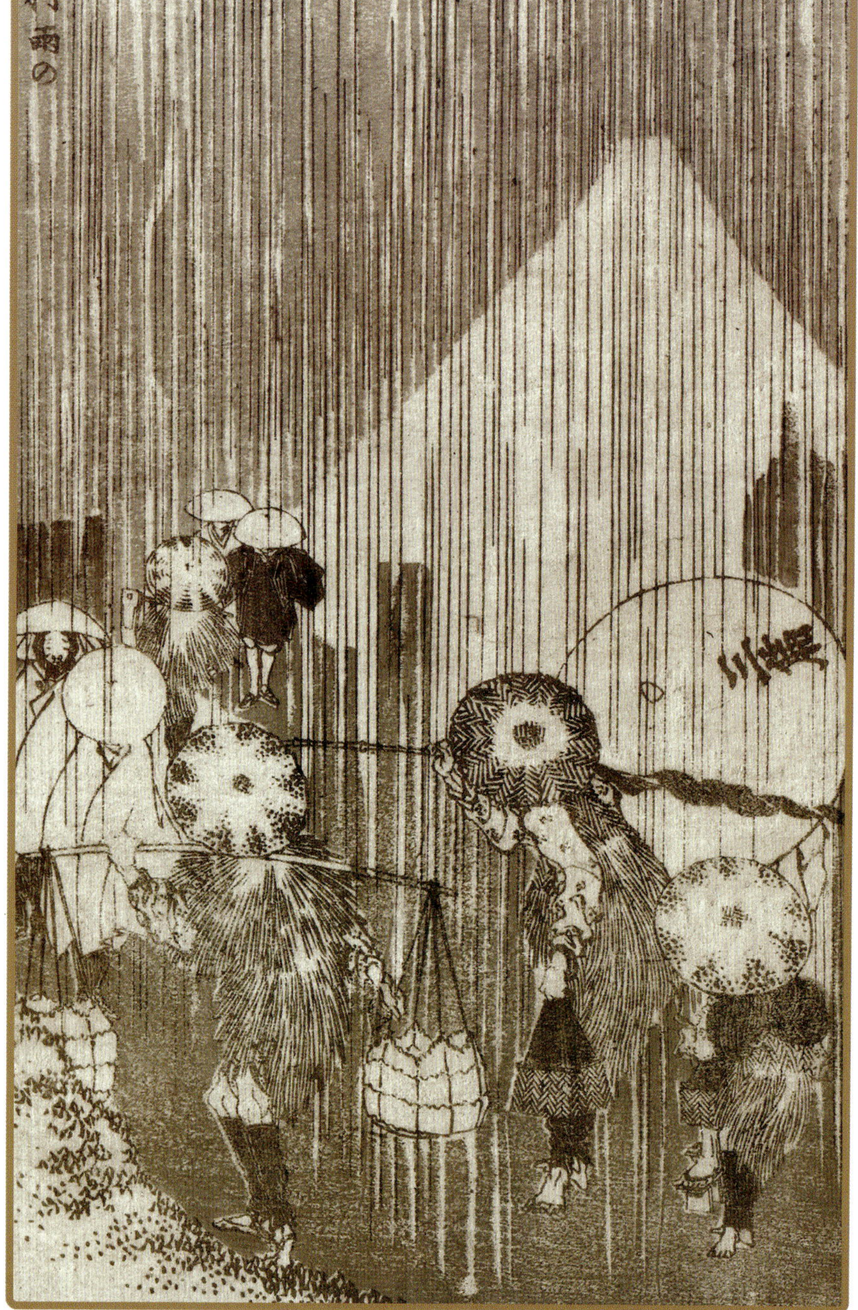

Above **Katsushika Hokusai (1760–1849)** *Viewing Mount Fuji Through Spring Rain at the Village* from 'One Hundred Views of Mount Fuji', Vol. 3 (1849)

And, just as the *auteured* art film makes more demands of its viewer than the mainstream movie, 'One Hundred Views of Fuji' is more exacting than its full-colour predecessor. Not only are the prints less colourful, they are often spare and comparatively unyielding; there is an austere inapproachability about these views at times. On occasion, there is a seeming tendency towards something bordering on abstraction, whether because the drawing is so intricate it seems to surpass its representational function or because, on the contrary, it is so uncompromisingly minimal. There is a quizzical, perhaps even gnomic, quality to many of the prints and, by extension, to the collection as a whole. We can never really feel we have it fathomed.

What's in a Number?

We are on safer ground numerologically with this title than we were with 'Thirty-six Views of Fuji'; there is no real doubt that Hokusai (and probably his public) would have attached importance to there being 100 views. Then, as now, in Japan as elsewhere, this number had its own very particular mystique – whether applied to years, to pictures or to just about anything else.

We have already seen that Hokusai saw himself living longer than 100 years and that he had high hopes, quietly confident that by his hundredth year he would be 'producing work of divine perfection'. There were precedents for 'Fuji 100s' too. The Buddhist scholar Keichu (1640–1701) had published a collection of '100 Poems in Praise of Mount Fuji', and his work of artistic devotion had been emulated many times by other poets. Even in the more obviously commercial compositions of the 'Thirty-six Views…', the spiritual significance of Fuji for Hokusai had been evident. Whilst he never quite admitted it, there has from the first been something close to a consensus that this was his attempt to do in graphic art what Keichu had achieved in poetry.

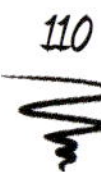

Pre-eminent Prints

The writer of the preface to the first volume *does* make the connection explicit, in fact, although we have no real reason to believe that this was Hokusai. More promotional than editorial, it is less what we would consider the kind of explanatory introduction an author might write for his own work and more a piece of selling copy, a cover blurb. It certainly does not undersell its product. 'Hokusai's pictures', the author opines, 'tower above those of other artists as Mount Fuji does above other hills'.

That is the sort of value-judgement we do not generally want to leave to a publisher, but we can hardly disagree with what he says of Hokusai's longstanding and developed interest in Mount Fuji:

> *He has loved this sacred peak for many years. Apparently he deemed it too obvious to view it, like everybody else, from Tago Bay or Miho – a cliché, like the image of blossoms beneath a bright full moon. Taking up his staff, then, he has set out to walk all the way to Fujimigahara and had his litter carried as far as Shiomizaka. He has looked up at his beloved summit through a mesh of willow branches and through quivering rice-sheaves; he has viewed it across open seas and storm-lashed coasts, over meandering roads and misty valleys, and across rugged crags. Such great integrity has he shown in his depiction of Nature here that it is fair to say that his spirit resides within this work.*

Fuji, from Top to Bottom

Turning to the views themselves, we are shown from the first that, in this new book, Hokusai is hoping to look deeper than he has before. The opening image (*see* page 104, top left) represents not Fujisan itself but its proprietary deity, the goddess Konohanasakuyahime, Princess of Blossoms. Like a European Virgin of the Assumption, she stands aloft on a little pedestal of what might be mountaintop, but looks more like cloud; her robe spills luxuriantly around her and you can practically feel its crinkly folds.

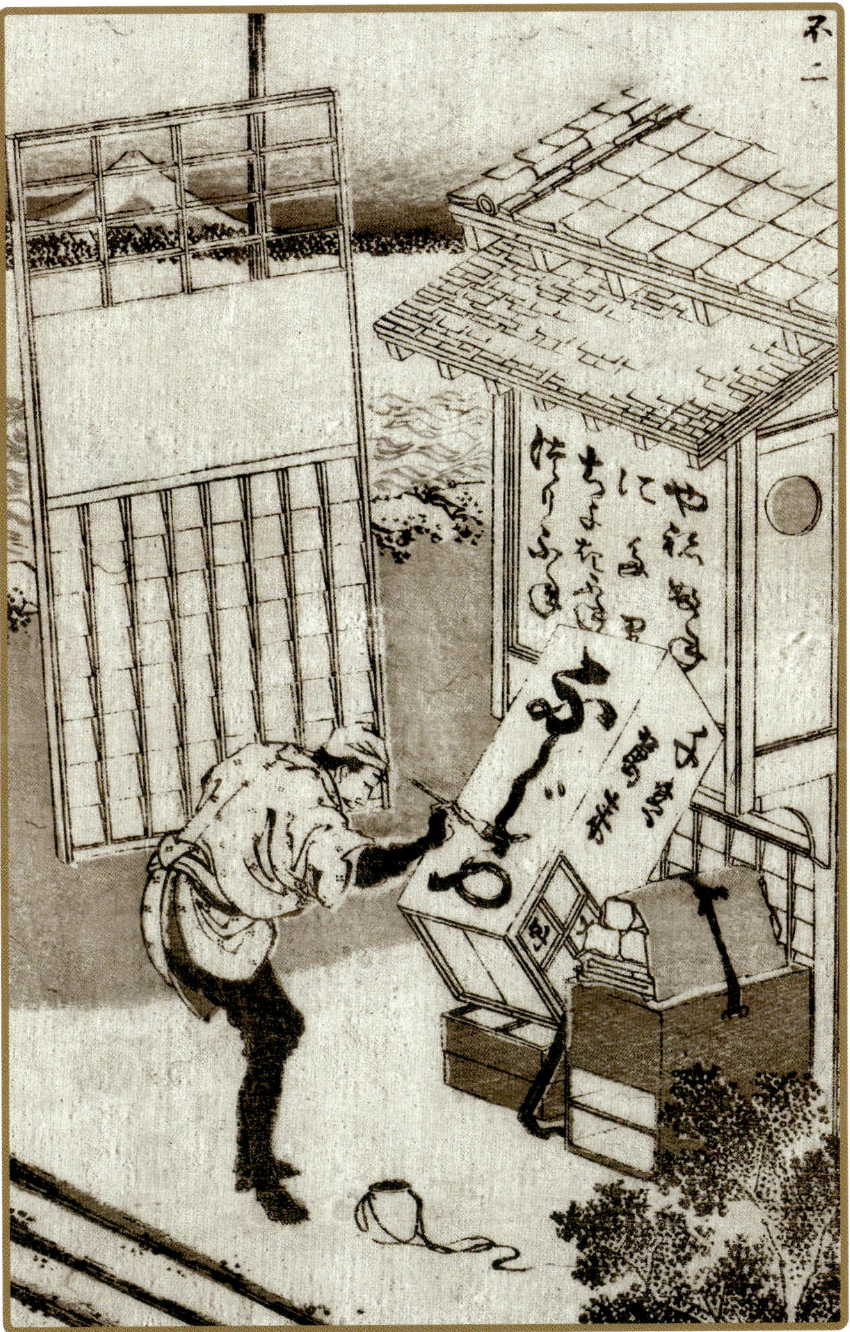

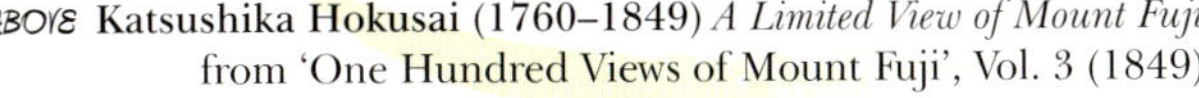
Above Katsushika Hokusai (1760–1849) *A Limited View of Mount Fuji* from 'One Hundred Views of Mount Fuji', Vol. 3 (1849)

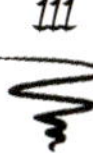

In her right hand, she holds a circular mirror, the Yata no Kagami, sacred to Shintoism because of its ability to reflect the world and hence to contain all things and its open frankness in reflecting things truthfully. The mirror, believed to be kept in the sun goddess Amaterasu's Grand Shrine at Ise, is one of the Imperial crown jewels of Japan. In her left hand, Konohanasakuyahime grips a long *sakaki* branch which towers over her shoulder and up behind her head. This evergreen tree is considered sacred in Shinto and is associated with eternal life.

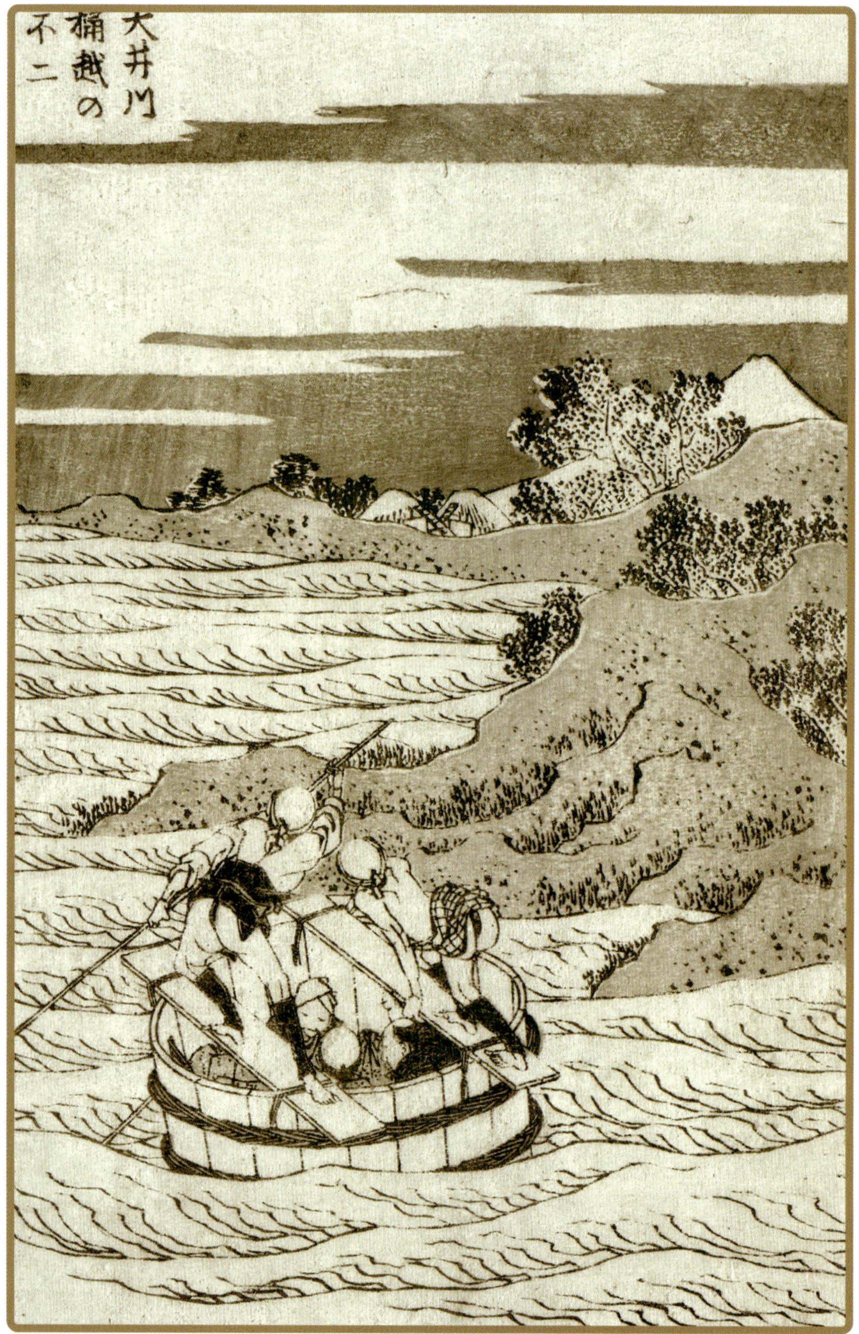

ABOVE Katsushika Hokusai (1760–1849) *Viewing Mount Fuji from a Bucket Boat Going Down the River Oi* from 'One Hundred Views of Mount Fuji', Vol. 3 (1849)

Her iconographical significance apart, Konohanasakuyahime's presence in this context announces Hokusai's artistic ambition. In this book, it is clear, his intention was to look at Mount Fuji not just as a topographical feature (however rich in symbolism), but as a transcendent, spiritual realm. His next picture, however, transports us at the turn of a page from the mountain's mystic summit to its mundane base, where a gawping group of people – both high officials and lowly peasants – gaze up towards a distant summit that projects above the perimeter of the picture's black-lined frame.

Or breaks through it; for this scene is supposed to represent the mythical moment in the third century BC when, without warning, the mountain suddenly appeared. Next comes the figure of holy man En no Gyoja (*c.* 634–*c.* 700), reputedly the first man to have climbed Mount Fuji. Seated in the lotus position, his sandals off, he meditates beside the open crater.

Facets of Fuji

In his first three images, accordingly, Hokusai has set out his spiritual stall. Only now does he show us Fujisan from a distance, in a classic, unpeopled view. In the pages that follow, he gives us close-ups of pilgrims clambering up the mountain's rocky slopes towards its summit and longer-range vistas in very different scenes.

Here we see Fuji reflected on the surface of a pool, with geese; here we see it across a pine forest where country folk gather mushrooms; now we see it through a winter wind, as all before us is being blown to tatters, except for

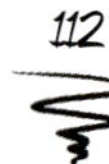

Fuji, which stands in the background, ever serene; now through a tracery of hanging willow branches; now over open reed beds or the rooftops of a town. Several pages take us back to the 'Thirty-six Views…' in recollection; a group of cranes, for instance, recalls *Umezawa in Sagami Province* (*see* page 92). A couple of prints commemorate the great Hoeizan eruption of 1707, when, amidst a massive earthquake, ash exploded from a vent low down on the mountain's side, raining down across Edo and the surrounding country.

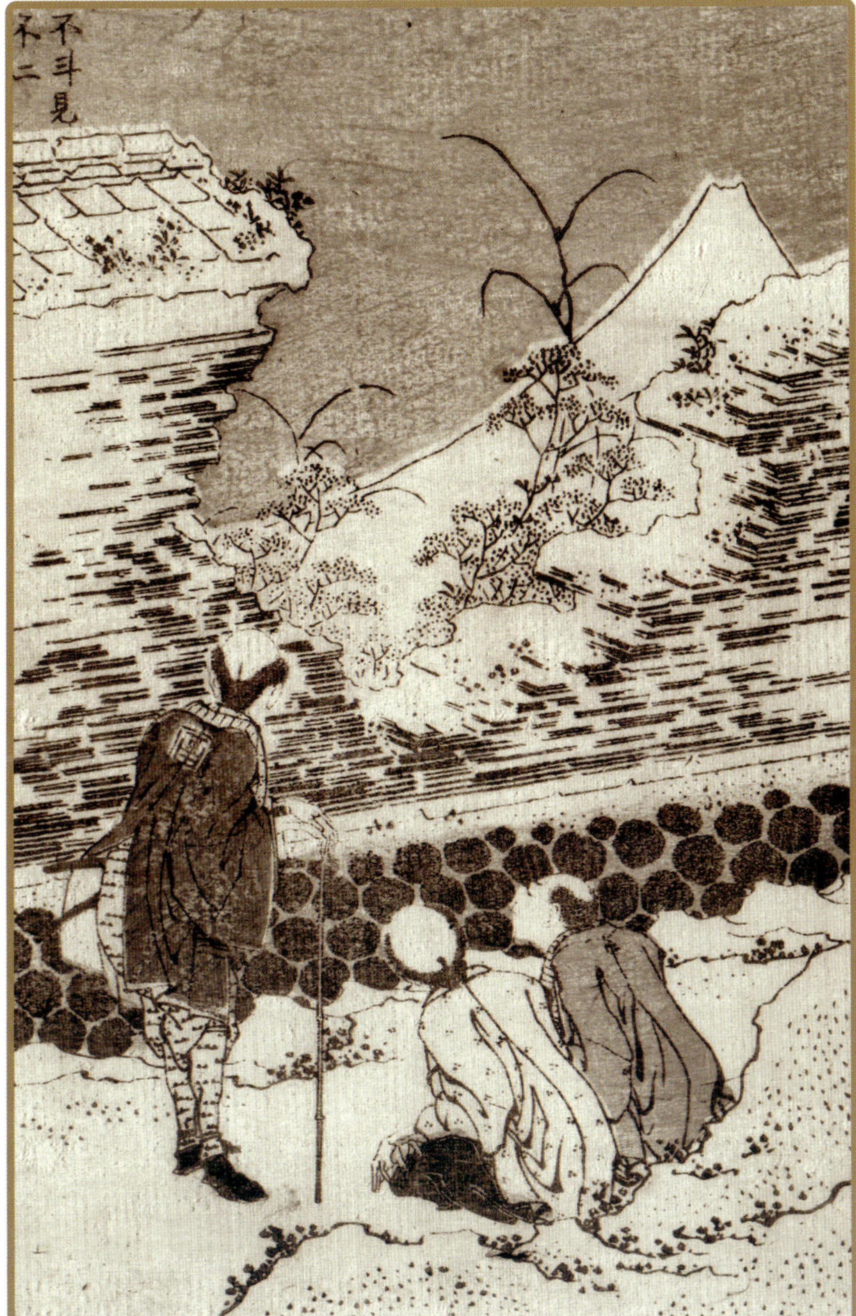

ABOVE Katsushika Hokusai (1760–1849) *Mount Fuji at Second Glance* from 'One Hundred Views of Mount Fuji', Vol. 3 (1849)

Reflected Glory

One memorable composition gives us Fujisan as the pedestal upon which the setting sun appears to rest (*see* page 105). As the American scholar Henry Smith has pointed out, it makes of mountain and sun a mirror of truthfulness, but does so crucially in the context of a much more humdrum, earthly scene. In the foreground, a peasant makes his way home with his dog; while a pair of boatmen struggle to manoeuvre their vessel past the supportive trestle of a tiny footbridge, as a little coastal village begins to wind down for the day.

Throughout the 'Thirty-six Views…' we saw Hokusai exploiting the reflective properties of Fuji, its stony sides glowing red, brown or blue in summer, its white winter snows touched into colour by the rising or setting sun. The writer of the Preface to Book II of the 'One Hundred Views…' homes in on this capacity of his country's sacred mountain to bear witness, in all its eternal stillness, to incessant change:

> *Like a carefully cut gemstone, silver-white, Fujisan has no front or back; no irregularity; no projecting edge. It is symmetrical from every side, like a lotus flower floating in a pool…. The red light of dawn shines on its slopes; the sinking sun of evening casts shadows of dark blue and green. Its colours are different by morning and by evening, seen from close-to and from afar. Through the sunshine of Spring and the storms of Autumn; through fogs and clouds, in light and darkness….*

This function of reflecting Japan to itself in all its beauty, he suggested, was reflected in turn by Hokusai's pictures.

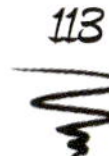

Hokusai's composition is invariably careful, but, as we saw several times in 'Thirty-six Views…', he sometimes seems to be playing geometric games. So it is here as well, his second book getting under way with a print showing the famous mountain being elegantly framed by the machinery of a hoist used by a workman who is cleaning out a well. With a view through arcing bamboo stems and another in which we scarcely see Fujisan at all, except as its shadow falls upon a corrugated sea-surface, this second book revels in this sort of play.

Representational Relations

A print in which the specks of foam from a breaking wave appear to metamorphose into a flock of flying seabirds brings together beauty, wit and a sense of spiritual mystery, whilst also anticipating postmodern preoccupations with the very nature of representation, the relation of artistic image to real thing. So too does the scene in which we have to search for the mountain, only at last to find it reflected on the surface of the cup of *sake* (rice wine) a fisherman is holding, a reference to an old folktale (and, of course, to the ancient mirror myth).

Perhaps the most intriguing picture in this regard is the one in which we see a servant removing a wall panel revealing a view across to Fuji, which his astonished guest assumes for a moment is actually a hanging picture. Might there ever, one wonders, be so perfectly accomplished an artwork that it could show the natural scene not only in all its beauty but in all its change?

Not surprisingly, the Preface to Book III singles out the eccentricity of Hokusai's views of Fuji, but it remarks as well on the way they bring the mountain and its environment to life. The pictures that follow show us Fujisan from an extraordinary variety of perspectives, some improbable, and an extraordinary range of unusual visual 'frames'. For instance, as seen through a forest of parasols, in silhouette through the mesh of a giant fishing net, even as projected by a knothole (as in a pinhole camera) on to a wall behind. Along with such trickery, however, there is also a great deal of human life and bustle (not to mention wit and humour), with Fuji standing as a distant sentinel.

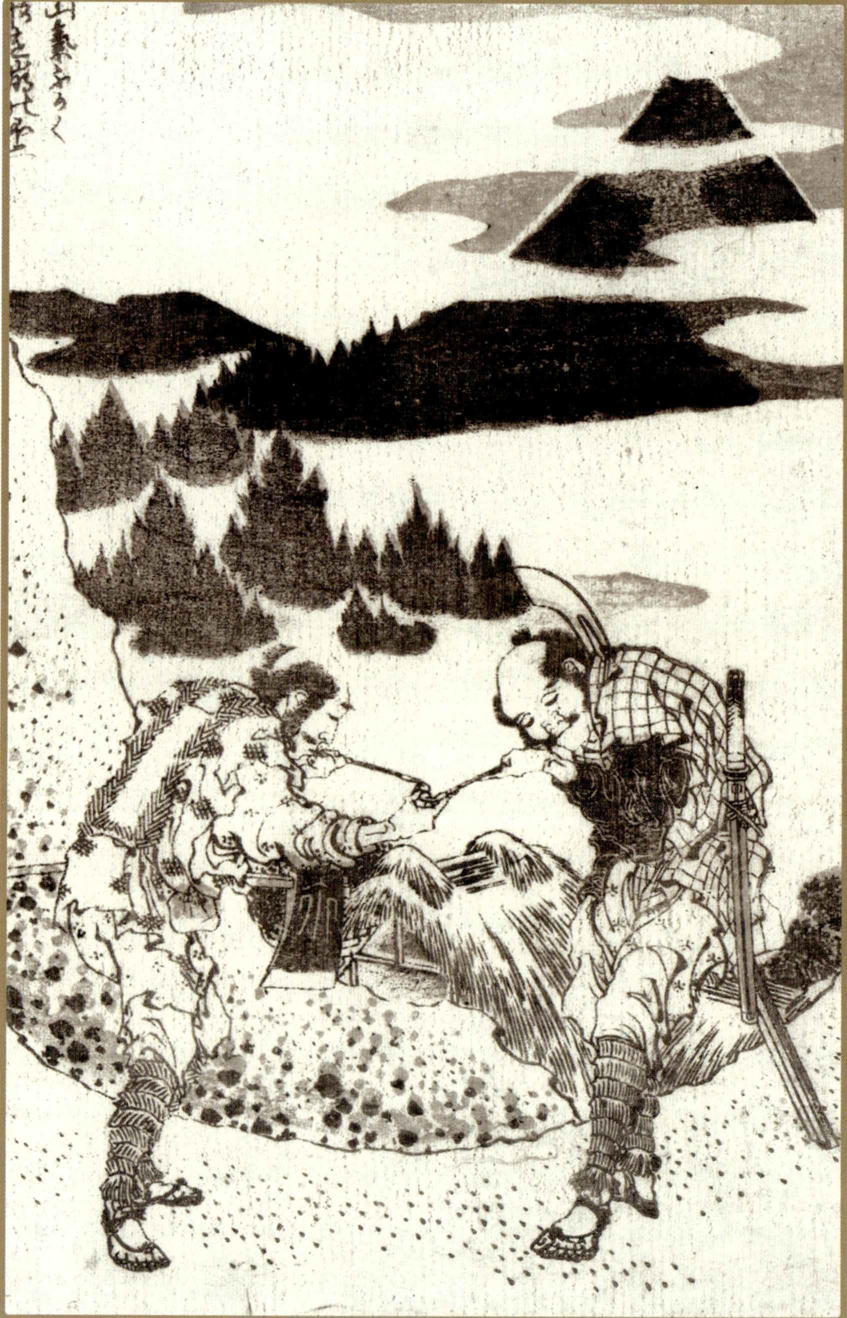

Above Katsushika Hokusai (1760–1849) *Measuring the Shape of Mount Fuji* from 'One Hundred Views of Mount Fuji', Vol. 3 (1849)

146 All Told?

'The snow that crowns the peak of Fuji does not melt until the middle day of June / and then that night the snow begins to fall again.' Thus an anonymous poem written in 795 AD neatly sums up the centuries Fujisan stood as a special place at the centre of an endless cycle of seasonal and spiritual life. Thanks to Hokusai, however, Japan's sacred mountain had been hallowed artistically as well; a veritable blizzard of representations were to come.

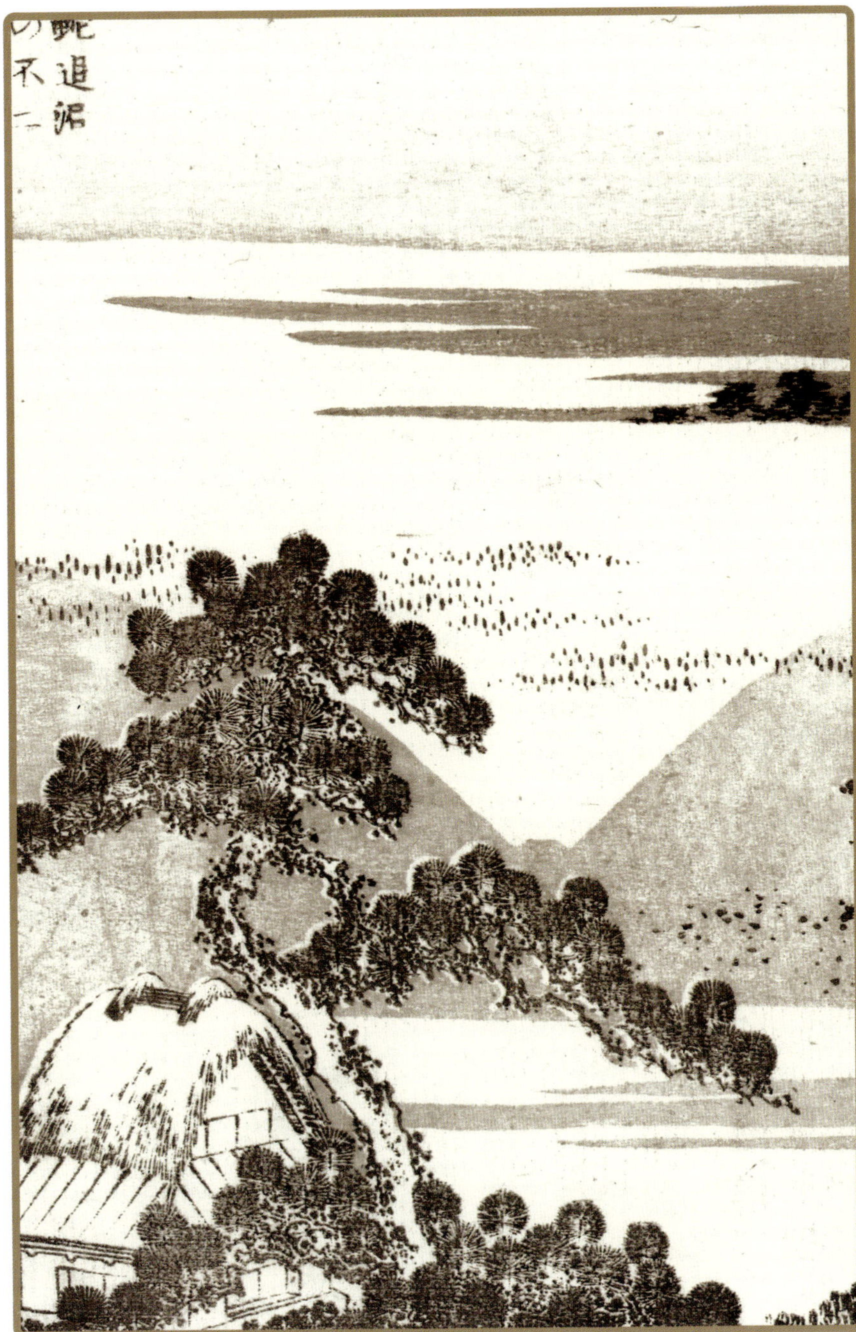

ABOVE Katsushika Hokusai (1760–1849) *Snake Chasing Mount Fuji* from 'One Hundred Views of Mount Fuji', Vol. 3 (1849)

Anyone who imagined for a moment that Hokusai's 'Thirty-six Views…' and 'One Hundred Views…' (plus one-off pieces) could have exhausted the artistic subject had not been paying attention to the master's work. The whole purpose of these projects had, in an important sense, been to reveal the infinite possibilities of the subject. If his contemporary, the English poet William Blake (1757–1827), could claim 'To see a world in a grain of sand / And a Heaven in a wild flower', how much more could Hokusai see in so vast, so spectacular – and, of course, so spiritual – a mountain?

An Artistic Opportunity

Nor was it just Hokusai. As we have seen, he had not been the first to make Mount Fuji the subject of this sort of theme-and-variations treatment. There is no doubt, however, that his two great print series of the 1830s had put what was already arguably Japan's most important geographical and cultural landmark very firmly on the artistic map. And if, as the preface to the 'One Hundred Views…' had suggested, Hokusai's work was a Fujisan in its own right, it naturally became the mark that others aimed at.

Most were to fall short, of course; dismally so, in many cases. *Ukiyo-e* had arguably never been all that far removed from kitsch. But if Hokusai had opened the way to a host of hacks, he had also opened up an exciting field for artists who could genuinely appreciate and emulate his breadth of vision.

Hokusai's Heir?

The best known of these, without much doubt, was Utagawa Hiroshige. Not only did his earlier works show an obvious debt to the older master

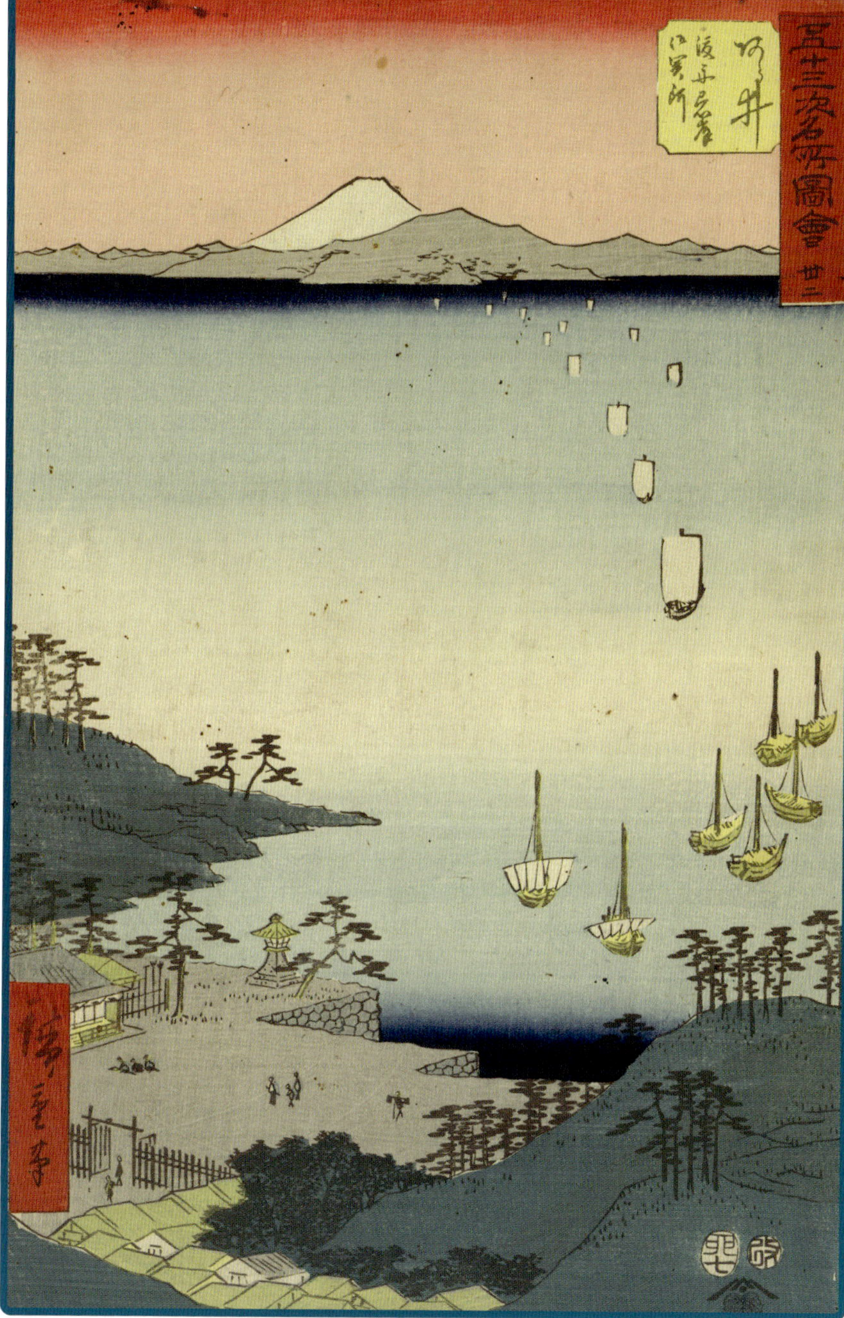

ABOVE **Utagawa Hiroshige (1797–1858)** *Arai*, the 31st station from 'Famous Views of Fifty-Three Stations of the Tokaido Road' (*c.* 1855)

but with his own 'Thirty-six Views of Fuji' (1852 and 1858; *see* pages 118–19 for the latter) he became Hokusai's self-appointed heir – his self-appointed rival even.

Hiroshige's background had been comparatively obscure. Whilst he had been born into the Ando family, an old and distinguished house of the Samurai class, this was at a time when the warrior nobility had experienced generations of decline. A decline which had, moreover, been instigated and carefully managed by the state and which was not in the authorities' interest ever to reverse.

One of the ways in which the Tokugawa shogunate had made itself invulnerable since the seventeenth century had specifically been by targeting those groups that could potentially pose a threat. Schooled in swordplay, archery and all the other arts of warfare, and invested with an inviolable code of mutual loyalty, the Samurai were far too dangerous to be left alone.

Successive shoguns had, accordingly, killed their power with kindness, flattering them with ornamental positions at and around their Edo court. Not only did this immediately make them dependent on shogunate patronage, it broke their centuries-old connections with ancestral lands. Hence the fact that Hiroshige's Samurai father was, when all was said and done, a fireman, albeit the commander of a special brigade designated to serve the shoguns' palace. That privilege arguably only added insult to injury: he was head of a fire brigade that was almost never called upon to fight a fire.

Fired with Ambition

It was a hereditary position and one that Hiroshige – then named Tokutaro – was to come into when, at the age of only 11, his parents died and he found himself head of his household. This came as a mixed

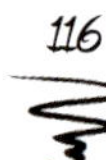

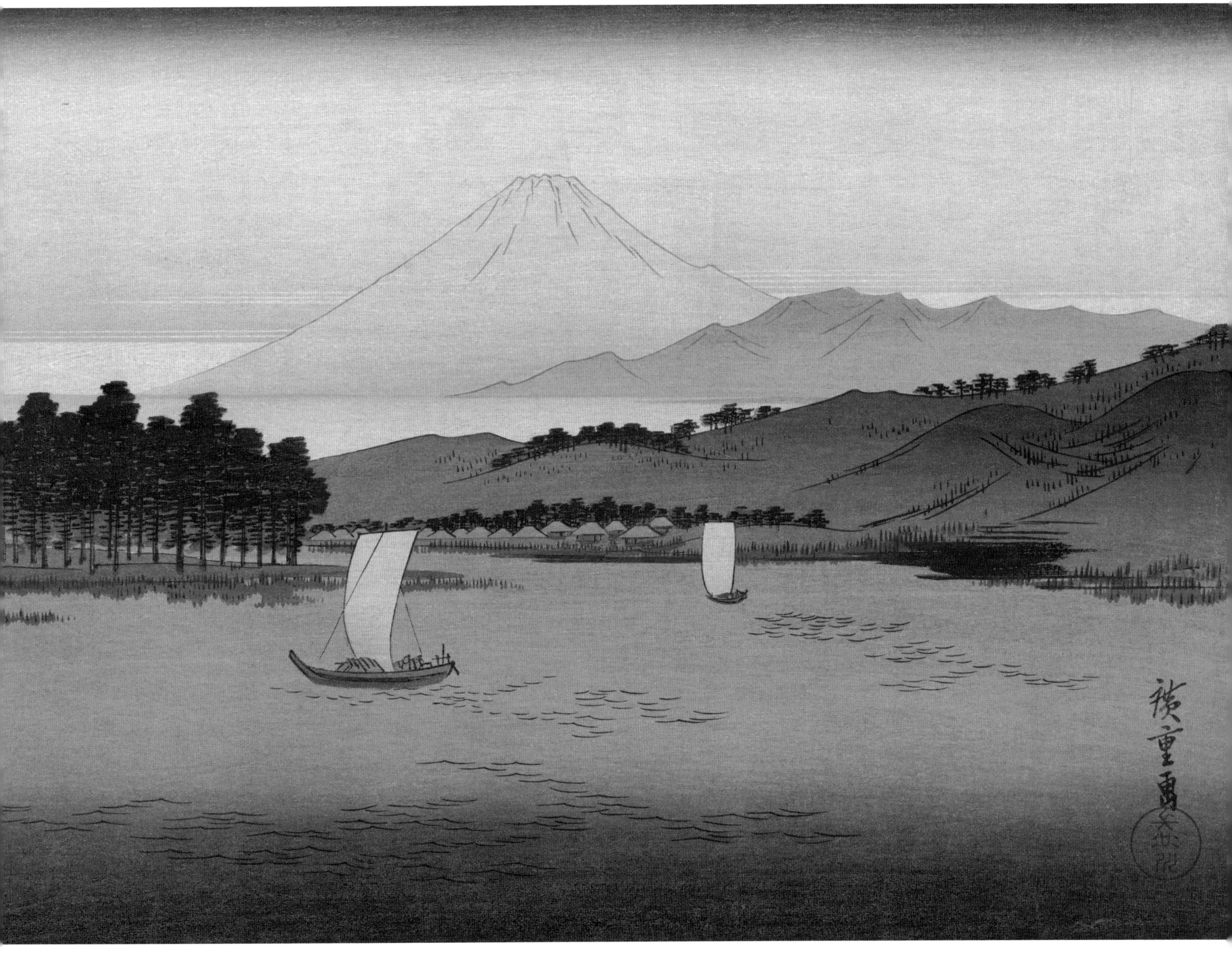

Above **Utagawa Hiroshige** (1797–1858) Untitled landscape with boats (printed 1900–1940)

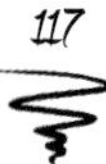

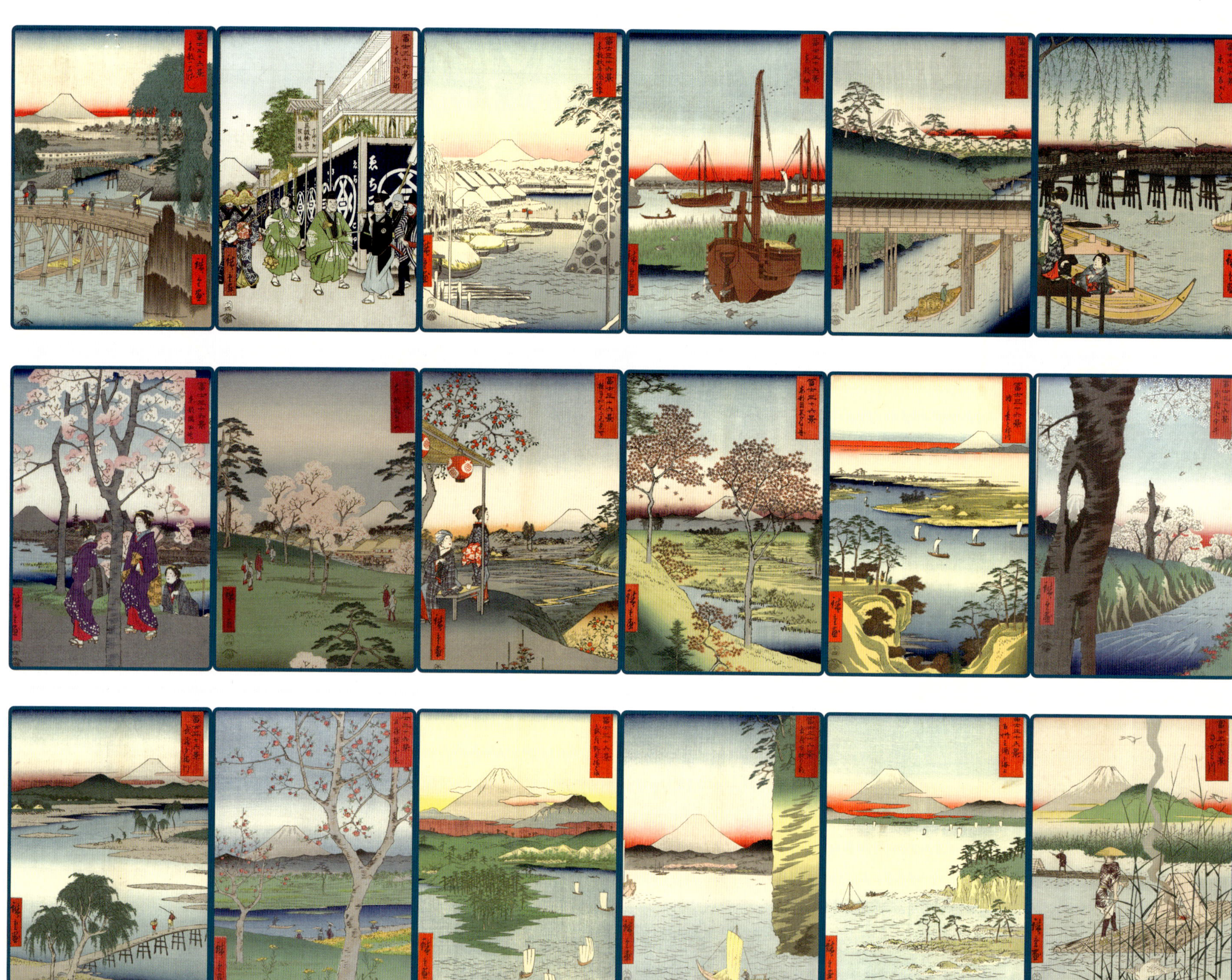

ABOVE Utagawa Hiroshige (1797–1858) Prints 1–18 from 'Thirty-six Views of Mount Fuji' (1858)

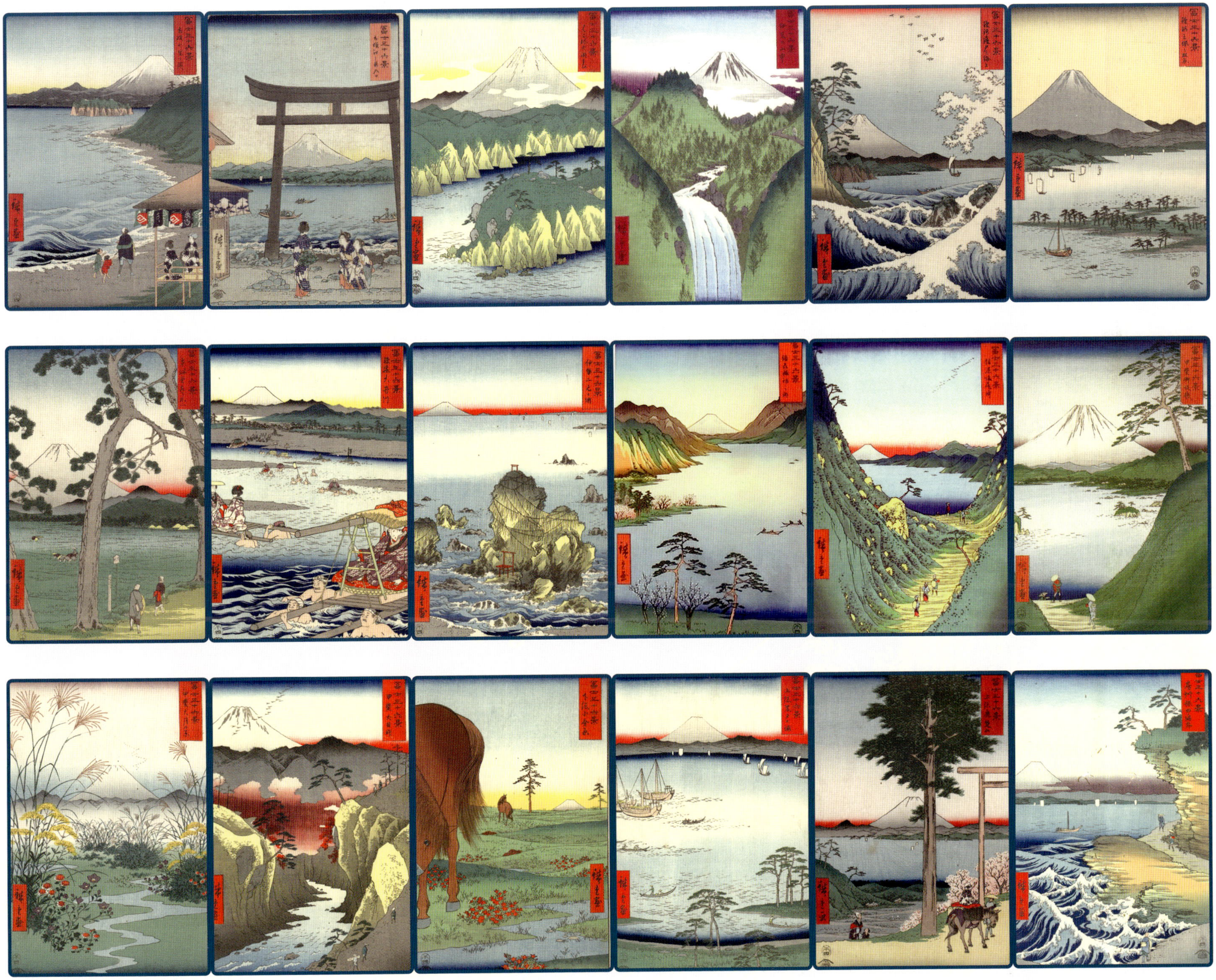

Above **Utagawa Hiroshige (1797–1858)** Prints 19–36 from 'Thirty-six Views of Mount Fuji' (1858)

blessing because whilst it guaranteed a modest income for an extremely modest workload, its ceremonial requirements still collided with an artistic ambition that he had already formed as a young boy. On the other hand, Tokutaro appears to have enjoyed a level of literary and philosophical education most more modestly-born *ukiyo-e* artists could not have dreamt of. Did this help shape the – famously poetic – character of his art in later life?

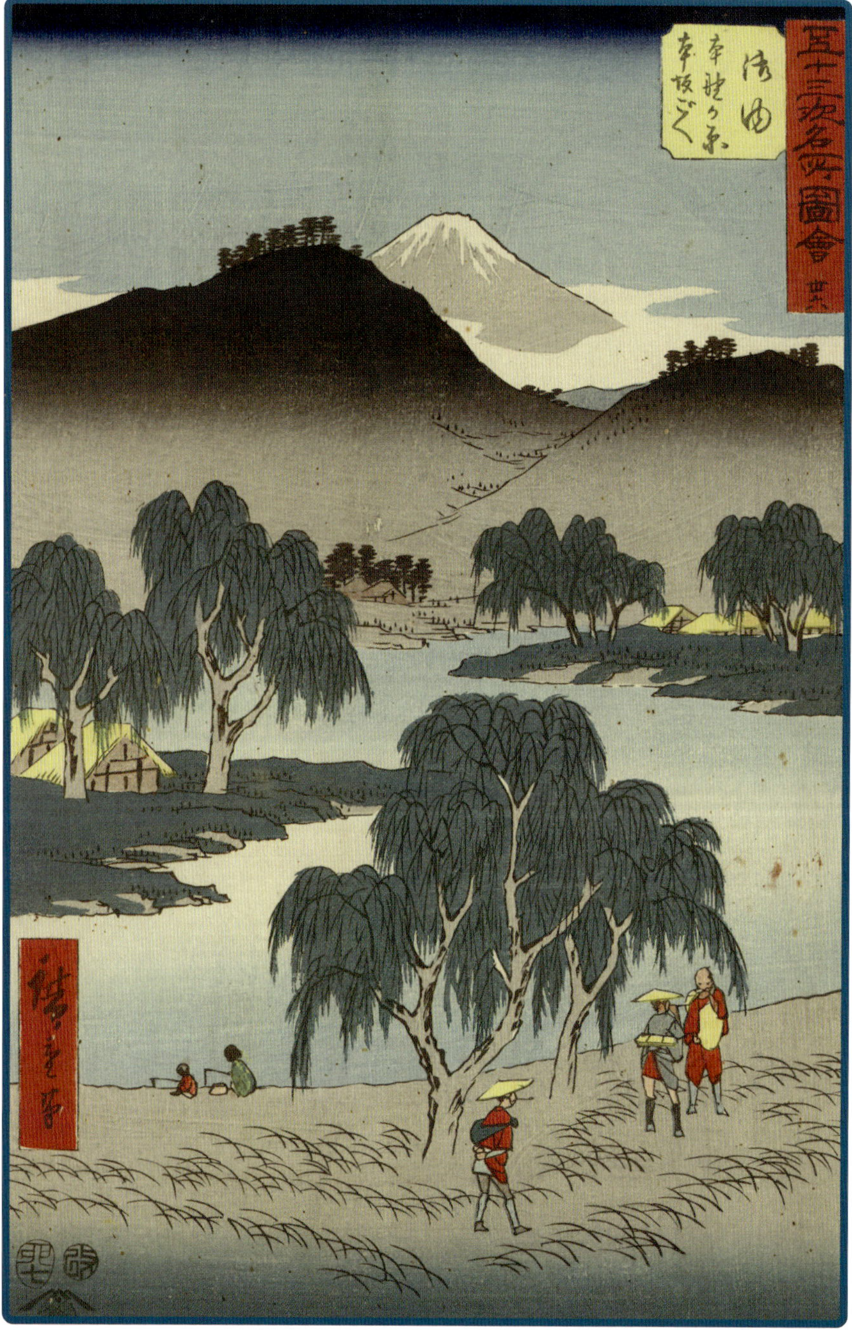

Above **Utagawa Hiroshige (1797–1858)** *Goyu*, the 35th station from 'Famous Views of Fifty-Three Stations of the Tokaido Road' (*c.* 1855)

We can only guess at the influences Hiroshige's specific background and social situation were to have on his wider attitudes – to himself, his world and his work. Far from forgetting his semi-aristocratic antecedents, he was ultimately to make plans for a Samurai-style funeral; in his daily life, he would have taken orders, accommodated clients and for the most part mixed with people of a much less exalted rank. Did he, like Thomas Mann's bourgeois-bohemian writer-protagonist Tonio Kröger in the eponymous novella, experience a sense of being 'between two worlds and a part of neither'? Did that uncertainty prove creative in the end?

Whatever the answer to that question, Tokutaro certainly proved persistent in pursuing an artistic career which, whilst ultimately bringing great success, would arguably do it at the expense of social standing. At the age of about 14, it seems, he managed to become an apprentice to Utagawa Toyohiro (1773–1828), himself a protégé of Utagawa Toyoharu (*c.* 1735–1814), who had founded his own Utagawa School. (As a favoured student, Toyohiro had been invited to assume his master's name, rather as Hokusai had a form of Shunsho's years before, *see* page 64.) An early adopter of Western-style perspective, Toyoharu had been adventurous, too, in the range of genres he tackled, though his own preferred discipline had been landscape art (*see* page 28).

By Toyohiro's time, however, the Utagawa School was big and powerful and encompassed just about every area of *ukiyo-e* art. Like Hokusai before him, as an apprentice Hiroshige found himself directed into an area that was not necessarily the most congenial to him, that of turning out endless *bijin-ga* – prints of female beauties. If he was never really to set the Sumida River on fire with this type of painting, he did well enough to earn the new name Utagawa Hiroshige (a mark of honour, of course, for any apprentice of the Utagawa School).

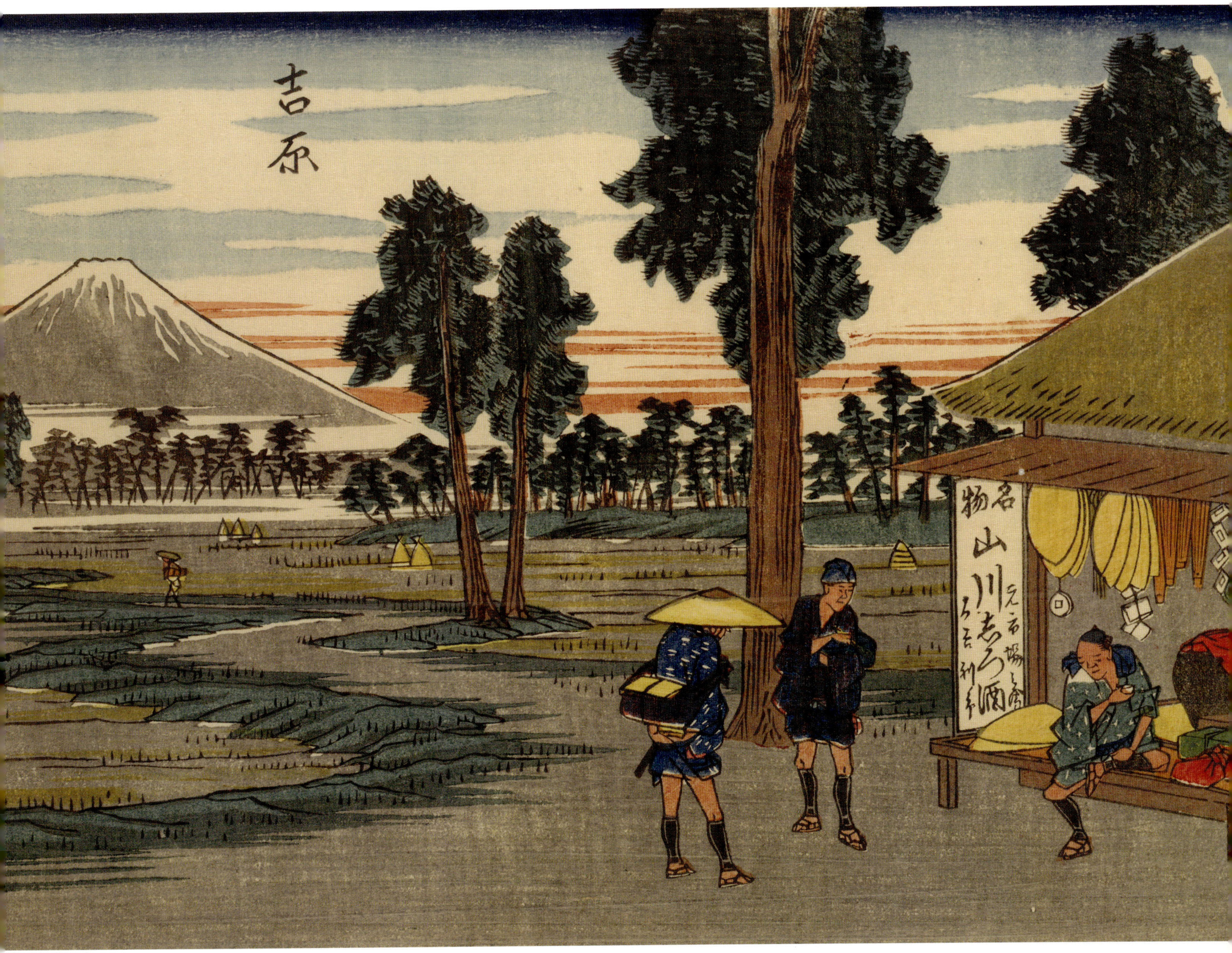

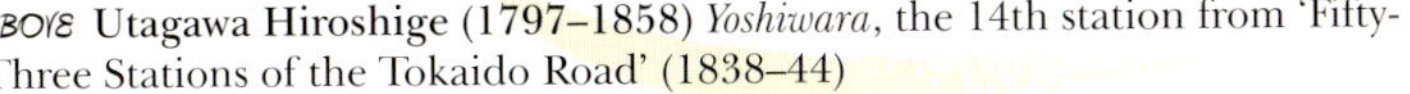

Above Utagawa Hiroshige (1797–1858) *Yoshiwara*, the 14th station from 'Fifty-Three Stations of the Tokaido Road' (1838–44)

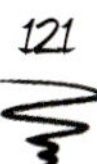

His main influences at this time were older contemporaries, such as his fellow Toyohiro protégé Utagawa Kunisada (1786–1865) and Kikugawa Eizan (1787–1867). And he certainly paid his dues, working in this same area for the next decade or so, branching out only into kabuki actor prints and book illustrations. (Indeed, whilst landscape became his first love – and certainly the basis for his artistic fame – he came to enjoy his work in *bijin-ga*, and continued to produce them.)

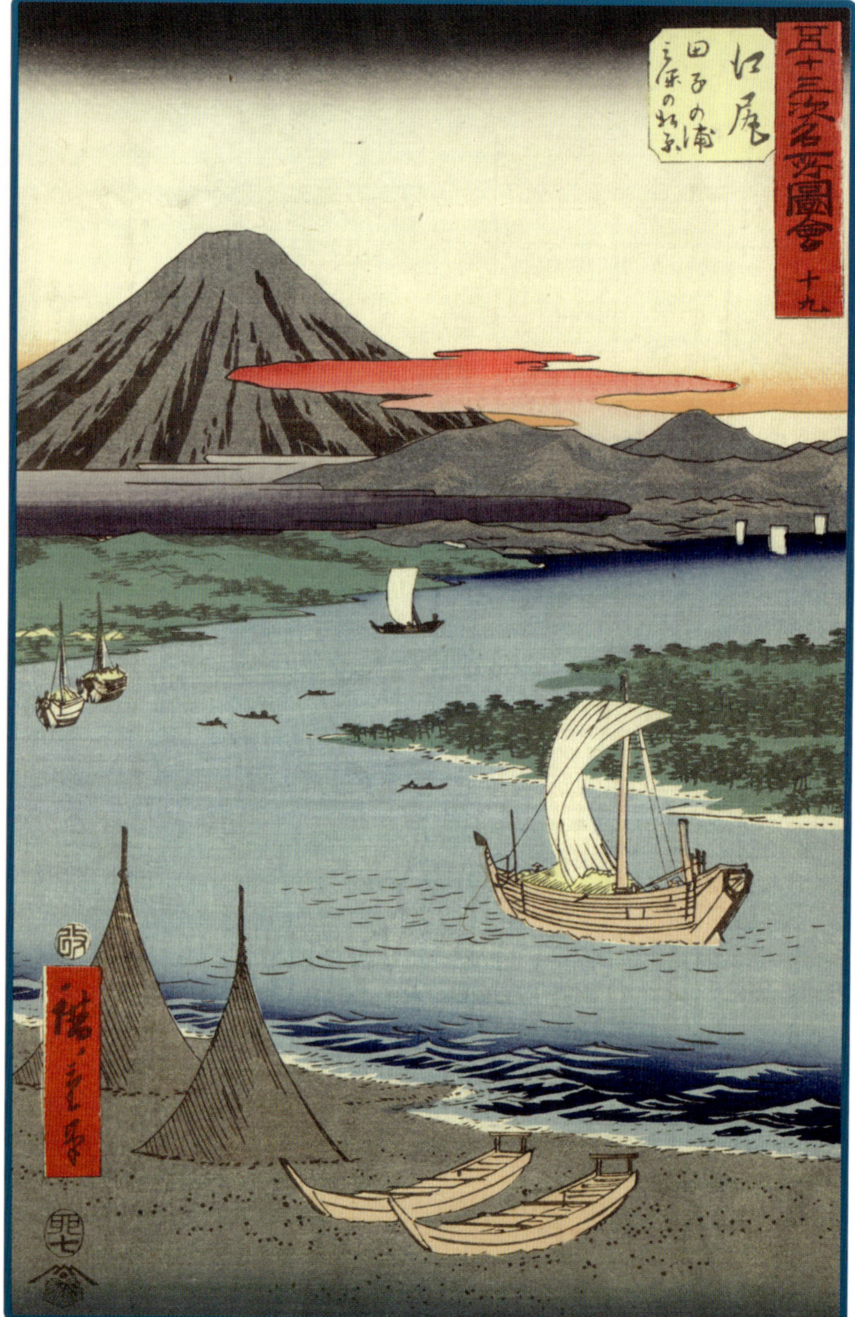

ABOVE **Utagawa Hiroshige (1797–1858)** *Ejiri*, the 19th station from 'Famous Views of Fifty-Three Stations of the Tokaido Road' (*c.* 1855)

Original Sketches

Hiroshige does not seem to have turned to landscape art until about 1830. The honour of being selected to make a special ceremonial expedition along the Tokaido Road to Kyoto that year may have been his catalyst (but then again it may not have – there is very little evidence to support the factual basis of what nevertheless remains a major episode in the mythobiography). The purpose of the journey was to take a purebred white horse from the Shogun to the Emperor, by tradition an annual gift, so it was conducted amidst the utmost pomp and circumstance.

The story goes that, stirred by what he saw along the road during this journey, Hiroshige made rough sketches, which he subsequently made into prints. This approach would have been a little more radical than it may sound. Traditional Japanese art (indeed, oriental art generally) had until this point been to a considerable degree convention-bound. It had never seemed self-evidently desirable to work from life.

That said, it was a recent notion in the West as well, as the art historian Ernst Gombrich (1909–2001) notoriously showed (in *Art and Illusion*, 1960). He described the stylized way in which the German artist Albrecht Dürer (1471–1528) represented a rhinoceros in a famous print of 1515. So celebrated was the rhino's hide for its formidable toughness that he represented it as though it took the form of armour plates. Dürer never claimed to have seen the animal he was depicting; he had worked from earlier engravings and from the folk-zoology in his head. Still, his vision of the rhinoceros essentially shaped European assumptions about the beast's appearance, even for artists who had seen the real thing.

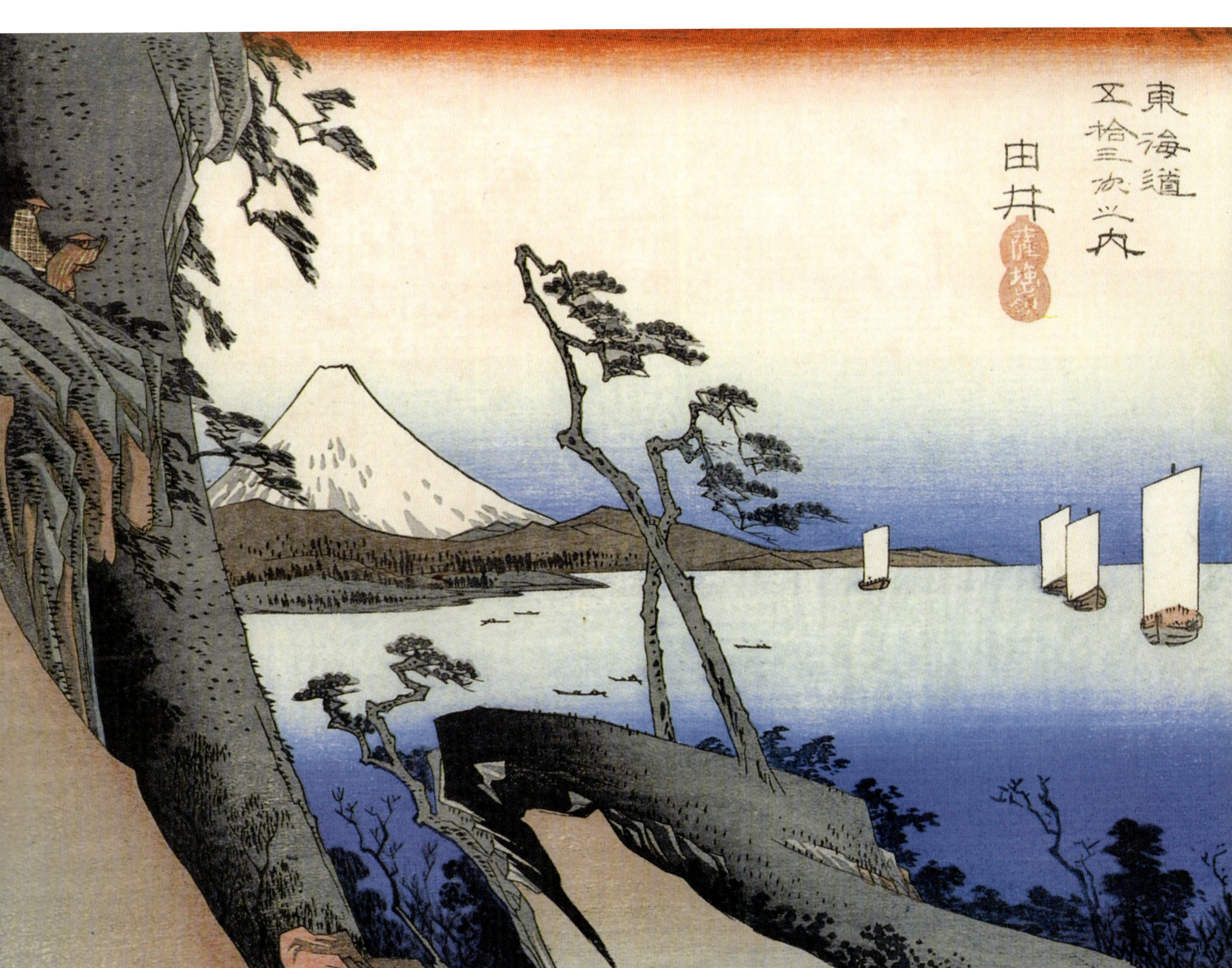

ABOVE **Utagawa Hiroshige** (1797–1858) *Yui*, the 16th station from 'Fifty-Three Stations of the Tokaido Road' (1833–34)

Gombrich gives the example of James Bruce, who in 1790 published a picture he said had been drawn from life, and yet which still had those armour plates.

We 'see' in stereotypes, then, Gombrich suggested, even when we think we do not and even when we sit in front of what we are trying to represent and believe we capture it from life. And this in the context of a Western tradition which had always been more self-consciously mimetic than the Japanese. So Hiroshige's own claims that these landscape prints were the finished copies of original sketches he had made from nature have to be regarded with a certain circumspection.

Painting in Print

Not that it is difficult to see why he made them or why his contemporaries acclaimed the living realism of his works. In some ways, Hiroshige did bring a certain special vividness to landscape art. His care and assiduousness in the use of the technique of *bokashi* ('gradation printing') exemplifies his concern to move beyond stereotypes – or at least to establish new, more sophisticated ones – in giving his pictures a sense of three-dimensional space and depth.

A difficult and in many ways unwieldy business, *bokashi* involves taking the woodblock when it is just ready to print and dabbing away at areas of ink with a damp fabric pad. The result in the areas treated is a thinner, faded effect which, properly managed, can give a sense of distance. On the face of it, the process is perverse: why ink up a woodblock, only to then remove the ink?

More to the point: why try to do in print what one would much more naturally do in paint? It is an interesting question. Many of Hiroshige's greatest works have the air of printed paintings. *Bokashi* features in a great many works by a great many Japanese artists (not least Hokusai), but Hiroshige was to make the technique his own. His lasting reputation as the great master of mists and clouds, of expansive skies and endless ocean waters was well earned, although his achievement arguably runs counter to the strengths of his chosen genre. Was it the artistic challenge

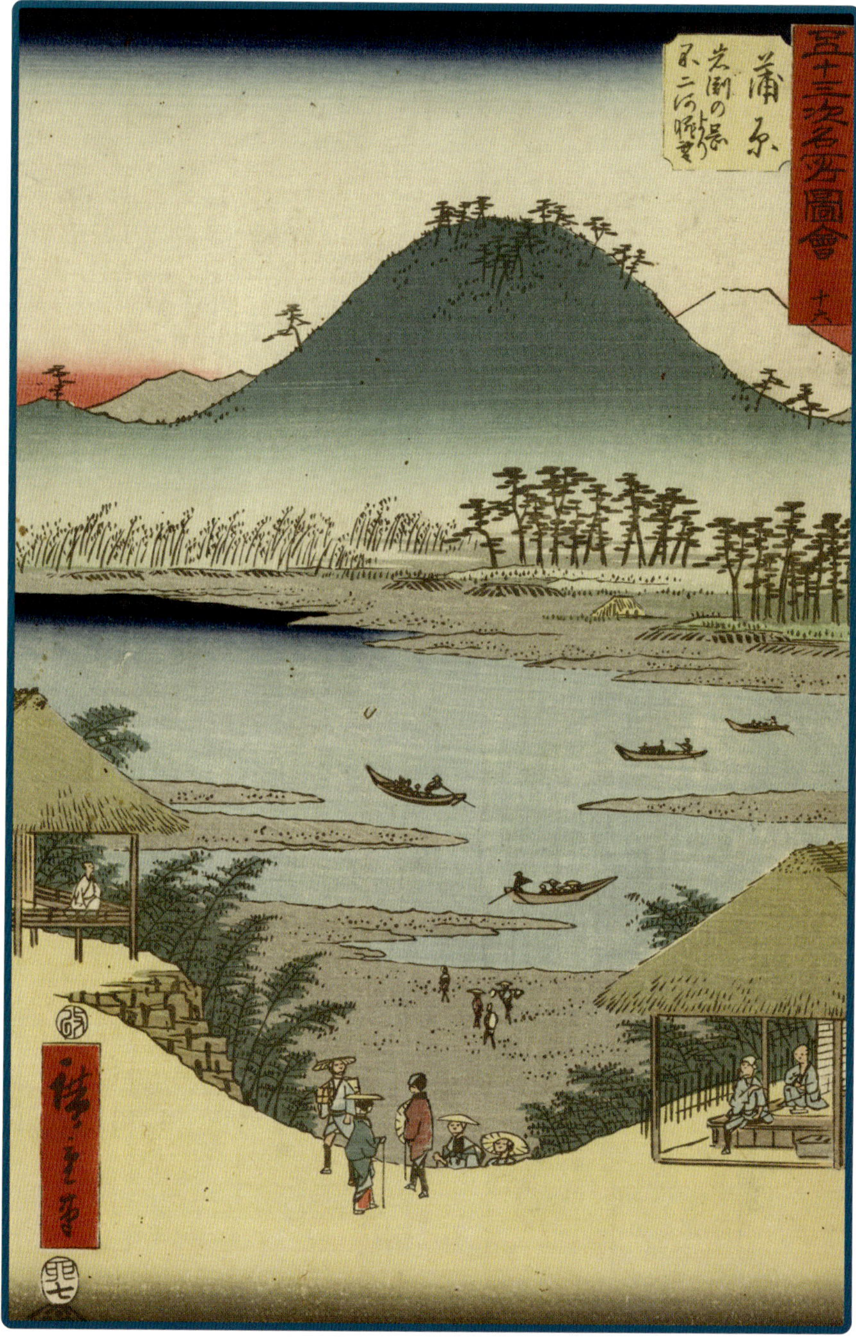

OPPOSITE Utagawa Hiroshige (1797–1858) *Otsu*, the 53rd station from 'Famous Views of Fifty-Three Stations of the Tokaido Road' (*c.* 1855)

ABOVE Utagawa Hiroshige (1797–1858) *Kanbara*, the 15th station from 'Famous Views of Fifty-Three Stations of the Tokaido Road' (*c.* 1855)

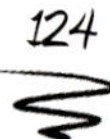

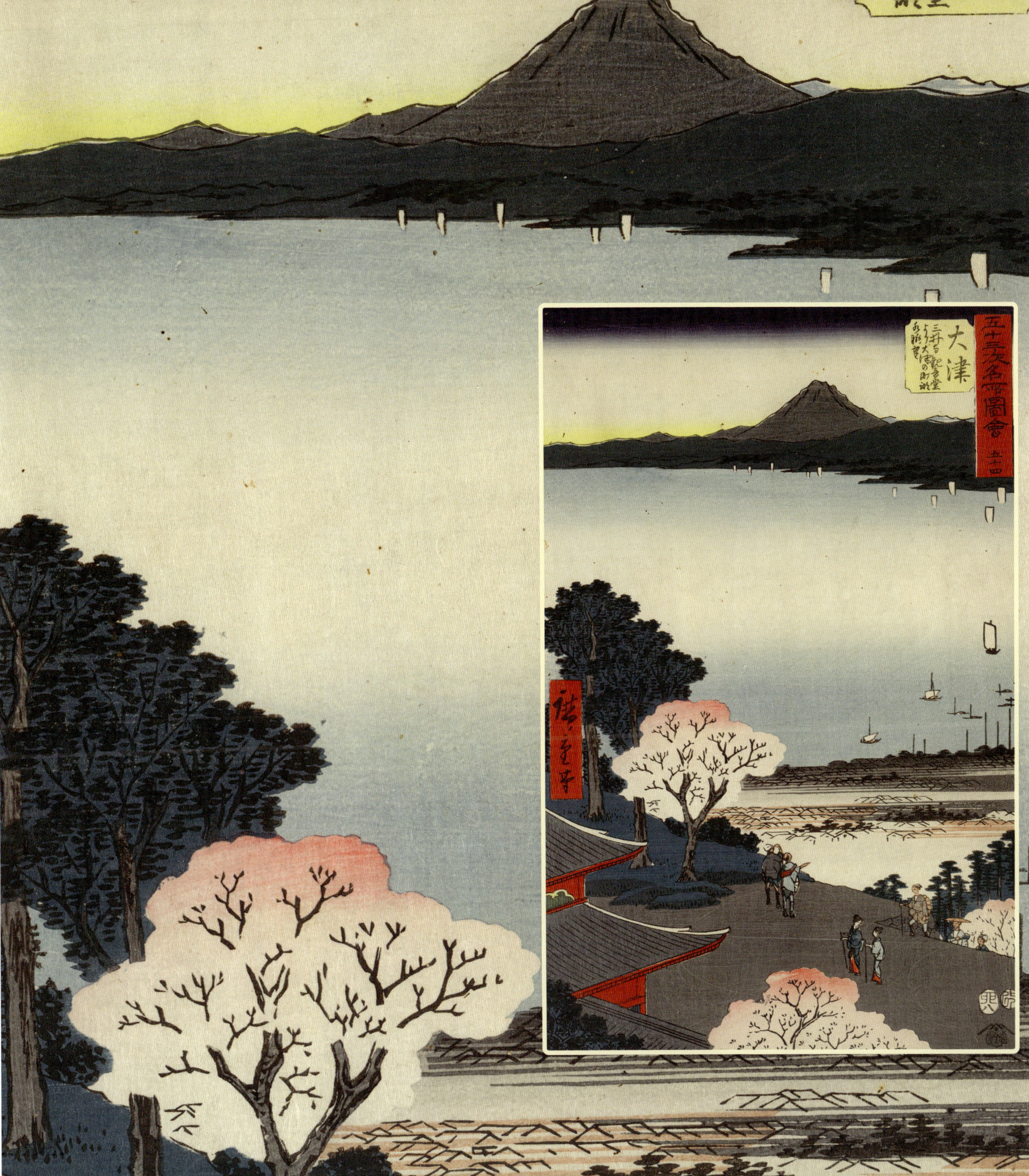
五十三次名所圖會
五十四
大津

he found so absorbing, or a quasi-spiritual one? Never quite so avowedly religious in his artistic expression as Hokusai (though in his final retirement he took orders as a Buddhist monk), he may still have found a deep and mystic satisfaction in this transcendence of apparent bounds.

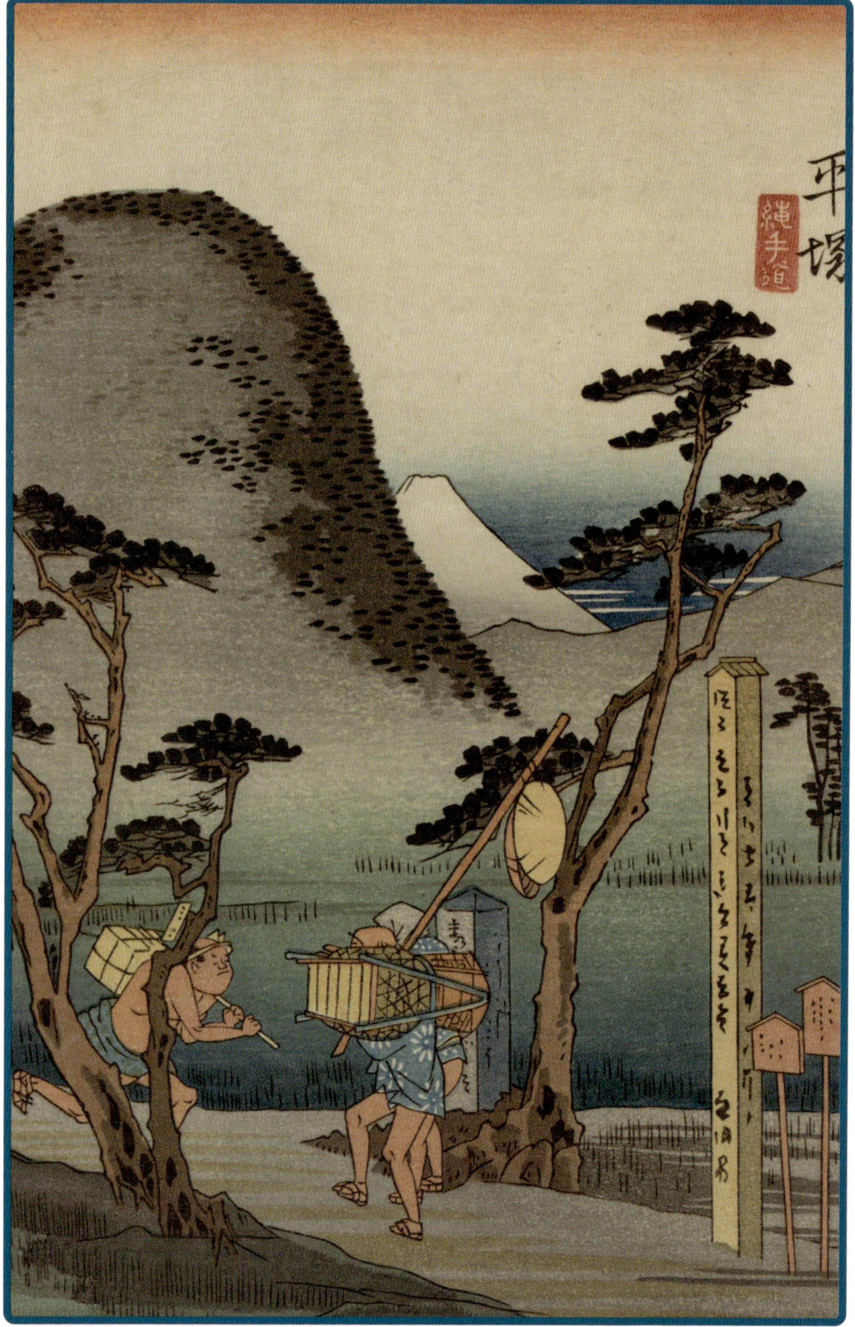

ABOVE **Utagawa Hiroshige (1797–1858)** *Hiratsuka* (detail), the 7th station from 'Fifty-Three Stations of the Tokaido Road' (1833–34, printed later)

Whatever their creative source, and however we evaluate these early prints in terms of their technical innovation, a preliminary 'Eight Views of Omi' appeared in 1831. Mount Fuji did not appear in this work, although it was to crop up a couple of times in 'Famous Views of Our Country' (*c.* 1832) and to loom quite large in sections of the great book-of-the-expedition itself, the 'Fifty-Three Stations of the Tokaido Road' (*c.* 1833–34 – more were to follow after this first key series).

Human Interest

As seen from *Kawasaki* (*see* right), the second station on the Tokaido Road, Mount Fuji is a comforting, protective presence. Wayfarers ride the little ferry over the river, or wait to cross. Leaning into his labour, the boatman toils while his passengers chat, oblivious to his efforts. There is real humour and humanity here, along with the artistry. It is hard to feel there is not also a comic element in the seventh print – this time burlesque. The view from *Hiratsuka* (*see* left) is all but completely blocked by a big and bulbous hill that is as dark and dull as Fujisan is bright, and just about as ungainly as the sacred mountain is elegant.

A more serious note is struck in the view for Station 11, *Hakone* (*see* page 130), the site of a sacred shrine beside a beautiful and atmospheric lake. It is not difficult to see how easily a geological coincidence (Mount Fuji's altitude) came to seem like irresistible evidence of divinity; with its snowy slopes, the mountain stands out here as though transfigured with numinous light.

The human scale is restored once more for the view of *Hara* (*see* page 131), Station 13: two finely dressed ladies make their way past a particularly rugged-looking Fuji (it bursts through the upper 'frame' of the print) with a porter carrying their belongings; a couple of cranes browse in a paddy field behind. Although they are dressed for travel, they still seem faintly incongruous in this setting, and it has been suggested that they are a pair of courtesans.

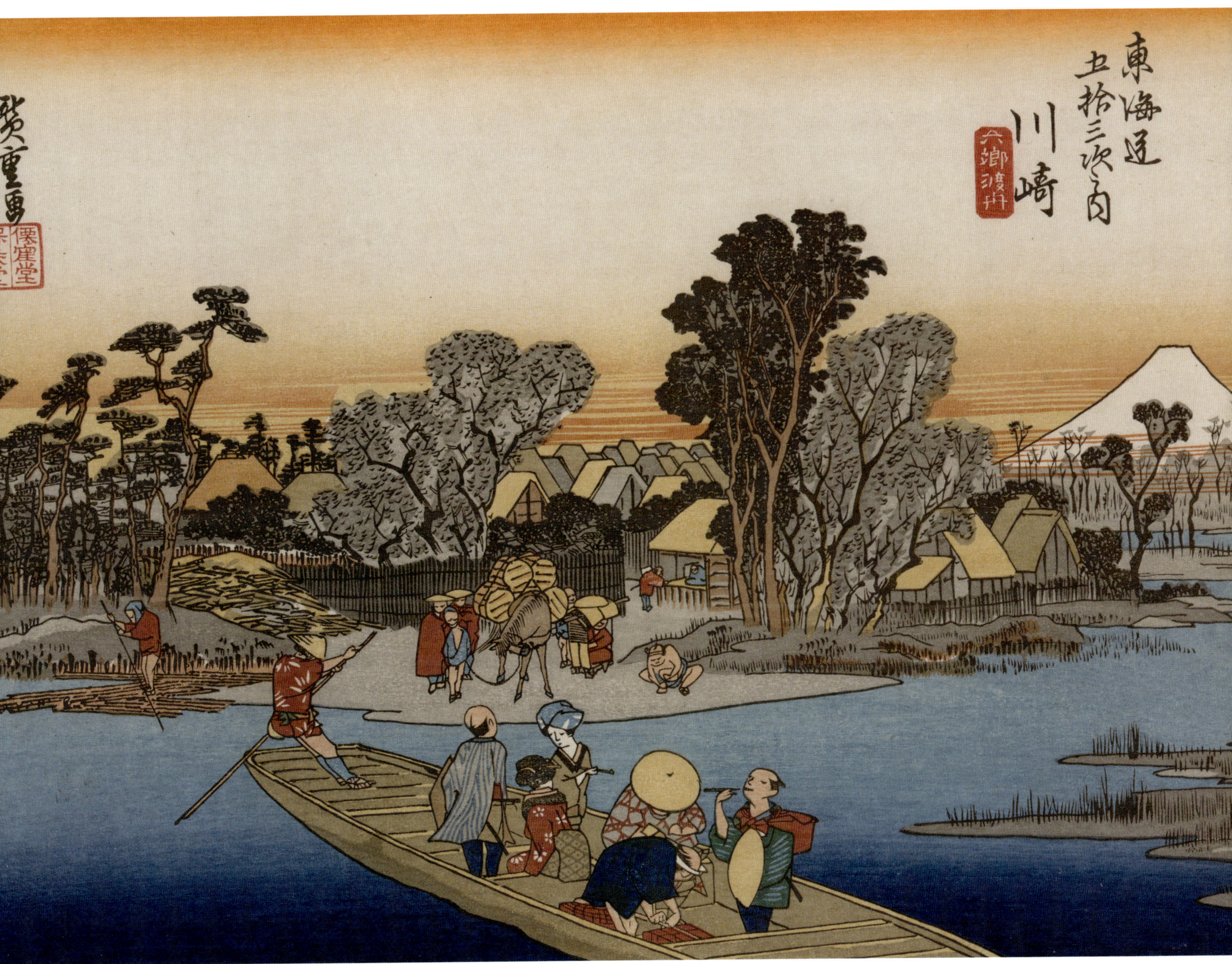

ABOVE Utagawa Hiroshige (1797–1858) *Kawasaki*, the 2nd station from 'Fifty-Three Stations of the Tokaido Road' (1833–34, printed later)

That such questions, from Hiroshige's time to our own, have occasioned serious speculation is a mark of the human impact of these prints. It seems certain that this is an aspect of which Hiroshige (and his contemporaries – he surely would not have been unique in this) would have been well aware and would to some extent have carefully contrived.

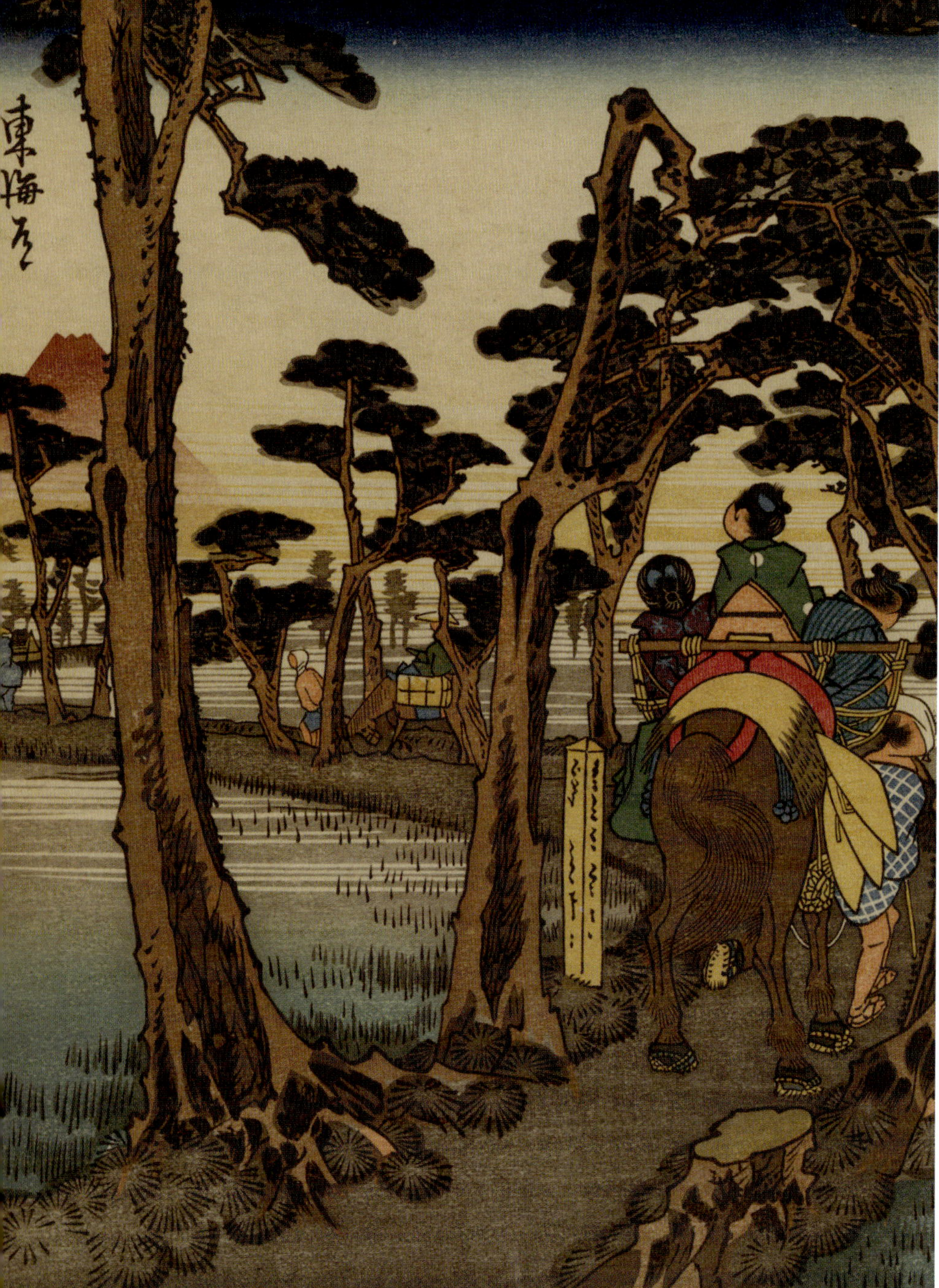

ABOVE **Utagawa Hiroshige** (1797–1858) *Yoshiwara* (detail), the 14th station from 'Fifty-Three Stations of the Tokaido Road' (1833–34, printed later)

Trees and Trails

The road outside *Yoshiwara* (Station 14, *see* left) runs through rice fields across a narrow causeway lined with trees, so close that they seem to form a natural arch. In Hiroshige's print, a group of ladies make their way along this precarious pathway, clinging on as they ride a single horse, led by a groom into this tunnel beneath the boughs, beyond which a russet-coloured Fuji is barely seen. (Again, the viewer cannot help asking: who are these women? Where are they all off to, or where have they just been? What is the story here?) In the view from *Yui* (Station 16, *see* page 123), another group of travellers – this time making their way on foot down a dizzying clifftop path – gaze out wonderingly across Kiyomo Bay to Mount Fuji. Jagged rocks, and trees and shrubs shaped to crazy angles by the battering of the seacoast storms contrast with the eternal smoothness of the sacred mountain.

By this time, of course, travellers who had passed under the very shadow of Fuji as they left Hara had left it quite some way behind. It is almost as a surprise reminder, or an afterthought, then, that it appears in a gap through a motley array of lesser mountains in print 31, which shows the view from *Maisaka* (Station 30, *see* right). Of a series of conical peaks, starting at the centre and diminishing from left to right, Mount Fuji (far right) only overtops the very smallest.

Under the Influence?

It is hard to know how much, if at all, Hiroshige had been influenced by Hokusai in these earlier depictions of Fuji. We know he made his sketches during his journey of 1830, when the 'Thirty-six Views...' had not yet

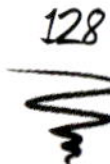

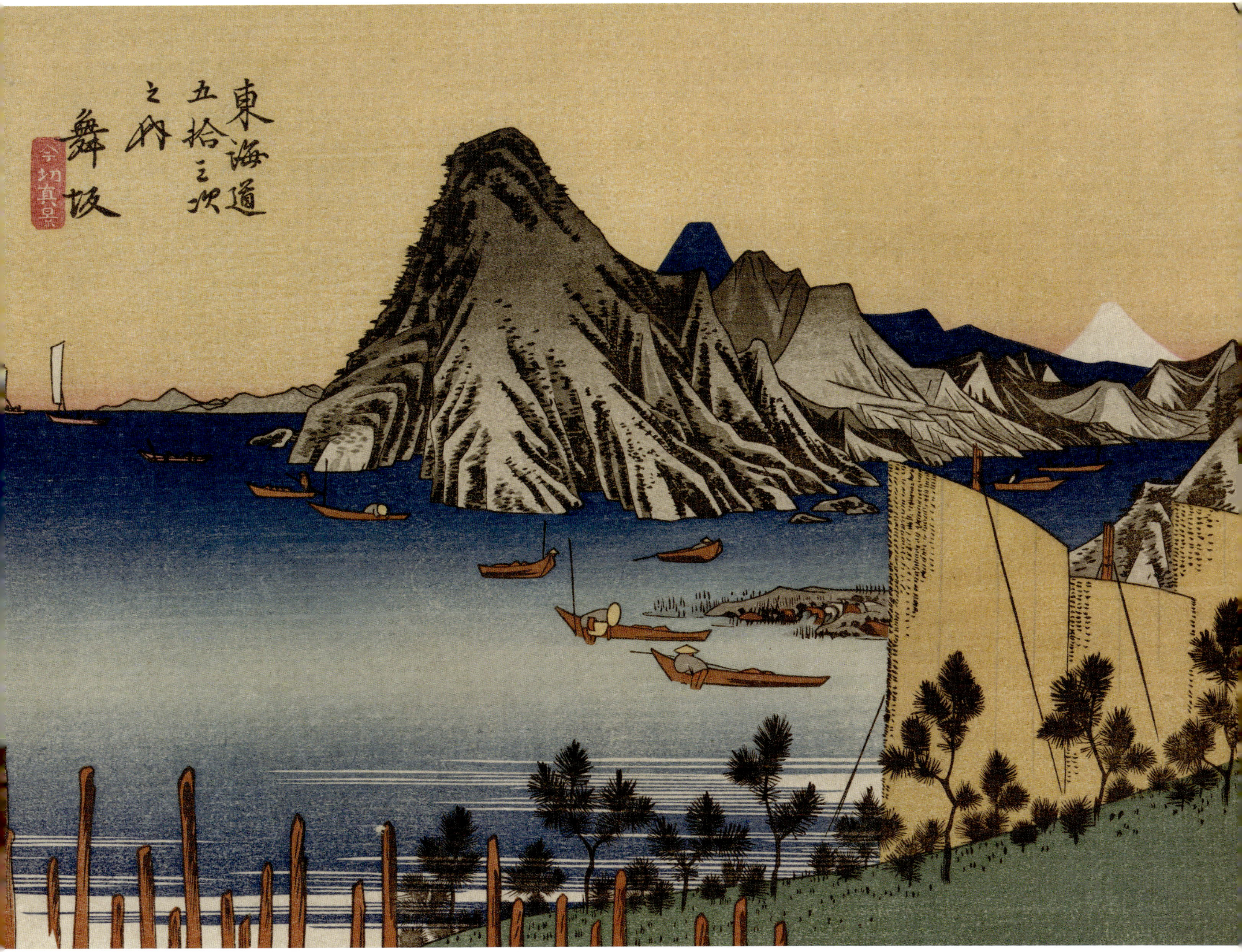

Above **Utagawa Hiroshige** (1797–1858) *Maisaka*, the 30th station from 'Fifty-Three Stations of the Tokaido Road' (1833–34, printed later)

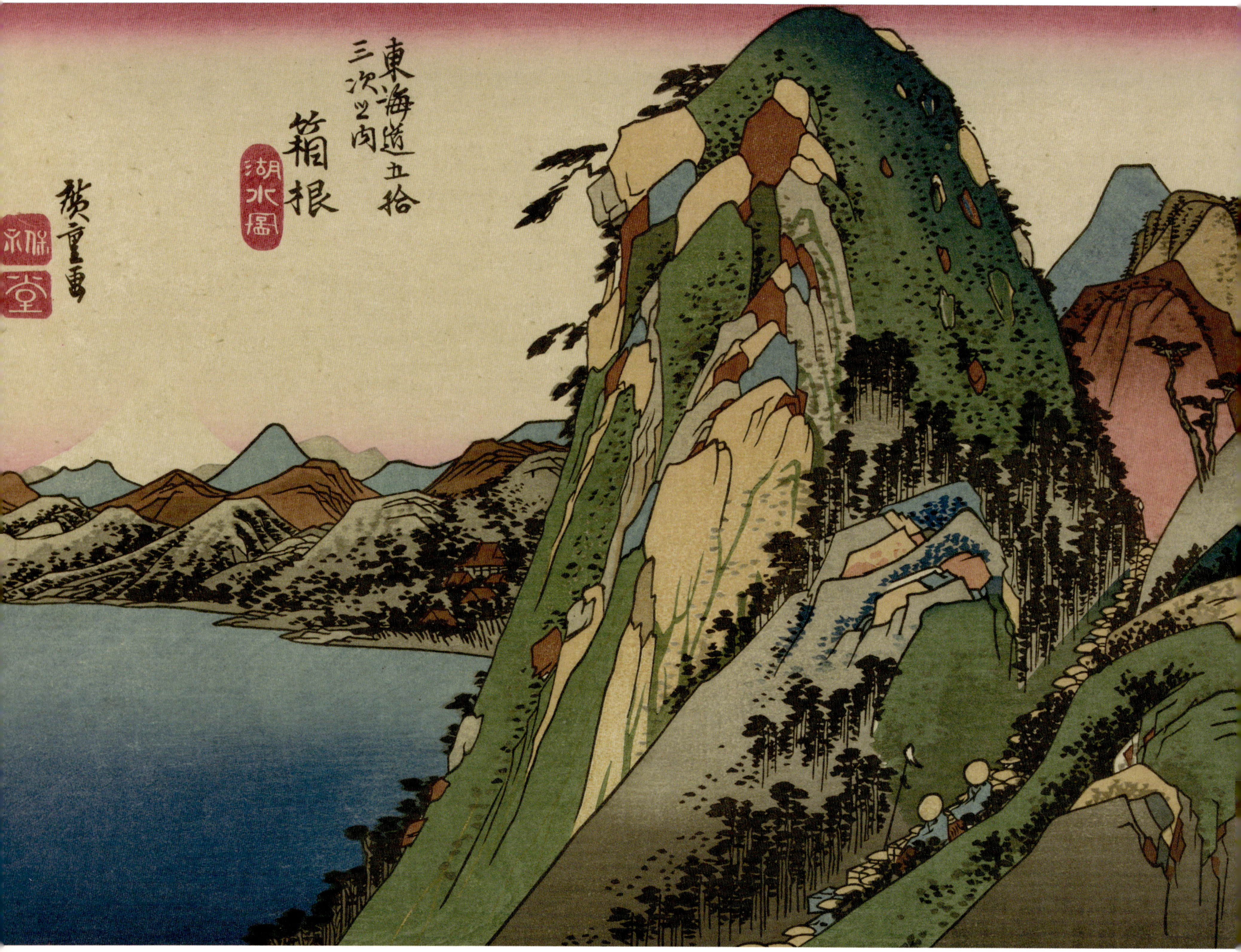

ABOVE **Utagawa Hiroshige** (1797–1858) *Hakone*, the 11th station from ‘Fifty-Three Stations of the Tokaido Road’ (1833–34, printed later)

been published. On the other hand, by the time 'Fifty-three Stations…' began appearing, publication of the 'Thirty-six…' was well under way, so it is by no means impossible that they prompted some of the artistic choices made by Hiroshige.

Even in this comparatively early collection, Fuji is never just another feature. Hiroshige's style is for the most part more realistic, less obviously stylized, than Hokusai's (as in *Hara*, for instance). Even so, Fuji's special charisma is clearly apparent. For this one mountain, he will bend the realist rules – as we have seen in the summer view from *Hakone*: whilst even the highest mountains in the surrounding countryside are lush and green, Fujisan is dazzling white from top to bottom, as though the normal climatological conventions need not apply.

On the Road

Ever since the time of Matsuo Basho (*see* page 30), the travel narrative had held a special place in the Japanese poetic imagination. The 'Narrow Road to the Deep Interior' was a physical road as well as a metaphorical road into the heart of human consciousness, the external and the internal being two sides of the same coin. Hiroshige's great achievement of the 'Fifty-three Stations of the Tokaido Road', it might be argued, was to marry the quest for this more personal self-discovery with a wider and more general curiosity among the Japanese about the identity of themselves and of their country.

That said – and putting Hiroshige's claims to have sketched his prints from life into their due proportion – the portrait the series painted was in many ways idealized. You would certainly never know from this or other, later print series that for much of the 1830s the Japanese countryside was ravaged by famine, with riots in Edo itself. Public confidence in the shogunate, already ebbing fast, was further damaged by the Kogo Fire of 1834 – in which vast areas of Edo were destroyed and an estimated 4,000 people died – and shaken by a terrible earthquake in Sanriku, in Honshu's far north-east. Of course, it might easily have been just such tribulations that fed the desire among the still comfortable classes to see their national realities reflected as cheerfully as they were in Hiroshige's work.

Stations, Harbours, Snow and Flowers

Following up on the success of the 'Fifty-three Stations…', Hiroshige and another artist, Keisai Eisen (1790–1848), were commissioned to capture the 'Sixty-nine Stations of the Kiso Kaido' – a route which tracks the Tokaido Road some way inland. Fuji may be seen from this road too,

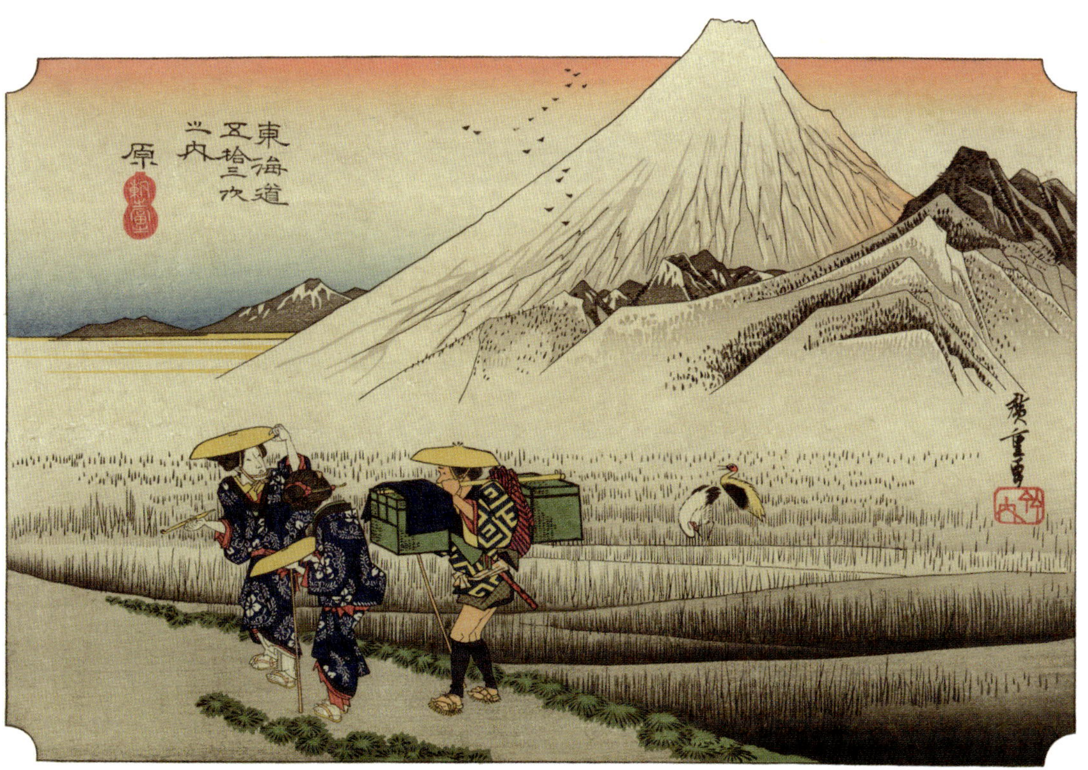

ABOVE Utagawa Hiroshige (1797–1858) *Hara*, the 13th station from 'Fifty-Three Stations of the Tokaido Road' (1833–34, printed later)

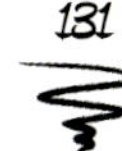

although the section that affords these views fell to Eisen, not Hiroshige. Fuji also makes a cameo appearance in Hiroshige's series 'The Harbours of Japan' (1840–42), in which its white mass rises like a ghostly presence behind the Nihonbashi Bridge, in the port of Edo, echoing his earlier *Evening Shower at Nihonbashi Bridge* (*see* right) from his 1833–43 series 'Famous Views of the Eastern Capital'.

Another lovely one-off appears in 'Famous Places of Snow, Moon and Flowers' (*c.* 1844–48). The very name of this collection underscores the extent to which the *ukiyo-e* artistic culture had come to take an unabashed delight in aestheticizing the Japanese scene – urban and rural – in assessing every outlook for its picturesque possibilities. One of Hiroshige's prettiest portrayals of Fuji is to be found here – though, as so often, it is no more than a background presence – in *Cherry Blossoms on the River Banks at Koganei*. Oddly stunted-looking trees – evidently radically pruned – protrude at crazy angles on either side of a path along which colourfully dressed strollers saunter to a little footbridge. Above an azure river, the blue sky fades to all-but-white – though never quite bright enough to match a dazzling Fuji which, in this view, is framed by a riot of pink-white bursts of blossom. This print also echoes an earlier one, the equally pretty *Evening Glow at Koganei Bridge* (*see* pages 12–13), from his 1838 series 'Eight Views in the Environs of Edo'.

Hiroshige's first wife (whose name is unknown) died in 1839. She had been a real boon to the early part of his career with her driving energy and the resourcefulness with which she had managed to make his meagre artistic earnings stretch. By the time of her death, Hiroshige was professionally established.

'The King is Dead'

In the decade or so that followed, Hiroshige's reputation grew steadily, if slowly, whilst Hokusai's renown was mounting in leaps and bounds. In

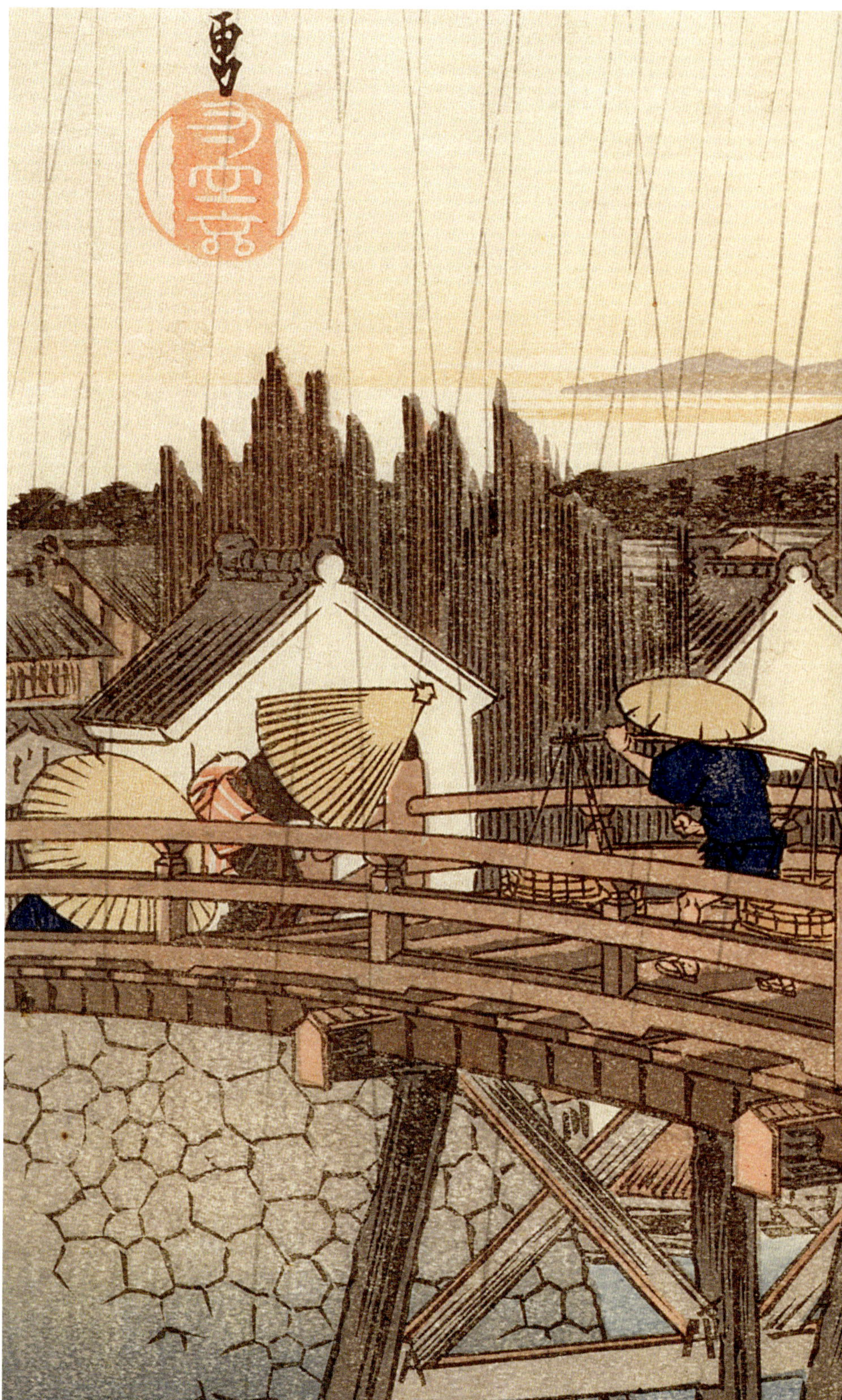

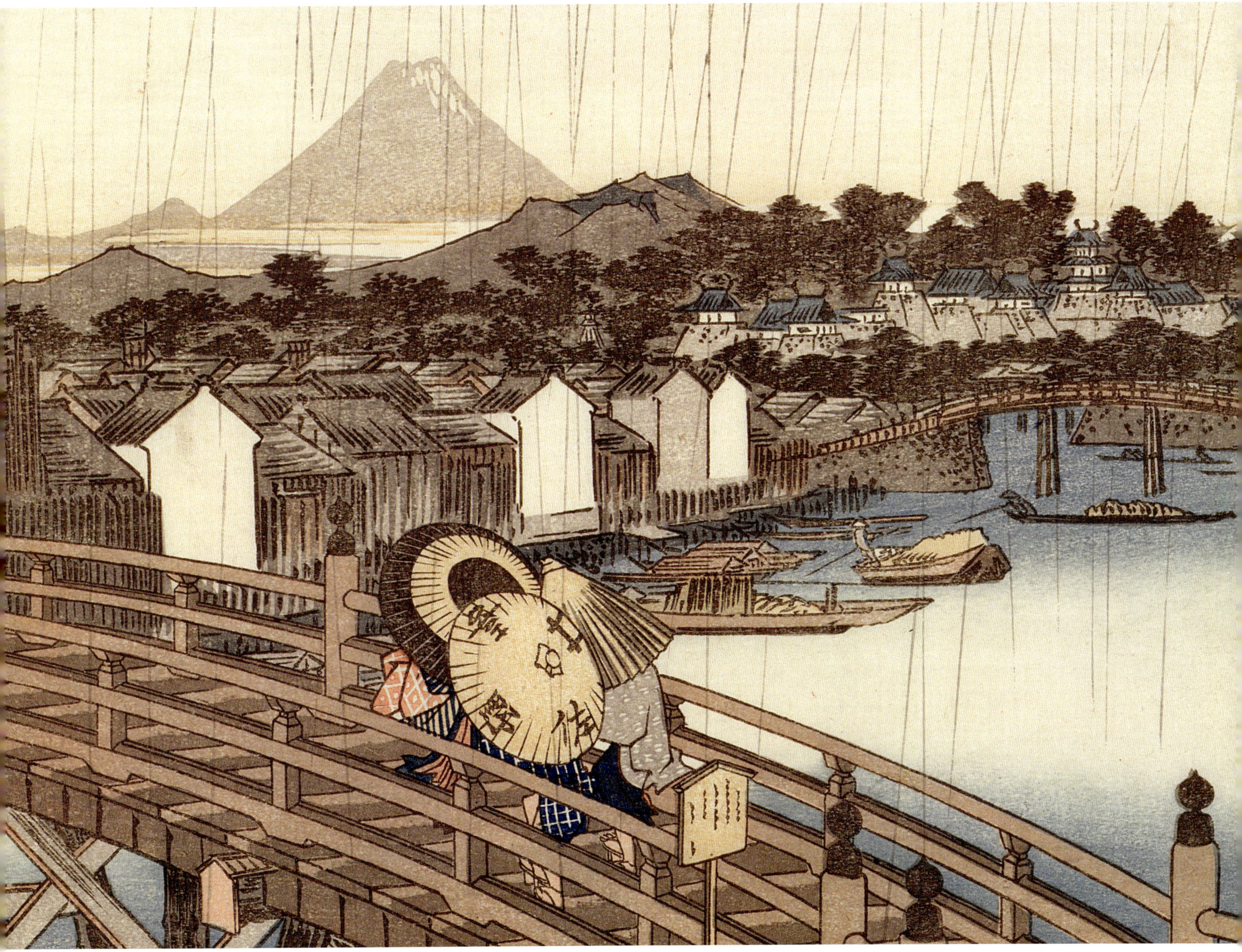

ABOVE Utagawa Hiroshige (1797–1858) *Evening Shower at Nihonbashi Bridge* from 'Famous Views of the Eastern Capital' (1833–43)

1847, Hiroshige remarried – this time to a farmer's daughter – not much is known about her other than her name, which was Oyasu. By 1849, when 'The Old Man Who's Mad About Art' (as Hokusai had taken to signing himself) died, he was the Japanese art world's acknowledged superstar.

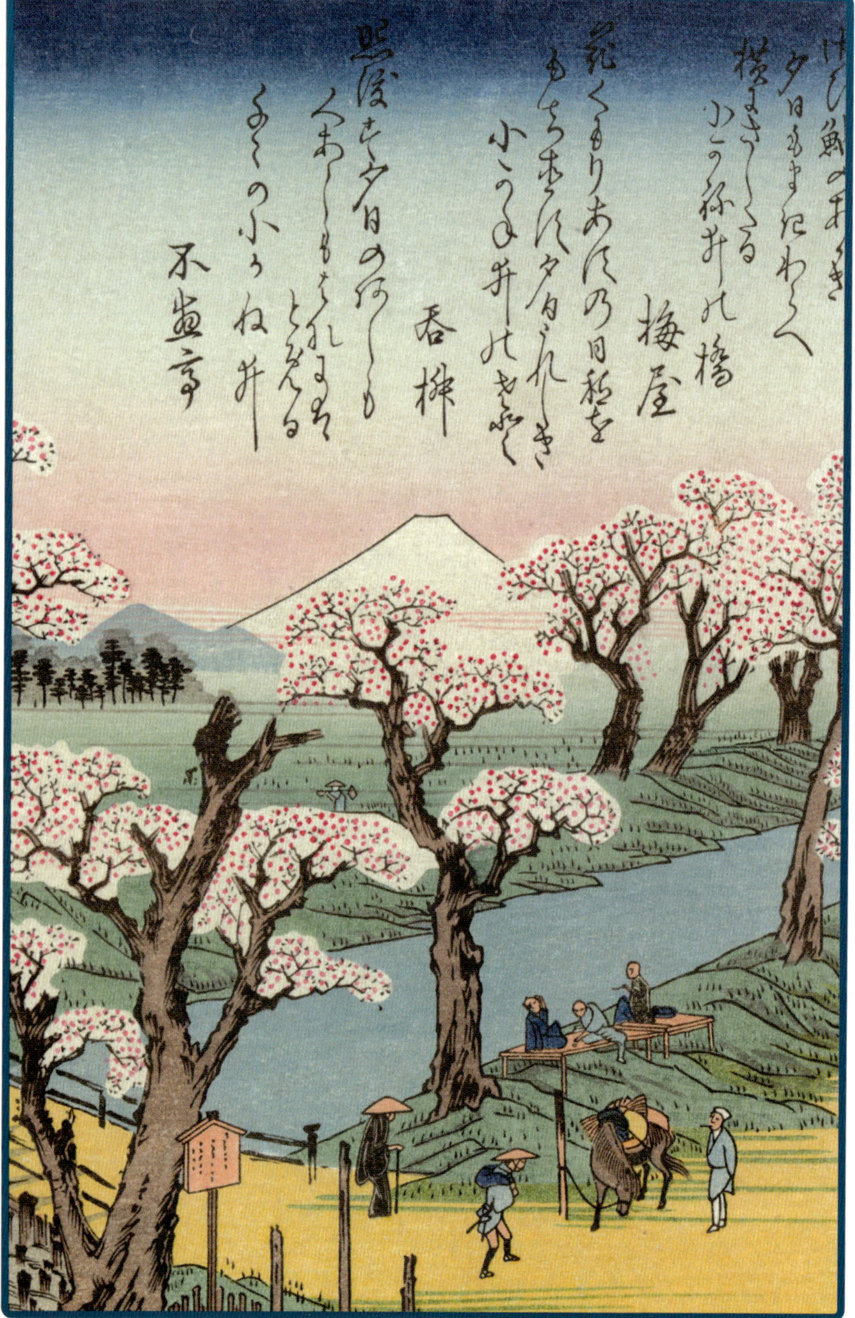

ABOVE Utagawa Hiroshige (1797–1858) *Evening Glow at Koganei Bridge* (detail), from 'Eight Views in the Environs of Edo' (1838)

It was only natural that Hiroshige would have aspirations to take his place. Quite how conscious he was of this intention when, from 1850, he started working on the first of his own two 'Thirty-six Views of Fuji' series, we cannot know, but Hokusai's collection was extremely well-known.

Completed by 1852, this first of Hiroshige's major runs at Fujisan has an austere look, despite its use of colour. In *Sawtooth Mountain in Awa Province*, the mountain rears up sheer, snow-white and weightless above a gunmetal grey range of hills and a reed-edged lake of blue with fishing boats. The division between workaday reality and the spiritual realm represented by Mount Fuji could hardly be more clear. In *Seashore in Izu Province*, by contrast, we have to strain to make out the famous form through the arch of a sea-stack and the haze of a sunlit bay – just as we see one of the figures on the shore having to do.

Symmetry is key in *Rough Sea at Shichirigahama ('Seven Ri Beach') in Sagami Province* (*see* right), in which we view Fuji through the gap between two highly stylized waves, whose trough mirrors the rise of a white Mount Fuji in the background. Framing the famous mountain on either side, a third wave, towering towards the background of the picture, balances out a vegetation-covered promontory. In *Tanabata Festival in Edo*, Mount Fuji rises smooth and clear above a foreground 'floor' of corrugated rooftops, above which leafy boughs wave, bedecked with brightly coloured streamers. Texture is important too in *The Musashi Plain*, a prospect across beds of swaying sedge to where a flock of geese flies across the face of Fuji.

Hiroshige's view of *Aoyama in the Eastern Capital* hinges on the opposition of expansive blocks of black and white, with a pallid Fuji fronted by a dark and jagged mountain skyline. In the morning or evening half-light, the trees in the foreground are seen almost in silhouette. Colour comes to the fore in prints like *Sagami River* and *Inume ('Dog Eye') Pass in Kai Province*, both represented in the rich red light of dusk or daybreak. In the former, it is the sky that is flushed; in the latter, it is the landscape, a scene of valleys, crags and woods that take on a tinge of pink.

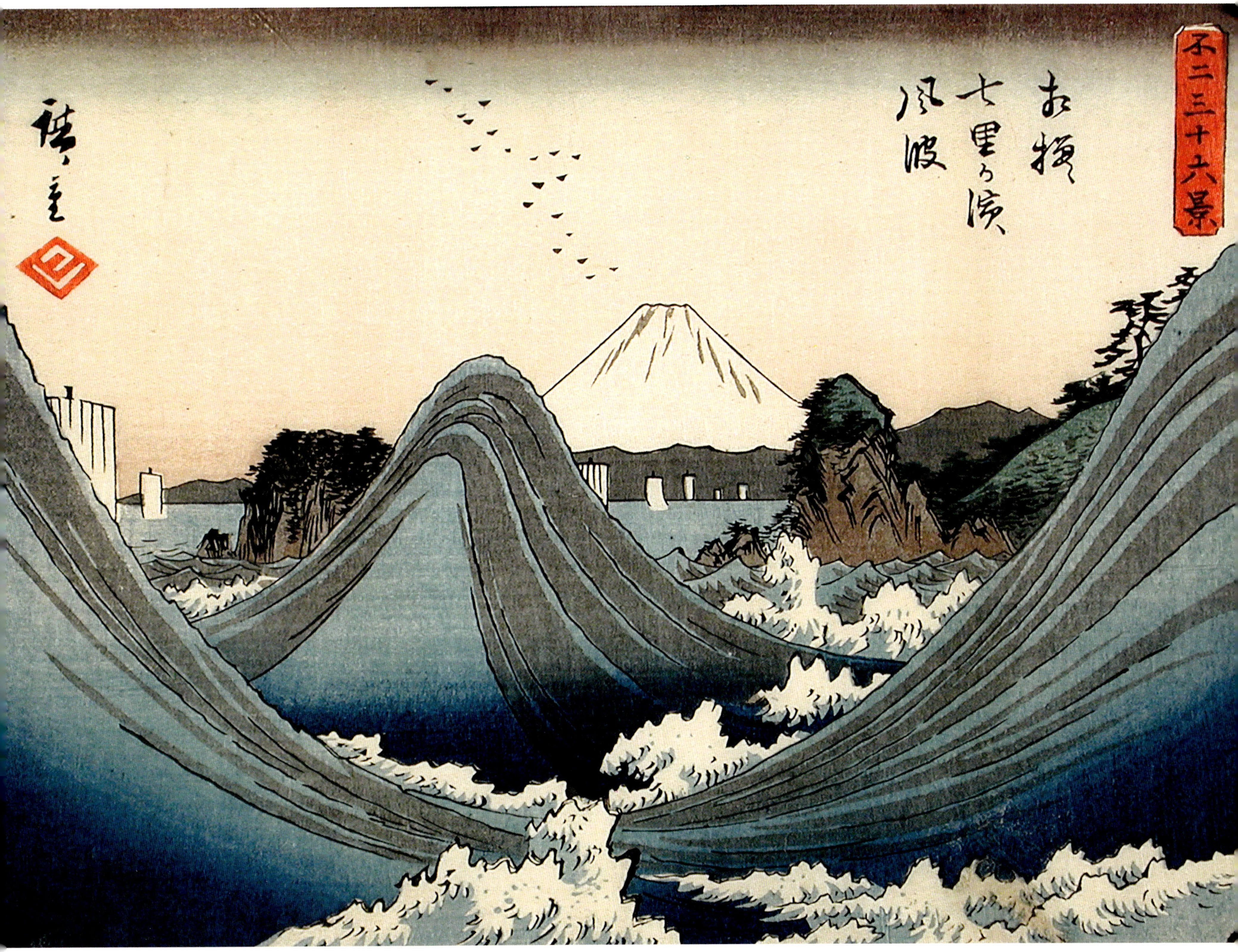

ABOVE Utagawa Hiroshige (1797–1858) *Rough Sea at Shichirigahama ('Seven Ri Beach') in Sagami Province* from 'Thirty-six Views of Mount Fuji' (1852)

Take Two

Whilst the 1852 series has its beauties, it is generally considered that Hiroshige really found his form with his second series, which appeared in 1858. Much had happened since the first series came out – not so much to Hiroshige as to Japan (though of course he can hardly be separated from his context). The arrival of the Americans (*see* page 29) and the final, brutal breaking of the *sakoku*, the opening up of Japan to trade, had thrown the country into economic, political, social – and, of course, psychological – confusion.

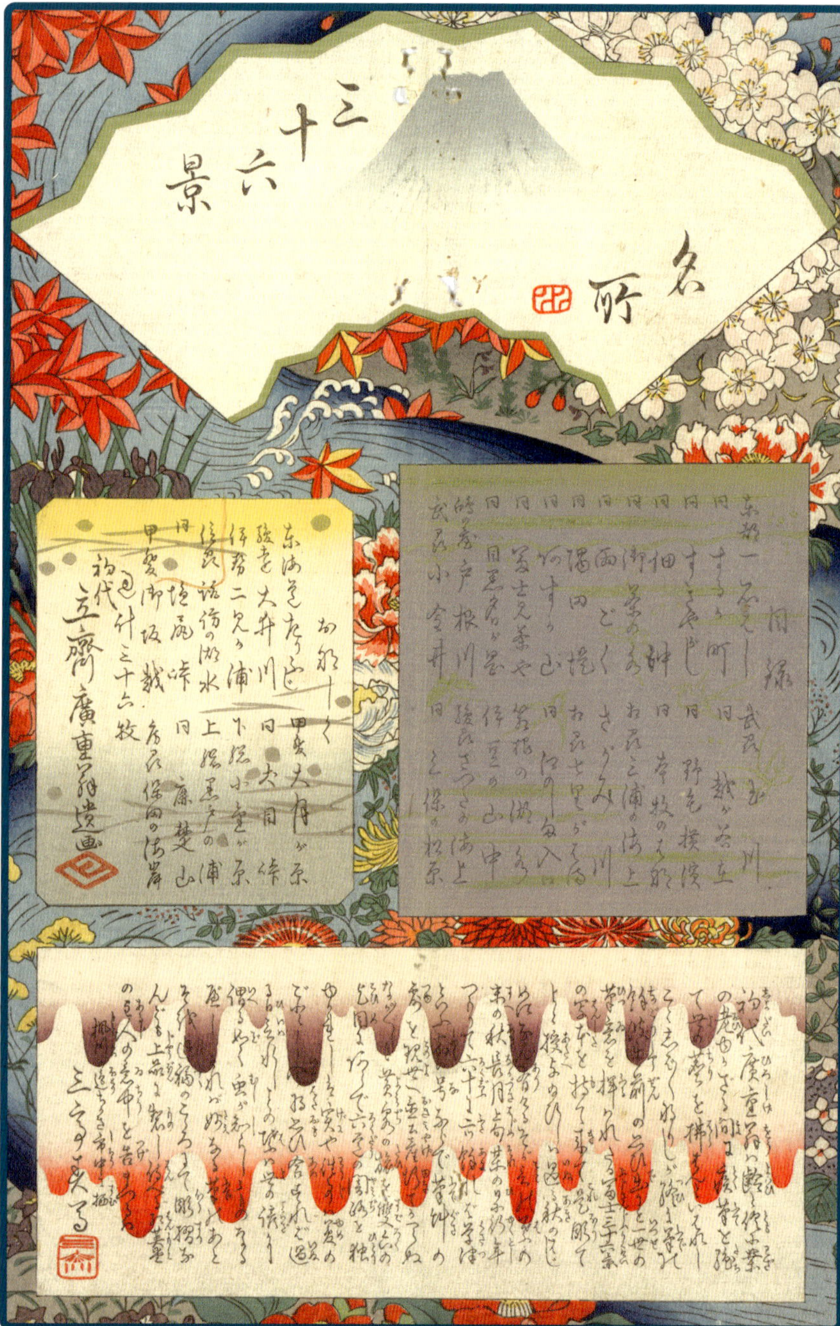

ABOVE Utagawa Hiroshige (1797–1858) Contents page from 'Thirty-six Views of Mount Fuji' (1858)

The most immediately striking difference between this second series and its predecessor, however, is that it presents its subjects in portrait rather than landscape format. Just as the first 'Thirty-six Views…' came into the world apparently oblivious to the famine, the Kogo Fire and the various political conflagrations of the early 1830s, the second seemed somehow to have stayed immune to all the country's ills in the years since. This in itself, it might of course be argued, was a way of handling unbearable realities. Hiroshige's art was representational not of Japan but of its conservative denial.

In any case, when we look closer, we see at least the suggestions of further developments – of more fully worked line and deeper, more sumptuous colour, for example. The difference is apparent even on the contents page (*see* left), in which the order of prints is set out against a background of blue water swirling with lotus flowers and other blossoms of red and white. Above, the arc of an outspread fan runs counter to the curves of an upward-sloping Fuji; geometric play is to be as important as colour in this collection.

Both are in evidence in the opening picture, which shows *The Ichikoku Bridge in the Eastern Capital* (or *Tokyo*, the name by which Edo was increasingly becoming known, *see* right.). Just as the bridge's curve (and that of another in the middle distance) balance the form of Fuji in the background, the rich green foliage of the trees on either side contrasts with the view to a snowy summit across a silver sea. If the distant volcano barely gets a look-in in Hiroshige's view of the crowded streets and colourful hoardings of *The Suruga District in the Eastern Capital* (*see* page

70), it is all-change for *Sukiyagahsi in the Eastern Capital* (*see* page 14). With a layer of snow spread out across the town before us, covering rooftops, trees and even fishing boats, it is as though the white form of Fujisan has extended itself to engulf the entire scene.

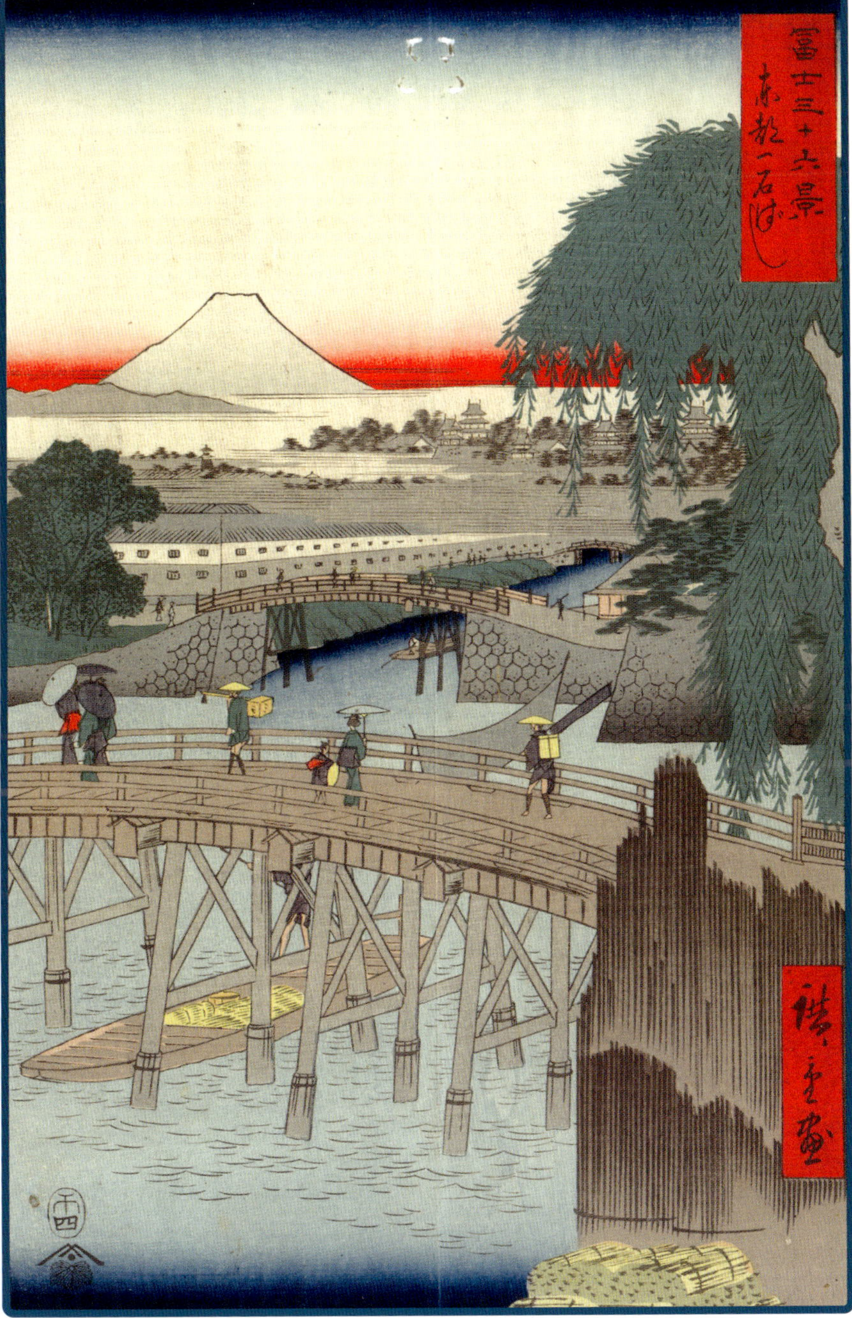

Above Utagawa Hiroshige (1797–1858) *Ichikoku Bridge in the Eastern Capital* from 'Thirty-six Views of Mount Fuji' (1858)

Compare and Contrast

Off Tsukuda Island in the Eastern Captial (*see* below) allows us to revisit a scene we saw in Hokusai's 'Thirty-six Views…'. His standpoint as low

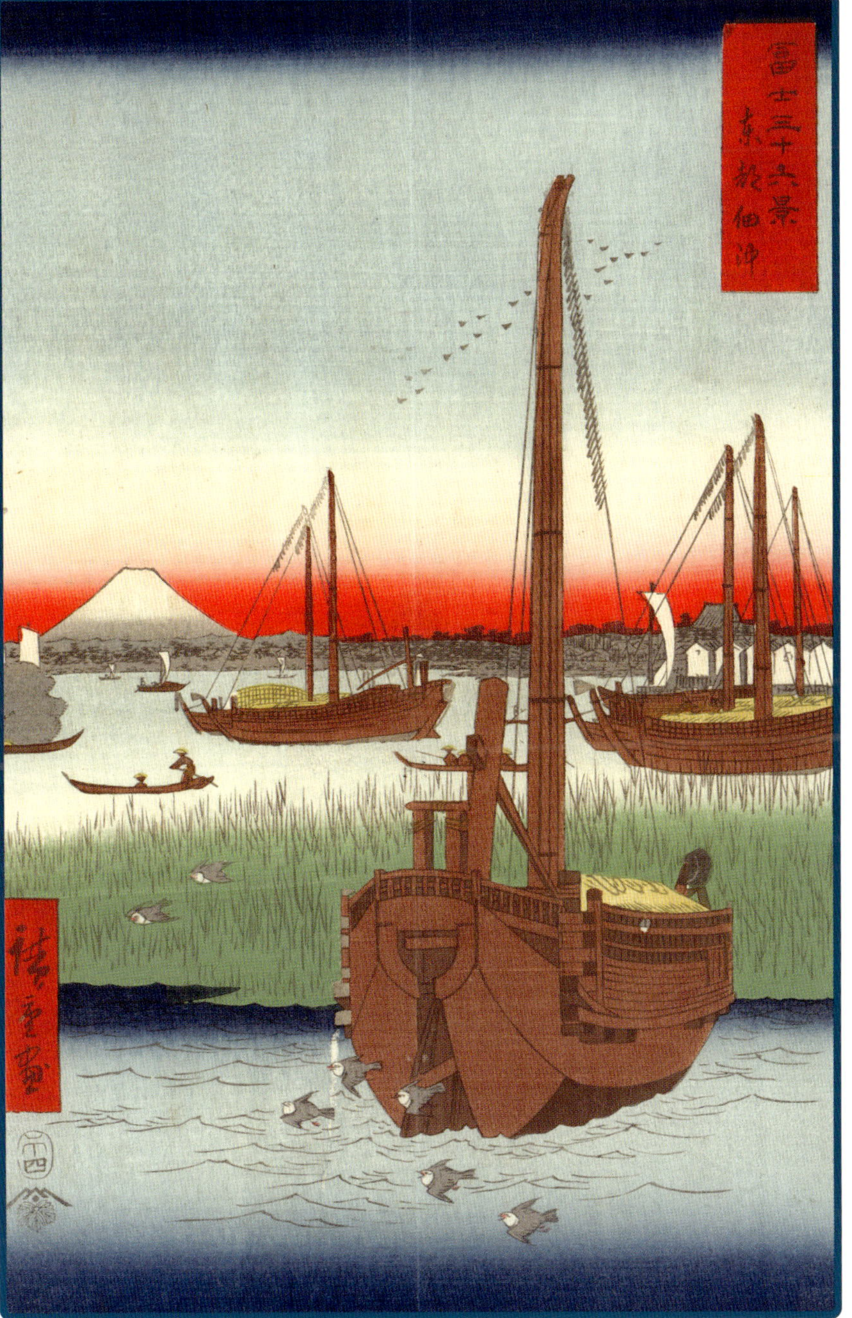

Above Utagawa Hiroshige (1797–1858) *Off Tsukuda Island in the Eastern Capital* from 'Thirty-six Views of Mount Fuji' (1858)

in the sky as the setting sun, Hiroshige looks across the water towards this artificial island in the mouth of the Sumida River, past boats and reed beds to a grey-white skyline and, beyond, a blush of grenadine. We find ourselves in old Hokusai haunts in *Ryogoku in the Eastern Captital*

(*see* below) too, though this pleasure party appears to be embarking from a jetty rather closer to the bridge. The seemingly greater intimacy of Hiroshige's scene is in part owed to the number of people, and partly to his use of the vertical portrait format. But he is also careful to 'frame' his

ABOVE Utagawa Hiroshige (1797–1858) *Ryogoku in the Eastern Capital* from 'Thirty-six Views of Mount Fuji' (1858)

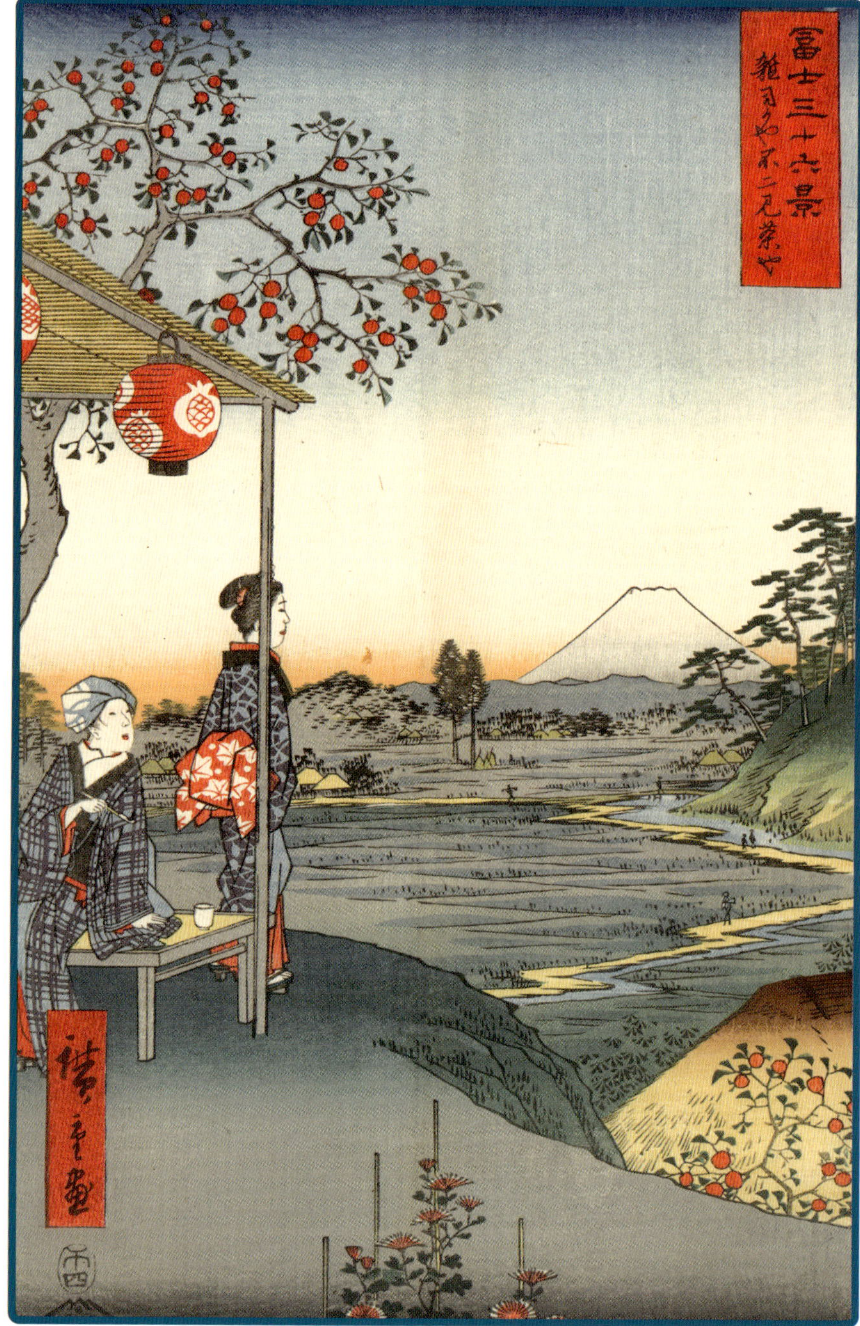

ABOVE Utagawa Hiroshige (1797–1858) *The Teahouse with the View of Mount Fuji at Zoshigaya* from 'Thirty-six Views of Mount Fuji' (1858)

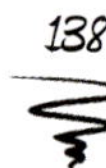

human subjects within the wider picture, closing the couple in between the downward-spreading branches and bridge and the boat with its upward-curving keel.

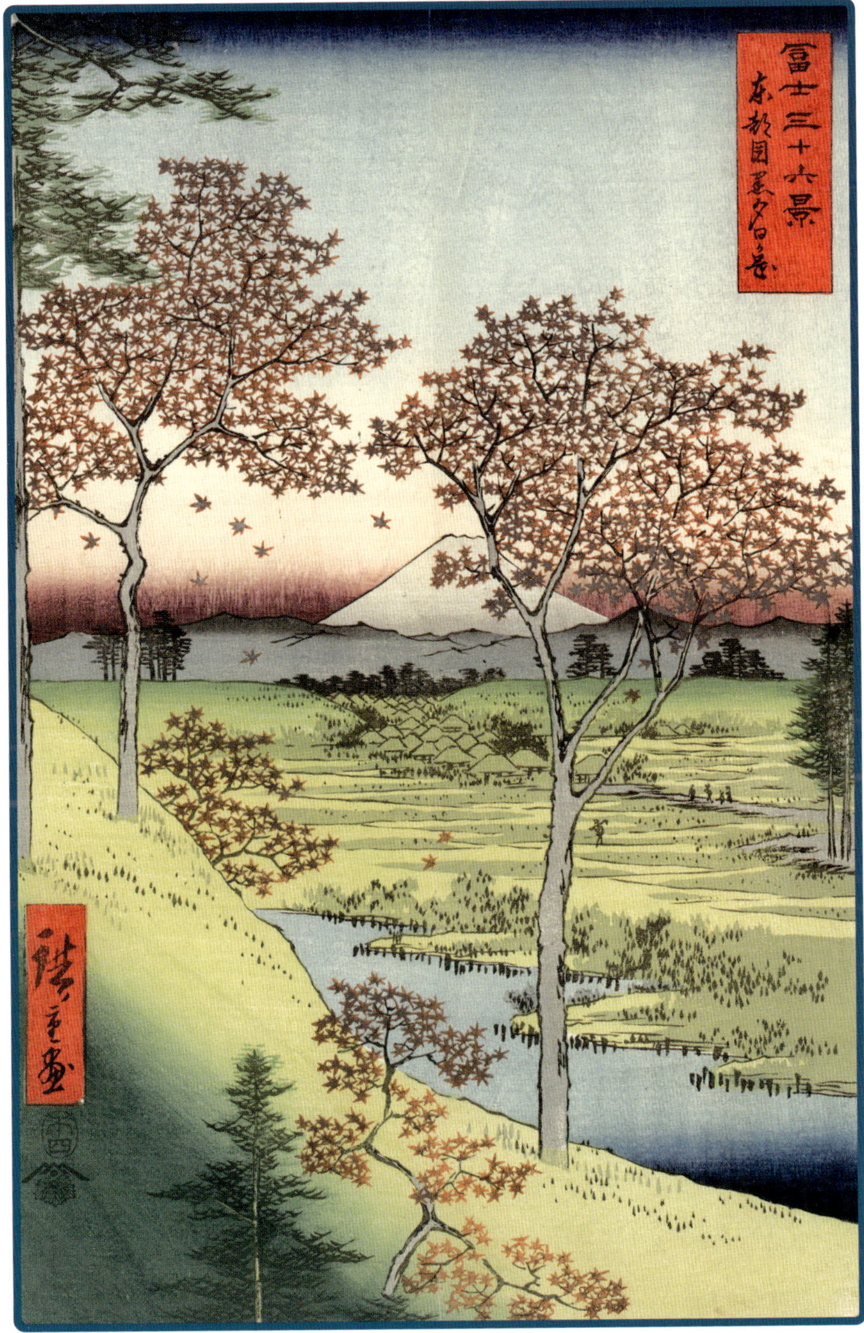

ABOVE Utagawa Hiroshige (1797–1858) *Twilight Hill at Meguro in the Eastern Capital* from 'Thirty-six Views of Mount Fuji' (1858)

Bijin Beauty

Hokusai's landscapes were, we saw, only seldom absolutely unpeopled, but the human figures for the most part were not 'scenic' in any way. In *The Sumida Embankment in the Eastern Capital* (*see* page 40), however, the two *bijin* we see out strolling together are every bit as picturesque as is their setting, a beautiful riverside park lined with cherry trees, their branches laden with blossoms. The young women's costumes are rich and warmly coloured, the shapely sinuousness of their figures given emphasis by the slender tree trunks beside them, the position of the older woman, coming up the embankment from below, underlining their height.

If in *Mount Asuka in the Eastern Capital* (*see* page 118, middle row, second from left) we barely register the people out walking for the explosion of cherry blossom above their heads, *The Teahouse with the View of Mount Fuji at Zoshigaya* (*see* opposite) restores human, feminine beauty to centre stage. Here, with the sun apparently all but set and the scene slipping into something approaching darkness, the standing girl's *obi* (sash) stands out in the same bright red as the lanterns behind her and the blossoms above her head.

Seasonal Cheer?

Dead leaves fall across a yellowing, faintly threadbare landscape and fleck the white face of faraway Fujisan in Hiroshige's view of *Twilight Hill at Meguro in the Eastern Capital* (*see* left). Given its name, it makes sense that we should see this setting at the close of day – and in autumn, at the closing of the year. *Koganei in Musashi Province* (*see* page 30) shows us Mount Fuji in the springtime, though the festive mood is tempered by the wizened and crooked tree trunk (through a gaping hole in which we actually view the mountain) in the foreground and the ragged wreck of a tree behind. Both the big trees are grotesquely time-ravaged, but both are putting out impressive displays of blossom. What does it mean? Is Hiroshige's glass half-empty or half-full?

The scene at *Koshigaya in Musashi Province* (*see* page 74) is more upbeat. Jewelled blossoms sprout before an ultramarine pool with an emerald plain behind it, all set off by the white mass of Mount Fuji on the horizon. On the other hand, viewed from a distance, a crimson mass matching the intense red of the sunset sky, *Cherry Blossoms at Honmoku in Musashi Province* (*see* right) take us into semi-abstract territory, into which we are only conducted deeper by *The Sea off the Miura Peninsula in Sagami Province* (*see* page 76), where Fuji seems almost to be dissolving into its waters through a swirling eddy of sunset-tinged cloud.

Unhelpful Comparisons?

Hiroshige followed Hokusai in making his own pilgrimage to Enoshima (*see* page 84). In *The Entrance Gate at Enoshima in Sagami Province* (*see* opposite) we see Mount Fuji framed by the gate to the famous shrine. His vision of *Lake at Hakone* (*see* page 69) frankly suffers by comparison with Hokusai's masterpiece of eerie atmospherics (*see* page 91), just as *The Sea off Satta in Suruga Province* (*see* page 119, top row, fifth from left, and the front cover) invites unfavourable comparisons with *The Great Wave off Kanagawa* (*see* page 55). On its own terms, however, this is a fascinating work, with its own distinctive play of line, curve, colour and rhythm. (And a perhaps more interesting Hokusai allusion in the spots of spray that 'become' flying birds, *see* page 114). As for the *The Oi River between Suruga and Totomi Provinces* (*see* page 184), we see an altogether more peaceful arrangement than in the Hokusai depiction of an epic encounter between brave travellers and a raging torrent (*see* page 100). While the water in the middle is very clearly deep, our focus is on the left foreground, where a pair of fine ladies, ensconced in their litter, look completely serene.

Hiroshige arguably makes more of *The Pine Forest of Miho in Suruga Province* (*see* page 179) than Hokusai (*see* page 45). Seen from a distance, in semi-darkness under a spooky yellow sky which is reflected in the ocean, it seems a fitting setting for one of Japanese mythology's most memorably unsettling stories (*see* page 86).

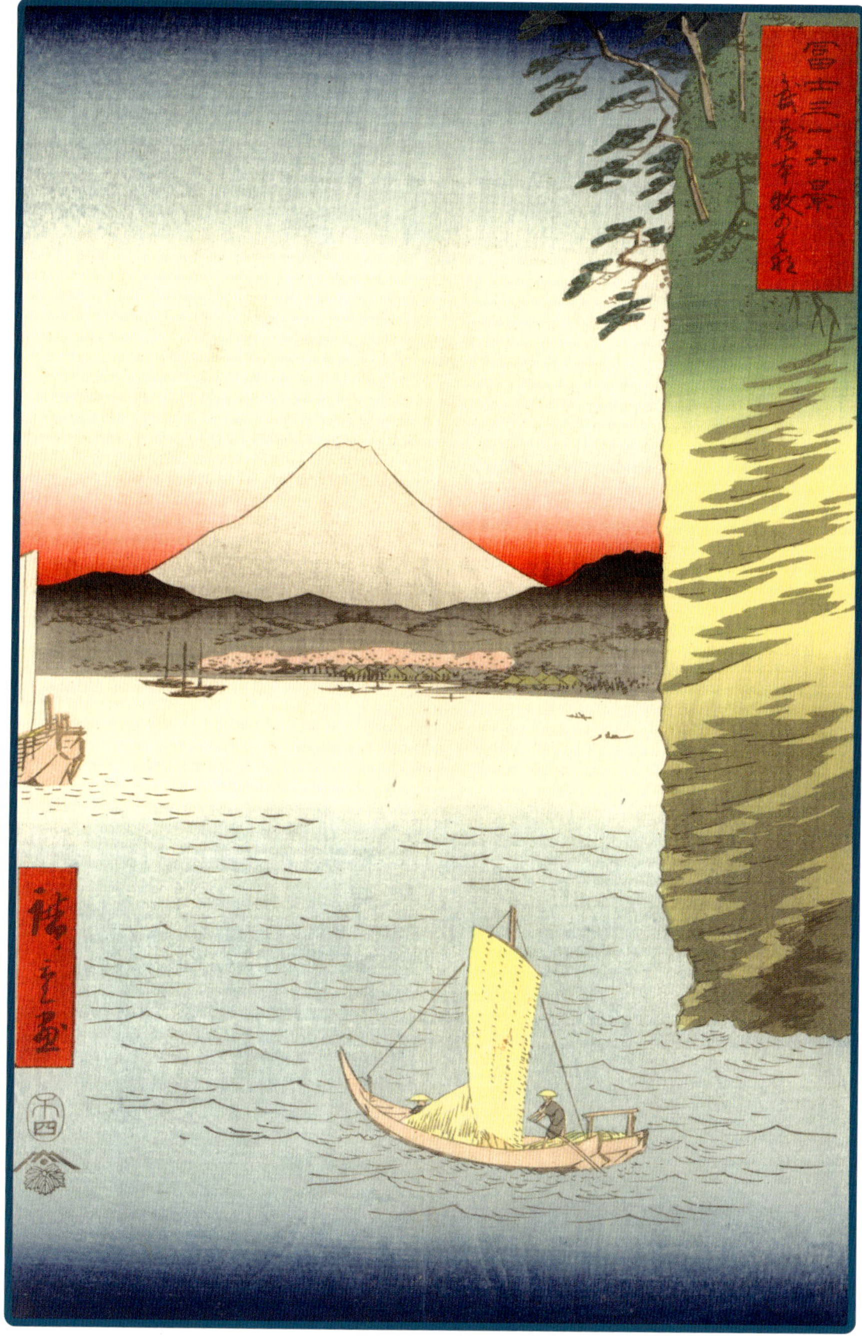

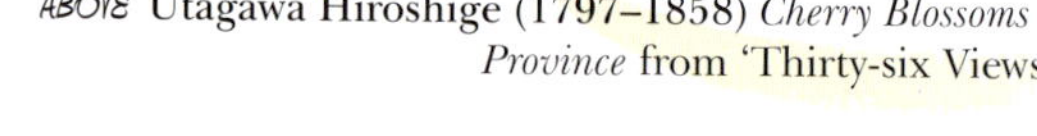

Above Utagawa Hiroshige (1797–1858) *Cherry Blossoms at Honmoku in Musashi Province* from 'Thirty-six Views of Mount Fuji' (1858)

Colour and Composition

Fuji on the Left of the Tokaido Road (*see* below right) is, purely and simply, a lovely picture: we see a twilit Fuji through a screen of pines and across a paddy field, as does the priest in the foreground who has removed his hat (he is holding it before him) so as to have an unimpeded view of Japan's most famous mountain. Figures like this one can in an important sense serve as our proxies in the picture, underlining for us the significance of what they see.

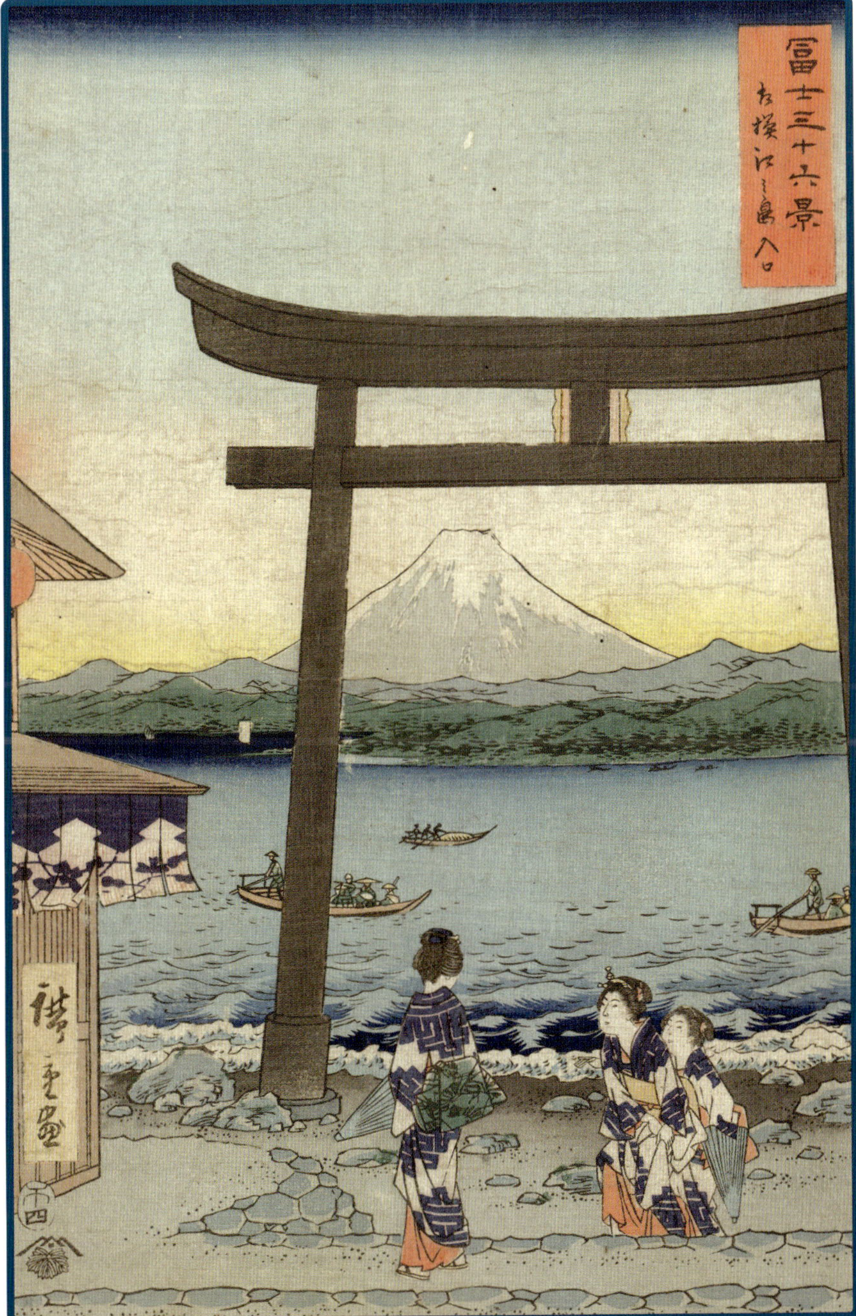

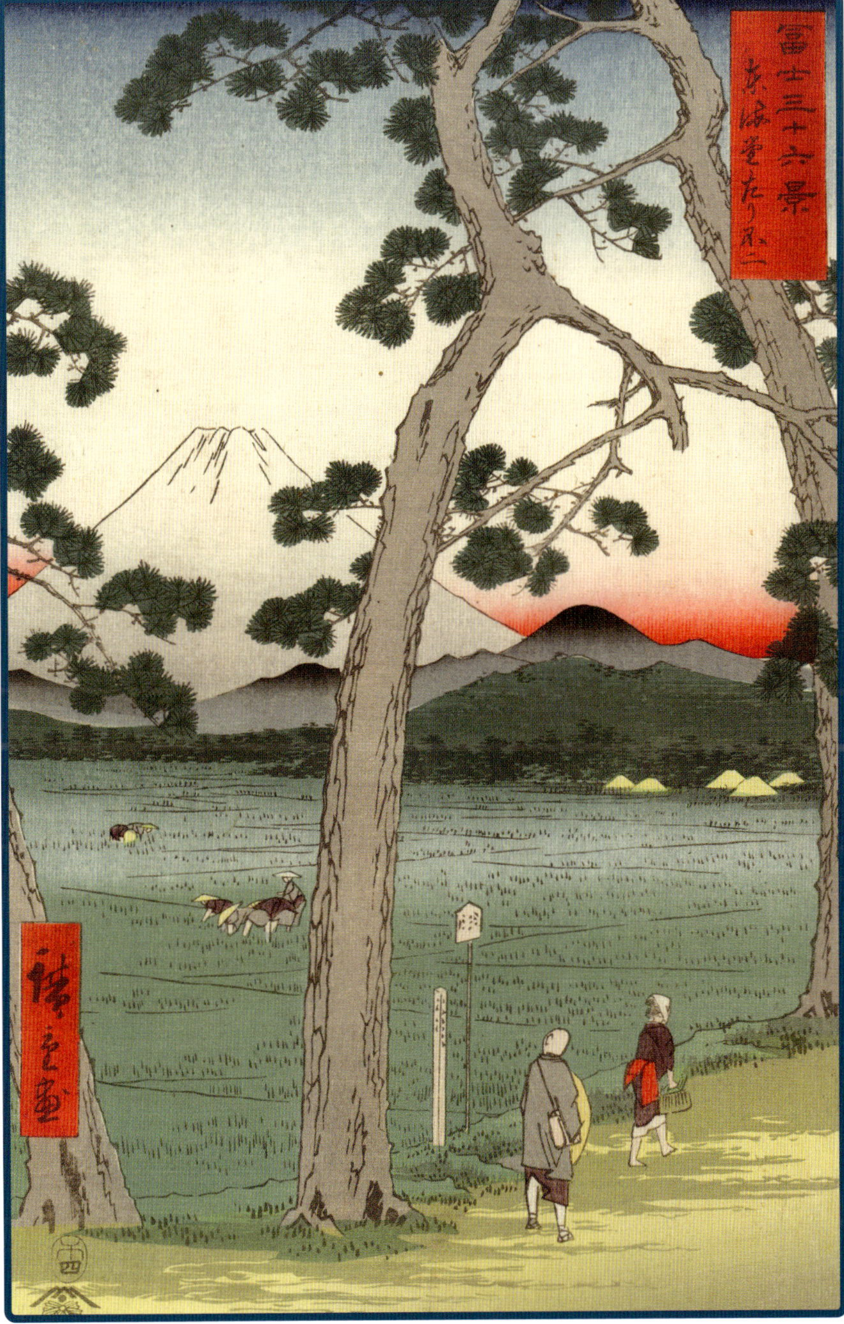

ABOVE Utagawa Hiroshige (1797–1858) *The Entrance Gate at Enoshima in Sagami Province* from 'Thirty-six Views of Mount Fuji' (1858)

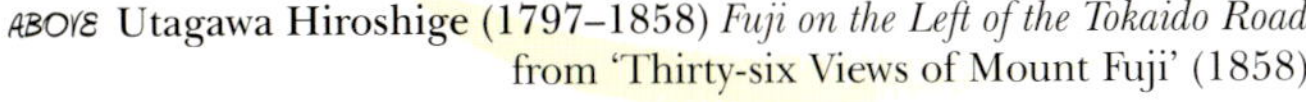

ABOVE Utagawa Hiroshige (1797–1858) *Fuji on the Left of the Tokaido Road* from 'Thirty-six Views of Mount Fuji' (1858)

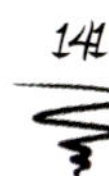

In *Futami Bay in Ise Province* (*see* below) we see the 'wedded rocks' – the *Meoto Iwa* – a pair of offshore sea-stacks in Futami Bay, one big 'husband' and another, smaller 'wife'. Connected together by long, straw-woven ropes (and with little *torii* at the top and bottom of the 'male' rock), this remains one of Shinto's most celebrated shrines. Less interesting formally than Hokusai's version of much the same scene (*see* page 94), *Lake Suwa in Shinano Province* (*see* page 119, middle row, third from right) has a special quality, as its deep blue shallows give way to a more distant gleam. This

ABOVE Utagawa Hiroshige (1797–1858) *Futami Bay in Ise Province* from 'Thirty-six Views of Mount Fuji' (1858)

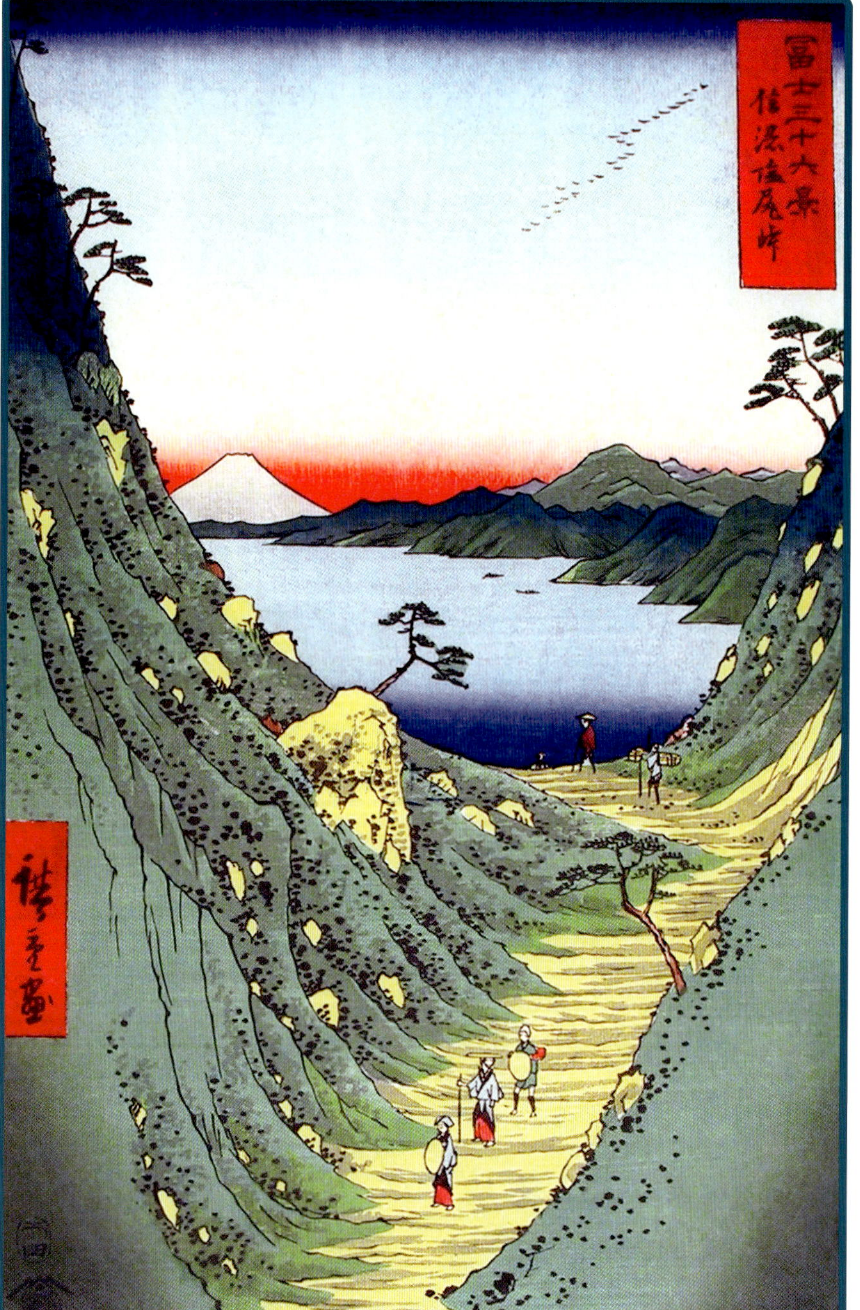

ABOVE Utagawa Hiroshige (1797–1858) *Shiojiri Pass in Shinano Province* from 'Thirty-six Views of Mount Fuji' (1858)

view is a study in colour, as are Hiroshige's prospects of the *Shiojiri Pass in Shinano Province* (*see* left) and the *Misaka Pass in Kai Province* (*see* page 176), with their very different arrays of yellow, blue and green.

In the view of *The Otsuki Plain in Kai Province* (*see* page 168), a straightforward divide between deep green grassland foreground and silver mountain-and-sky background is beautifully embroidered with threads of grass and wildflower along a winding stream. Perspective-wise, it is problematic, as strictly speaking these little tufts of vegetation tower like rainforests in form and colour. However, it could hardly be more satisfying.

Unless, perhaps, it were to be given the sort of sash of ruby-tinted cloud that floats across the river running down the middle of the *Dog Eye Pass in Kai Province* (*see* page 167), a favourite location for Hiroshige (*see* page 56). *Kogane Plain in Shimosa Province* (*see* page 119, bottom row, third from left) is interesting for including grazing horses. They are surprisingly solid, given that they are the work of the same artist who had executed such exquisitely delicate birds, butterflies and blossoms in the past.

But the main purpose of this picture, created (as Gian Carlo Calza has pointed out) in a Chinese Year of the Horse, seems to have been to present these benign-looking beasts as emblems of good luck. (Perhaps too, in the context of this work of landscape art, Hiroshige was happy for his horses to appear almost as topographical features, interruptions in an open field which extended all the way to the horizon, where Fuji stood, flanked on either side by slender pine trees.)

Concluding Colourburst

In a final flurry of colour, Hiroshige ended his sequence with a run of twilight takes on *Kuroto Bay in Kazusa Province* (*see* right), *Mount Kano in Kazusa Province* (*see* page 119, bottom row, fifth from left) and *The Hota Coast in Awa Province* (*see* page 34), each apparently more luxurious in its colour than the last. *Kuroto Bay…*, unusually, places Mount Fuji just about dead-centre on its far horizon, beyond what appears to be a virtually circular stretch of sea. Fishing boats and cargo vessels have sought the sanctuary of this sheltered bay, under the protection of Fujisan, as it seems here.

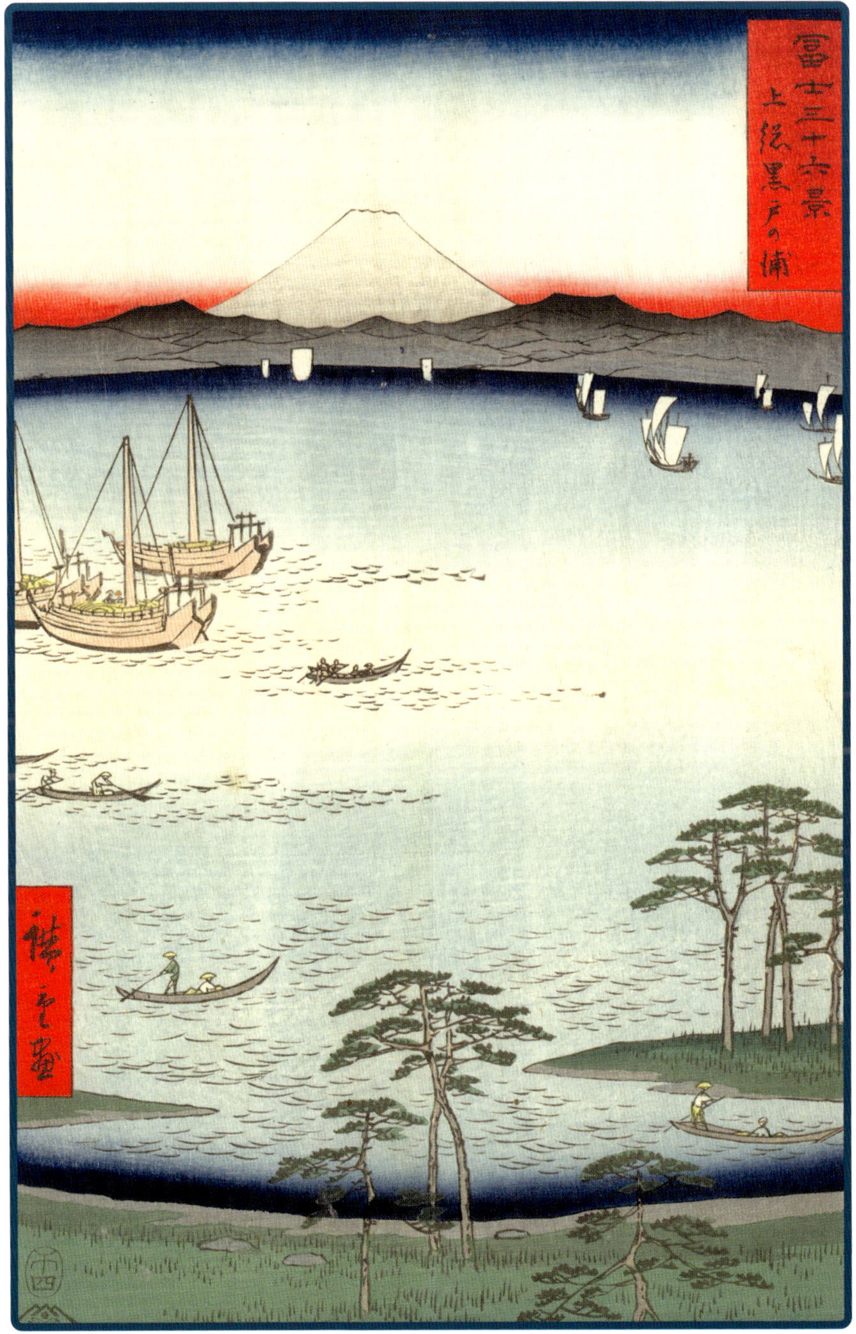

Above Utagawa Hiroshige (1797–1858) *Kuroto Bay in Kazusa Province* from 'Thirty-six Views of Mount Fuji' (1858)

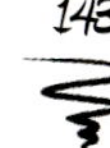

The view from the slopes of Kano is directly obstructed by a large and spreading pine, but its dark canopy appears to give the sacred mountain shelter. As so often, angled planes at the bottom seem to balance out the lines of the volcano's slopes – here a dark green bank (left) and an array of beautiful pink blossom to the right. Along the road in the immediate foreground, wayfarers pass by – a mounted dignitary, led by a servant, and, coming up the hill, a woman with a child.

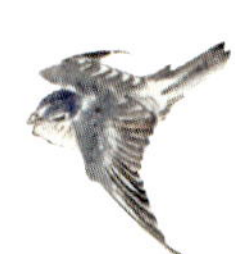
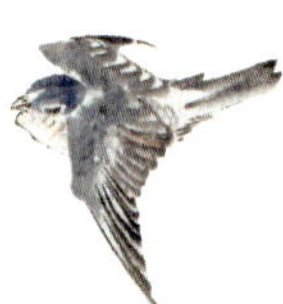

Starting Point

The late 1850s was a particularly productive time for Hiroshige with his 'One Hundred Famous Views of Edo', dated to *c.* 1856–58. As a colourful contents page made clear, these were grouped according to season. (And by the time the series was completed, the last few prints being the work of Hiroshige's apprentice, son-in-law and appointed successor Suzuki Chinpei, a.k.a. Hiroshige II (1826–69), there were getting on for 120 prints in all.)

Fuji makes its first appearance in the opening print, a view of *Nihonbashi* with its famous bridge. This was both the main port of Edo-Period Japan and the spot from where all distances were calculated. The scene is subtitled *Clearing After Snow* (*see* right), but if the snow is really clearing, it has only just begun to do so: this scene shows us spring at its very start. It is a morning scene and it is not just the Japanese day that is getting under way; the boatmen coming upriver and the market traders setting out their stalls seem to be preparing the city for a busy and prosperous New Year.

In print 3, *Hibiya and Soto-Sakurada from Yamashita-cho* (*see* opposite, left), we see Fujisan again from a vantage point above the broad blue moat of Edo Castle, whose massive rampart balances the mountain to the right. The *kadomatsu* (gate pines) outside the door front-right, the *hagoita* (lacquered wooden paddles) thrusting in from either side of the picture and the flying comedy-kites are all associated with the celebration of New Year. There is a festive feel again in print 5, *Ekoin Temple in Ryogoku and Moto-Yanagi Bridge* (*see* opposite, right), where the towering wooden structure that seems to dwarf the distant peak was the

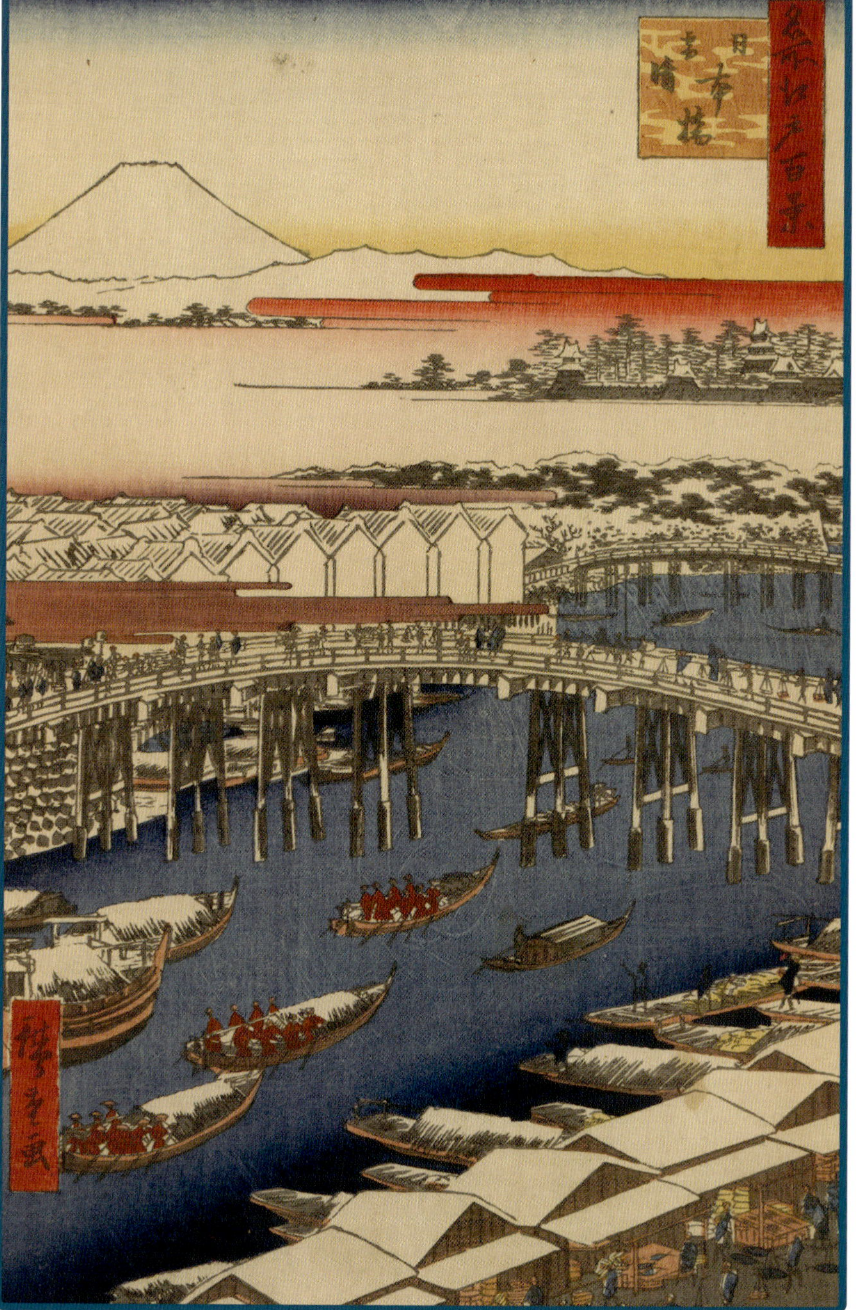

ABOVE Utagawa Hiroshige (1797–1858) *Clearing After Snow* from 'One Hundred Famous Views of Edo' (1856–58)

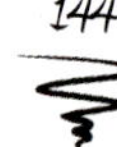

drum tower for the Ekoin Temple in Ryogoku. From the top of this, the priest would beat his drum to mark the start of the ceremonial sumo wrestling tournaments for which this Buddhist shrine was famous throughout Japan.

Iconic

Fujisan's symbolic importance goes without saying in all Hiroshige's representations, of course, but there are moments when this dimension

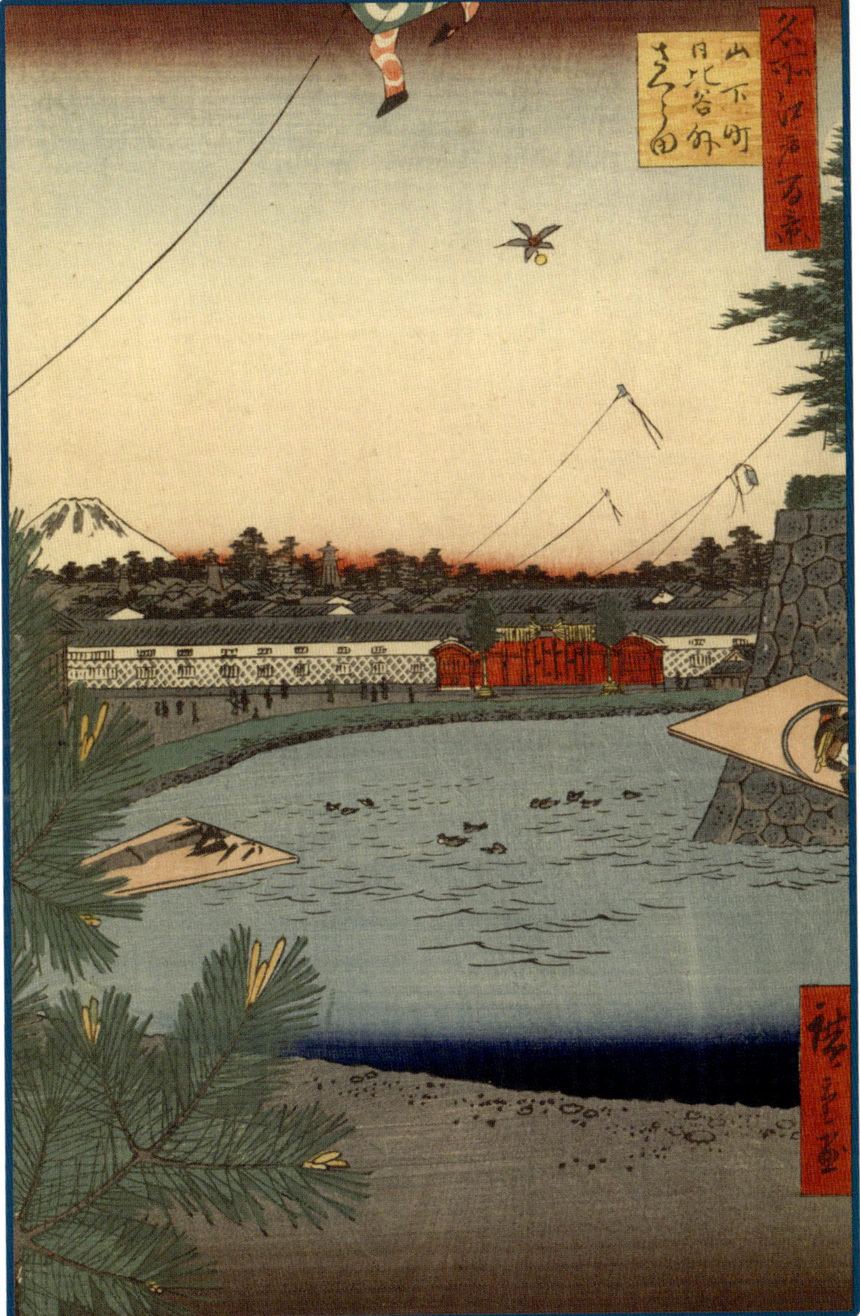

Above Utagawa Hiroshige (1797–1858) *Hibiya and Soto-Sakurada from Yamashita-cho* from 'One Hundred Famous Views of Edo' (1856–58)

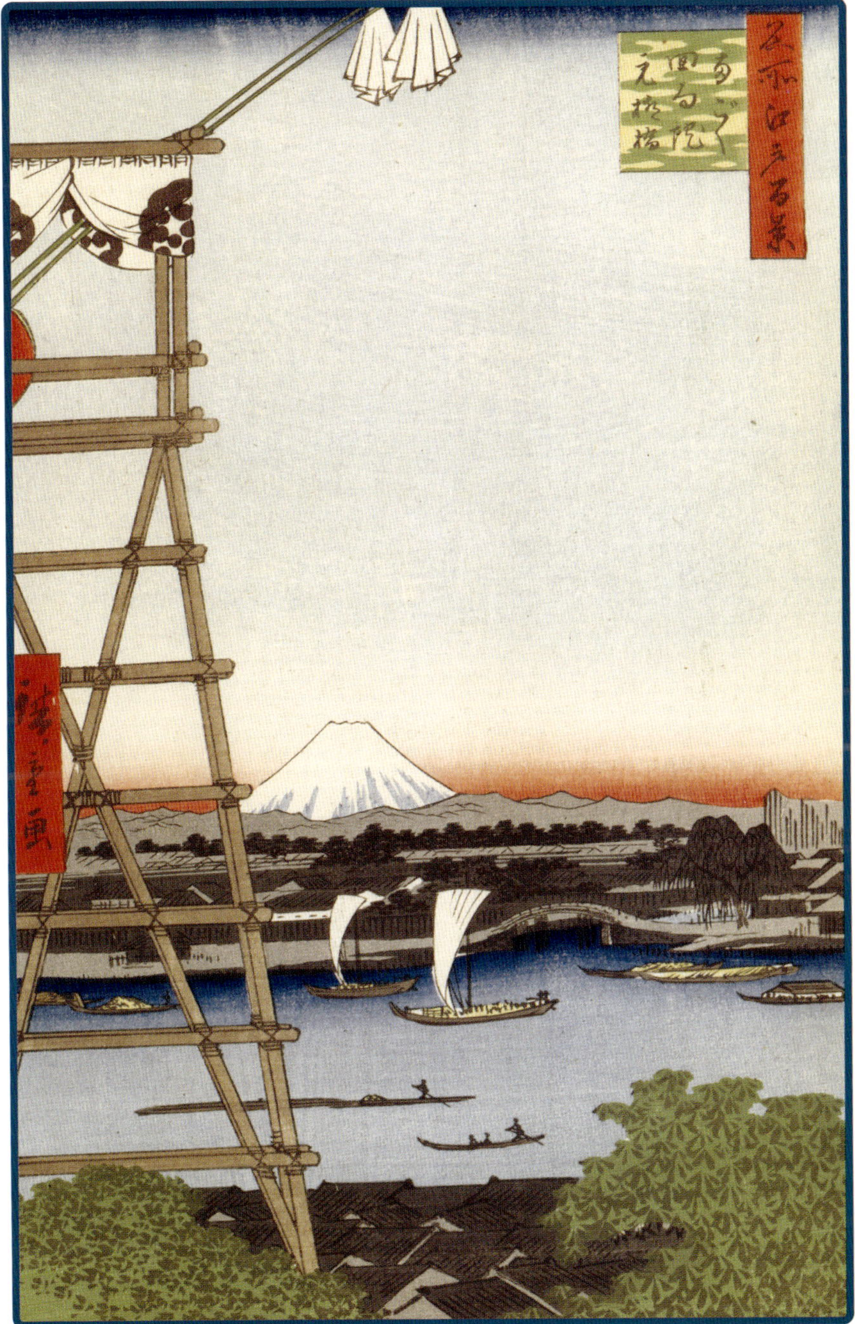

Above Utagawa Hiroshige (1797–1858) *Ekoin Temple in Ryogoku and Moto-Yanagi Bridge* from 'One Hundred Famous Views of Edo' (1856–58)

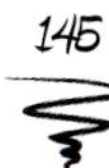

seems more obviously to the fore. In print 8, *Suruga-cho* (*see* below), for instance, whilst a frantic foreground shows us a busy scene of Edo's great Mitsui textiles market, in the background, borne up by cloud, Mount Fuji seems to float.

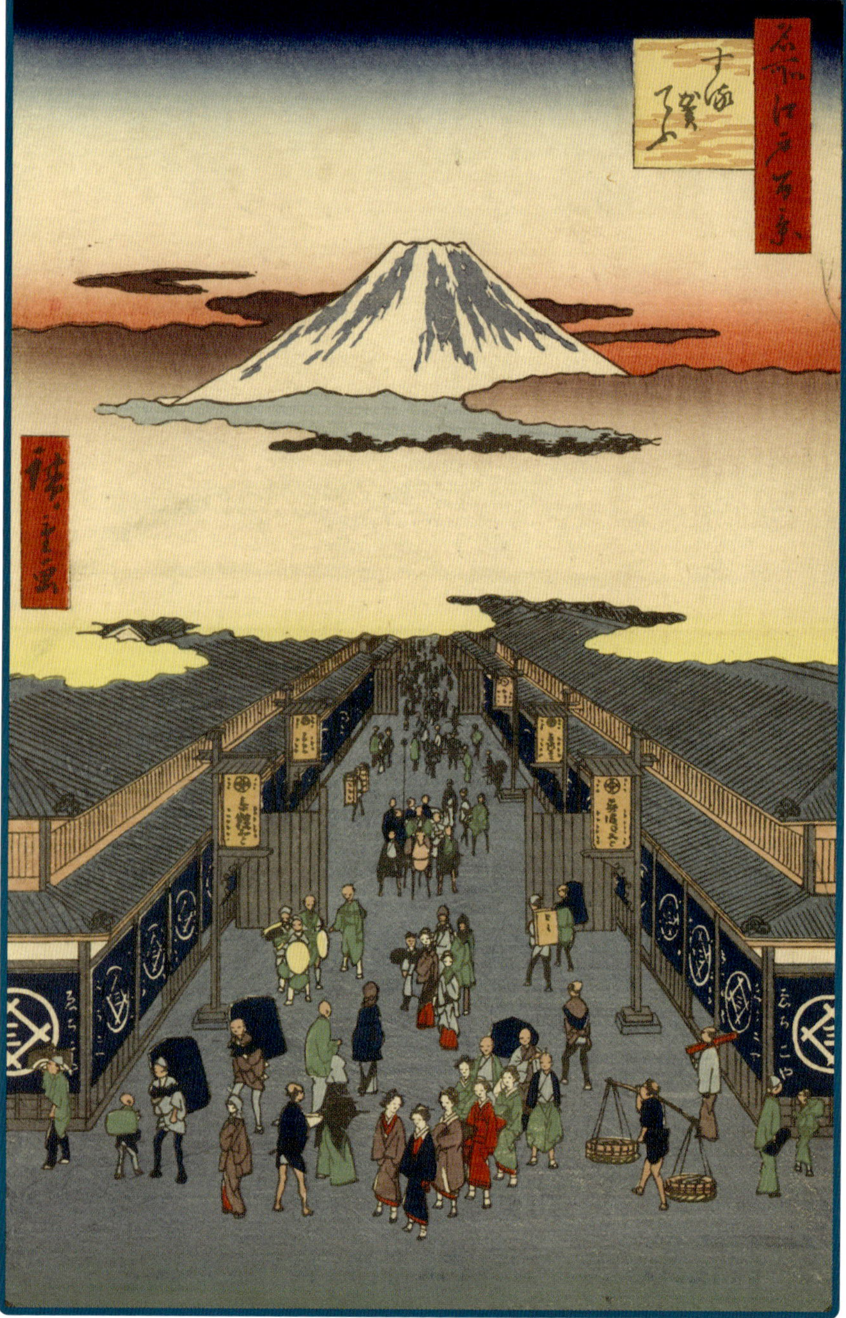

Above Utagawa Hiroshige (1797–1858) *Suruga-cho* from 'One Hundred Famous Views of Edo' (1856–58)

In print 24, meanwhile, we see a small-scale replica of the sacred mountain in the foreground – *New Fuji in Meguro* (*see* right) – and then, further back on the horizon, the real thing. These mini-Fujis were quite a common feature: they enabled the pious-but-busy to make at least an approximation of the great pilgrimage up Mount Fuji proper and derive some of the same spiritual benefits they would have hoped to gain from the actual climb.

Original Fuji in Meguro (print 25, *see* far right) shows us the actual mountain as viewed across the slopes of another little replica; this one is thought to have been the first one ever built (in 1812) at Kamimeguro. It appears to have been the similarity in theme that led the collection's compilers to overlook the obviously autumnal air about the cherry trees (they are in full blossom in the previous print), hence its misplacement in the sequence here.

In print 39 (*Distant View of Kinryuzan Temple and the Azuma Bridge*, *see* page 148), we look inshore to see Mount Fuji framed by the awning of a boat on the Sumida River, beyond the famous pagodas of Edo's most ancient shrine, the Temple of Senso-Ji, and of course the Asakusa Shinto shrine next door. In the foreground, petals swirl in the air like fragrant snow. Their fall is actually a sign that spring is far advanced, however, and that we are now upon the very cusp of summer.

Fuji, Fauna and Flora

The carp was an acknowledged symbol of energy, strength, fertility and moral vigour, so the sort of *koinobori* carp streamers to be seen in print 48 (*Suido Bridge and Suruga Hill*, *see* page 148) were hoisted in honour of the 'Festival of the Boys'. One of the highlights of the Japanese summer, this was a celebration of the younger generation of boys and the hopes the country invested in them for the future. Glimpsed through a crook in the *koinobori*'s shape, Fujisan is there as a reminder of the traditional values that will endure whatever changes the future should one day bring. Closer, we see the Sumida River spanned by the Suido Bridge and beyond that the Surugudai district where many high officials lived.

Mannen Bridge, Fukagawa (print 56, *see* page 149) is basically a visual pun. Realism gives way to whimsy (and to religious superstition) here. Like the tortoise, the turtle is famous for its extreme longevity. Here, then, we see Mount 'Never-Dying' framed between the turtle of long life and the

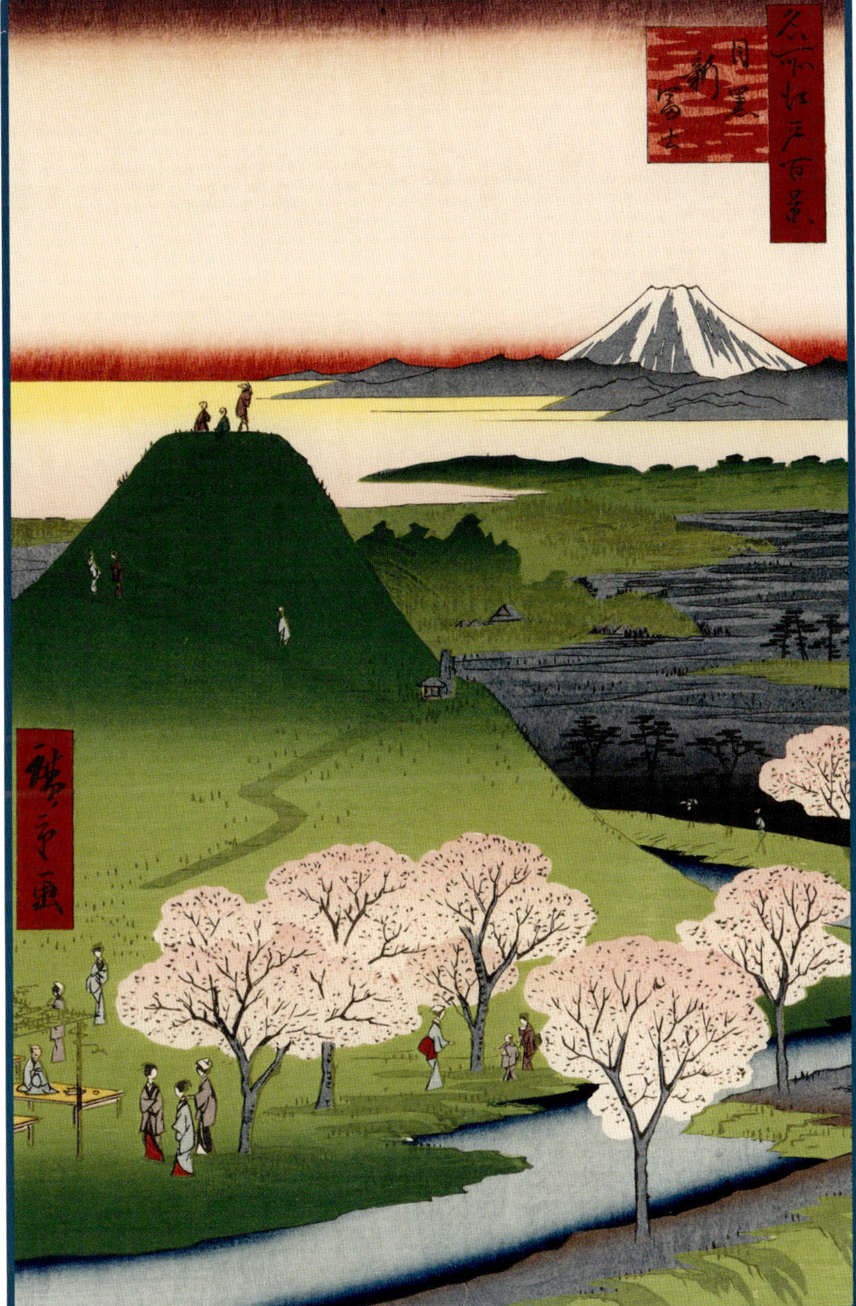

ABOVE Utagawa Hiroshige (1797–1858) *New Fuji in Meguro* from 'One Hundred Famous Views of Edo' (1856–58)

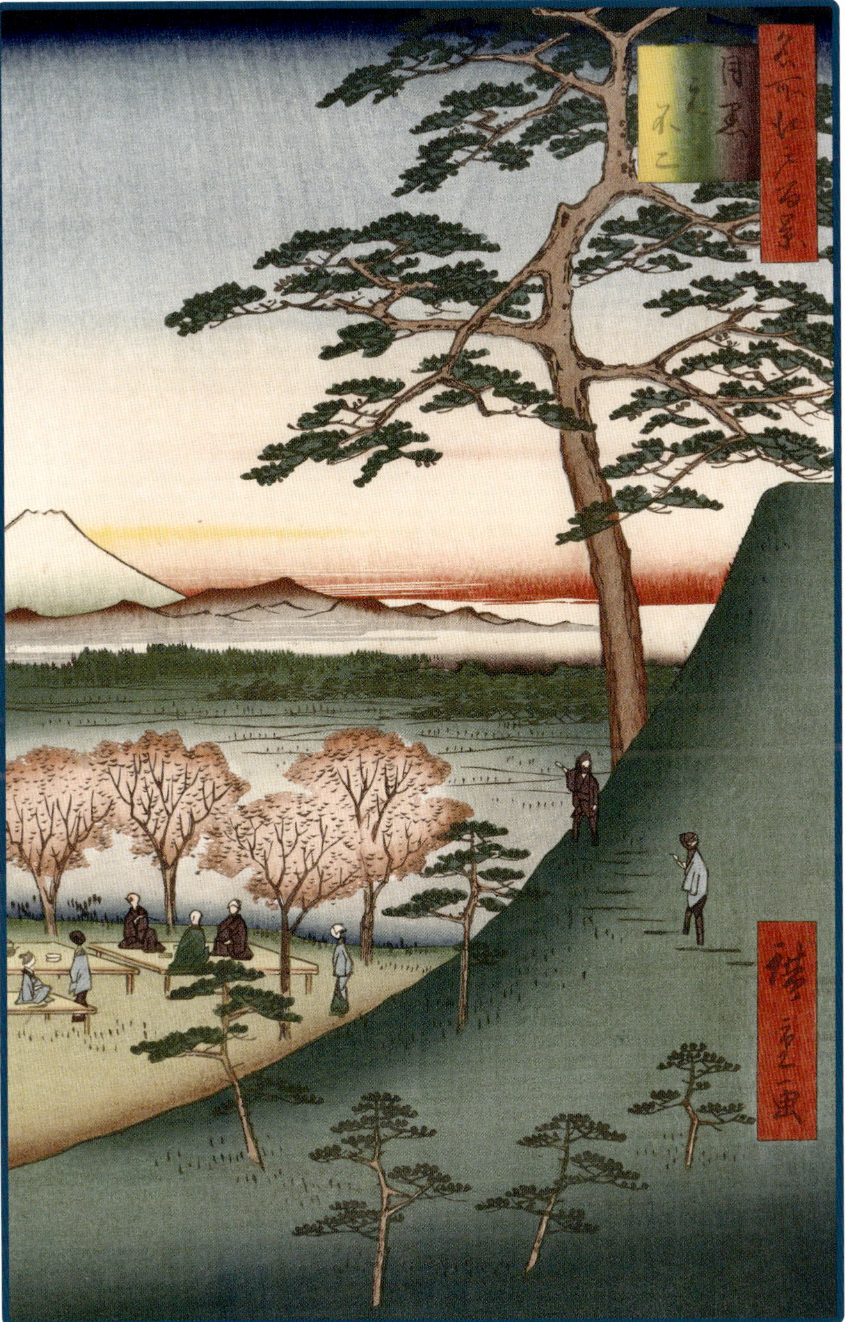

ABOVE Utagawa Hiroshige (1797–1858) *Original Fuji in Meguro* from 'One Hundred Famous Views of Edo' (1856–58)

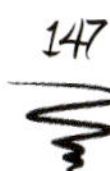

structure of a bridge whose name 'Mannen' meant 10,000 years. View 57 (*see* opposite, right), looking out from a little way down the Sumida River at Koto, wreathes Fuji round with a distinctly ethereal mist of white, touched with red by the light of the declining sun.

But the reeds we see in the middle of the river remind us of a racier episode in recent Edo history: this glorified mud bank is all that remains of the decadent glories of Nakazu Island, a pleasure ground shut down and razed by an angry shogunate in the middle of the eighteenth century.

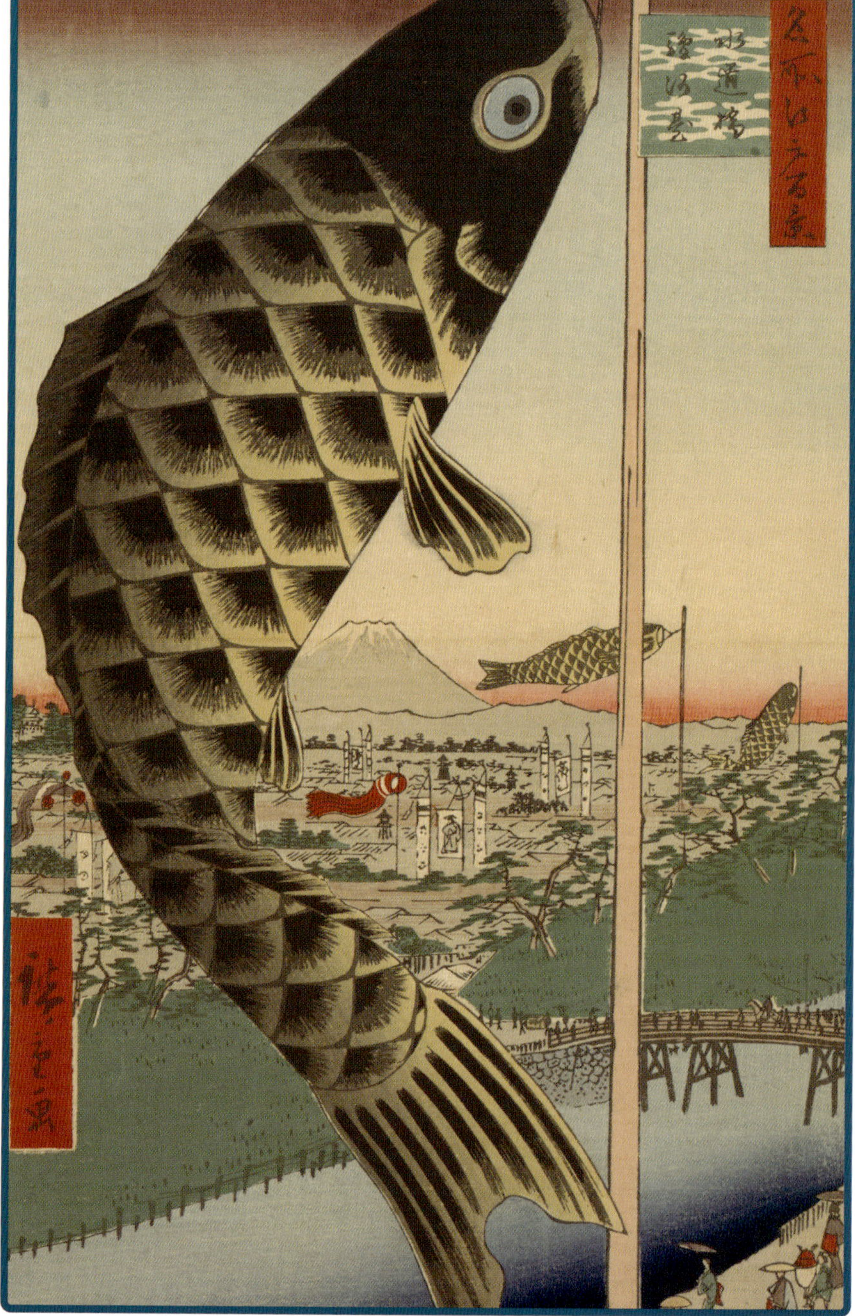

ABOVE Utagawa Hiroshige (1797–1858) *Distant View of Kinryuzan Temple and the Azuma Bridge* from 'One Hundred Famous Views of Edo' (1856–58)

ABOVE Utagawa Hiroshige (1797–1858) *Suido Bridge and Suruga Hill* from 'One Hundred Famous Views of Edo' (1856–58)

Intimations of Autumn

Many felt that Edo culture was in a state of decadence, perhaps powerless to resist colonization by the West; but traditional Japanese culture stood firm.

It has been suggested that print 73 (*see* page 150, left) may show the view from Hiroshige's house – unusually, no site is specified. Wherever we are looking from, however, we see Fujisan across the rooftops of Edo – and through a veritable forest of boughs and streamers. These were raised in

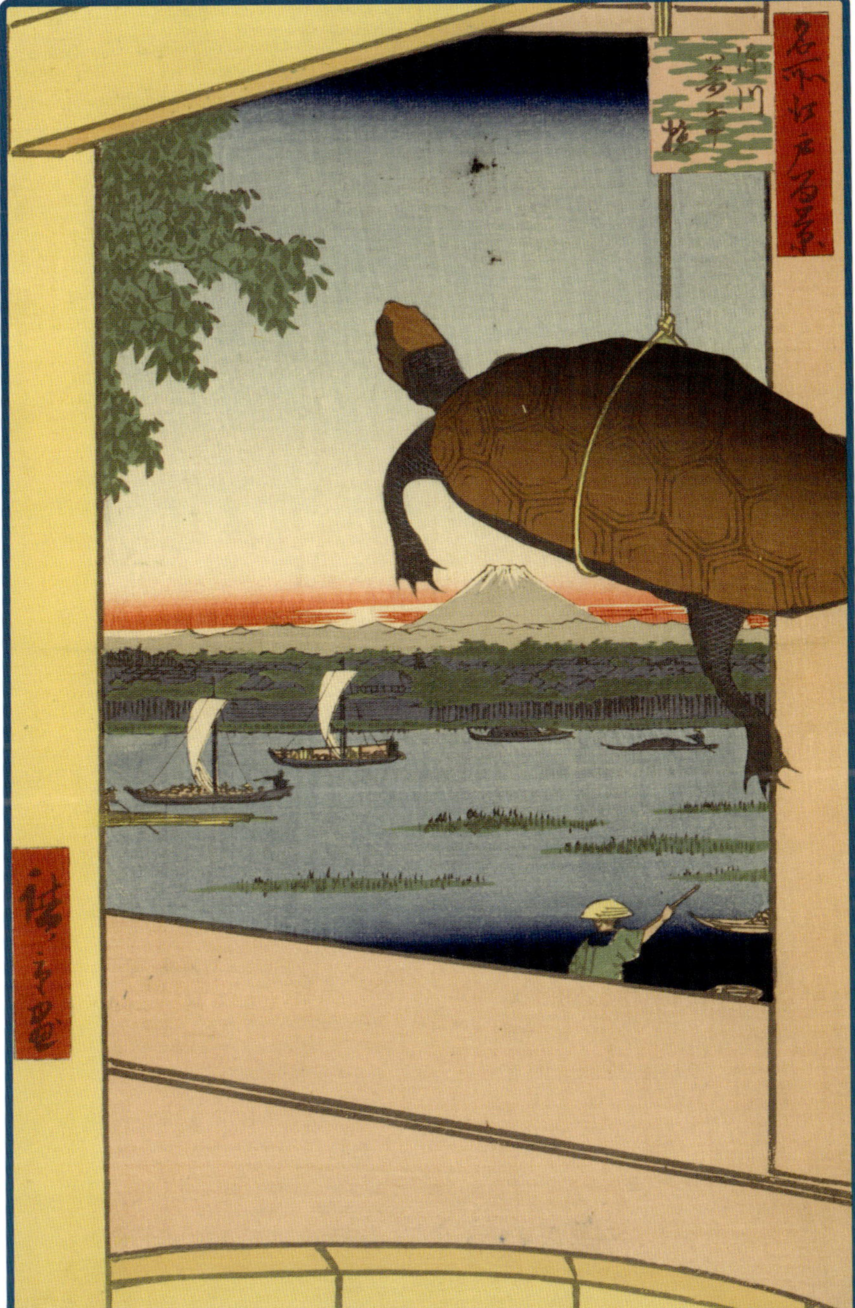

ABOVE Utagawa Hiroshige (1797–1858) *Mannen Bridge, Fukagawa* from 'One Hundred Famous Views of Edo' (1856–58)

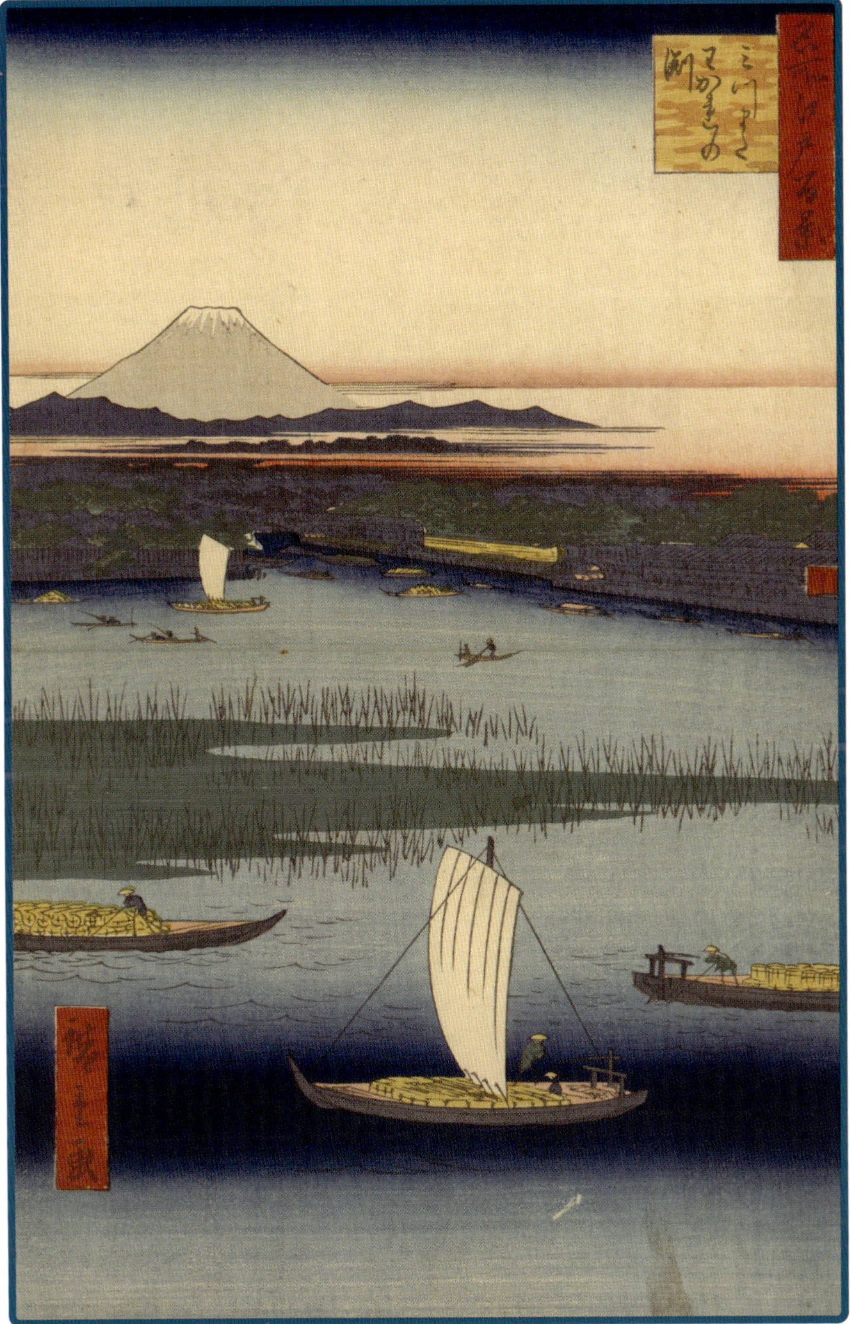

ABOVE Utagawa Hiroshige (1797–1858) *Sumida River at Koto* from 'One Hundred Famous Views of Edo' (1856–58)

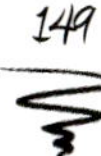

acknowledgement of the Tanabata Festival, which traditionally marked the beginning of autumn in Japan (although held in what Westerners would think of as late summer, being late July/August). *The City Flourishing* was the title Hiroshige gave to this particular print: it certainly suggests that he saw the autumn as a time of auspiciousness and enjoyment. Attached to some of the streamers here are what appear to be notes with the written wishes people would petition to the gods at Tanabata-time.

Above Utagawa Hiroshige (1797–1858) *The City Flourishing, Tanabata Festival* from 'One Hundred Famous Views of Edo' (1856–58)

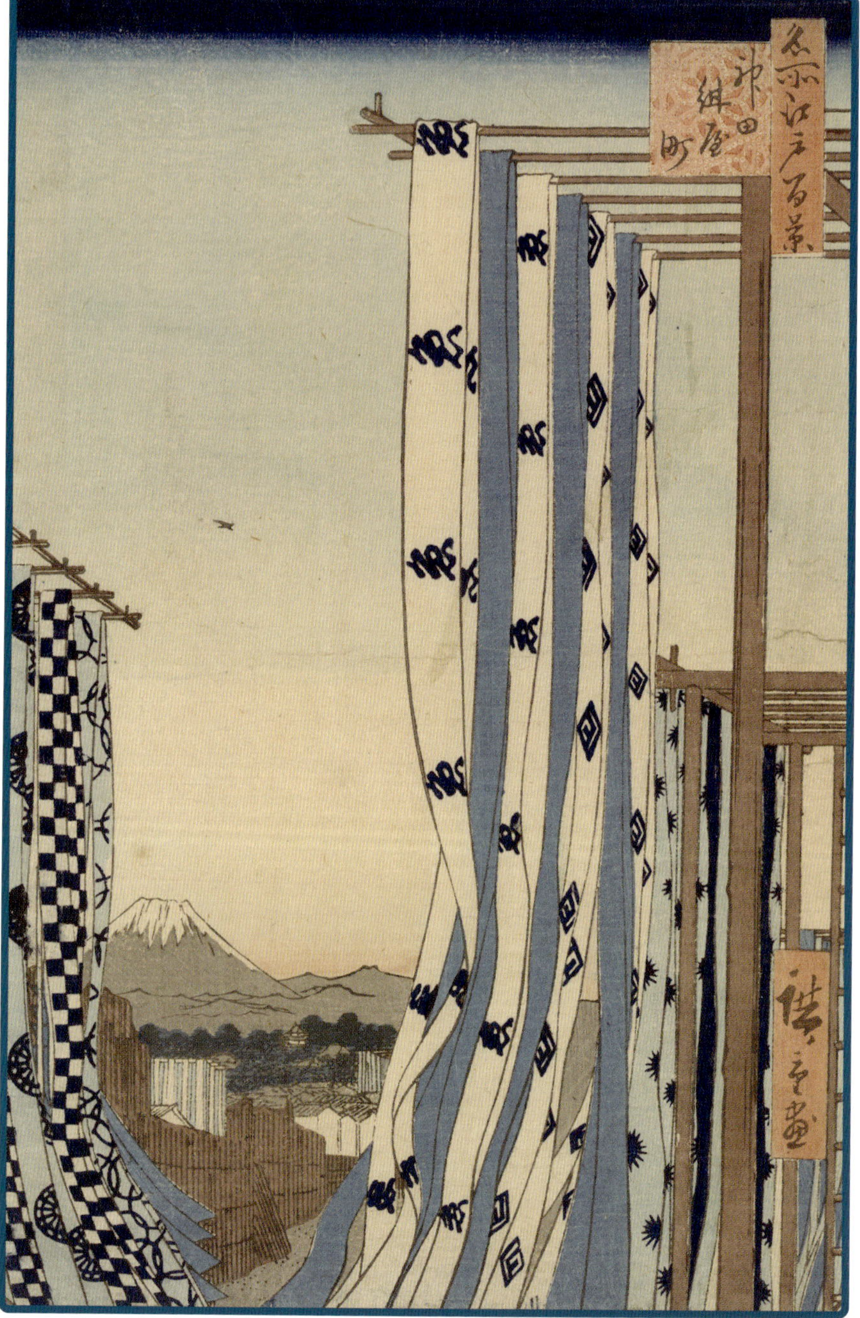

Above Utagawa Hiroshige (1797–1858) *Dyers' Quarter, Kanda* from 'One Hundred Famous Views of Edo' (1856–58)

In print 75 (*see* left), we see what would at first glance seem to be the decorative streamers of another festival – but are actually lengths of fabric drying in Kanda, Edo's dyeing district. The looping 'U' they form mirrors the rising outline of Mount Fuji in the background – pale grey and white in the luxurious crimson of closing day. The cloth itself looks rich and costly, the *kanji* or written character design on the first few lengths a bit of 'product placement': it says '*sakana*' for Sakayana Eikichi, the publisher whose firm was publishing these prints. The *kanji* on the farther fabric lengths is Hiroshige's own diamond seal.

Trade and Tea

In print 77 (*see* right), we look out from some sort of elevated structure over *Inari Bridge and Minato Shrine, Teppozu*, something of a transport hub for Edo and for Japan. Ships bringing freight around the coast from the western provinces were too big to pass beneath the Inari Bridge or up the Hatchobori Canal, so they anchored here and decanted their cargoes into little lighters. Largely out of sight behind the big red fence, the Minato (Harbour) shrine was held to be important in protecting sailors and seagoing merchants and their vessels. Japan's geographical situation meant that, even through the centuries of the isolationist *sakoku* policy, it had relied upon a busy maritime trade.

From the bustling heart of the country's greatest port, we are transported to a quiet place of peace and leisure. *Grandpa's Teahouse in Meguro* (print 84, *see* page 60) is itself seen from something of a distance here, as we look out over day trippers gazing at Fuji across the fields. It is an agreeable prospect, the valley – its autumnal fields now as yellow as the teahouse thatch – nicely framed by big and shapely pine trees.

The view of *Konodai and the Tone River* (print 95, *see* page 66) looks out from what is now Edogawa, in the east of Tokyo. Beneath an overhanging outcrop fringed with trees at precipitous angles, Mount Fuji – seen across a misty stretch of sea – seems to be nestling comfortably in a river bend. Its snow-white slopes might just be the continuation of the row of sails we see stretching away before us, bellying out as though pregnant with the prosperity of Japan. Not far away, where this same river meets the sea at

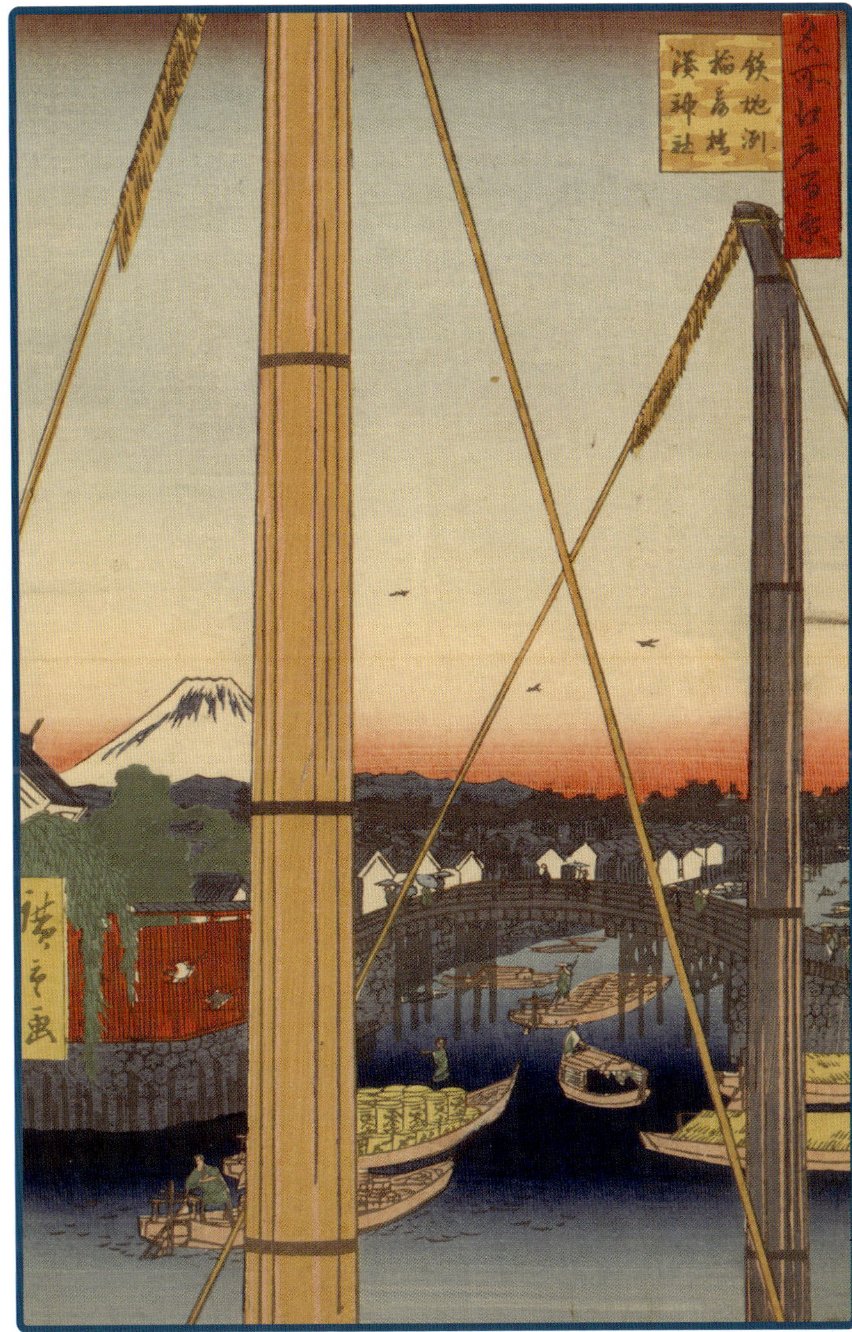

ABOVE Utagawa Hiroshige (1797–1858) *Inari Bridge and Minato Shrine, Teppozu* from 'One Hundred Famous Views of Edo' (1856–58)

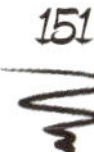

Edo Bay, we look down over the little fishing villages of *Horie and Nekozane* (print 96, *see* below). As so often in Hiroshige's (and, for that matter, Hokusai's) prints we see an irredeemably mundane scene in the foreground, and Fujisan the centre of an utterly other-worldly one beyond.

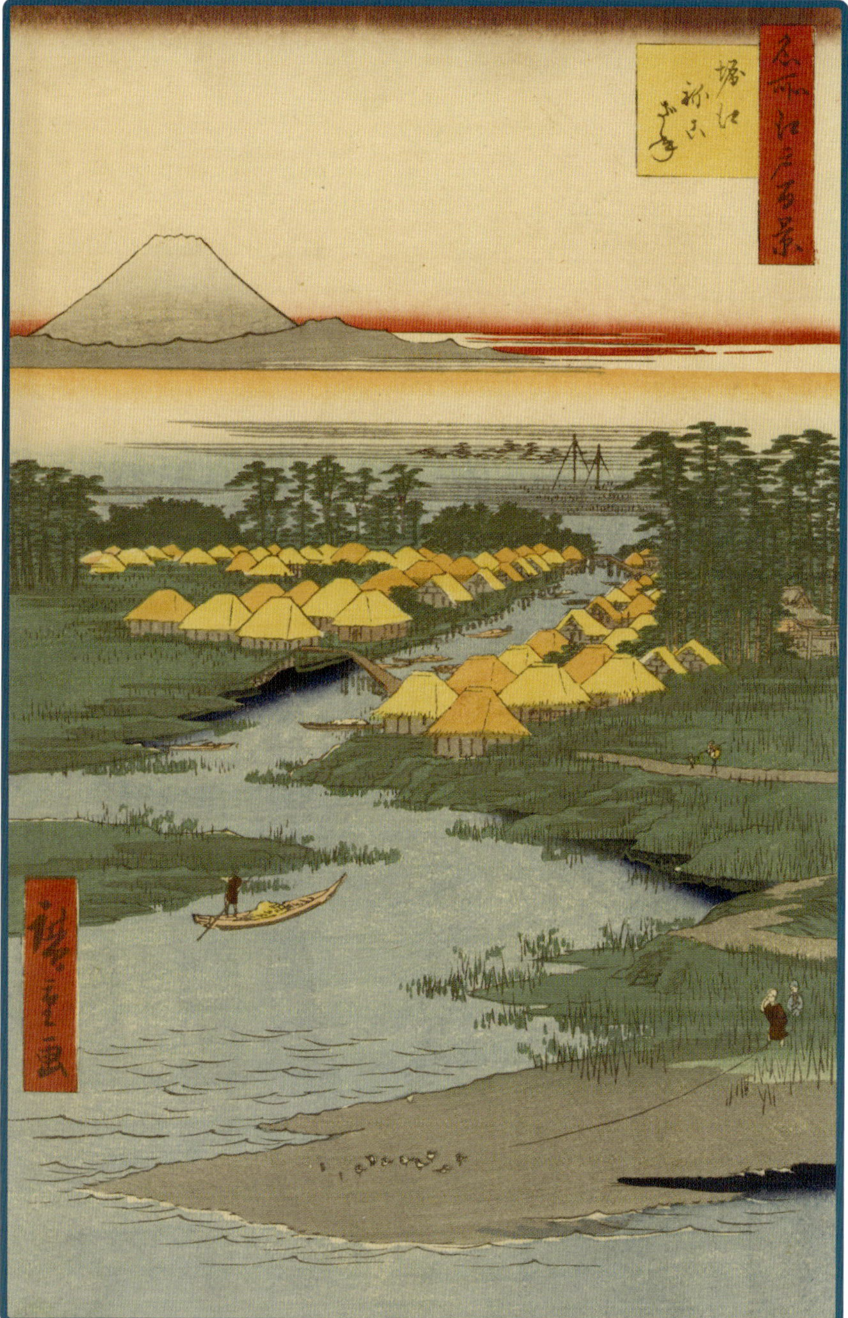

ABOVE Utagawa Hiroshige (1797–1858) *Horie and Nekozane* from 'One Hundred Famous Views of Edo' (1856–58)

A View from the Brothel

Print 101 (*see* below), entitled *Asakusa Ricefields and Torinomachi Festival* does indeed show a view out over paddy fields to a distant Fuji.

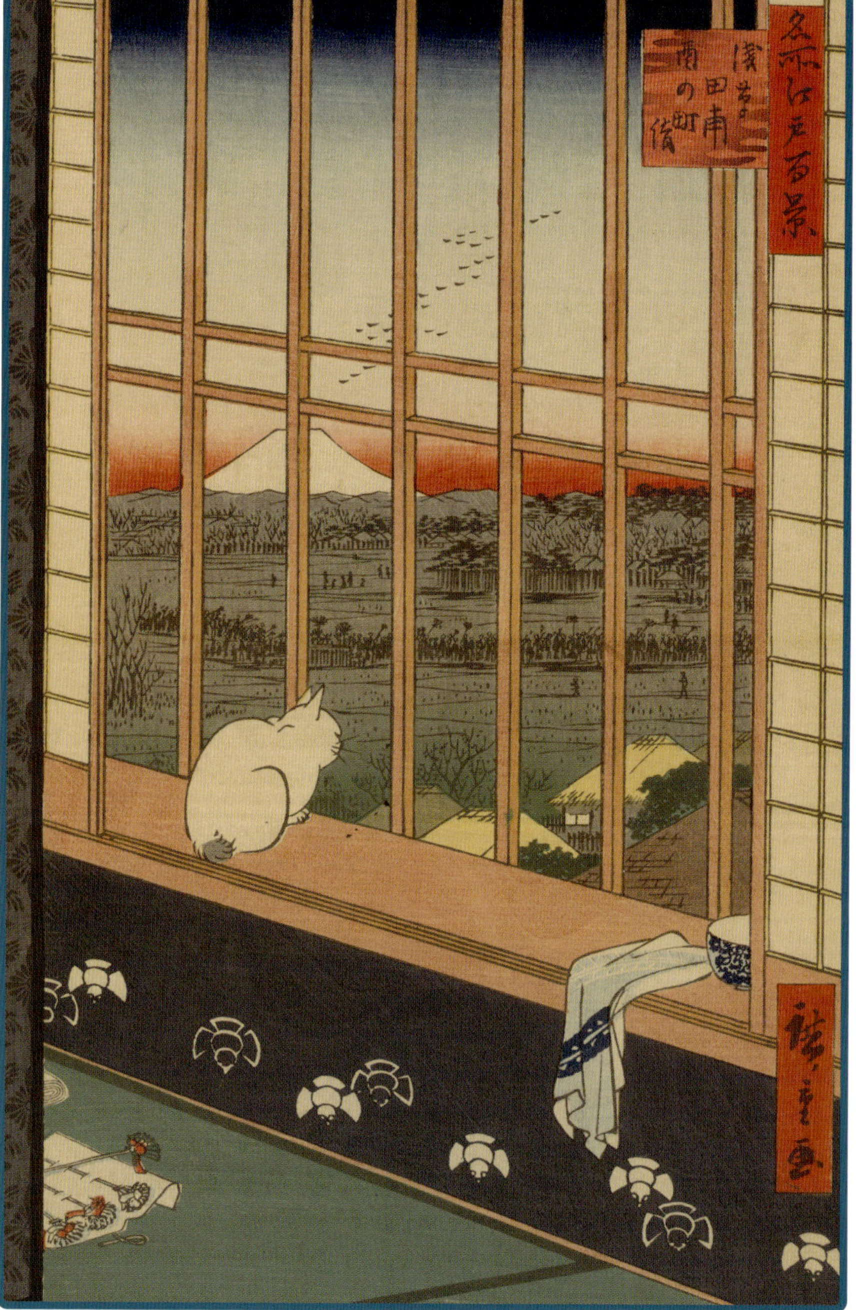

ABOVE Utagawa Hiroshige (1797–1858) *Asakusa Ricefields and Torinomachi Festival* from 'One Hundred Famous Views of Edo' (1856–58)

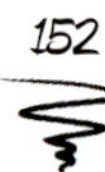

However, it is the vantage point that is unusual this time, with the vista extending away beneath the upstairs window of a brothel. The Torinomachi Festival (the Feast of the Cock or Rooster) was a time when the Yoshiwara pleasure quarter was open to everybody in Edo – not just the wealthy, and not just men. Hence, this glimpse of an otherwise hidden way of life.

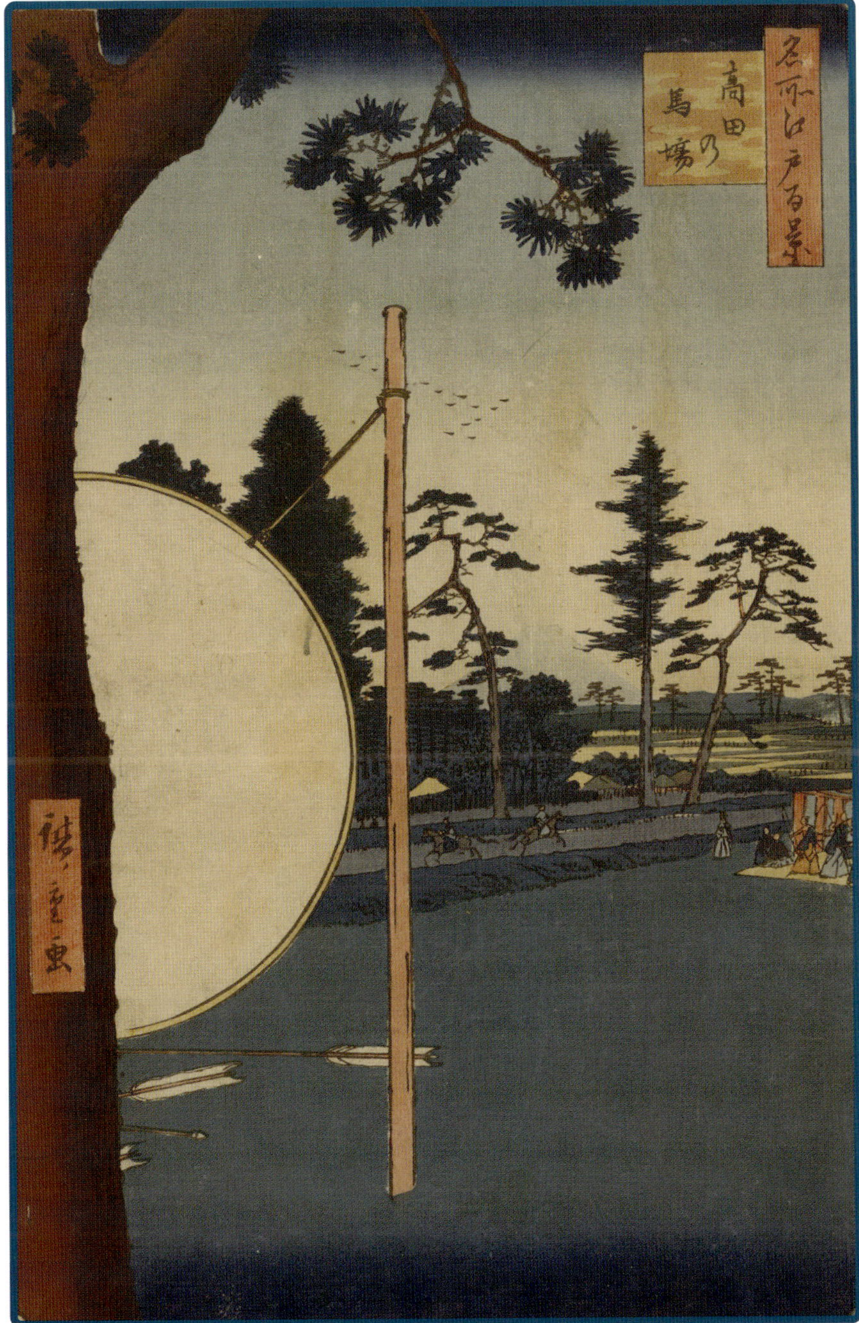

ABOVE Utagawa Hiroshige (1797–1858) *Takata Riding Grounds* from 'One Hundred Famous Views of Edo' (1856–58)

The white cat peering through the window bars is thought to represent (by that same sub-Freudian symbolic code that brought us the idea of 'pussy') feminine sexuality in general, and the geisha who uses this room in particular. Other symbols are more subtle – the discarded hair-fasteners on the floor below the windowsill, though known from their shape as 'bear's claw combs', also resemble the rakes revellers carried during Torinomachi, so that they might readily 'rake in' the good fortune of the day. Among other bits and pieces, some of the paper tissues the woman working here would use to wipe up mess may be seen lying down by the screen at left. And what of the geisha herself? Is she out enjoying the festival or behind the screen, perhaps with a client, just out of sight?

And in the meantime, as ever, Fujisan simply stands there, seemingly impassive. Life – in all its aspects – must go on.

Targeting Change

Continuity surely seemed especially important in the face of such seemingly irresistible threats to the traditional Japanese way of life. Hence, perhaps, Hiroshige's inclusion of the *Takata Riding Grounds* (print 115, *see* left). Hiroshige was, we know, immensely proud of the Samurai heritage which he might in many ways be thought to have abandoned. The martial arts practised at this school in the Shinjuku district were evidently for him a vital link to a fast vanishing past.

The warriors we see here, however – some riding, some squatting down to receive instruction – are relegated to the background behind the broad white disc of an archery target. Hanging there, beside the distant form of Fuji, it looks for all the world like a sacred mirror of

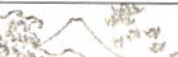

the sort that had so long symbolized truth in Japanese tradition (*see* page 113).

If, between them, Hokusai and Hiroshige had done much to change Japanese art, they had been abetted – if not actually impelled – by wider changes in their society. In hindsight, at least, we can see that both had addressed in their work what was to be the central challenge confronting this ancient and elaborate culture: how to keep its integrity whilst still adapting to the modern world.

The Western Way

One way was to go out and meet modernity, to embrace Western culture and reap its benefits. This philosophy had long had its adherents in Japan, especially among the artists of the *Yōga* (Western) movement. For Shiba Kokan (1747–1818), European techniques and styles could make Japanese art more Japanese. 'Only Dutch painting can accurately capture Mount Fuji,' he notoriously maintained.

An all-round intellectual and eager student of *rangaku* (*see* page 48), Kokan had a strong sense that the vital contribution of art was as a sort of science in itself; to show us our world as it actually was. To this end, he had produced his own illustrated guide to Copernican astronomy, made his own camera obscura to study the science of optics and, in 1792, created what is believed to have been Japan's first modern map. 'Eastern pictures,' he complained in his treatise *Seiyo Gadan* (*On Western Painting*, 1799):

> *offer no accuracy in their detail, and without this a picture can hardly be called a picture. Painting reality is about painting all things – whether they be landscapes, birds, flowers, cows, sheep, trees, rocks or insects – just as they actually appear, in this way giving the picture its air of animation.*

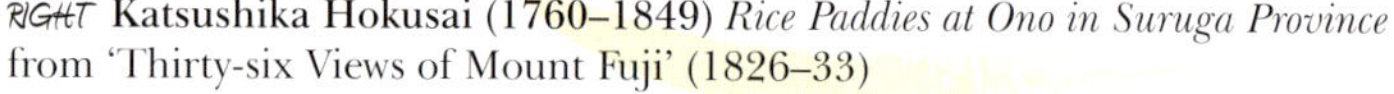

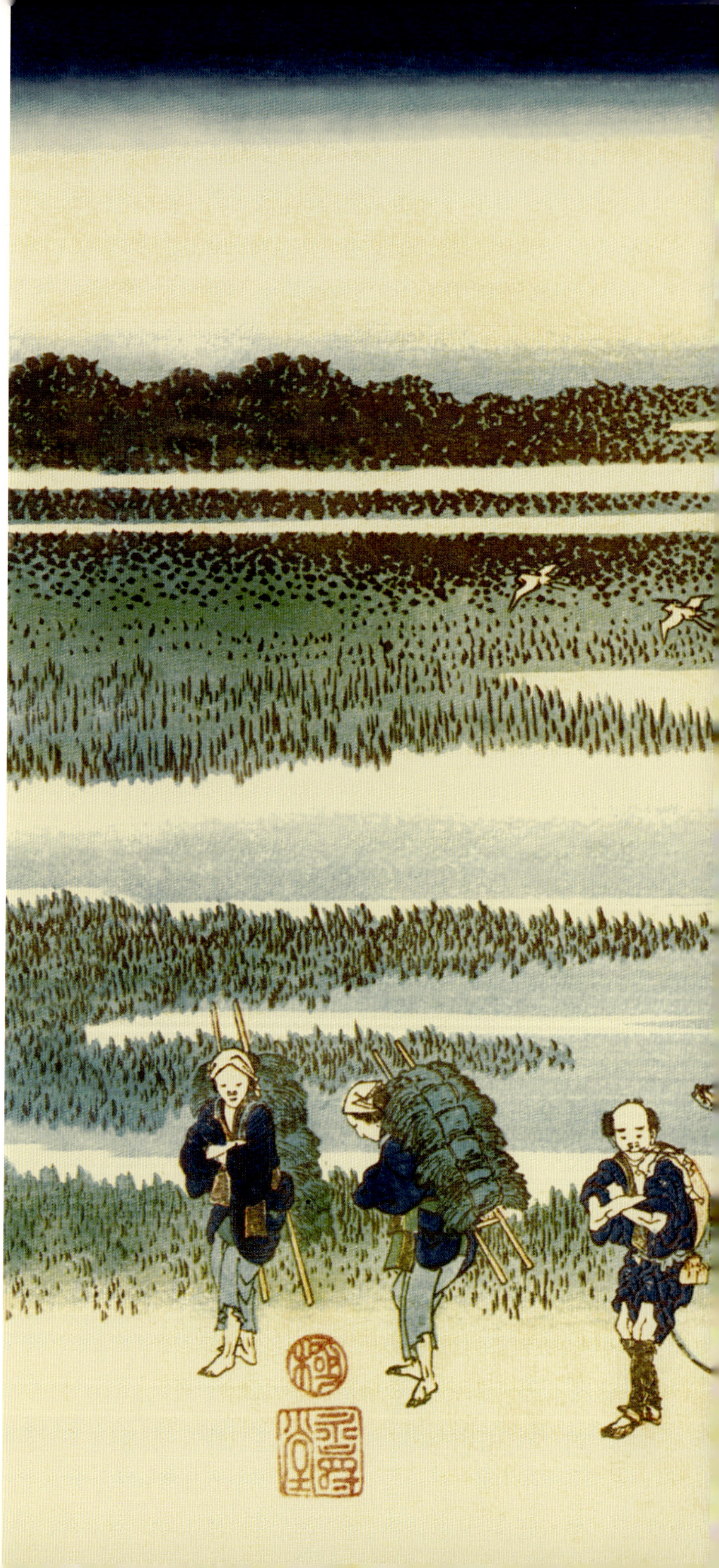

RIGHT **Katsushika Hokusai (1760–1849)** *Rice Paddies at Ono in Suruga Province* from 'Thirty-six Views of Mount Fuji' (1826–33)

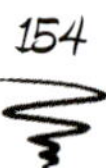

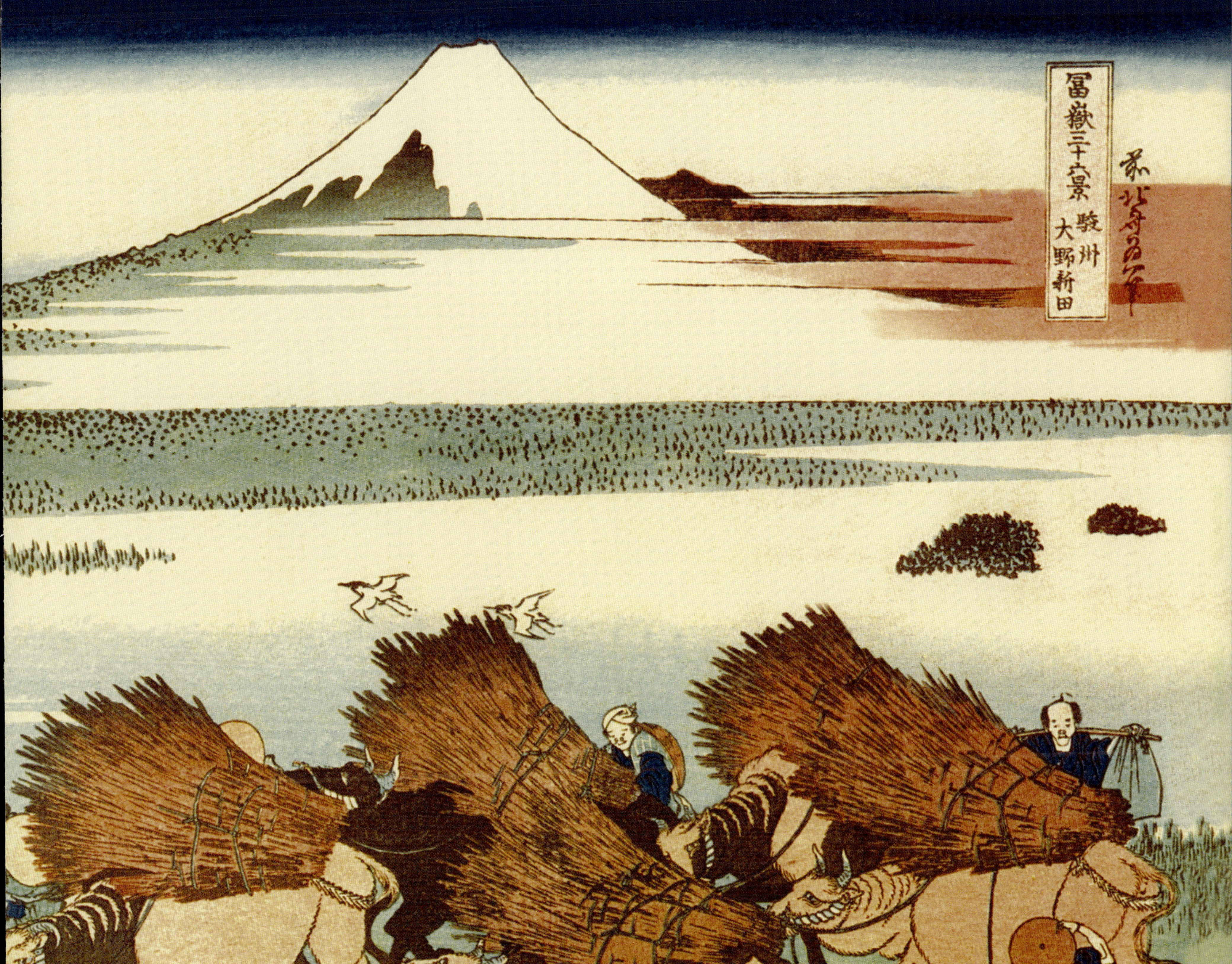
冨嶽三十六景
駿州大野新田

Is it really the photographic accuracy of a drawing which animates it? The view seems naïve now, and – like many of Kokan's remarks – likely to make one cringe. It comes as no surprise that many of his compatriots resented his pronouncements when we find him making observations such as these:

When a Western painter looks at the work of an Eastern artist, he must surely see it as the mere playing of a child, hardly worthy of the name 'painting'.

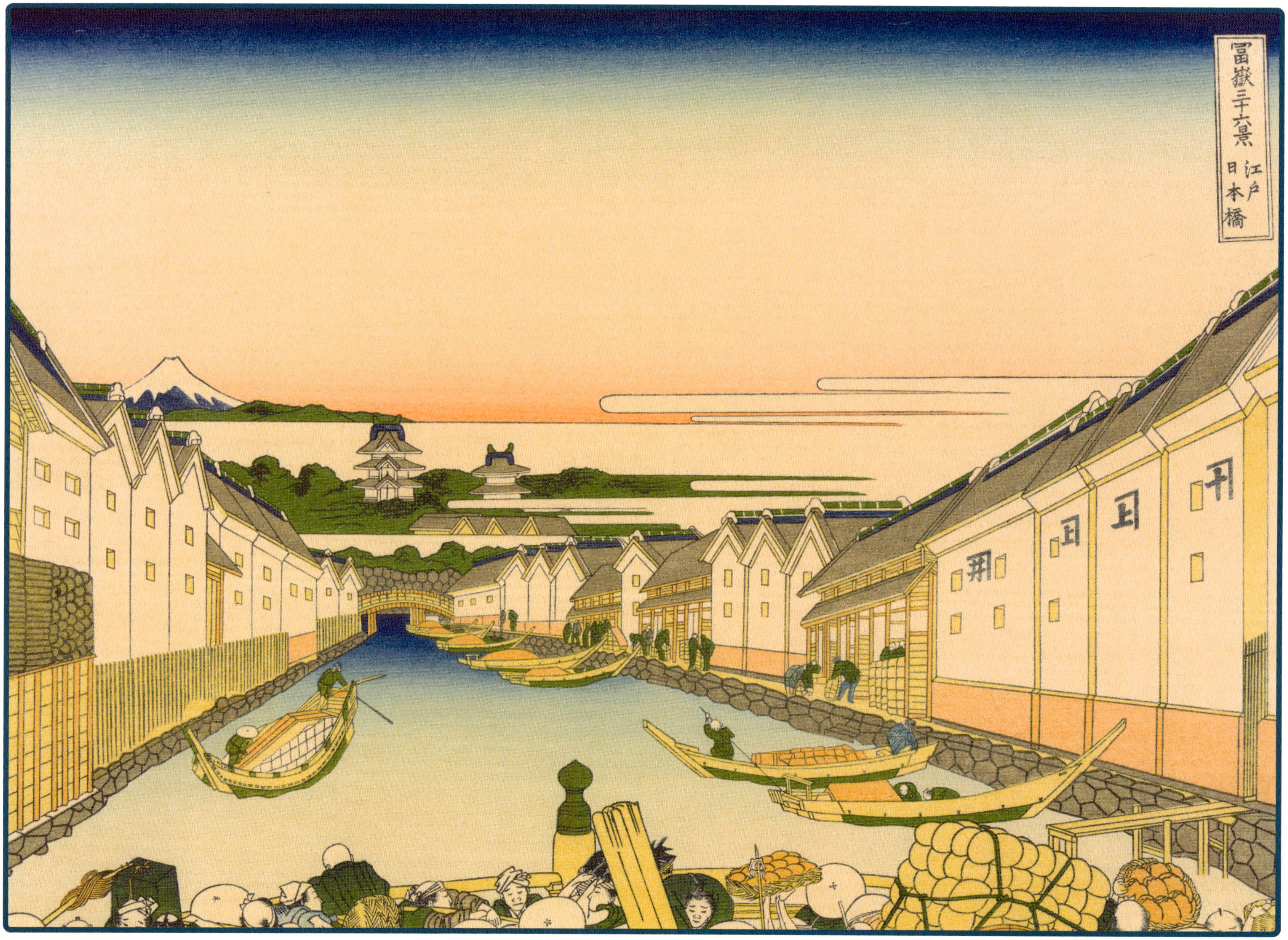

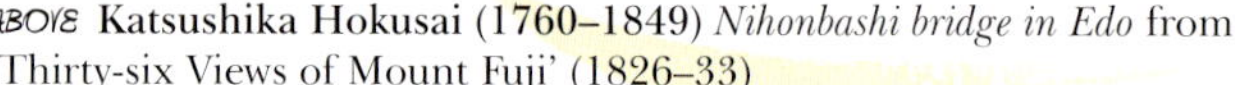

ABOVE **Katsushika Hokusai** (1760–1849) *Nihonbashi bridge in Edo* from 'Thirty-six Views of Mount Fuji' (1826–33)

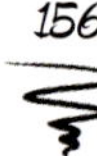

Oriental art was 'wretched', he said, and yet in their complacency Eastern artists looked on the far superior Western art as just another style; scientific perspective as nothing more than a handy trick. It seems to have been in part in an effort to convince his contemporaries of the inferiority of Japanese art that Kokan taught himself to forge the works of the *ukiyo-e* master Suzuki Harunobu (*c.* 1725–70).

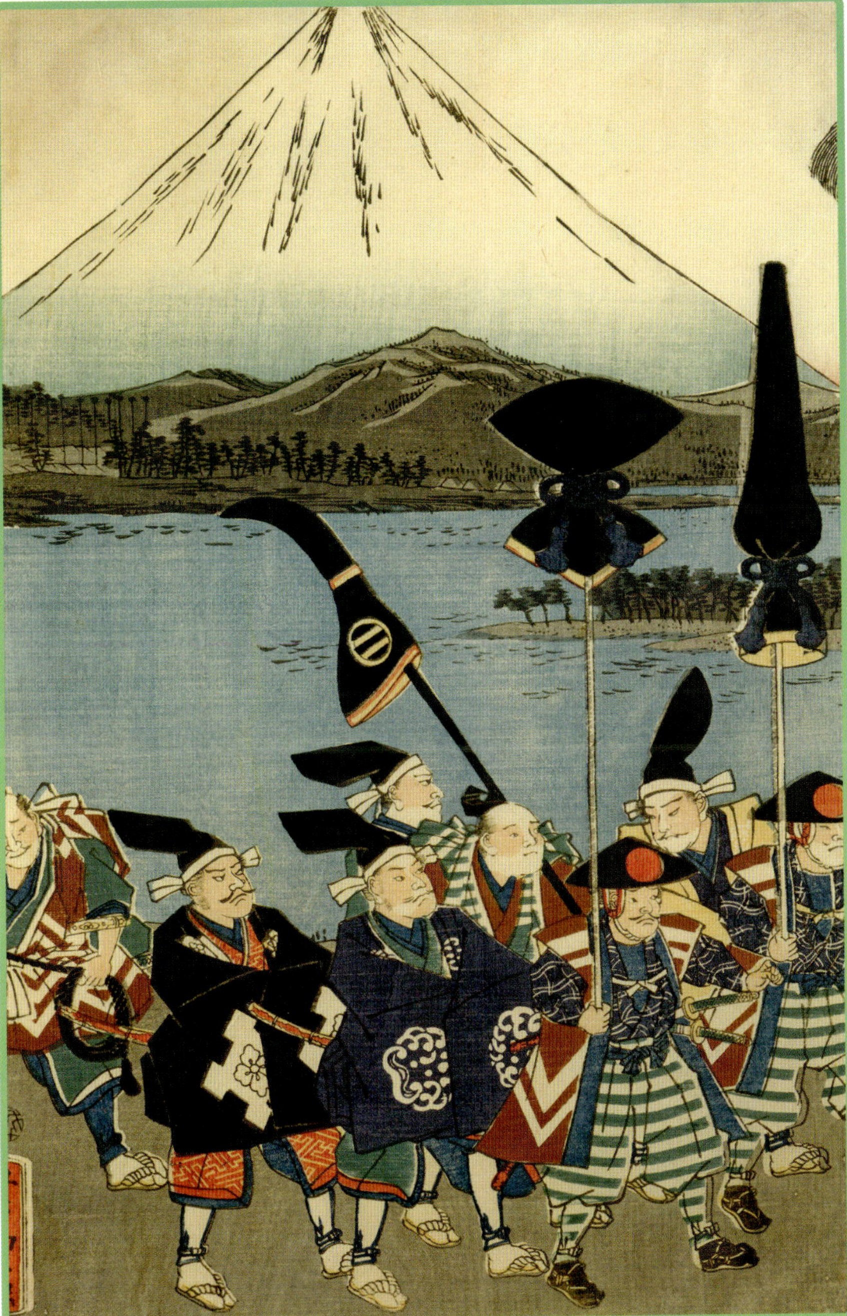

Far better, he felt, to paint 'properly', as he did in 1776 when (working, it is believed, from an imported engravings book) he produced an English scene believed to show the Serpentine – the famous lake in Hyde Park, London. His oil on silk, *Mount Fuji Seen from the Imai Ferry on the Tone River, Shimosa Province* (1812), makes an interesting comparison with Hiroshige's later *Konodai and the Tone River* (*see* page 66). Few would feel that Hiroshige's view was really in any sense more crude. And what, for example, of a work like *The Daimyo's Entourage before Mount Fuji* (1858, *see* left), by Utagawa Yoshitora (*fl.* 1850–80)? What the Fuji rising up in the background here may lack in 'proper' perspective, it surely more than compensates for in its contribution to the atmospherics of this scene.

In this sense, Kokan's career can be seen as offering an intriguing parallel to those of both Hokusai and Hiroshige, a fascinating view of a 'road not taken' in Japanese art. Even if art history has not been on his side, Shiba Kokan still warrants deep respect as an artist and a thinker of integrity and real (if, in hindsight, quixotic) ambition.

Back to the Future?

Tsukioka Yoshitoshi (1839–92) represented an almost diametrically opposing view. His career can be seen as a valiant (if futile) rearguard action against the modern world. While other printmakers discovered the joys of working with lithography and early photographic methods, he held ferociously to the old ways of woodblock printing. Such dogged, even fanatical, conservatism is not generally expected to lead to successful art, for which an adaptive openness to new developments is seen as vital.

It helped that, however hidebound he was in his methods, Yoshitoshi was nothing if not transgressive in the moody emotionalism – and often

Above Utagawa Yoshitora (*fl.* 1850–80) *The Daimyo's Entourage before Mount Fuji* (1858)

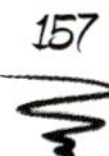

violence – of his work. What seems to have been his deep disenchantment at his country's collapse into international subservience seems to have inspired an angry pessimism which found expression in works of murder, mayhem, torture and oppression.

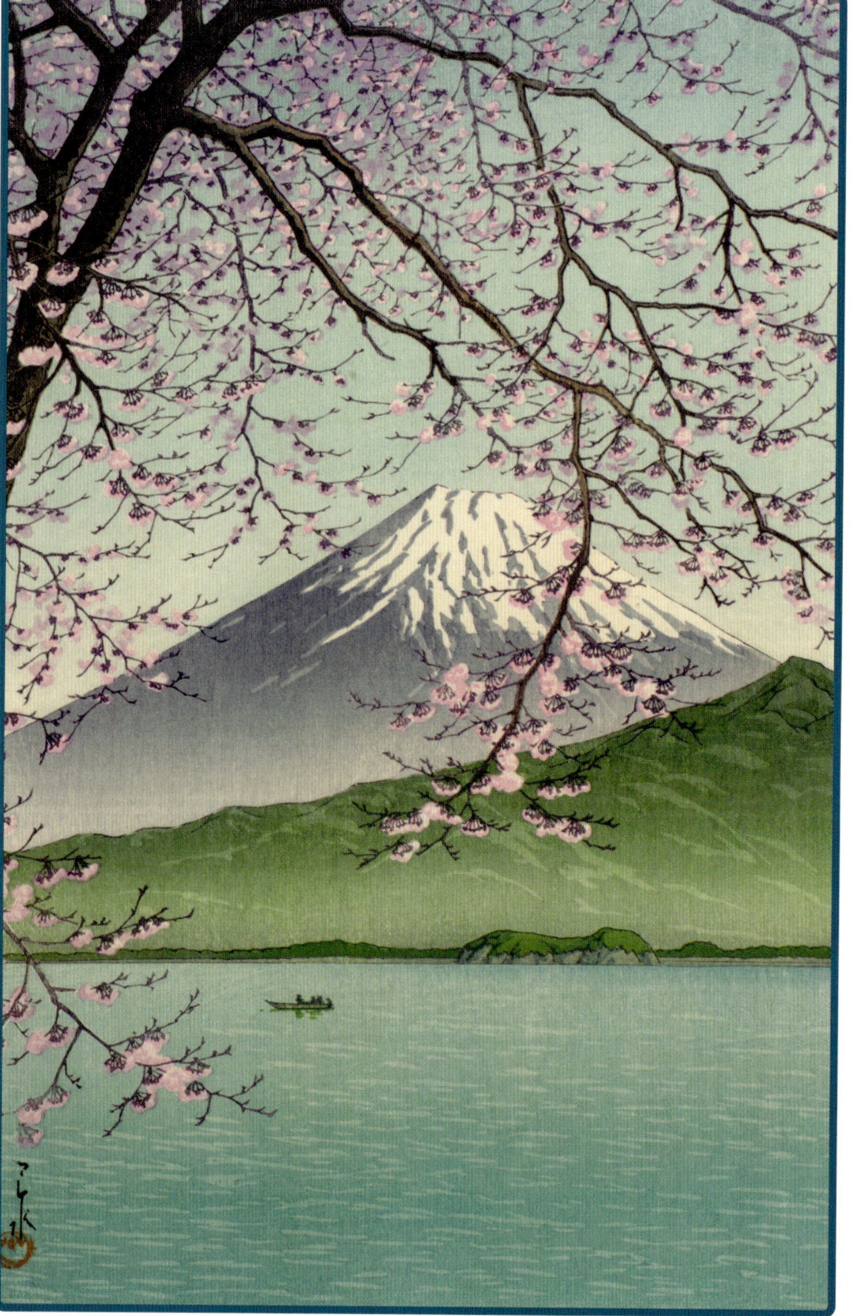

Even for Yoshitoshi, however, Fujisan seemed to offer a still centre, a point of peace; it is a commanding presence in one of his most famous works. *Moon Over the Pine Forest of Miho* shows a seated sixteenth-century warlord, Takeda Shingen (1521–73), contemplating the forest through which he has to lead his men. (The same forest, of course, had appeared in a very different light not only in stories of the remoter mythic past, but also in the recent works of both Hokusai and Hiroshige, *see* pages 45 and 179.) And then, rising behind, there is the intimidating form of Fujisan.

The fear of Takeda was the only thing that united the rival families warring for the shogunate, and prompted even Tokugawa Iesayu and his bitter enemy Oda Nobunaga (1534–82) to make common cause. Even then, Takeda had defeated them both at Mikatagahara in January 1573. Here, however, he is daunted, stopped in his tracks by the forbidding obstacles placed in his way by an unsympathetic Nature: 'even the sky bars the way', says an accompanying caption. It is hard not to read this picture as an allegory of Japanese history, in which Mount Fuji plays a vital protective and unifying role.

New Prints for Old

Yoshitoshi's radical reaction was renewed and redoubled in the early years of the twentieth century by the artists of the *Shin-hanga* 'new prints' movement. What was new about their work was its resort not only to traditional styles but to traditional methods of print-making. Artists like Hasui Kawase (1883–1957, *see* left) rejected the modern European-influenced tendency for an artist to produce his own picture – carved, coloured and printed as a one-man *fait accompli* – in favour of an old-style division of labour. The impulse was as much a matter of vision as of pure technology or technique, they felt: rather than being a miracle of artistic alchemy, printmaking was a process, requiring the contributions of a whole team. The work of Hokusai influenced *Shin-*

Above Hasui Kawase (1883–1957) *Kisho, Nishi-Izu* (1937)

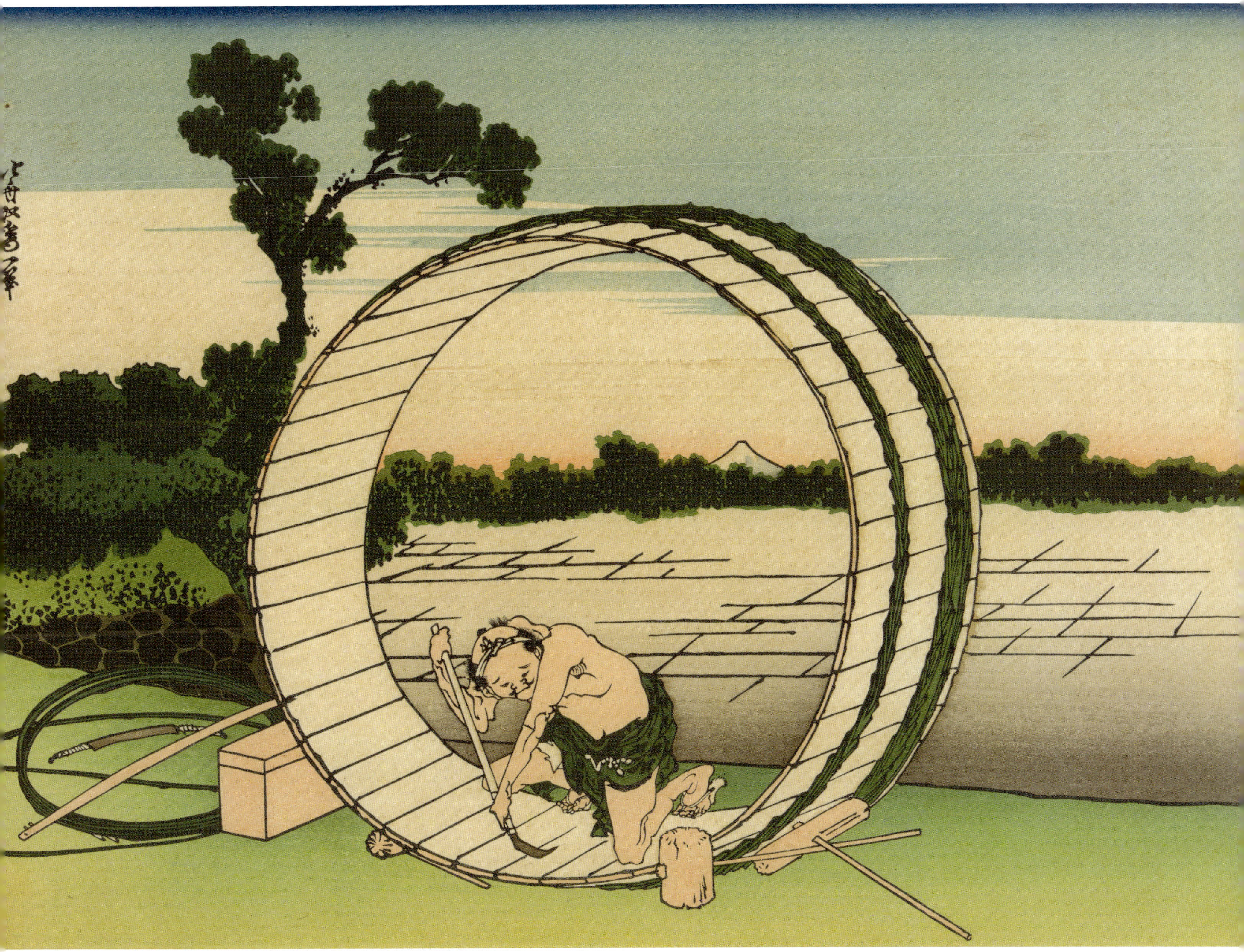

ABOVE **Katsushika Hokusai** (1760–1849) *Fuji View Field in Owari Province* from 'Thirty-six Views of Mount Fuji' (1826–33)

hanga-adherent Ogata Gekko (1859–1920, *see* opposite) not just in its techniques but in its subject matter: he created his own series of 'One Hundred Views of Mount Fuji' in 1904.

Nationalist Fuji

For better or for worse, Yokoyama Taikan (real name Sakai Hidemaro, 1868–1958, *see* right) represents the gradual transition of late-nineteenth-century national pride to that early-twentieth-century Nationalism which was finally to find geopolitical company in Hitler and Mussolini's Axis. Fuji's iconographical significance was to drift to the right as well. Indeed it became, as the historian Trevor Harrison notes, 'such a powerful expression of Japanese nationalism that, for a time after 1945, the American Occupation Authorities cut the mountain from Japanese films, viewing it as an incitement to the feudal culture they were attempting to eliminate'.

That was later. As of the 1880s, those young painters who were reinventing old traditions in a new *Nihonga* (Japanese-style) were merely resisting what they saw as their country's cultural dispossession in favour of a Westernizing *Yōga*. And it was not just national pride at stake: for many Japanese – as for many Western – intellectuals, the rise of modern industrialism had brought with it the rise of a coldly mechanistic, impersonally technocratic approach to life. Modernist poets such as W.B. Yeats and T.S. Eliot (1888–1965) and novelists such as Joseph Conrad (1857–1924) and D.H. Lawrence (1885–1930) were all at least to some extent attracted by European Fascism for this reason.

Taikan, too, seems to have deplored developments in his homeland as heralding not just the death of the nation but of beauty and of art. The two went together in the iconic image of Mount Fuji. Only gradually, over time, would its significance slowly shift and the mountain become the emotive emblem of a new and aggressive Nationalism.

Alternative Aesthetics

If Yokoyama Taikan had drawn inspiration from *ukiyo-e* art, younger artists such as Matsuoka Eikyu (1881–1938) reached even further back historically. Matsuoka was able to sidestep what was already starting to seem a problematic Nationalism by harking back to a time when there arguably had not been a Japan at all. His *yamato-e* art attempted to make a modern art of imagery and techniques which had first been developed in the Yamato state (*see* page 17) of the first millennium AD.

Not that *Yōga* did not have its continuing adherents – or Fujisan its Europhile admirers. Kyoto-born Umehara Ryuzaburo (1888–1986) seems to have taken to heart Shiba Kokan's claim that 'Only Dutch painting can accurately capture Mount Fuji', although in his case, the 'Dutch' were the French Impressionists such as Pierre-Auguste Renoir (1841–1919), with whom he studied. Whether it is truly 'accurate' is debatable, but in Umehara's work we see Fuji depicted with a well-nigh Fauvist brashness and panache.

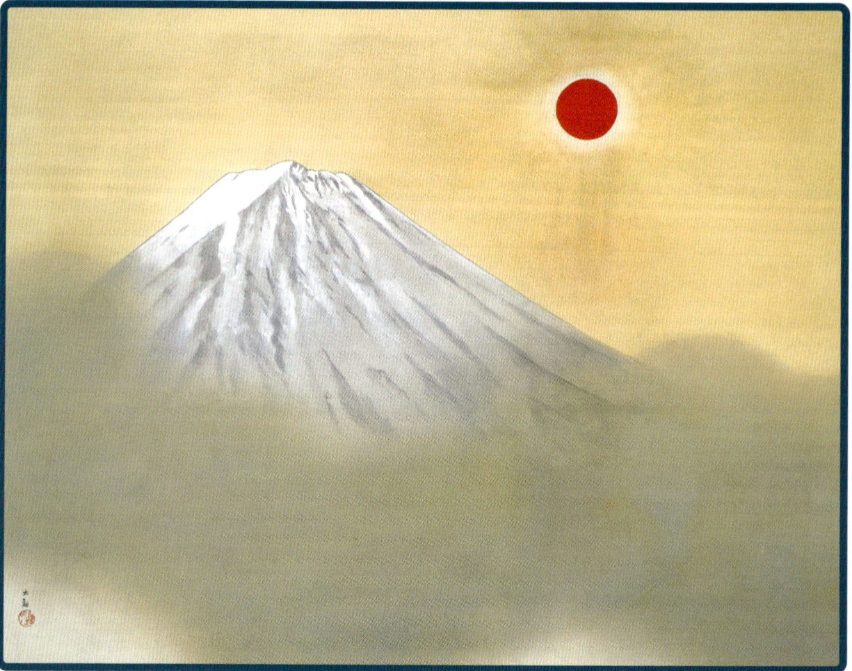

ABOVE Yokoyama Taikan (1868–1958) *Mount Fuji* (1940), scroll painting, pigment on paper

OPPOSITE Ogata Gekko (1859–1920) *Fuji from the Beach at Mio* (1900–10)

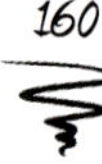

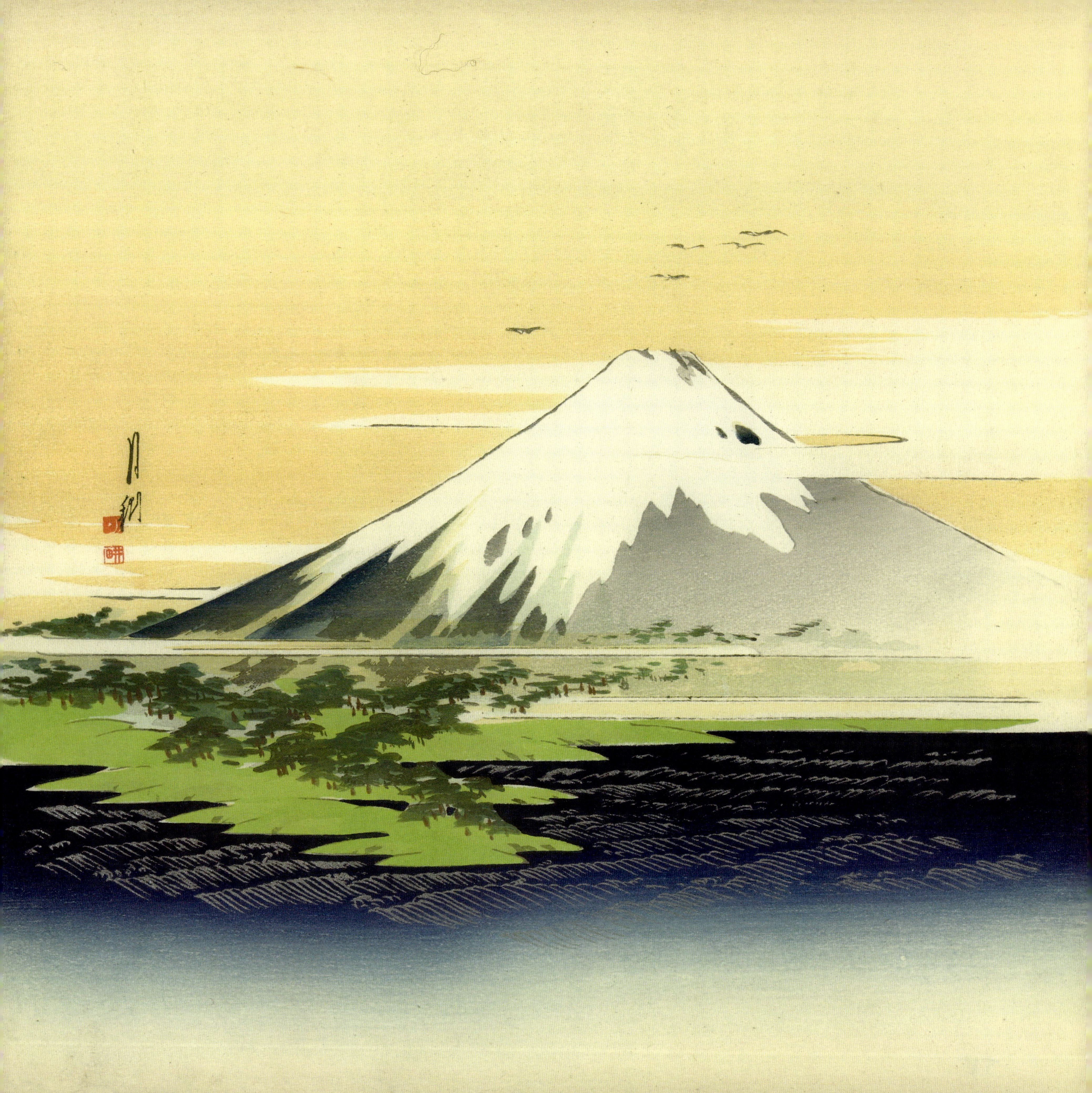

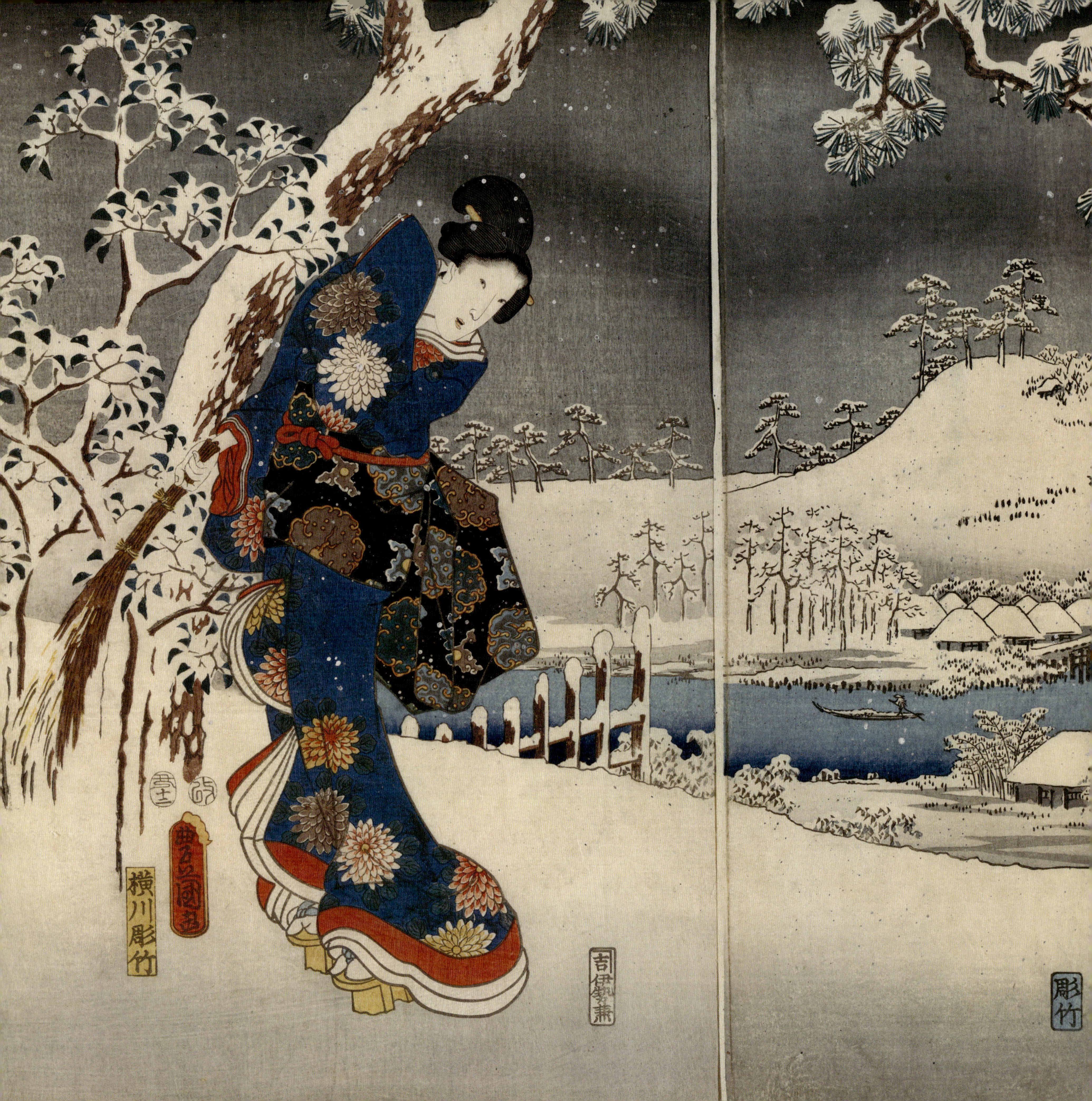
豊国画
横川彫竹
吉伊勢兼
彫竹

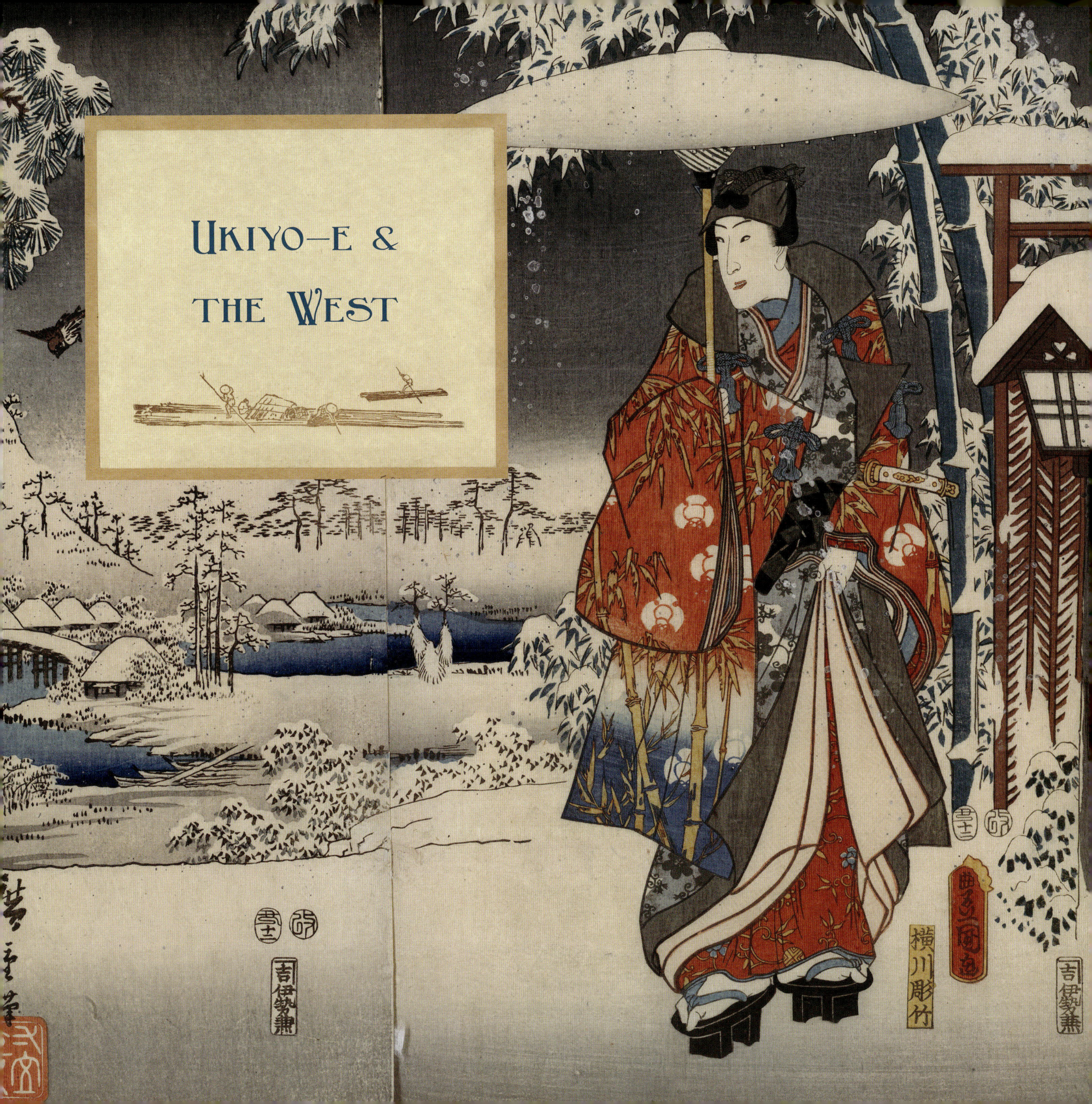
Ukiyo-e &
the West
横川彫竹

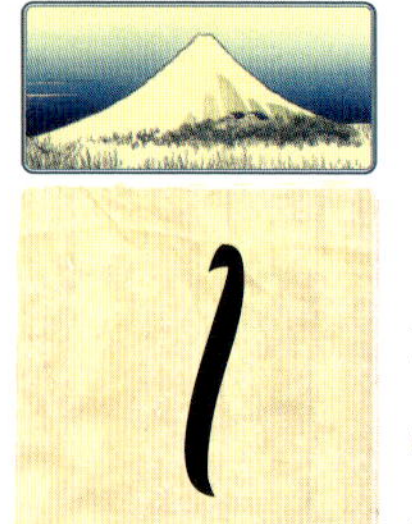

IN THE CLOSING DECADES of the nineteenth century, the Western powers made 'unequal treaties' – as tactful historians have called them – with all the Far Eastern nations, employing some quite robust encouragement, it must be said. If shots did not need to be fired to persuade the shogunate to open its doors to 'free trade' with the foreigners, that was because they had seen what happened to China at the hands of the British in the Opium Wars of the nineteenth century. So it was that Japan's Treaty of Amity and Commerce (or Harris Treaty) with the United States was agreed in 1858, when the Anglo–Japanese Treaty of Amity and Commerce was also signed. Similar treaties with Russia, the Netherlands and France followed in quick succession, with all five accorded 'most favoured nation' status.

Just three months later, as it happened, Utagawa Hiroshige passed away. On his deathbed, it is reported, he composed a poem:

I leave my brush at Azuma,
I go to the Land of the West on a journey
To view the famous sights there.

If Azuma was in downtown Edo, the 'Land of the West' was clearly the afterworld – the place the sun went to each night when it dipped below the waves. That he could look forward to his approaching trip with what sounded like an excited tourist's expectancy suggests the serenity he had attained in his final years. It was not a serenity his surviving compatriots could share, however, faced with a future in which their country looked set to be asset-stripped before their eyes.

But Hiroshige was also to go West in a much more positive and productive sense. Soon his works would be reaching a new and exhilarated audience across the world. Granted, the cultural exchange which was to bring his discovery would be part and parcel of the economic commerce his country had been forced into, but there is no disputing that *Japonisme* would be artistically liberating for the West.

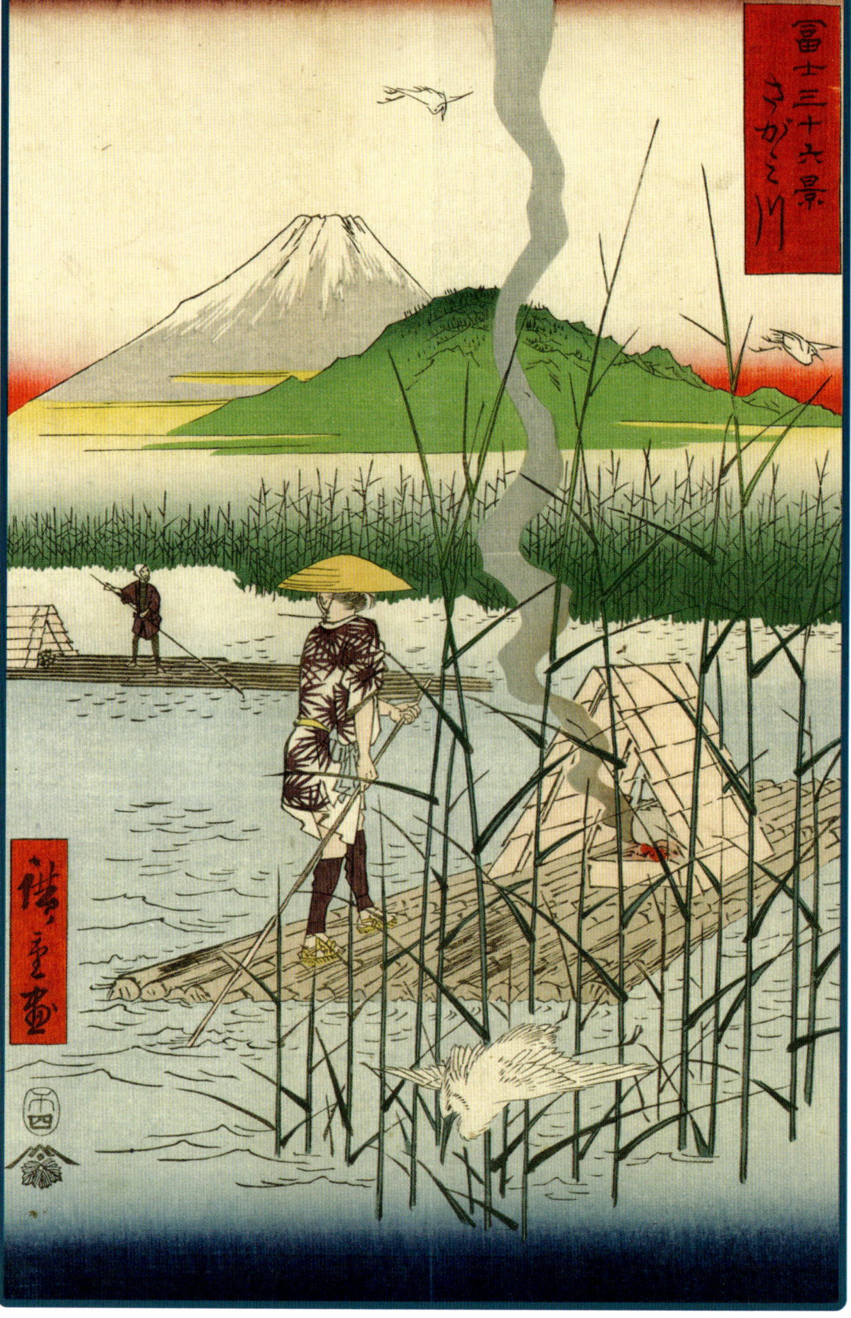

PREVIOUS PAGES Utagawa Hiroshige (1797–1858) and Toyokuni III (Utagawa Kunisada, *c.* 1786–1865) *A Modern Version of the Tale of Genji in Snow Scenes* (1853)
RIGHT Katsushika Hokusai (1760–1849) *Mount Fuji in the Sea* (detail) from Vol. 2 of 'One Hundred Views of Fuji' (1835)

ABOVE Utagawa Hiroshige (1797–1858) *The Sagami River* from 'Thirty-six Views of Mount Fuji' (1858)

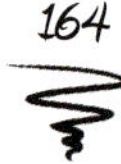

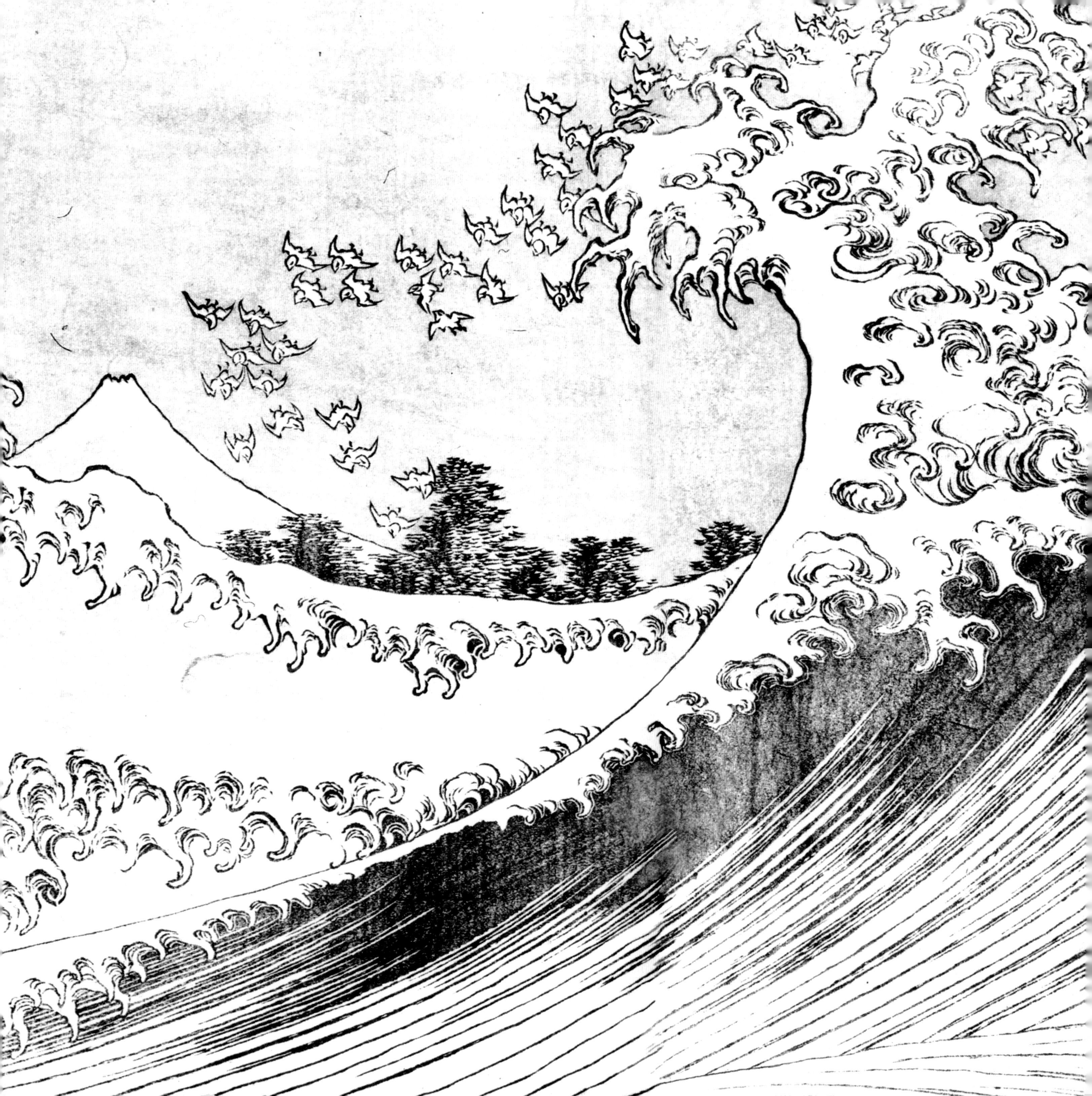

In Vogue

In 1887, in Paris, the guests at a dinner party in the play *Francillon* by Alexandre Dumas *fils* (1824–95) were told by their hostess that what they were eating was a 'Japanese salad'. For no greater reason than that, as she explained, the oriental was *à la mode*, and 'everything is Japanese these days'.

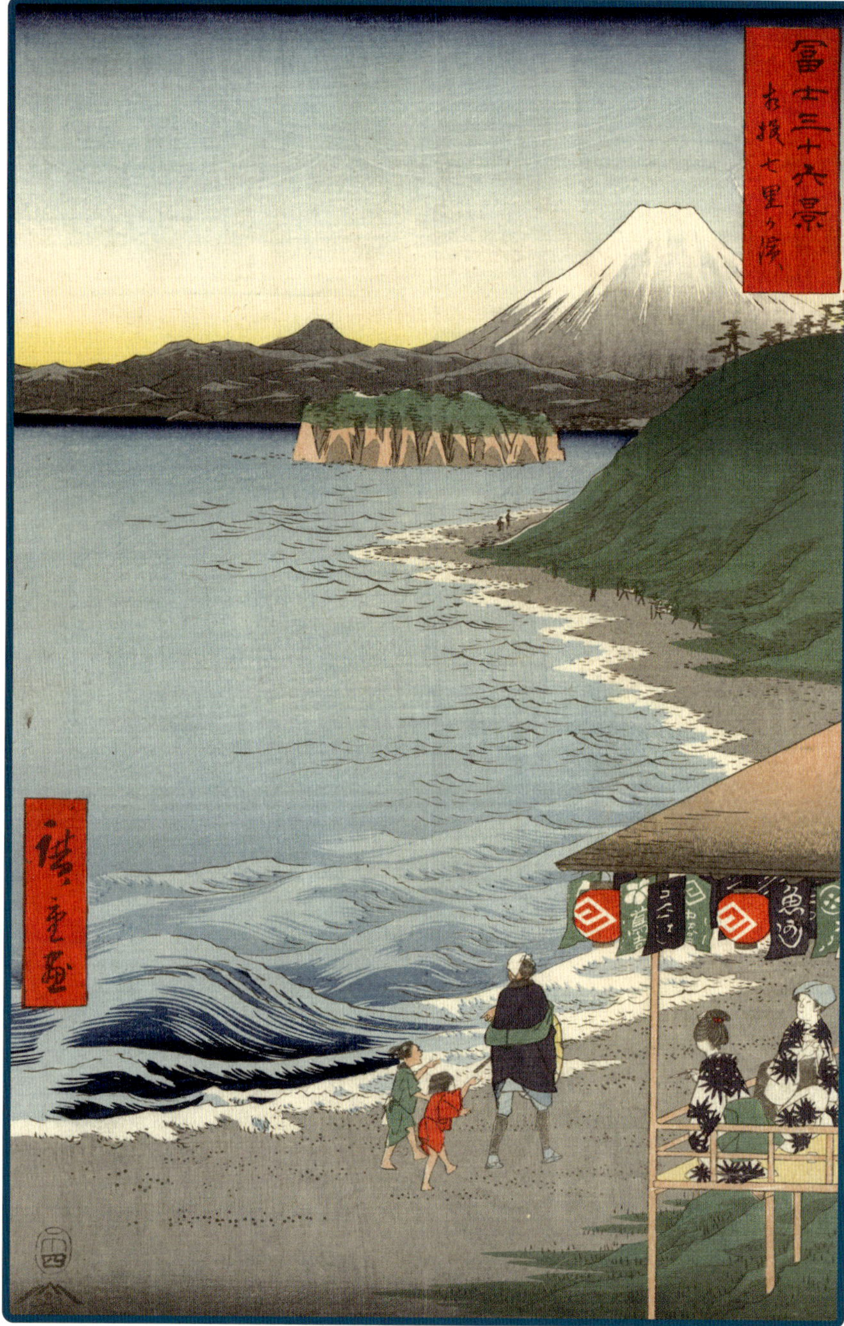

There is no doubting the sheer exoticism of Japanese art and design from a Western point of view. To find a comparable example of so rich and different a 'new world' being opened up to European eyes, we have to reach back as far as the fifteenth and sixteenth centuries, and the discoveries of the Age of Exploration. No one had seen anything like the sort of pictures to be found in the *ukiyo-e* art which surged across Europe and North America in the 1860s with all the power and grace of a Hokusai wave.

The Orient on Show

The Shogun sent a deputation to London's International Exhibition of 1862; the same year saw the opening of *La Porte Chinoise* in Paris's Rue de Rivoli, where many of the goods on sale were Japanese. That no meaningful distinction was as yet being made between the cultures of these two great – and greatly different – oriental nations is obviously a mark of Europe's colonialist condescension towards 'the Orient' – although in some ways, the remarkable aspect is how quickly (in the area of art, at least) that disdainful vagueness disappeared. It was France's turn for a World's Fair five years later, and Japan set out a truly astounding stall.

From the pagoda-style pavilion through the dazzling silken gowns of the attendants to the 'china' teacups, every inch of the exhibit was radically, staggeringly different from anything spellbound visitors had ever seen. Even so, it was the *ukiyo-e* prints that stole the show and whose impact continued to reverberate, long after the exhibition had closed its gates. Nor was that impact confined to the field of 'high' or museum art. As prints, these new imports were intrinsically more affordable than oil paintings and more obviously suited to possession and exhibition in the bourgeois home. Part of the attraction, indeed, was the way in which the

Above Utagawa Hiroshige (1797–1858) *The Seven Ri Beach in Sagami Province* from 'Thirty-six Views of Mount Fuji' (1858)

Right Utagawa Hiroshige (1797–1858) *Dog Eye Pass in Kai Province* from 'Thirty-six Views of Mount Fuji' (1858)

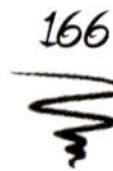

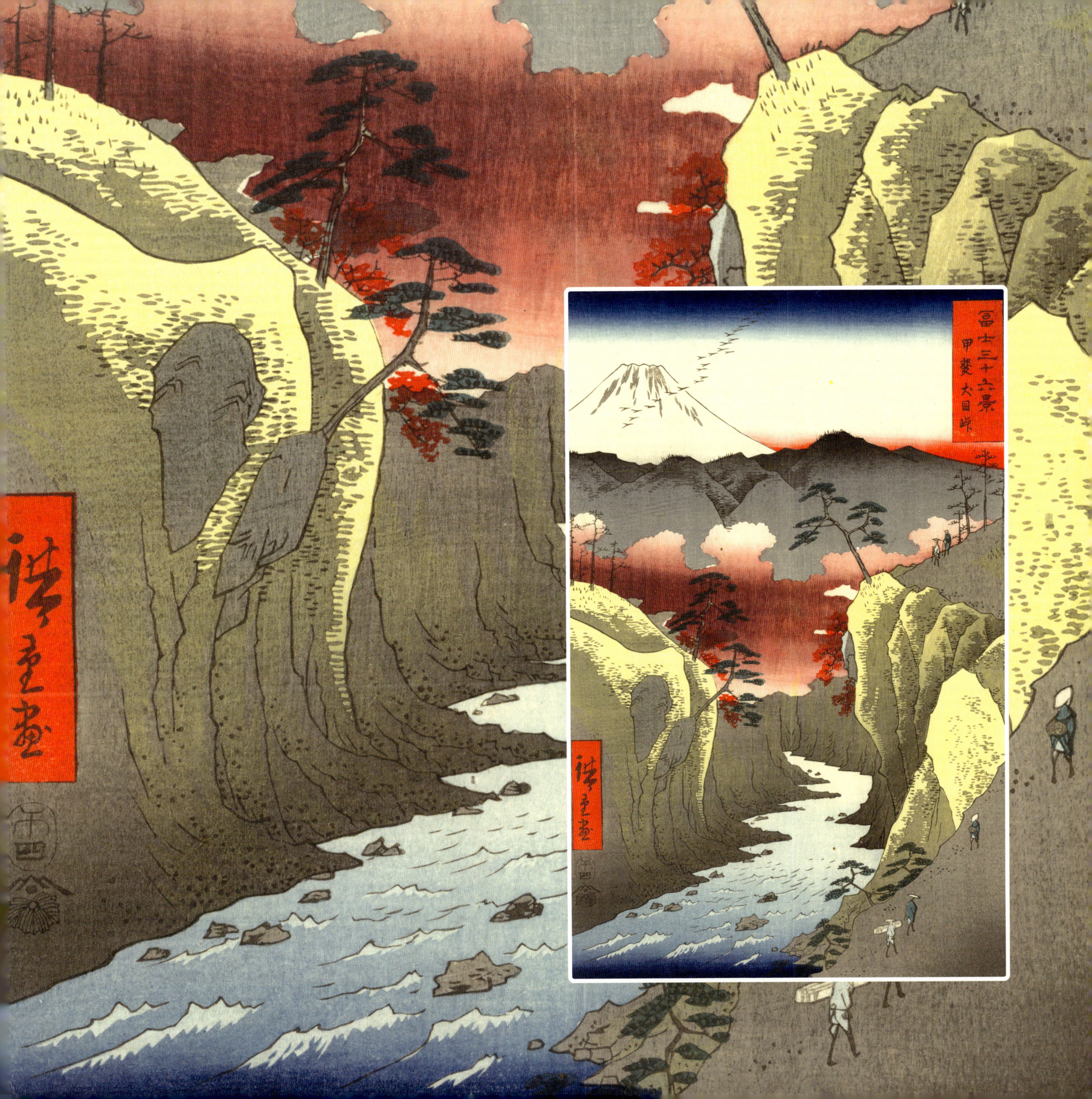

oriental aesthetic transcended the traditional European boundaries: beauty did not stop at the picture frame.

Design Comes Home

Nor even at the stunningly shaped, exquisitely inlaid, lacquered and enamelled furnishings (the screens, the cabinets, the dressing tables, the vases) with which they now shared the fashionable home; the Japanese designed beauty into every area of life. Whilst it would be quite wrong to suggest that *Japonisme* was decisive in bringing in the idea of the 'art of the everyday', it certainly lent impetus to what was already an exciting movement, Europe-wide. In England, the Arts and Crafts movement, established by the socialist artist and thinker William Morris (1834–96), was already by the 1880s making the case that art should not be a separate sphere: a well-designed wallpaper or tablecloth could be as beautiful and as life-enhancing as an oil painting. Morris's views stemmed from his concern both for a labour force left deskilled and alienated by industrial production and for consumers schooled to settle for shoddy factory goods. But their appeal extended far beyond the revolutionary left.

Unusually, Morris missed a trick, asserting in 1893 that the Japanese had 'no architectural, and therefore no decorative, instinct'. But his younger contemporary Aubrey Beardsley (1872–98), making the pilgrimage to Paris in the early 1890s, became an enthusiastic convert to the values of French *Art Nouveau* – which was steeped in *Japonisme* to its very core. Poster-painter and printmaker Henri de Toulouse-Lautrec (1864–1901) was utterly in love with *ukiyo-e*, in all its values – with its frank commercialism as much as its use of space and line. Along with a great many other young artists, Alphonse Mucha (1860–1939, *see* opposite) saw the *Japoniste* light at Paris's World Exhibition of 1889.

It was not just the artists who were drawn to the new look. Wealthy clients were beginning to get the message as well, not least because they saw that the plutocrat's home need no longer just be a castle, it could be a palace, and an important public statement of who they were. In 1902, for example, Glasgow publisher Walter Blackie (1816–1906) had a new home built, Hill House, in Helensburgh, across the Firth of Clyde. He had been

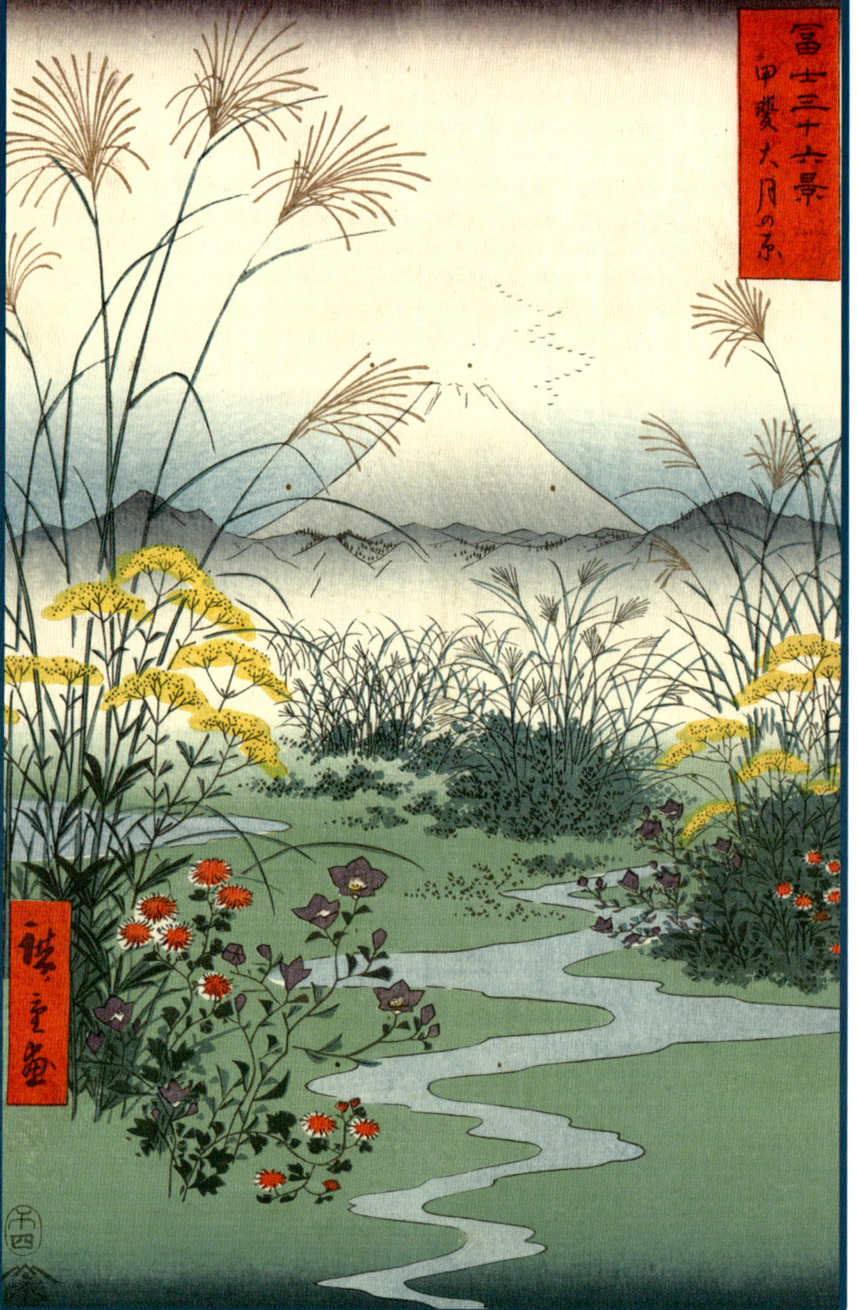

OPPOSITE **Alphonse Mucha** (1860–1939) Plate 33 from 'Documents Decoratifs' (1902), colour lithograph

ABOVE **Utagawa Hiroshige** (1797–1858) *The Otsuki Plain in Kai Province* from 'Thirty-six Views of Mount Fuji' (1858)

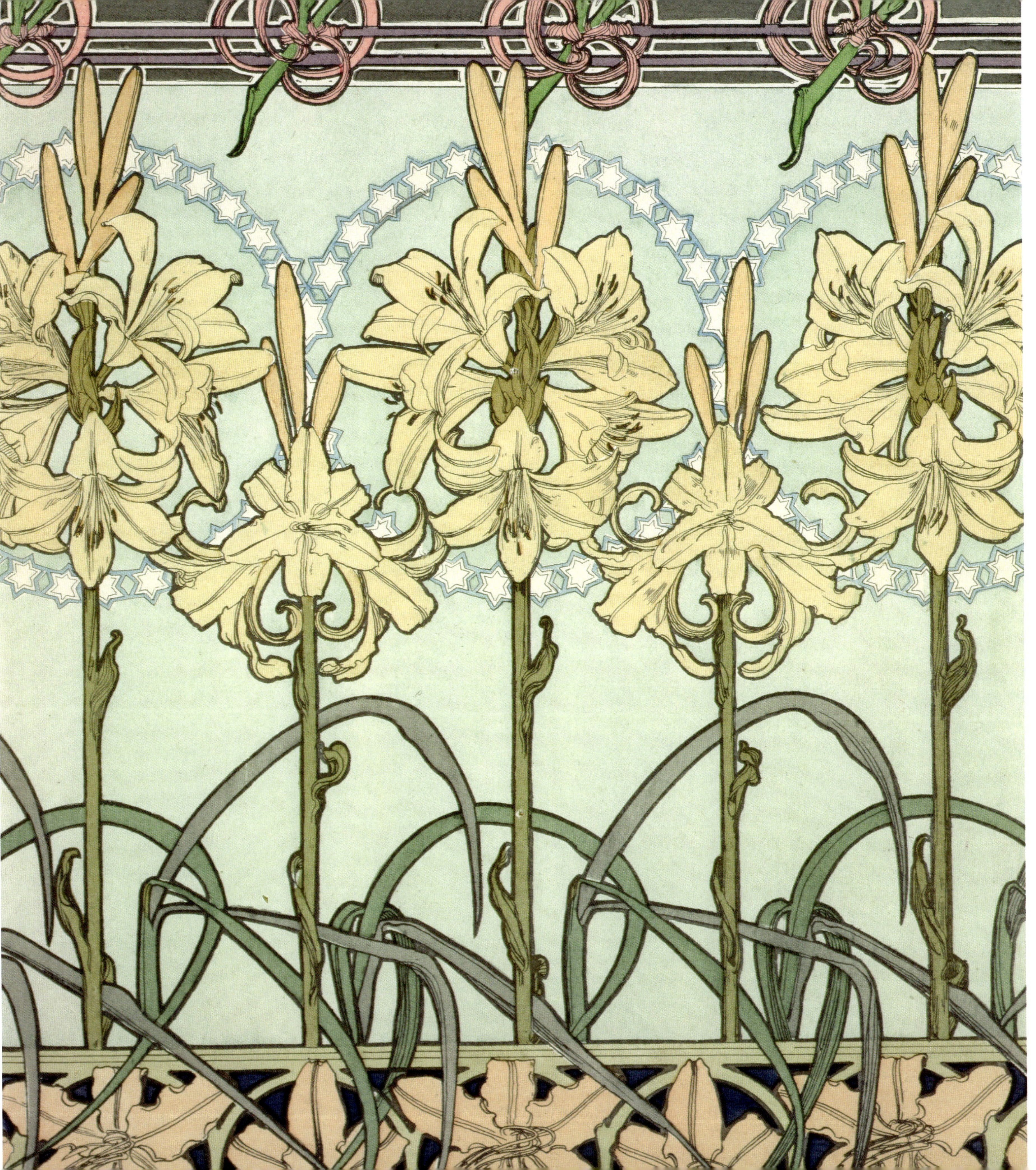

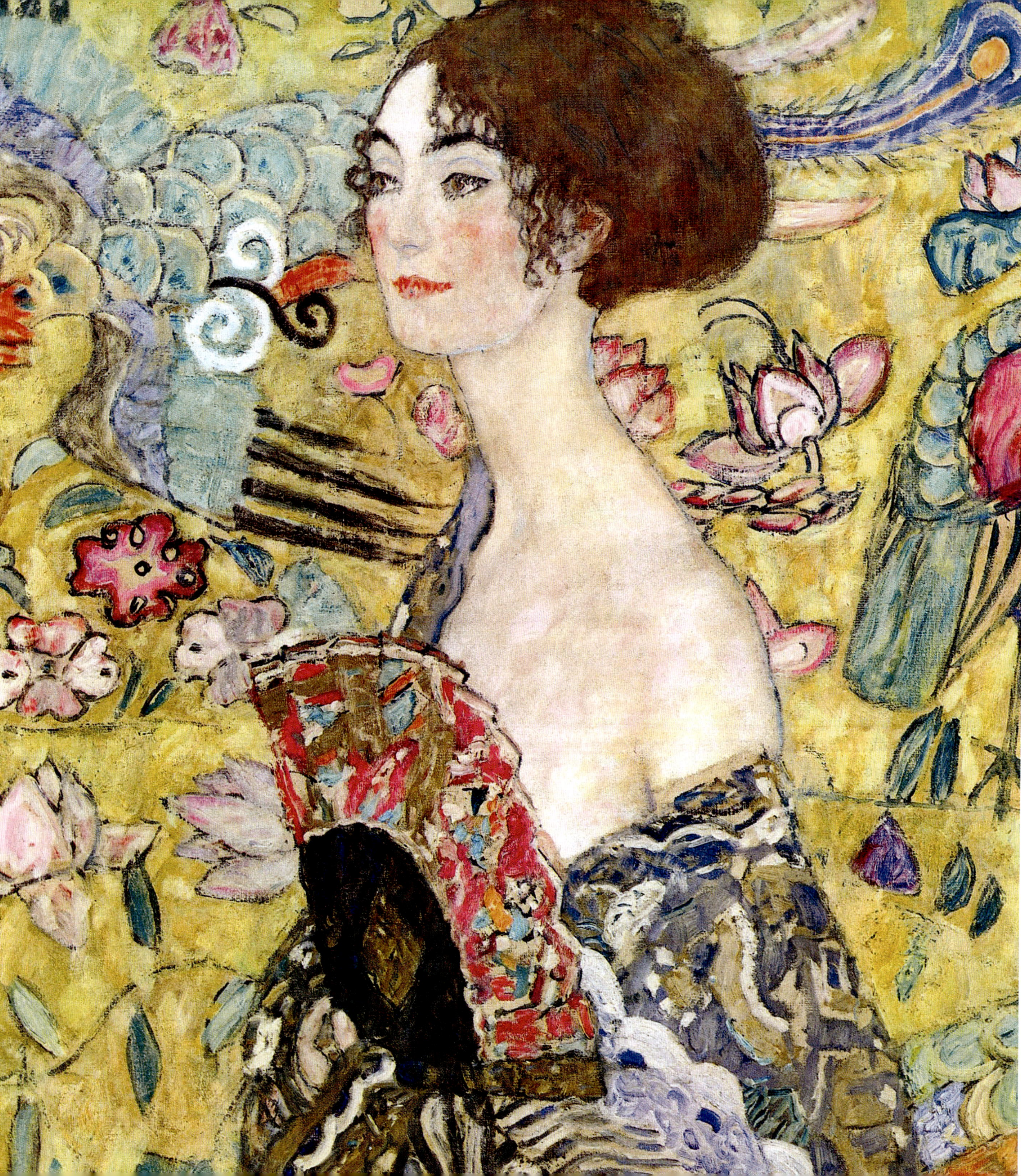

given the name of his architect, Charles Rennie Mackintosh (1868–1928) by Blackie & Son's art manager, who had used him as an illustrator and designer – another example of how art was coming to seem to be a seamless continuum, rather than a set of separate fields.

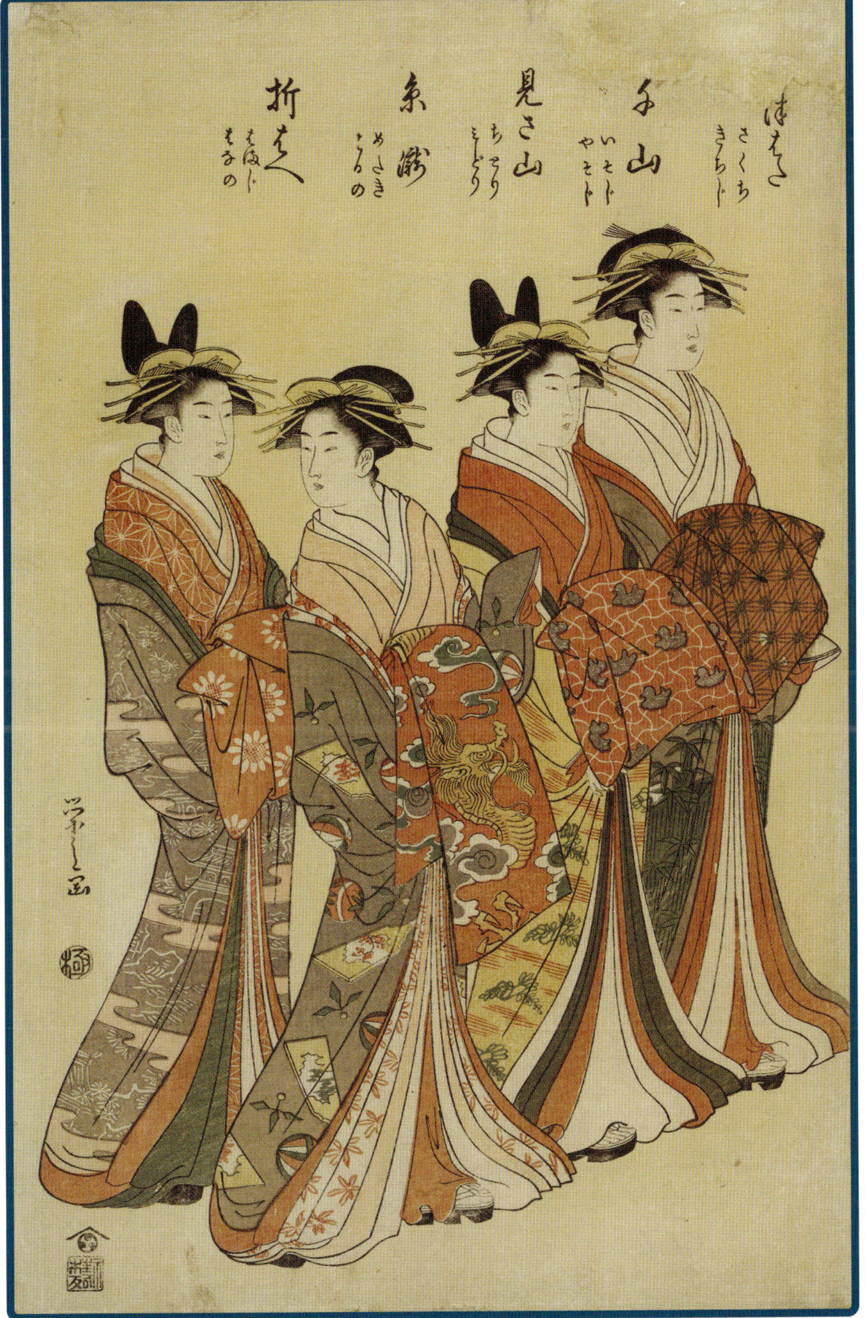

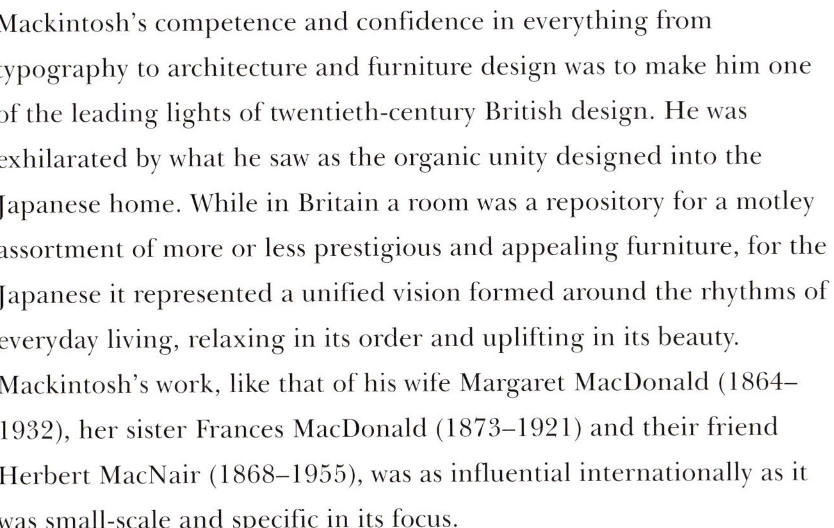

Mackintosh's competence and confidence in everything from typography to architecture and furniture design was to make him one of the leading lights of twentieth-century British design. He was exhilarated by what he saw as the organic unity designed into the Japanese home. While in Britain a room was a repository for a motley assortment of more or less prestigious and appealing furniture, for the Japanese it represented a unified vision formed around the rhythms of everyday living, relaxing in its order and uplifting in its beauty. Mackintosh's work, like that of his wife Margaret MacDonald (1864–1932), her sister Frances MacDonald (1873–1921) and their friend Herbert MacNair (1868–1955), was as influential internationally as it was small-scale and specific in its focus.

Their example was to be an inspiration for Koloman Moser (1868–1918), Josef Hoffmann (1870–1956) and their fellow workers of the Wiener Werkstätte to undertake wall-to-wall designs of complete domestic interiors in their quest to produce what they called the *Gesamtkunstwerk* ('total work of art'). Their friend and fellow artist Gustav Klimt (*see* opposite) was much taken with Japanese art as well. The influence is apparent not only in the luxuriously lacquered, spangled, decorated look of his most celebrated paintings, but also in the chaste austerity of the monochrome prints he created for the contemporary art magazine, *Ver Sacrum*.

The Art Market

Nor was it just in the home that *Japonisme* was to exercise its influence. The style transformed the art world from top to bottom. It may, in fact, have been the bottom that transformed the top, if the anecdote of the *fin de siècle* is to be believed. The Japanese aesthetic did not just find its way into Europe in the form of finished artworks but in the incidentals of ordinary commercial life. Whether it is actually true that – as the artistic gossip was to have it – Monet (*see* page 173) had his orientalist epiphany when he saw some of the wrappings in a spice shop hardly matters. Nor is

Above Eishi Hosoda (1756–1829) *The Courtesans Mitsuhata, Senzan, Misayama, Itotaki and Oribae* (1791–93)

Opposite Gustav Klimt (1862–1918) *Lady with a Fan* (1917–18), oil on canvas it really important whether Whistler had his when he bought some packs of Chinese tea.

As important as any specific insight these great artists might have had from the designs they saw in such seemingly unpromising contexts was the revelation that artistic design could extend into the realm of the everyday.

It seems symbolically important, at the very least, that Hokusai's prints were first discovered in Europe when the French artist Félix Bracquemond (1833–1914) unpacked some porcelain and was thrilled to see the pictures on the papers crumpled up as wrapping – as important, surely, as the inherent value of Hokusai's work evident in its presence around household utensils for daily use.

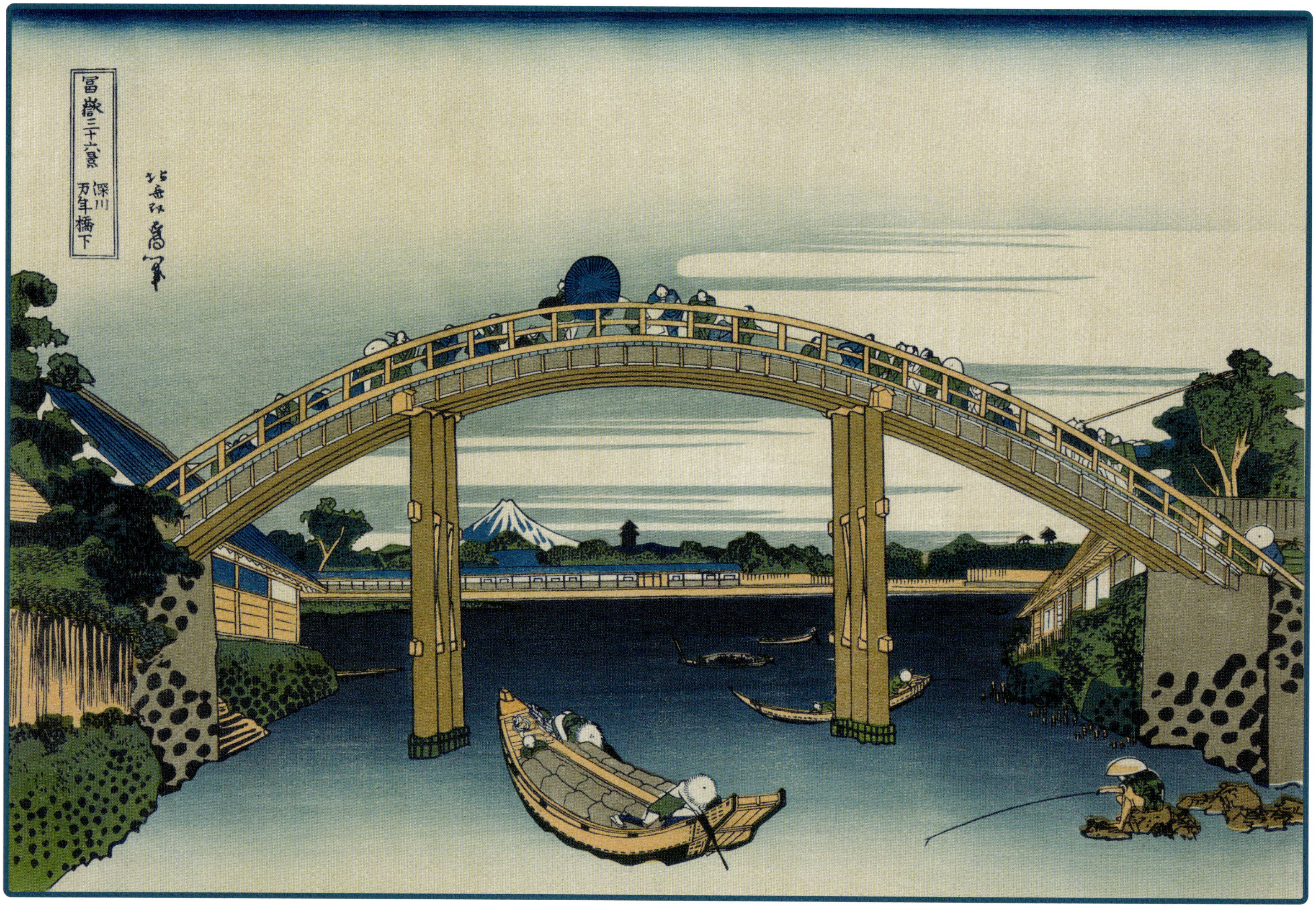

Above **Katsushika Hokusai (1760–1849)** *Under Mannen Bridge at Fukagawa* from 'Thirty-six Views of Mount Fuji' (1826–33, printed later)

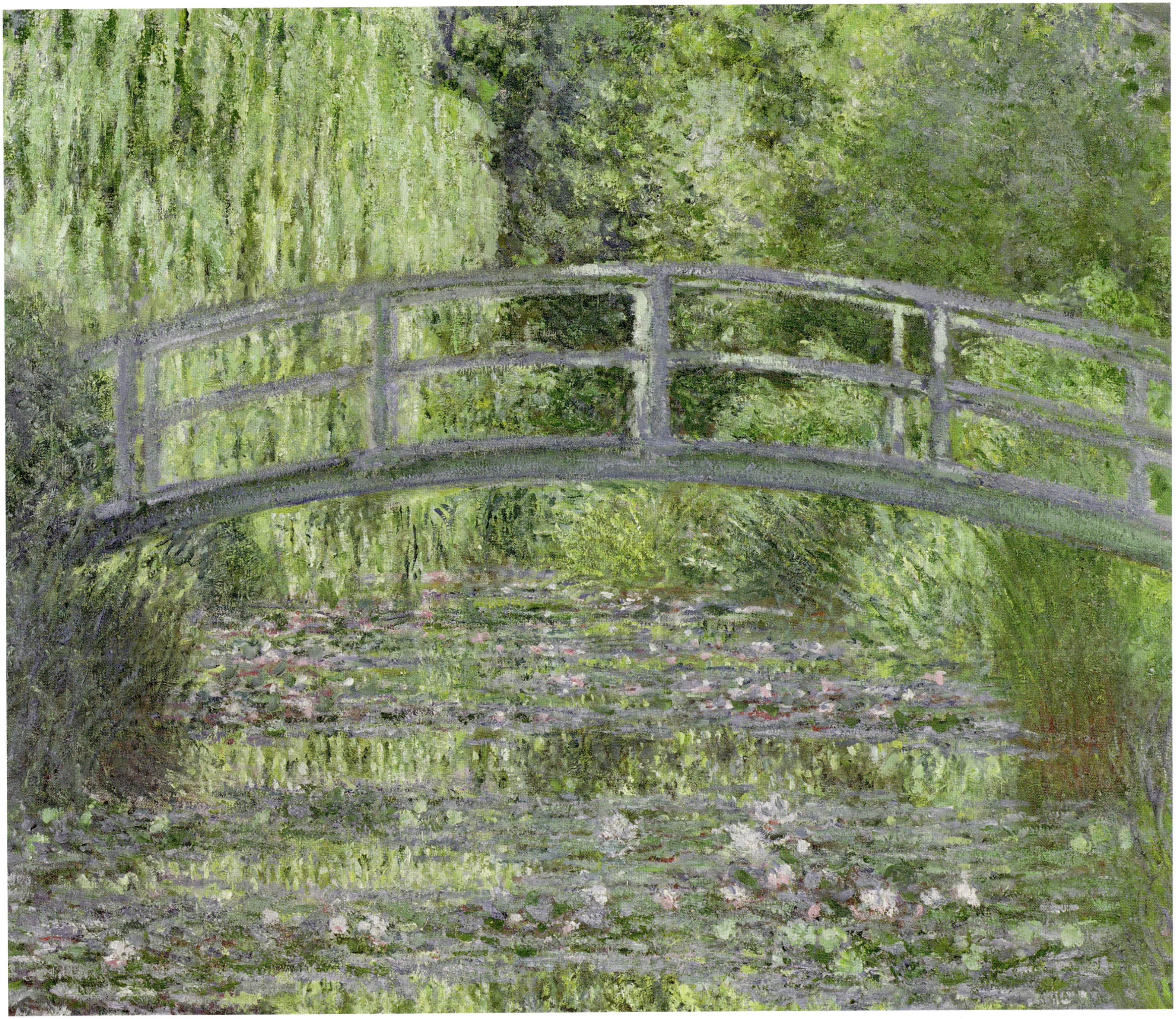

ABOVE Claude Monet (1840–1926) *The Waterlily Pond: Green Harmony* (1899), oil on canvas

Inspirational Disposability

And, of course, at least in hindsight, the treatment of such august artistic work as essentially disposable was also important. As we have seen (*see* page 22), whilst its overall output may have been small by the standards of our own time, *ukiyo-e* was in some ways more like the product of a modern mass culture than of the systems of elitist patronage which had prompted so much creativity in the West. Whilst the Pop Art of Andy Warhol (1928–97), Roy Lichtenstein (1923–97) and Jasper Johns (1930–) obviously lay many decades in the future, European artists could still find something intriguing (however disconcerting) in the thought that real art might be mass-produced and then thrown away.

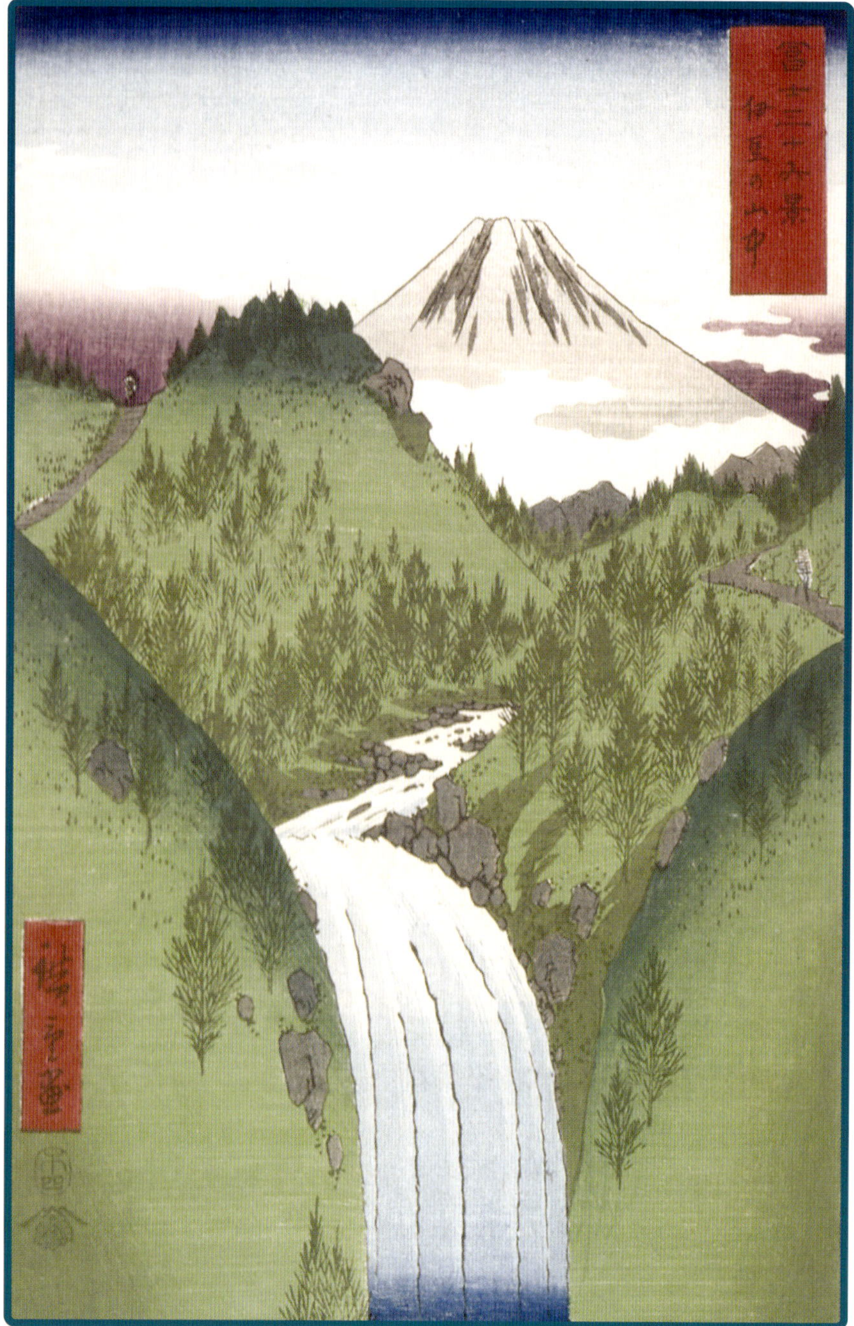

Above Utagawa Hiroshige (1797–1858) *The Izu Mountains* from 'Thirty-six Views of Mount Fuji' (1858)

Even packaging could be beautiful, then; even padding for porcelain could please the eye. There was no need for ugliness or for a lack of aesthetic judgment, anywhere. Japanese art was not just a collection of images and objects (or even a set of principles), then, but a complete way of life, a totalizing view.

Myth, Metamyth and Mountain

And Mount Fuji – or Fujiyama, as the Europeans had taken to calling it – towered over that totality in its unifying form. Take, for instance, the embossed triptych screen that Hiroshige and his fellow Utagawa alumnus Kunisada (1786–1865) had decorated together with woodblock print in 1857. *A View of Tago Bay* shows a stunning land- and seascape in which all eyes are drawn to Fuji, especially because, before it in the beachfront garden in the picture's immediate foreground, two tall black cones of sand rise up like mini mountains. Which was, of course, the precise intention of those who created these *tsukiyama* – smaller versions of the larger, grass-covered mounds raised up around Edo by ardent followers of the Fuji cult (*see* page 146).

And, indeed, at right foreground, we see the legendary poet-Prince Genji reciting to a female companion the poem he wrote about his garden, with its two little Fujis made of sand. *The Tale of Genji*, reputedly written by the imperial lady-in-waiting Murasaki Shikubu (*c.* 973–*c.* 1014), is of course a

Right Katsushika Hokusai (1760–1849) *Ono Falls on the Kisokaido* from 'Visiting Famous Waterfalls of Japan' (*c.* 1833, printed later)

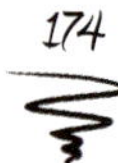

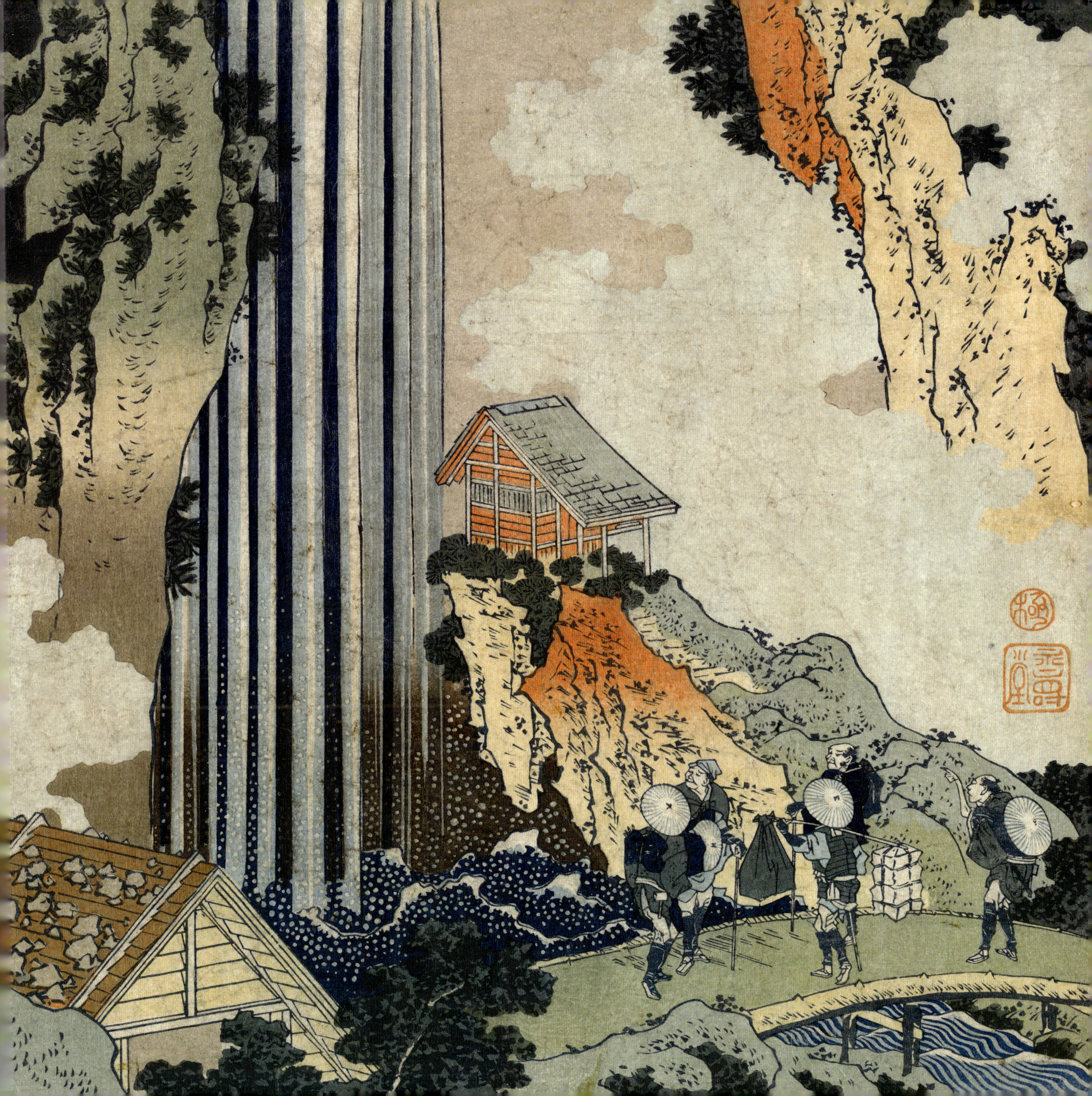

classic of Japanese literature. Arguably the world's first novel, and certainly among the very earliest work of which this claim could reasonably be made, it is in addition an absolutely enchanting – exciting, romantic, moving and in many ways witty – story. It is also a work of

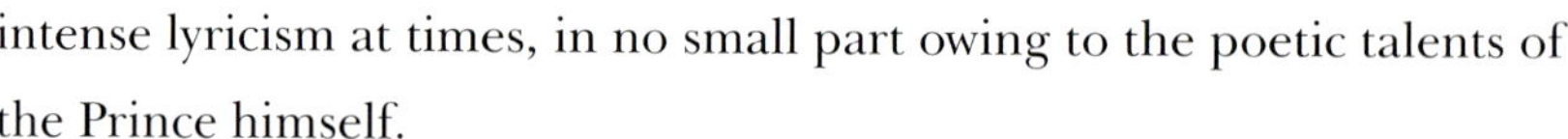

intense lyricism at times, in no small part owing to the poetic talents of the Prince himself.

Here, then, Hiroshige and Kunisada take us on a little artistic mystery tour. We see the picture painted by a poem within a novel within a picture within a screen – within, presumably, when the work was originally commissioned, a decorated room. And, framing the whole experience (as, to some extent, it has the whole history of Japanese art), the figure of Fuji, and the mythic and aesthetic values it represents.

In a quite extraordinary way – and at quite extraordinary speed – those values appeared to be acquiring centrality for artists in the West as well. Whistler went so far as to say (in the *Ten O'Clock Lecture* he gave in Princes Hall, Piccadilly, London, in 1885) that 'the story of the beautiful is already complete – hewn in the marbles of the Parthenon, and broidered, with the birds, upon the fan of Hokusai – at the foot of Fusihama'. The significance of this pronouncement can hardly be overstated: Whistler puts *ukiyo-e* on a par with a classical achievement which had until then been revered as representing the sole origin and arbitrative yardstick for Western art.

The Erotic Exotic

We should not, of course, assume that – even in the 'higher' echelons of European art – the enthusiasm for *Japonisme* was entirely high-minded. In Western culture, the East has long been as much a psychic site as a geographical location, the place to which the romantic and transgressive spirit goes. And it was an explicitly feminine place at that, with all the enchanting exoticism and danger that haunted the consciousness of the nineteenth-century Western male. 'There is not a bourgeois alive,' wrote Gustave Flaubert (1821–80), 'who hasn't imagined himself capable of great passions and noble deeds. What petty seducer hasn't dreamt of Eastern queens?'

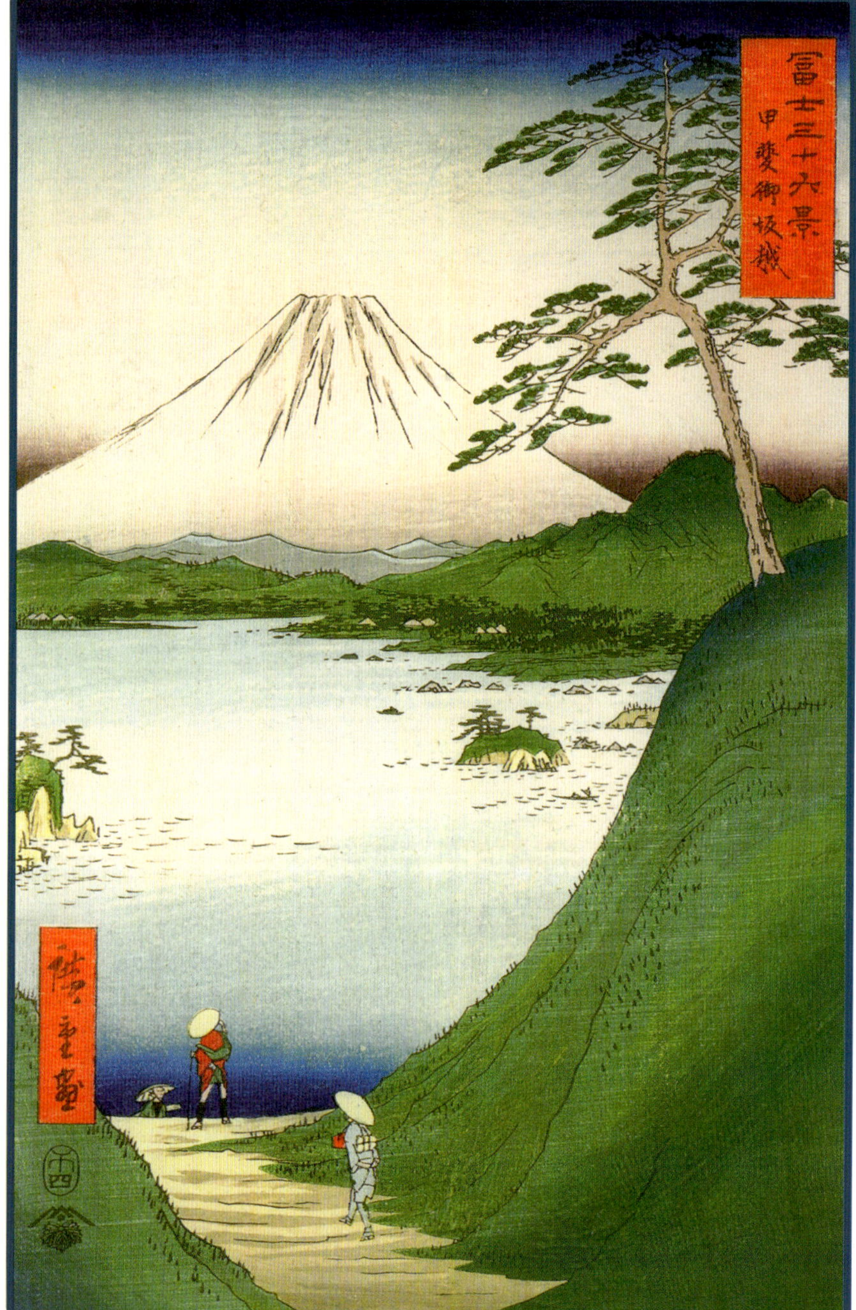

Above Utagawa Hiroshige (1797–1858) *Misaka Pass in Kai Province* from 'Thirty-six Views of Mount Fuji' (1858)

Right Katsushika Hokusai (1760–1849) *Kirifuri Falls at Mount Kurokami in Shimosuke* from 'Visiting Famous Waterfalls of Japan' (*c.* 1833, printed later)

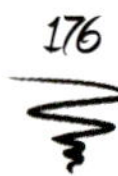

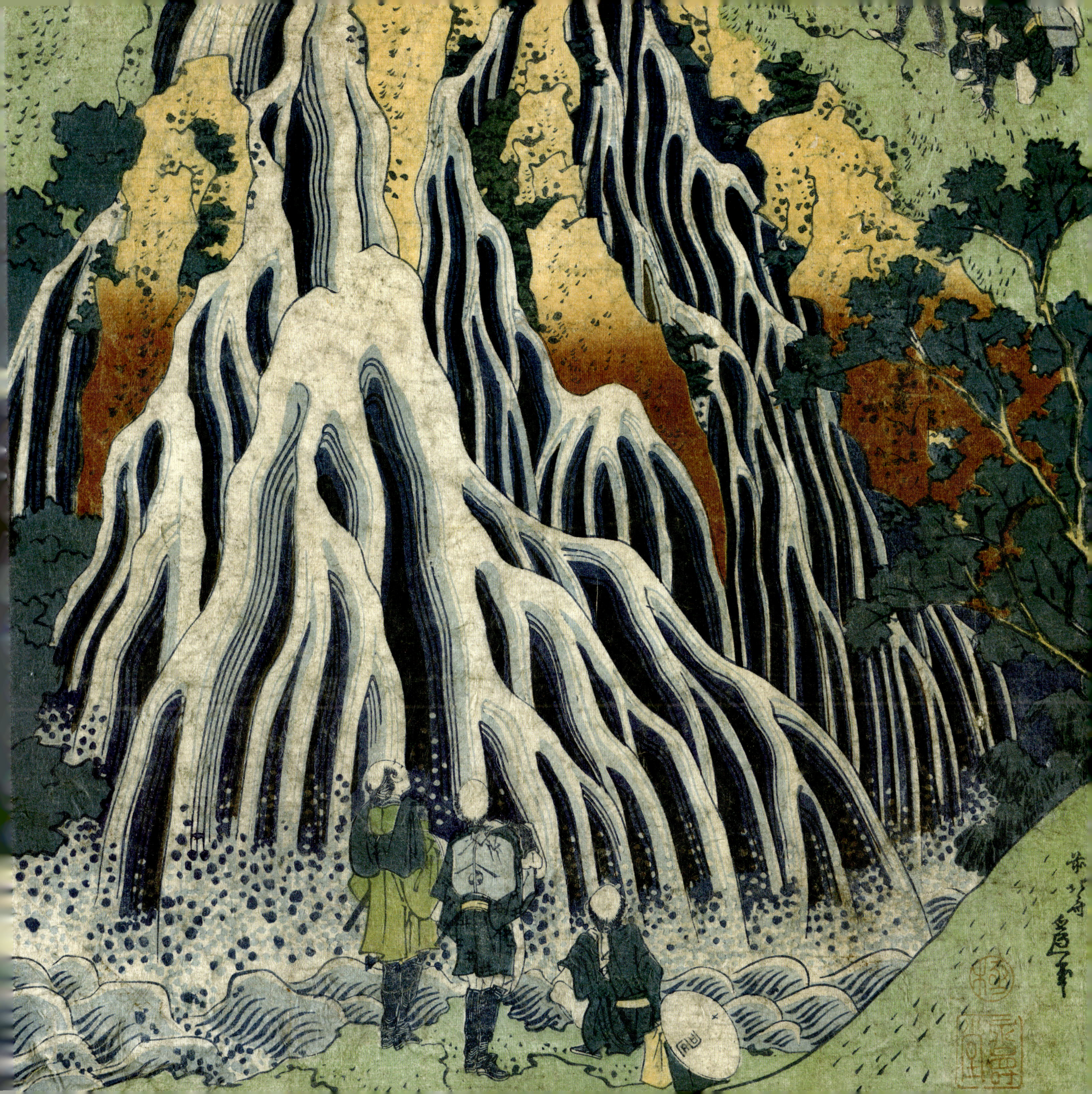

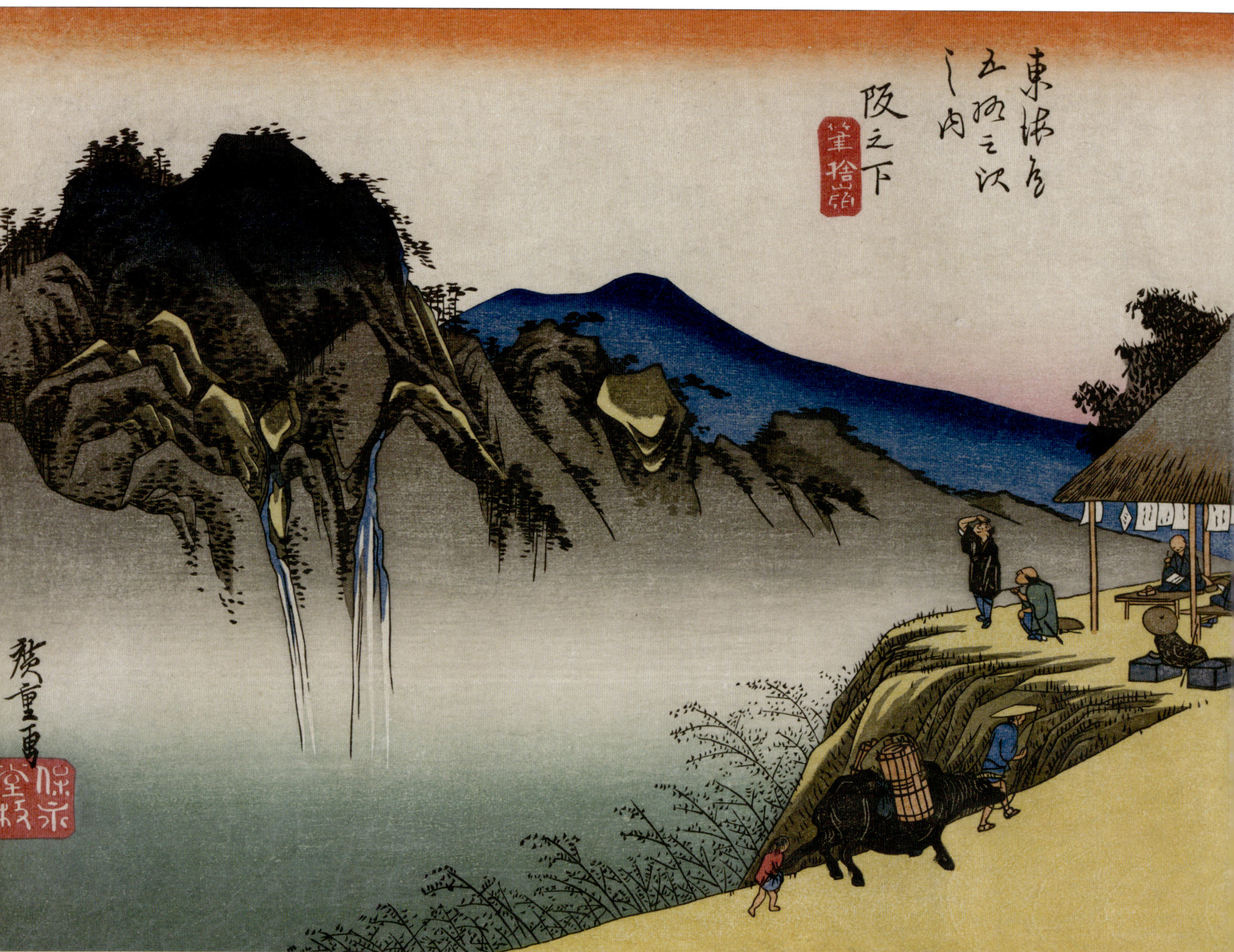

ABOVE Utagawa Hiroshige (1797–1858) *Sakanoshita*, the 48th station from 'Fifty-Three Stations of the Tokaido Road' (1833–34, printed later)

The French novelist had written this in *Madame Bovary* (1857) before *Japonisme* could really be said to have 'arrived'. Even so, he was hardly saying anything new. The idea of the oriental seductress – at the same time irresistibly exciting and unutterably dangerous – went all the way back to classical times (and no doubt before). It was at least as old as the Caucasian Medea's murderous passion for Jason in the Greek myth of the Argonauts or as the Egyptian Cleopatra's seductive way with Roman generals.

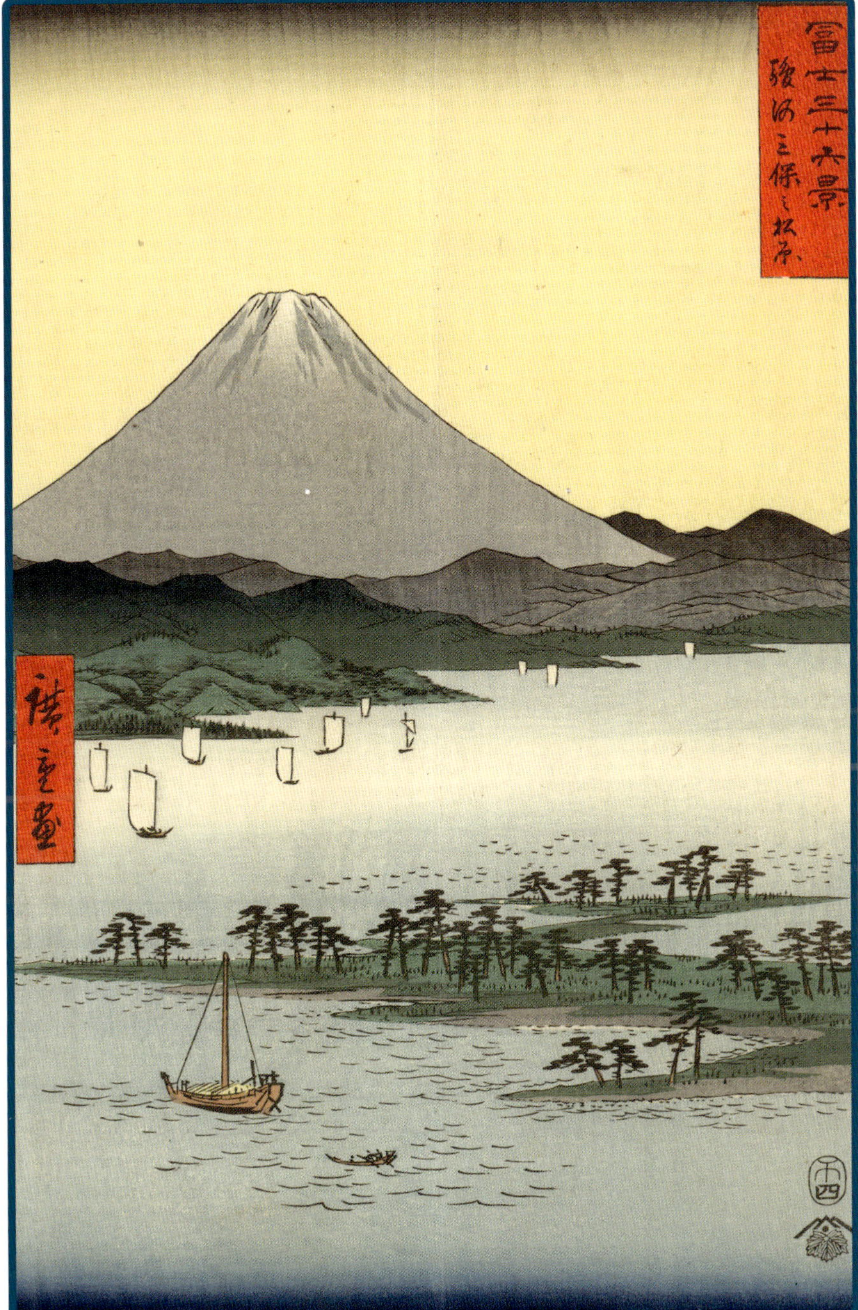

ABOVE Utagawa Hiroshige (1797–1858) *The Pine Forest of Miho in Suruga Province* from 'Thirty-six Views of Mount Fuji' (1858)

Edouard Manet, an eager collector of *ukiyo-e*, found its frankness as attractive as its use of space and line – though the aesthetic and the ethical dimensions are not so easily teased apart. The *ukiyo-e*-esque 'flatness' of *Olympia* (1863) is – even now – challenging to the European viewer in the same way as the subject's bold and unapologetic stare.

A Cruel Code?

Another enthusiast, Edgar Degas is known to have acquired a considerable number of Japanese prints, although as with Manet, it is by no means always easy to point to specific influences. Colours, textures, spacing, light and shade were all shown in a slightly different way by the 'new' *ukiyo-e* imports but, in the European context, older-established conventions continued to exercise their own artistic pull.

It is widely believed that in his pictures of women at work – the laundresses leaning into their daily labours, tough and physical; the dancers delicately balanced, but equally hard at work – Degas was influenced by sketches he found in Hokusai's manga notebooks. His innumerable variations on the theme of the 'woman combing her hair', meanwhile, might be said to show clear signs of kinship with Japanese *bijin-ga* art, whilst his portraits of street prostitutes also perhaps reference *shunga* porn.

What are we to make of the impersonality of these pictures? 'Degas's detachment is beyond cruelty,' says the feminist writer Germaine Greer. And she is right, at least to the extent that these paintings very obviously obliterate their subjects as individuals. Are they sympathetic or sadistic in their view of women reduced to the status of working bodies? Should

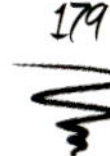

Degas be lauded for the lack of moral censure he shows in his pictures of prostitutes? Or, on the other hand, should he be castigated for an arguably misogynistic indifference to (even enjoyment of) women's subjection and suffering?

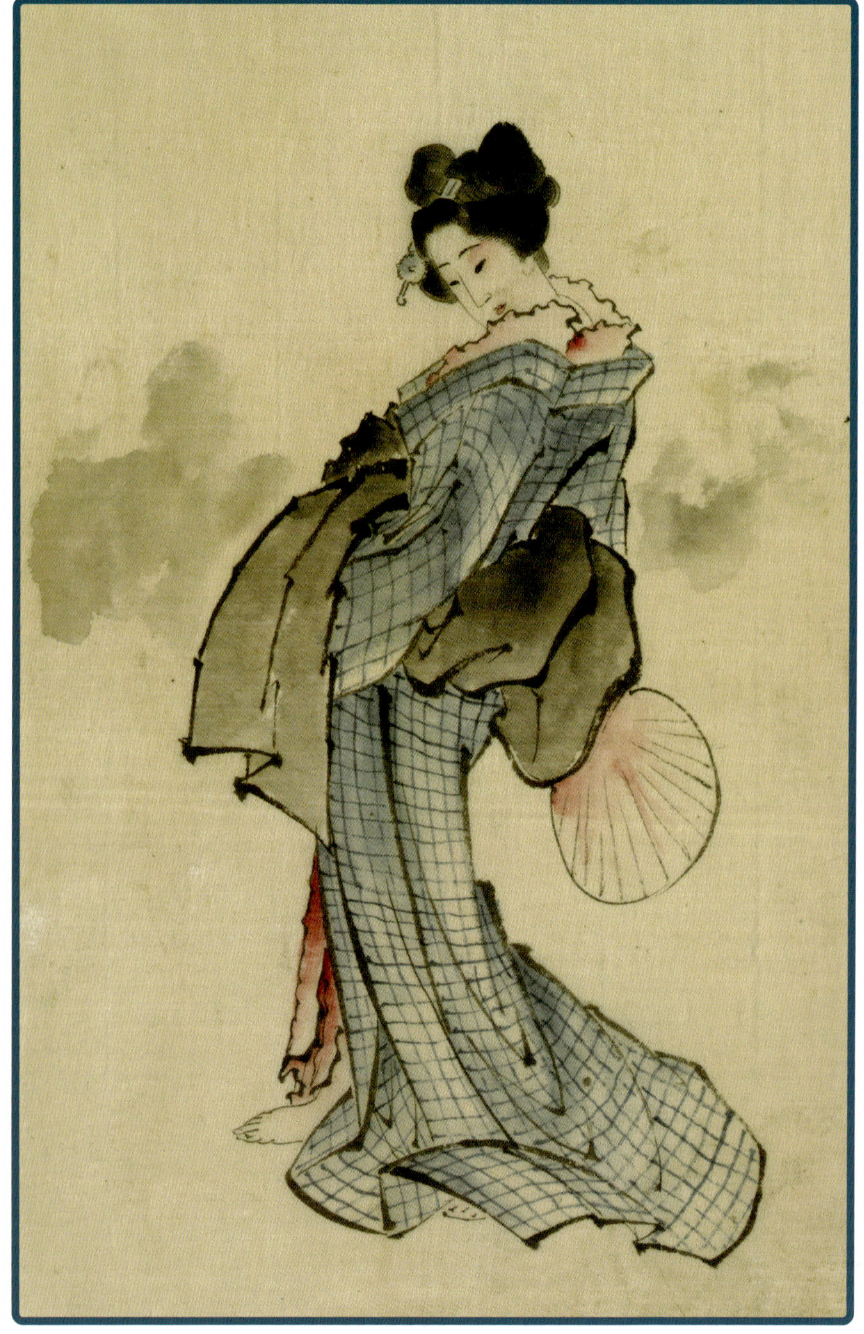

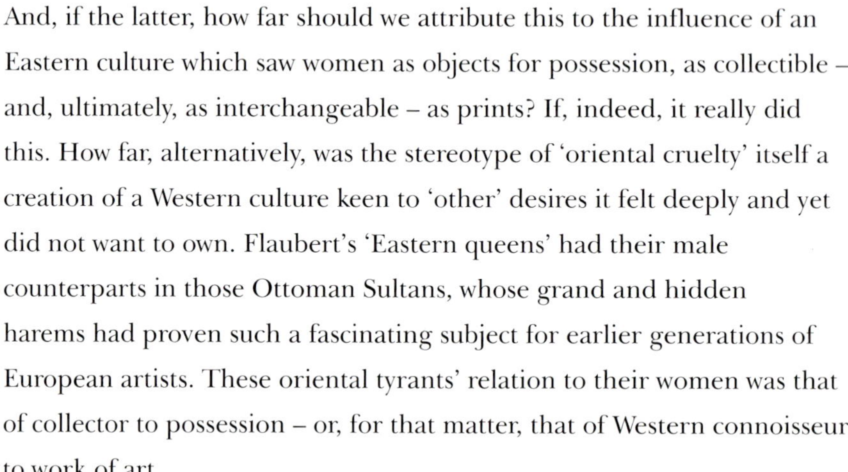

And, if the latter, how far should we attribute this to the influence of an Eastern culture which saw women as objects for possession, as collectible – and, ultimately, as interchangeable – as prints? If, indeed, it really did this. How far, alternatively, was the stereotype of 'oriental cruelty' itself a creation of a Western culture keen to 'other' desires it felt deeply and yet did not want to own. Flaubert's 'Eastern queens' had their male counterparts in those Ottoman Sultans, whose grand and hidden harems had proven such a fascinating subject for earlier generations of European artists. These oriental tyrants' relation to their women was that of collector to possession – or, for that matter, that of Western connoisseur to work of art.

Far Eastern Fantasies

We have certainly come a long way from Mount Fuji, although this in turn might seem to prompt the question of just how Japanese *Japonisme* ever really was. To a certain extent, it prompted the question at the time. In 2015, protestors forced the Boston Museum of Arts to cancel a popular programme of 'Kimono Wednesdays' in which fan-waving visitors posed in brightly coloured gowns like those to be seen on the model in Monet's *La Japonaise* (*see* right), in the gallery's collection. Painted in 1876, this painting showed the artist's first wife Camille in oriental dress. The incongruity of this image was only underlined in Monet's painting by the fact that Camille, a Lyonnaise brunette, was wearing a hyper-Europeanizing blonde wig. Matisse, another artist whose work shows the unmistakeable influence of *ukiyo-e*, was also to paint his wife in Japanese dress.

The charge of cultural appropriation as it is made today is founded on the idea that certain racial and ethnic prejudices endure in Western culture as a post-colonial legacy. When Renoir complained about the appropriation he saw in so much *Japonisme*, he seems to have been more concerned about the blunders of taste and judgement he felt his fellow Europeans were

Above **Hokusai school** Woman holding fan in kimono (1830–50), ink wash and colour on paper

Right **Claude Monet** (1840–1926) *La Japonaise (Camille Monet in Japanese Costume)* (1876), oil on canvas

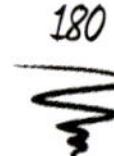

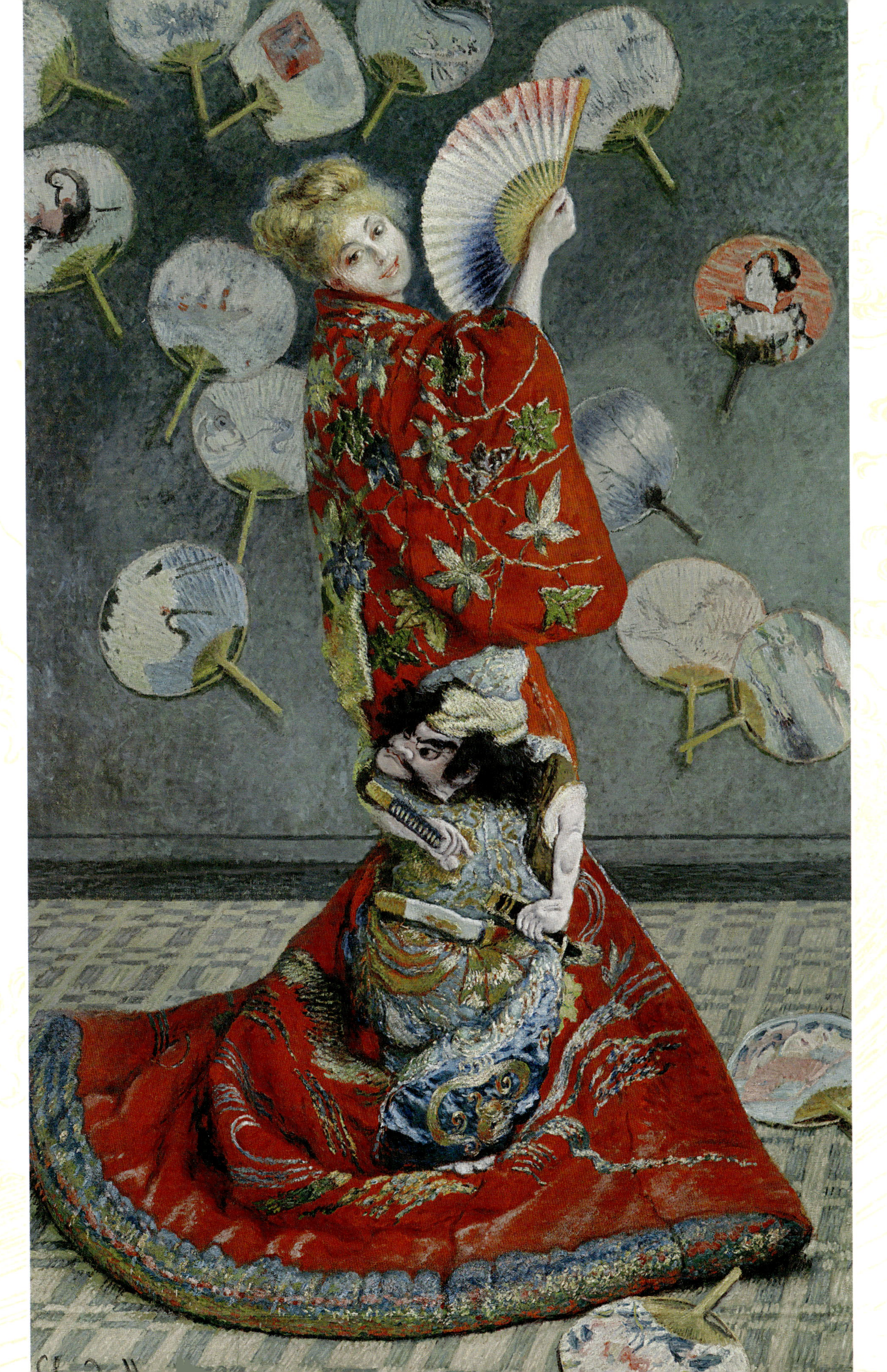

prone to when dabbling in an aesthetic they could not hope to understand. (A fair point, perhaps, although few would regret his having overlooked these scruples to create the – plainly *ukiyo-e*-influenced – geometrical explosion of umbrellas in *The Umbrellas* of 1886; *see* opposite).

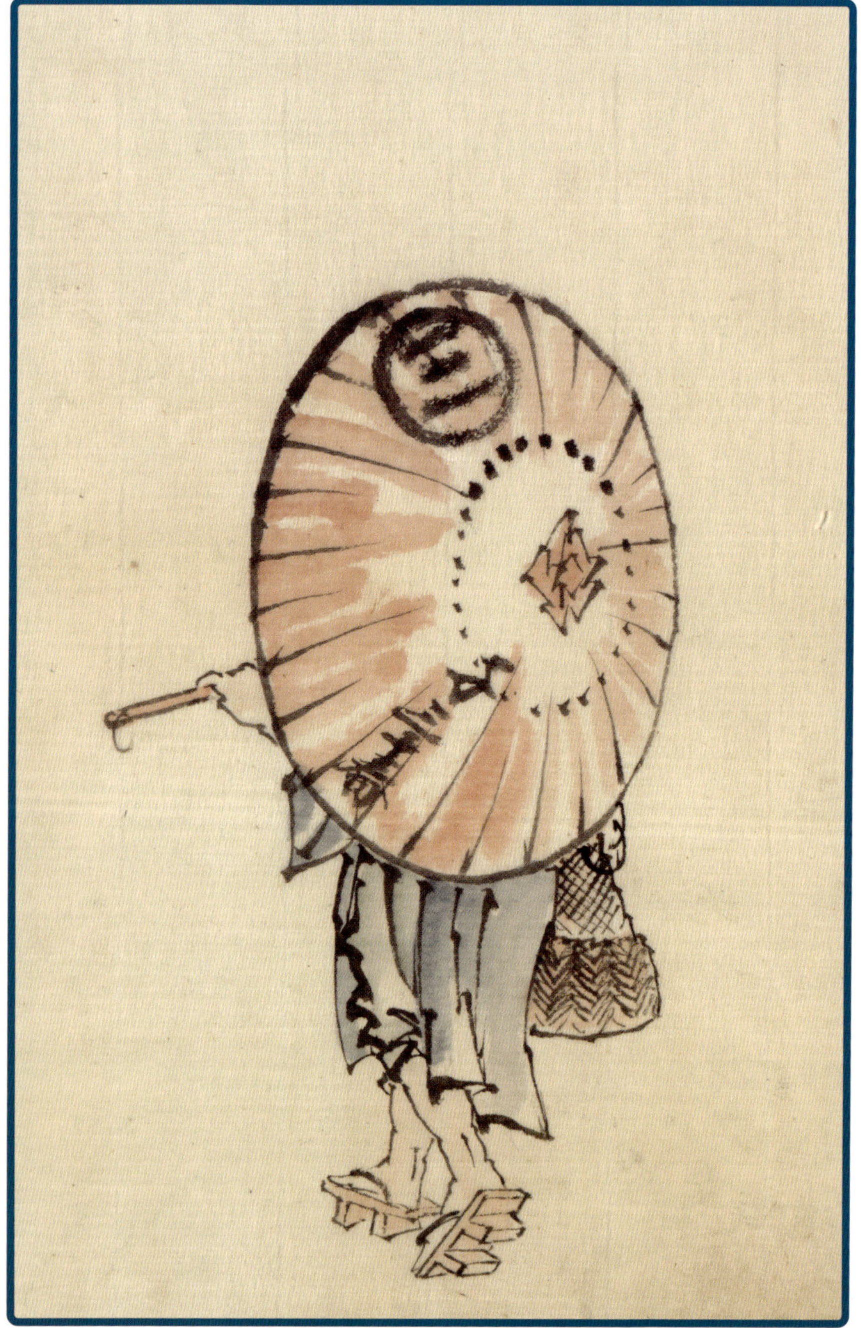

ABOVE **Hokusai school** Woman with parasol and bag (1830–50), ink wash and colour on paper

To some extent, undoubtedly – inevitably, perhaps – to these painters, 'Japan' was a fantasy, viewed always through a European, and essentially artistic, prism. Van Gogh was to admit as much (if 'admit' is the word, it seems practically a boast): 'I no longer need to have Japanese prints,' he said in a letter to his sister Wilhelmina in 1888, 'for I constantly tell myself that I am in Japan here' ('here' being Arles in southern France).

Yet, with all its limitations, Van Gogh's love for what he called *Japonaiserie* was deep and genuine. Not only did he copy a couple of Hiroshige's works, he even owned a print by his sometime collaborator, Keisei Eisen. 'All my work is to some extent based on Japanese art,' he had claimed. And, as odd as it may seem to us, he appears to have created in his own mind some strange identification between Japan and the south of France. 'Why not go to the equivalent of Japan, the South?' he asked his friend Émile Bernard (1868–1941). 'I wish you could spend some time here,' he enthused in a letter to his brother Theo (1857–91),

> *you would feel it after a while, one's sight changes: you see things with an eye more Japanese, you feel colour differently. The Japanese draw quickly … because their nerves are finer, their feelings simpler.*

There it is again, that Euro-condescension – how, really, are we to quantify simplicity or complexity of feeling? Why would we be so sure that their nerves are finer than our own? Such truth as there was in what Van Gogh had said was to be expressed much more respectfully by the American architect Frank Lloyd Wright (1867–1959) in his 1912 monograph on *The Japanese Print: An Interpretation*. Japanese art, he argued, was 'highly structural … the first and supreme principle of Japanese esthetics consists in a stringent simplification by elimination of the insignificant'. Far from being modern in itself, this view was as old as Plato. Wright went on to acknowledge this himself. In Western terms, he said, this principle resembled Plato's notion of the 'idea harmony' at the centre of the 'outward form'.

RIGHT **Auguste Renoir (1841–1919)** *The Umbrellas* (1886), oil on canvas

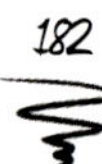

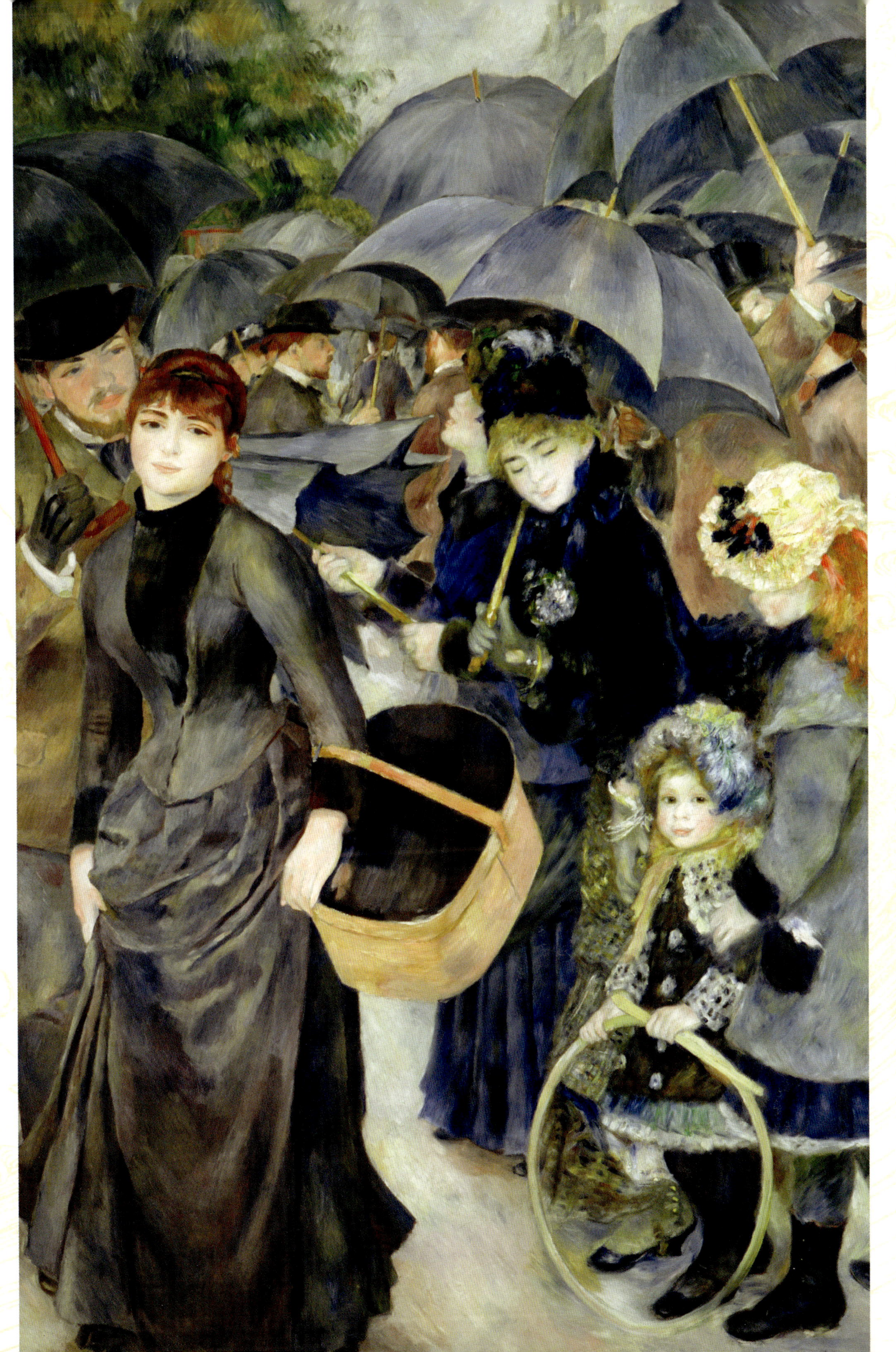

Decadent Discipline

That any given object was susceptible to any number of different representations from different standpoints had perhaps been the single most striking revelation of Hokusai's and Hiroshige's series. So it should be no surprise that Gauguin's personal take on *Japonisme* was altogether different from that of Van Gogh, with whom he had a mutual friend in Émile Bernard. 'Look at the Japanese,' he wrote to him in November 1888,

> *and you will see life depicted in the open air and in the sunshine without shadows, colour being used only as a combination of tones, diverse harmonies, giving the impression of warmth, etc.*

It is paradoxical, perhaps, that Japanese art should have appealed to Western viewers at once for its racy raffishness and its severity.

So it seemed to be, however. On his travels through the Pacific, Gauguin's records of the lives of the indigenous islanders were very much works of the 'open air'; like Hokusai's and Hiroshige's street scenes, Gauguin was to keep his collection of *ukiyo-e* with him. Wherever he went, he would hang them up on the walls of whichever hut he was using as his studio, so that he could see and be corrected by its 'stringent simplification'. Pissarro, by contrast, found Japanese art a source of calm: 'nothing that leaps to the eye, a calm, and extraordinary unity, a rather subdued radiance'.

The Modern Moment?

It is generally accepted that when Virginia Woolf (1882–1941) observed that 'on or about December 1910, human character changed,' she was setting a very late date for the advent of Modernism in the arts. Understandably enough, the English novelist was viewing things through the prism of literature, and of fiction in particular, in which she herself – along with others such as James Joyce (1882–1941), Gertrude Stein (1874–1946) and Marcel Proust (1871–1922) – had overhauled the novel, in line with the exhortation of the poet

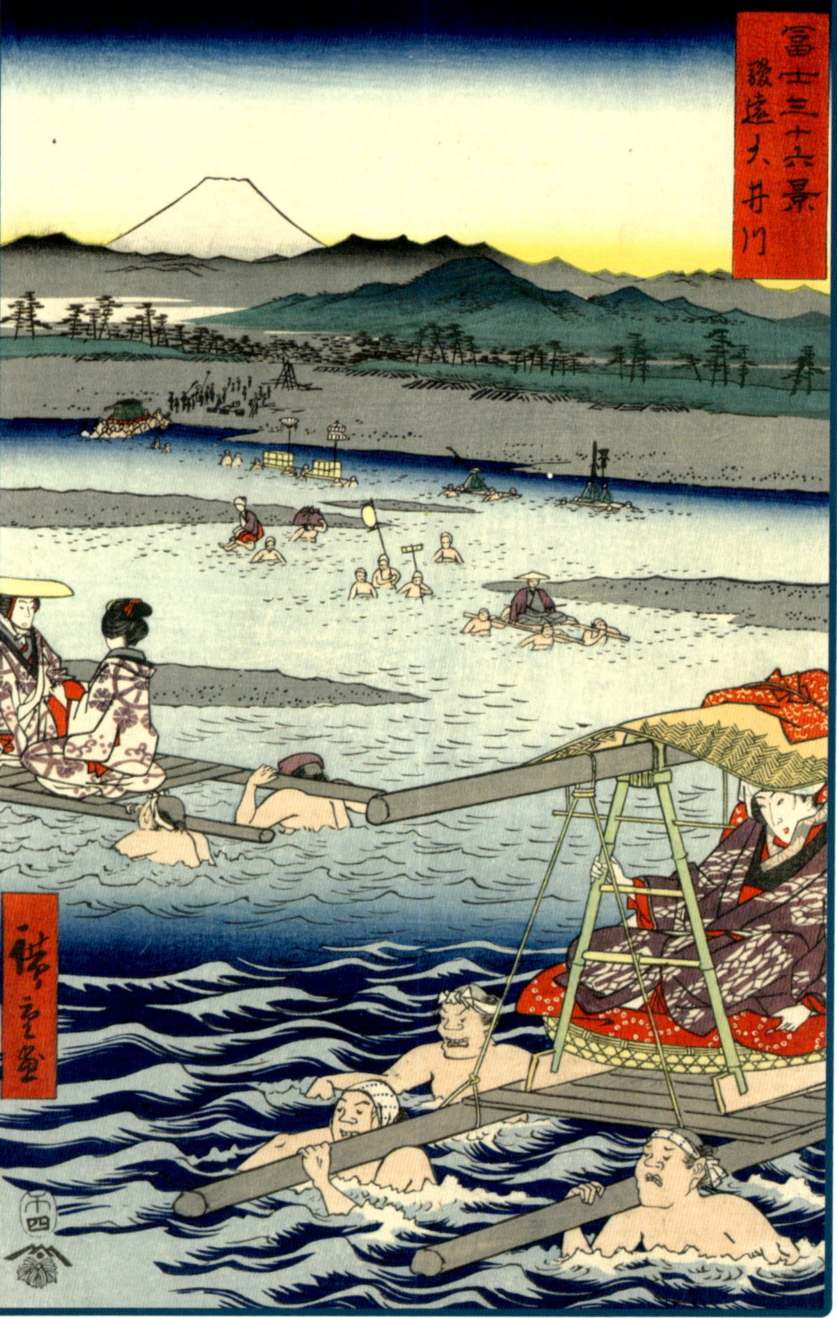

ABOVE Utagawa Hiroshige (1797–1858) *The Oi River between Suruga and Totomi Provinces* from 'Thirty-six Views of Mount Fuji' (1858)

RIGHT Utagawa Hiroshige (1797–1858) *Mount Kano in Kazusa Province* from 'Thirty-six Views of Mount Fuji' (1858)

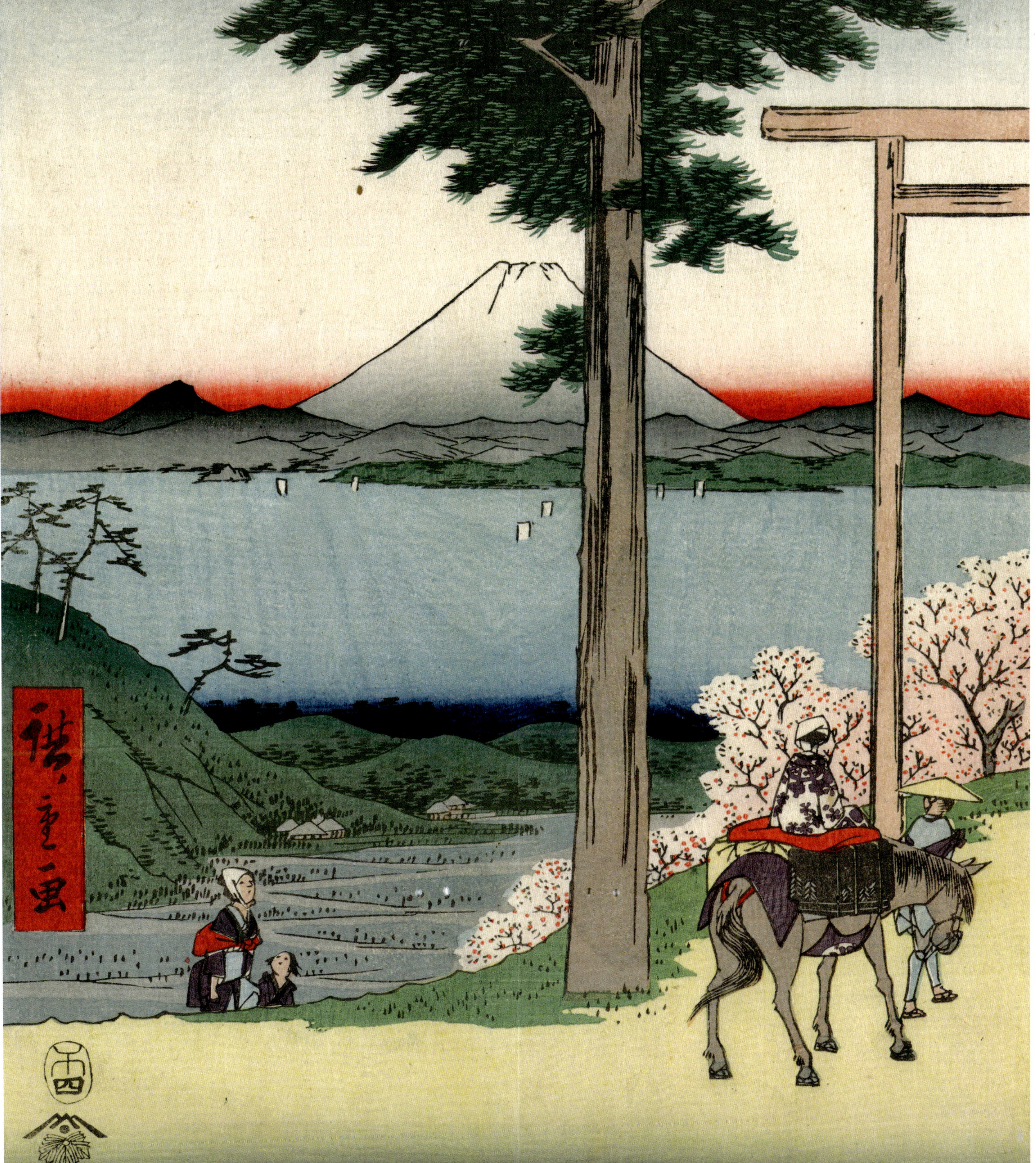
廣重画

Ezra Pound (1885–1972), to 'make it new'. That said, it is harder to say with any precision when the so-called 'Modern Moment' arrived, and a great many suggestions – all with things to be said for them – have been made.

Here, then, is another. In a letter of 1878, the French painter Paul Cézanne (1839–1906) recalled a recent journey with his drawing instructor Joseph Gibert (1806–84) in the south of France. He wrote:

> *'While travelling along the railroad near the Alexis countryside, a stunning motif appeared to the east: Sainte-Victoire and the rocks which dominate Beaurecueil. I said: 'what a beautiful motif'; he answered: 'the lines are too balanced'.*

Gibert's reaction accords completely with the post-Romantic view that beauty lay in irregularity; that a scene should not be too perfect, too finely poised. Cézanne, by contrast, was learning to respond to that same 'stringent simplification' Frank Lloyd Wright was to identify as being the underlying basis of the beauty of Japanese art. Like Van Gogh, it seemed, Cézanne had discovered his own Japan in the south of France – in his case, though, he had actually found his Fuji.

A French Fuji?

For, in the last quarter-century of his life, Cézanne was to paint Mont Sainte-Victoire more than 60 times from different perspectives – a project which Hokusai and Hiroshige would surely have understood. Indeed, it came to be as inescapable a presence in his consciousness as Fujisan had been in theirs. According to his friend, Joachim Gasquet (1873–1921), '[t]he bluish phantom of Sainte-Victoire floated at the edge of his thoughts and was present with him at the horizon of all landscapes.' Whilst, like much else produced under the auspices of 'Modernism', Cézanne's paintings of Mont Sainte-Victoire were difficult – by conventional standards unartistic, even something of a mess – a deeper simplicity seemed to underpin a higher purpose.

Much the same might be said for Monet's *Water Lilies* (*see* right; an oriental choice of subject in themselves, it might be said – kindred as they were to the sacred lotus), and for his decision to create a whole series of studies – some 250 – in his last decades. If that repetitiveness reflected his Impressionist's concern to record minor and momentary differences of light and colour, it also recalls the Japanese masters' great Fuji series. Not, however, as closely as the 1890–91 *Haystacks* series, whose subjects even resemble Fujisan in shape, as – less exactly but more appropriately nobly, perhaps – does the towering gothic frontage of *Rouen Cathedral* (1892–94).

But the final confirmation that Japanese art had conquered the twentieth-century art world came in 1902, the year that Henri Rivière (1864–1951) created his 'Thirty-six Views of the Eiffel Tower'. If the title is a clear nod to Hokusai, the finished series surpasses wit and goes far beyond pastiche. In casting France's most famous landmark as a modern-day Mount Fuji, Rivière reminds us of the mountain's special sanctity as a central symbol, not just of Japanese culture but of world art.

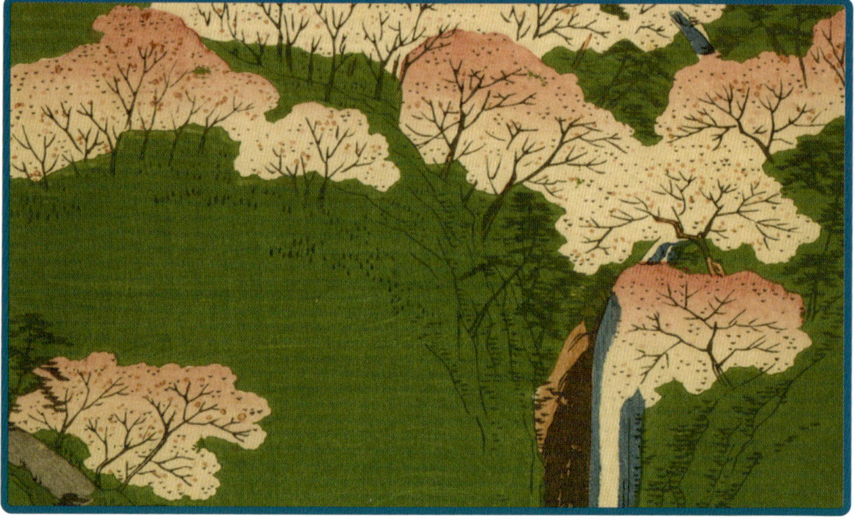

Above Utagawa Hiroshige II (1826–69) *Yoshino Mountain in Yamato Province* from '100 Famous Views of Japan' (1859)

Opposite Claude Monet (1840–1926) *Waterlilies* (1914–17), oil on canvas

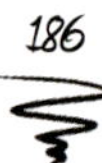

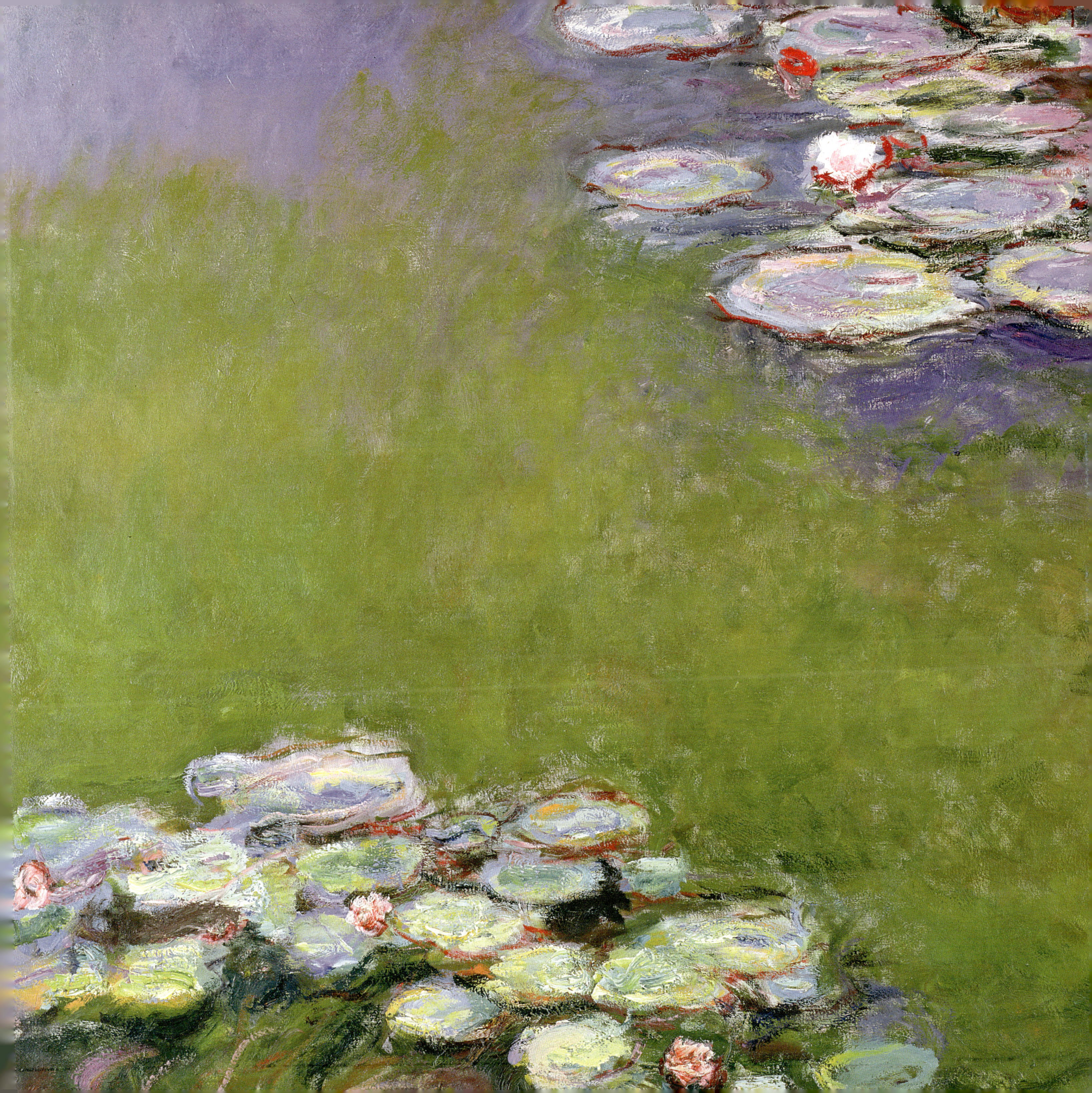

Further Reading & Acknowledgments

Bouquillard, J., *Hokusai's Mount Fuji: The Complete Views in Color*, Harry N. Abrams, Inc., 2007

Calza, G. C. , *Hiroshige: Visions of Nature*, Skira Books, 2009

Calza, G. C., *Hiroshige: The Master of Nature*, Skira Editore, 2009

Calza, G. C. *et. al.*, *Ukiyo-E*, Phaidon Press, 2007

Calza, G.C. *et. al.*, *Hokusai*, Phaidon Press, 2004

Clark, T., *100 Views of Mount Fuji*, Weatherhill, 2001

Davis, J. N., *Partners in Print: Artistic Collaboration and the Ukiyo-E Market*, University of Hawaii Press, 2015

Earhart, B. H., *Mount Fuji: Icon of Japan (Studies in Comparative Religion)*, The University of South Carolina Press, 2011

Fahr-Becker, G., *Japanese Prints (Taschen 25th Anniversary)*, Taschen Books, 2007

Forrer, M., *Hokusai: Prints and Drawings*, Prestel, 2009

Forrer, M., *Hokusai: Mountains and Water, Flowers and Birds*, Prestel, 2004

Guth, Christine, *Art of Edo Japan: The Artist and the City, 1615–1868*, Yale University Press, 2010

Harris, F., *Ukiyo-e: The Art of the Japanese Print*, Tuttle Publishing, 2011

Jansen, M., *Hiroshige's Journey in 60 Odd Provinces*, Hotei Publishing, 2004

Kobayashi, T., *Ukiyo-e: Introduction to Japanese Woodblock Prints*, Kodansha International Ltd., 1997

Kobayashi, T., *Utamaro: Portraits from the Floating World*, Kodansha International Ltd., 2001

Lambourne, L., *Japonisme: Cultural Crossings between Japan and the West*, Phaidon Press, 2005

Lane, R., *Hokusai: Life and Work*, Barrie & Jenkins, 1989

Marks, A., *Japan Journeys: Famous Woodblock Prints of Cultural Sites in Japan*, Tuttle Shokai Inc., 2015

Marks, A., *Japanese Woodblock Prints: Artists, Publishers, and Masterworks: 1680-1900*, Tuttle Shokai Inc, 2010

Meech, J., *Designed for Pleasure: The World of Edo Japan in Prints and Paintings*, 1680–1860, University of Washington Press, 2008

McGregor, Dr. M., *Ukiyo-E: Secrets of the Floating World*, Vyiha Publishing, 2016

Molenaar, M. *et. al.*, *Mount Fuji: Sacred Mountain of Japan*, Hotei Publishing, 2000

Reeve, J., *Japanese Art Close-Up*, British Museum Press, 2014

Robinson, M., *Japanese Woodblocks: Masterpieces of Art*, Flame Tree Publishing, 2014

Schlombs, A., *Hiroshige (Basic Art Series)*, Benedikt Taschen Verlag, 2016

Smith, Henry D., *One Hundred Views of Mount Fuji*, Thames & Hudson Ltd., 1988

Stanley-Baker, J., *Japanese Art*, Thames & Hudson Ltd., 2014

Takahashi, S., *Traditional Woodblock Prints of Japan*, Art Media Resources, 1973

Taschen, *Hiroshige: One Hundred Famous Views of Edo*, Taschen Books, 2015

Till, B., *Japan Awakens: Meji Prints*, Pomegranate Europe Ltd., 2008

Tinios, E., *Japanese Prints: Ukiyo-e in Edo*, 1799-1900, British Museum Press, 2010

Tjardes, T., *One Hundred Aspects of the Moon: Japanese Woodblock Prints by Yoshitoshi*, Museum of New Mexico Press, 2003

Watson, W., *The Great Japan Exhibition. Art of the Edo Period 1600–1868*, Royal Academy of Arts, 1981

Michael Kerrigan

Michael Kerrigan (author) is author of *Modern Art* from the 'World's Greatest Art' series and *100 Great Art Masterpieces*, and co-author of *The Architecture Style Spotter's Guide* along with many other books and articles on art, culture and history. He lives in Edinburgh, where he writes regularly for the *Scotsman* newspaper and is a book reviewer for the *Times Literary Supplement* and the *Guardian*.

Picture Credits

All images courtesy of **Library of Congress**, except the following: **Wikimedia Commons** and: Visipix.com 1 & 165, 128; Google Art Project/National Gallery of Art, Washington D.C. 48; Google Cultural Institute/Nomura Art Museum 51. **Bridgeman Images** and: Bibliotheque des Arts Decoratifs, Paris, France / De Agostini Picture Library / G. Dagli Orti 4clt & 24, 24, 25, 25; Indianapolis Museum of Art, USA / Gift of Mrs. Charles C. Kryter 7bl & 74 & 118(b2nd), 30 & 118cr, 40 & 118cl, 118(c2nd), 119 (t4th) & 174; Civico Museo d'Arte Orientale di Trieste, Italy 8cr & 157; Arthur M. Sackler Gallery, Smithsonian Institution, USA / The Anne van Biema Collection 27; Mead Art Museum, Amherst College, MA, USA / Gift of William Green 28; Private Collection 29, 37, 86, 147l, 147r; British Library, London, UK / © British Library Board. All Rights Reserved 58; Museum of Fine Arts, Houston, Texas, USA / Gift of Marjorie G. and Evan C. Horning 63; Private Collection / Photo © Liszt Collection 64, 114, 115; Los Angeles County Museum of Art, CA, USA 70 & 118(t2nd); Minneapolis Institute of Arts, MN, USA / Bequest of Richard P. Gale 71bcr & 84, 73br & 102; Rijksmuseum, Amsterdam, The Netherlands 73bl & 100, 161; Pictures from History 119(c4th), 119(c5th) & 142r; Brooklyn Museum of Art, New York, USA / Gift of Louis V. Ledoux 132–33; Freer Gallery of Art, Smithsonian Institution, USA / Robert O. Muller Collection 158; Mucha Trust / Bridgeman Images 169; Leopold Collection, Vienna, Austria 170; Musee d'Orsay, Paris, France 173; Museum of Fine Arts, Boston, Massachusetts, USA / 1951 Purchase Fund 183; Musee Marmottan Monet, Paris, France 187. **Getty Images** and: SuperStock 7cr & 73(4thRowl); Sergio Anelli/Electa/Mondadori Portfolio/Hulton Fine Art Collection 50; Fine Art Images/Heritage Images/Hulton Archive 66, 145r; Fine Art Images/SuperStock 71(3rdRowcl) & 78, 73tl & 92, 73(3rdRowl) & 94; Heritage Images/Hulton Archive 71(3rdRowl) & 79; Buyenlarge/Archive Photos 72(2ndRowcr) & 88, 73(4thRowcr) & 154–55. Courtesy **Degener Japanese Fine Prints**/www.degener.com/© Rolf M. Degener Gallery 8tcr, 104–09, 54. **SuperStock**/Fine Art Images 119cr & 176. www.lacma.org in/**Los Angeles County Museum of Art**, CA, USA 135. **akg-images** 160.

Index

Page numbers in *italics* refer to the illustration captions throughout.

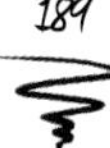

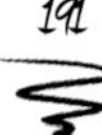

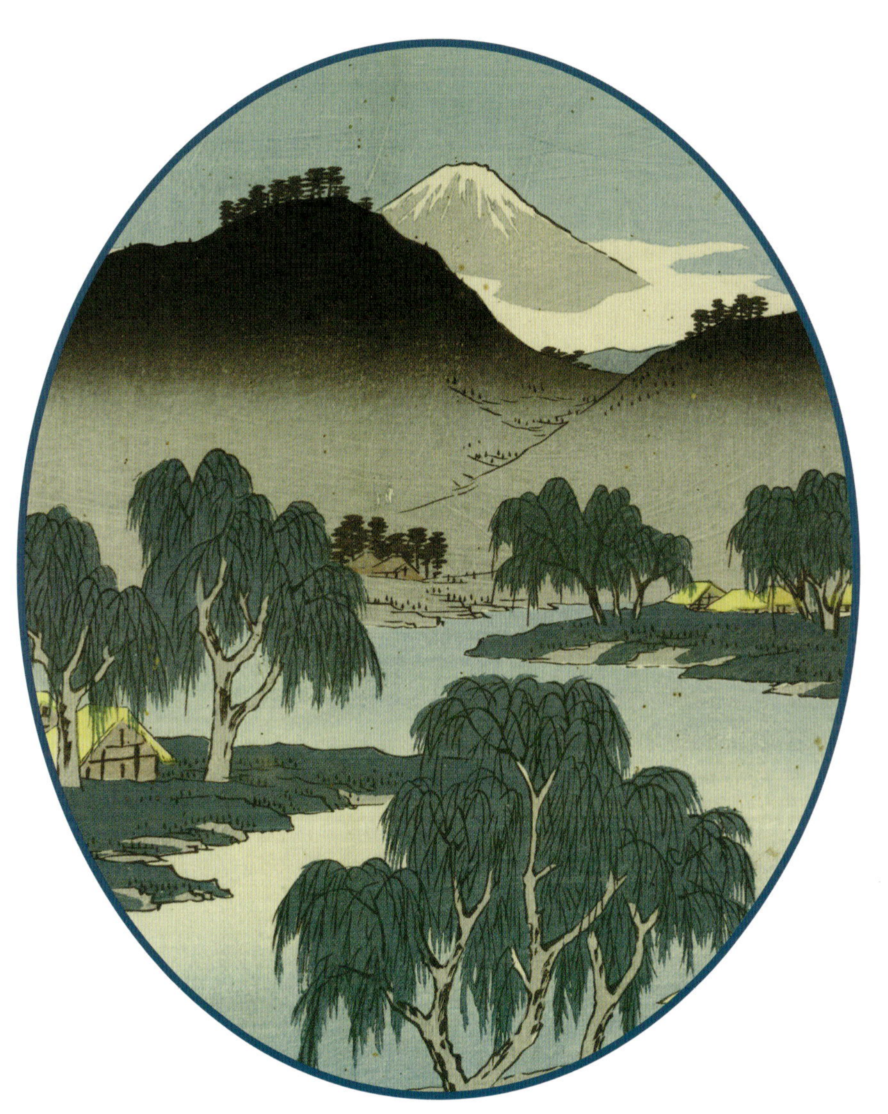